The First Churchill

By the same author

George Malcolm Thomson

The First Churchill

The Life of John,
1st Duke of Marlborough

WILLIAM MORROW AND COMPANY
New York   1980

To Diana

Library of Congress Catalog Card Number 79-66008

ISBN 0-688-03556-6

Printed in the United States of America.

First U.S. Edition

1   2   3   4   5   6   7   8   9   10

Contents

List of Illustrations

List of Maps

Acknowledgments

In attempting to make a list, however incomplete, of those to whom my gratitude is due for help in writing this biography, it would be wrong of me to omit mention of distinguished predecessors such as Sir Winston Churchill and Archdeacon Coxe. Much of the shape and substance of this book is inspired by the monumental work of Sir Winston (although I have ventured not to follow all his judgments), while Coxe's compilation of letters has been an indispensable prime source. I also wish to single out for my special thanks two recent books on military affairs of the time: David Chandler's *The Art of Warfare in the Age of Marlborough*, and R. E. Scouller's *The Armies of Queen Anne*. These have materially enlarged my understanding of the problems that Marlborough faced and his task in surmounting them.

As it will be obvious from the notes that I have derived a great deal of information from *The Blenheim Papers*, I must register here my indebtedness to the Duke's descendants who have, through the years, preserved this priceless archive for the nation and have now passed it on to the British Library. There, in the Department of Manuscripts, it is being expertly kept. To the staff I owe my gratitude for much courtesy and kindness, especially for leading me so quickly to the remarkable series of letters I have referred to under the heading "Marlborough's Spy". The Prints Department of the Library have also been most helpful.

From the London Library I have had the assistance and forbearance I have come to expect but should not take for granted.

To my excellent driver on the journey through Germany on the route of Marlborough's march to the Danube I am indeed grateful, as I also am to Mr James Macmillan, who cast a discriminating eye over my typescript.

For encouragement and editorial advice I owe more than I can say to Mr David Farrer, and in the preparation and production of the book I owe much gratitude to Mr John Blackwell and Mr William Neill-Hall.

Sybil Rang, who typed and so often re-typed a difficult manuscript, has my thanks for, once more, making my path easier.

G. M. T.

Money Values

In Marlborough's time, the exchange rate of the £ sterling was:

        13 livres,
         4 écus,
        10 guilders   10 stivers,
        $1\frac{1}{4}$ pistoles (a Spanish gold coin),
         4 Reichsthalers.

I write at a time when values are fluid and it is only possible, for obvious reasons, to find a very rough equivalence between the worth of money in Queen Anne's time and now.

The average income of a knight at the time of the Revolution of 1688 was £650 a year, of a shopkeeper £45, of a labourer £15. One can add a quarter by the time of Queen Anne. (R. E. Scouller, quoting the estimate of Gregory King.) I have assumed that the purchasing power of money was twelve or fifteen times that of today.

The Time Scale: London to Edinburgh – six days (postboys); London to The Hague – four days (with good weather and favouring wind); Paris to Madrid – eight days (express post), ten days (ordinary post).

The Golden Swamp

It was an age of cautious change and limited revolutions, of second thoughts about God and the state, of divisive loyalties and of treachery; an age of monarchs avid for glory; of subjects who dreamt of becoming monarchs. Outside England, Parliaments were unpopular. The army offered the most promising career for a young man of energy and brains, although it was better that, in addition, he should belong to a good family and possess influence in the right quarters. Deep underground, thought flowed slowly and in meagre volume, a trickle which gave the impression that at any moment it would be congealed. The thaw had not yet come.

Geometry ("the only science which it hath pleased God hitherto to bestow on mankind"[1]) was queen of the intellect. The age was that of Newton, Liebnitz and the calculus, of Vauban and fortification; of Descartes. Every now and then stampedes of population occurred when groups of people fled from persecution or tyranny. These movements enriched one country and impoverished another. Kings were more bigoted than popes for, while orthodoxy might save a soul for the next world, uniformity was a source of political strength in this one.

In politics and in family disagreements, poison was sometimes used and more often suspected. Witchcraft was on the wane, although in 1679 Paris shuddered over a horrifying outbreak. The beautiful gave way to the grandiose. Insolence rather than spiritual pride was the fashionable sin. Men built palaces as once they had built churches, palaces which were more than residences, more than headquarters, rather temples in which the god-ruler was adored and the munificence of the faithful was displayed. For the successful commander or the upstart official, the plates in the "Fürstliche Baumeister" were an incitement to extravagance. Hygiene was neglected; Versailles stank. So, for that matter, did Paris. Its smell, said the Princess Palatine, is "so detestable that it is impossible to remain there". London's air was possibly no purer. "From what I hear of the air in London, I don't believe I could last there for twenty-four hours without falling ill. I am told there is a constant smell of coal."[2] Towns were growing faster than the countryside. Before the end of the age, London would have 700,000 people, with shanty towns outside its walls, rookeries of crime and poverty. The "queen of cities" (Thomas Dekker) dragged her robes in the dirt.

Hunger was often at the poor man's elbow. Epidemics swooped, sudden as incursions of horsemen, not sparing even the rich. Doctors killed steadily and with the best of motives. There was a small revolution in the art of war; a new type of musket came into use, doubling the rate of fire of a trained soldier. This might have been a new argument for peace; if so, its results are hard to detect. As for war, it was slow-moving, largely a matter of patience and sieges. An army could not march more than three days beyond its baking ovens.

The winters were growing more severe. It was "a little ice age", which reached its climax in the Great Frost of 1709. Vines and sheep were in retreat all over Europe, moving towards the south and the lower slopes of mountains; wheat and cherry trees advanced. Astronomers reported in the second half of the century an unusual shortage of sunspots.[3] It was likely that people were having to tighten their belts. Finland lost a third of its population in the famine of 1669/70, which has been called the most terrible event in European history. Between 1695 and 1701, Scotland complained of seven hungry years.[4] Some authorities hold that what they call the crisis of the seventeenth century had a climatic origin. It may be so. It is more certain that, during those years, weather dealt more harshly with men than was usual. And men were more at the mercy of weather than they became later, for nine persons out of ten in Europe were peasants.

The centre of gravity of power in the world was shifting to the north and west.

To the east, the Germanies passed into a region where nations were not so much divided by frontiers but rather faded into one another across indeterminate zones. Muscovy, gloomy and puzzling, sent to the west embassies glittering with precious stones and crawling with lice, men bearded to the waist and with eccentric drinking habits – "He makes nothing of a pint of brandy at a draught, with a spoonful of white pepper in it. Sure he cannot live long."[5] One May day in 1703, Peter the Great

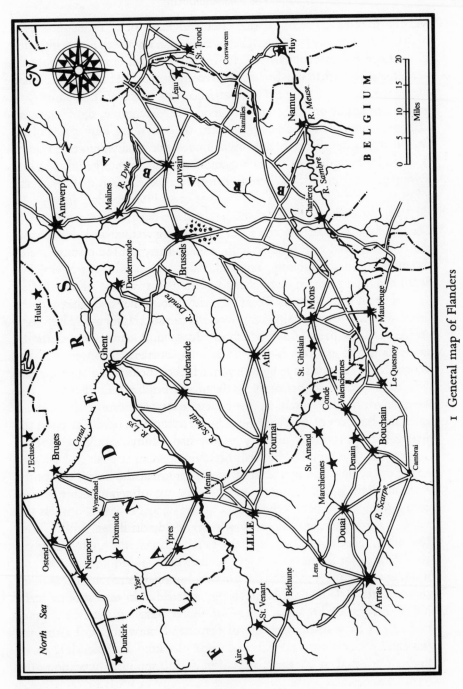

1 General map of Flanders

3

laid the foundation stone of the Peter and Paul fortress, designed by a pupil of the famous French engineer, Sebastian de Vauban and intended to overawe his new capital. St Petersburg was born. Russia was hoisting herself out of barbarism. But before that process could be accomplished much would happen. The Turk was about to make his last, most dangerous onslaught on Western Christendom. Meanwhile, the Hungarian Calvinists simmered in rebellion against the Hapsburg emperor. Poland was being strangled by her own impossible constitution. Sweden, haunted by memories of military grandeur, was about to be inherited by a young soldier of unstable genius. Prussia was on the verge of becoming a kingdom.

On the Atlantic coast, in the lands west of the Rhine and the Rhone, four powers eyed one another with suspicion and, in the case of one of their number, with cupidity. England, France, Holland – and Spain. The Spanish Empire was dying, choked with the treasures of the 'Indies, ossified with bureaucracy. To trade with her settlements "beyond the Line" was, for foreigners, piracy; to covet them, blasphemy. They were protected by a papal Bull, which all Protestants and many Catholics agreed could be ignored. More efficiently, Spain's possessions in the New World were defended by the mosquito. In the previous century she had suffered a spectacular defeat at sea from the English and after that was worn down by the Dutch. In due course, private enterprise shared with states the business of harrying Spain's overseas properties. On land, the prestige of her famous infantry was destroyed by Condé at Rocroi. Graver were the wounds she dealt herself.

Fear of the new and hatred of intrusion; indolence, which is one of the more insidious camp followers of unearned wealth; vast incompetence and inordinate snobbery – these, the obverse of Spanish stubbornness and courage, brought the nation slowly to a standstill: merchant fleets dwindling, tilled lands turning into ranches; even the influx of silver from Peru at last failing to arrive in Seville; the Inquisition, seeing all and bringing all to nullity; absolutism growing more absolute as it grew more stupid, until at last an imbecile King, crazed with superstitious fears, gibbered on the throne of His Catholic Majesty, while alien hands reached out to grab the heritage of Ferdinand and Isabella. To this sad pass had Spain been brought by the pride of race, "the Spanish cloak of despair and disdain",* the acceptance of idleness as a vocation, the

* John Strachey.

tradition, that while a gentleman might be poor, he must not work. "How nourishing is the crust of bread eaten under the genealogical tree!"[6] The Spanish Empire was dying, but it was dying slowly and it was dying hard. Before the story was finished, there would be more than one demonstration of how formidable the Spaniard could be in his own sierras, musket or pike in hand, and roused by the old war-cry, "Arriba, España!"

In the rich, beautiful land north of the Pyrenees the sun of national glory blazed, to be reflected upon a dazzled and envious world. It was supremely the age of French civilization, French language, French fashions (fanciful and full of colour, driving out the black cloth which Spanish taste had imposed on Europe), in short, of French greatness. Even a mortal enemy, like William of Orange, used French as the language of conversation. The French army was the most powerful in Europe, able to mobilize 120,000 men so as to crush the Dutch when their "insolence and arrogance" – and commercial success – had become intolerable. And before long, far bigger French armies took the field. Nobody noticed that, in fact, they were bigger than France could afford. "Swarming with people, sowed thick with cities and towns, this nation has also been always warlike."[7]

Having been a fascinating congeries of provinces, speaking three languages and heaven only knows how many dialects, confessing two variants of the Christian faith, France was becoming a unified nation-state, well-founded and, in normal years, self-sufficient in the necessities of life. The process was beginning of which François Mauriac saw – and deplored – the end-product three centuries later. "We no longer think about that period when every province formed a world which spoke its own language and built its monuments, a refined and hierarchical society which was not aware of Paris and its fashions." Already France was becoming highly centralized. She was grossly overtaxed. But this last fact, crucial as it was, was not noticed by all but the most perceptive of the observers who watched Versailles rise in splendour and saw the *Maison du Roi* – the Household troops – ride past, jingling and glittering, magnificent and numerous. To some, the sight was alarming, for what if, some day, there was an outbreak from one side or another of the great hexagon called France? To neighbours, anxiously watching, nothing seemed more likely. The power existed; the national temperament was dynamic, and at the heart of the great organism, from 1643 to the end of the age, moving all and deciding all, was a short, bright-eyed, hard-working man of consuming ambition. "No right was better established or more inseparably attached to my crown than that of universal subordination and direction within my territories."[8] Thus Louis XIV. Subordination and direction.

Briefing the marshals, directing the ships, instructing the ambassadors, building the factories, promoting research, controlling thought – every eddy in the nation's life contributed to a tide that flowed to and from the monarch's desk in his study in Versailles. In an autocracy, the King is the first slave. His was an absolutism as complete as Spain's. With this difference, however. That here, at the centre of things, instead of mind in a state of paralysis, was energy and intelligence. But also an excess of self-assurance? Absolutism has its pitfalls for the unwary, however intelligent they may be. For example, few men in France were intelligent enough to see that the centralized economic activity which the King's great minister, Colbert, had launched and which the King continued was bought at the price of paralysis in the industrial areas outside the "universal subordination and direction". In fact, French production during the reign never reached the level it had known under Louis XIII.

In the meantime, the eighteen million subjects of the Great Monarch enjoyed, if that is the word, the sense of belonging to the first power in Europe whose head was more important than the Hapsburg Emperor, able to talk on equal terms to the Pope, slightly scornful of England and, if annoyed at times by Holland, sure that one day in one brief, terrible campaign that over-rich little neighbour, that "republic of cheese-mongers", would be brought to obedience. Hardly anybody noticed that the poorest Frenchman worked the hardest, earned the least and paid the most in taxes. This elementary fact was not readily apparent to the ten thousand inhabitants of the royal settlement at Versailles. Fénelon, Bishop of Cambrai, was one of those who saw what was happening. He wrote to Louis XIV, "All France is but one great hospital, desolate and without maintenance," but it is unlikely that the King ever read the warning.[9] Probably until the last phase of his reign he believed himself to be the indulgent father of an adoring people. In the meantime, as the age advanced and his power expanded, Louis thought that his glory corresponded to the happiness of France. One grew with the other. No alternative to his unqualified power was possible, or desirable.

But, strangely enough, not many days' march from his borders, on the

North Sea coast, divided from France by a belt of land under a Spanish viceroy, a state had come into existence dramatically different from anything to be found in the dominions of the Sun King: different politically, economically, in culture and religion. Into a wide, grey sky climbed the brick belfries of churches stripped of their images. Windmills were many. Palaces were few and homely, as if to remind the viewer that here the towns were the kings. For a small republic, rather a group of republics, of three and a half million people clinging precariously to the sandbanks and mudflats at the mouths of three great rivers, dwelling on land much of which had been painfully won from the fishes over a thousand years, Holland – to give her the name of her dominant province – had a remarkable power to impress and annoy her neighbours. She was, in truth, not so much a nation as a miracle of stubbornness and ingenuity. Even now, in the last quarter of the twentieth century, Holland is compelled to spend a fifth of the national revenue in pumping the water out of her soil.[10] But this dire need, which should have made her the admired pattern of other states, only added a tincture of envy to the confused sentiments she provoked.

The Dutch were unpopular. They were rich, republican, Protestant, tolerant, frugal, grasping and contentious. "It being the custom here to save every year an overplus . . . upholds their credit."[11] Each of the national attitudes was a fault in somebody's eyes, although probably Holland's wealth was the most unforgivable of her crimes. "The trade of the Hollanders," wrote an envious Englishman, "is so far extended that it may be said to have no other bounds than those which the Almighty set to the world at the creation."[12] One year the salinity of the Baltic had changed and the herring had come to spawn in the North Sea. At that point in history, Amsterdam came into being.

There was a good deal against her, a town built on piles, a port difficult to sail from when the wind was in the east; shallow water.[13] How, then, did she become rich and make her neighbours rich after her?

> How com'st thou, golden swamp, by the abundance of heaven:
> Warehouse of East and West, all water and all state.
> Two Venices in one, where do thy ramparts end?[14]

The truth was that her good fortune far exceeded her bad. She was situated at the right place for a great market centre, a point where the fish, timber and naval stores of the North could be exchanged for the salt and wine of the South. Soon Amsterdam became a great entrepôt with the most capacious warehouses in Europe, in which the King of Sweden stored his copper and the Emperor his quicksilver.[15] Soon she had a central bank, a bourse and powerful chartered companies trading with the Indies. The Dutch East India Company, ruled by a council known as the Seventeen Gentlemen, was one of the great powers of Europe. Amsterdam was, as Genoa had been, the financial hub of the world. Soon the Dutch merchant fleet – including the three thousand herring *busses* that scoured the North Sea for fish, and the *fluits* that carried cargoes more cheaply than any other vessels – was twice as big as England's and nine times that of France.

One factor in her growth was not purely geographical: her policy of toleration, the first harvest of which was gathered when Antwerp was sacked by the Spaniards and most of the fleeing Protestants trudged northwards to find refuge and fresh outlet for their skills in Amsterdam. Toleration is, however, a virtue easier for a commercial city to practise than for a centralized monarchy, especially in an age of ideological warfare. It was all very well to insist that profit, however and wherever earned, was the highest good of the community and therefore shone with peculiar lustre in the eyes of God. In time of war, was it sound morality to trade with the enemy? The pure doctrine of Dutch commerce held that it was. "If it were necessary to pass through Hell in pursuit of gain," said Byland, an Amsterdam merchant accused of trading with the enemy, "I would risk burning my sails."[16] At war with the French, the Dutch supplied the enemy's battle fleet with all its gunpowder, match and lead.[17] Quixotry, commercial wisdom or plain treason? The question was hard to answer and even harder to explain to a foreigner, especially to a jealous and suspicious ally like England, who might also raise critical eyebrows on learning that French soldiers fighting against Holland's allies in Italy were paid by bills of exchange on Amsterdam.[18]

This was not, however, the only cause of foreign annoyance with the Dutch. There was also their leadership in the European typefounding and printing trade. Forty presses worked in Amsterdam, catering for the foreign as well as the domestic market. Cheap textbooks of Calvinist theology were smuggled into Scotland, where they found eager readers. Print, carrying words, conveying thought, influencing opinion, spreading subversion – in it, Holland possessed the most insidious of weapons. Louis XIV was incensed by the little books printed at The Hague containing scurrilous attacks on the morals of his court. But annoyed as he might be by such pinpricks, he was careful to have the Dutch news-sheets read to him regularly as part of his work as a monarch. The Dutch "sausage shop", as Mme de Sévigné called it, could be and, in fact, was useful in political war. It was a by-product of the efflorescence which, for a time, put Holland in the forefront of European thought. It was no accident that at Leiden the Dutch possessed the most vigorous university in Europe. It was the golden age of Holland, or, more exactly, it was the time in which that age was waning. In the decade that ended in 1679, Rembrandt, De Witt, Jan Vermeer, De Ruyter, Spinoza and Vondel all died. The future would not be so brilliant.

But, in the meantime, the seven sovereign provinces of Holland thrived and waxed in prosperity until the income of their people was, per head, five per cent higher than that of the English and forty per cent higher than a Frenchman's. The small, patrician, ruling class, the "Regents" of the Dutch cities, had no links with the nobility; they had their own pride, and one Dutchman in every thousand belonged to a regent family. These burghers combined wealth, taste and austerity; their fine houses on the Keisersgracht were crammed with works of art. As time passed, they retired from active business and lived on government annuities and on their dividends from the East India Company. They were rentiers. Land being the scarcest of all commodities in Holland, these merchants were not as subject as those in other countries to the normal temptation of commercial castes, to turn themselves into country gentry. For the most part, they invested the proceeds of business in business, although at times they put their surplus cash into schemes of land reclamation – the polders which, year after year, were adding six or seven square miles to the area of Holland.

But could a nation so small and so rich avoid falling as a prey to some powerful neighbour? In considering this question, the quality of the people's fibre must be taken into account. The Dutch might be lacking in panache, but they had plenty of sober courage and steady nerve; moreover, they could with their wealth maintain an army almost as big as England's, part native and part mercenary, and recruited in different countries. They paid good wages and they paid promptly. They enticed seamen by the hundred from the English navy. They kept on the strength three English and three Scottish regiments, which carried British colours and were commanded by a British officer.[19] These troops, although paid by the Republic, owed their allegiance to the House of Orange, the head of which was, by tradition, the Stadtholder (Viceroy) of Holland and commander-in-chief of the Dutch armed forces. The Orange princes were rich, with an income of £150,000 a year derived from estates in the Netherlands, France and Germany. As descendants of William the Silent, they were indelibly associated with Dutch valour and freedom. They would like to have become Kings, but the Provinces remained obstinately republican. As time went on and victory in war brought higher prestige to the family, the Orange princes, who had been "excellencies", wrung from the Emperor the right to call themselves "highness"; royal status evaded them. Holland remained a loose federation of urban oligarchies which, at times, were almost but never quite a monarchy. Thus, power in the country was divided in an untidy way which was plainly unsatis-factory and should have been unworkable. The States General (which Seeded a unanimous vote for any decision committing all the states), the ntadtholder, and the chief official of Holland, called the Grand Pensionary, all had their part to play in governing the country. One of the provinces, Holland, contributed nearly sixty per cent of the national revenue.

On the mudflats of the North Sea, then, a state had come into being unlike any other and, above all, different from Bourbon France. Ill-matched as they were, a clash between the two was, like the dismember-ment of the Spanish empire, one of the most likely events of the age.

However, there was the fourth member of the Atlantic quartet to be taken into account: England – the most idiosyncratic of the four, the one which most obstinately defied any attempt to fit her into a simple category, political, religious, or even economic. She had survived a tiresome civil war and a republican autocracy which most of her people had found highly uncongenial. Now she meant to make up for lost time, aware that, if Holland possessed certain advantages in the era that was opening, England possessed assets greater by far. Consider only her geographical position – an island looking towards America, on which, incidentally, she already had a foothold, a modest one admittedly, "the fag end of the discovery, northern, cold and barren", yet had she not "brought gold out of that dross, the dregs of the Spaniards' first extrac-tion"? In future, she would do still better. Her people: their nature was various and passionate, their interests complex. They were, for the most part, Protestants, although – and this, too, was characteristic – Protestant in a style of their own, not of the Dutch (or the Scottish) variety. They looked on the bustling commercialism whose hub was in Amsterdam as something they could learn from and imitate, eventually rival and surpass. They were supremely confident of their own abilities at any level of endeavour. One who knew them well and was certainly not blinded by chauvinism, said that their workmen had "a genius for improving the inventions of other races even if their temper is gay, ostentatious, vicious and full of excesses".[20] This was simply to say that the English artisan did not differ greatly from his compatriots in other walks of life. The merchants, the seamen (who were many), the soldiers (who were few) – foreigners could admire them, could even like them – but always there would be a sense that the English possessed hidden, undeveloped qualities which might be manifested in disconcerting ways. This suspicion that something lurked in the nation which had yet to burgeon was shared by the English themselves and appeared in a hint of arrogance and more than a hint of pride. England was moving up the staircase of power and achievement. Thus an unnamed poet sang:

"England's a perfect World! Has Indies, too!
Correct your maps! Newcastle is Peru!"[21]

The verse was rough but the meaning was clear enough.

One day, no doubt, it would be necessary for the English to settle accounts with the Hollanders, which would be a task well within their power! If only Holland were alone in Europe! But the matter was not so simple, as a glance at the map revealed. The entrance to the Scheldt, of which Holland held the key, must not, by an axiom of English policy, fall into the hands of a great power. Once this had meant Spain – now it meant France, a state quite different from England and, on land at least, a great deal stronger. At this point religion entered to make the pattern even more confused. A party grew up in the higher reaches of English political life which dreamt and, in secret, planned for a return of England to the fold of Rome. This party found natural allies at the French Court. The two royal houses, Stuart and Bourbon, were linked by blood and outlook. The English kings would like to become as powerful as their cousins the French kings were. But the Civil War in England had established a Parliament which, in the House of Commons, held a power over the nation's purse-strings that it had no intention of giving up. Taxes were held down, to the great advantage of business. The kings lived by cadging on foreigners. The army and navy were starved. "The people laid aside all warlike exercises," said a foreign observer, "and fell into such weakness and vices as are commonly the product of plenty and peace!"[22] Trade flourished as never before. In the three decades after the restoration of the monarchy, a share in the East India Company appreciated a thousand per cent while continuing to pay dividends of ten per cent on the market price.[23] While "the City" was the first to benefit, other classes shared in the general upsurge.

Was England a democracy? Of a faltering and partial kind. There were, in this nation of five million people, about a quarter of a million men who had the right to vote. The most solid political factor in church and state was the landed interest, the country gentry – substantial men who farmed their acres, hunted, shot and fished, good churchmen, hearty men with a hearty suspicion of the great cities, above all of London where something was growing up which they did not fully understand but instinctively disliked. They called it the "moneyed interest" – finance – and they scented in it a power, novel and rootless, which would one day surpass their own. That it would not always be rootless, that it would soon invade the preserves of the country gentlemen was hardly suspected. Yet, towards the end of the age, Daniel Defoe was writing, "I dare oblige myself to name five hundred great estates within a hundred miles of London which, within eighty years past, were the possessions of the English gentry which are now in the possession of citizens and trades-men."[24] Above the gentry was a smaller class of grandees, vastly richer and more sophisticated, inclined to be anti-clerical, with some awareness of what was going on in Europe and enough spare capital to take an occasional flutter in the City.

It was an age when political parties were only beginning to form, but where already one could say that there were two nations in England, not rich and poor, but high and low churchmen, men who had crossed the Channel and those who had hardly visited the next county, men who owned a town mansion and those who did not, those who drank wine and those who preferred October ale, Court and Country, and, as they would in due course come to be known, Whig and Tory. Among all the attributes of English life, puzzling and even shocking to foreigners, and competing for men's loyalty with patriotism itself, was the spirit of party. Sermons and tracts were no longer the main agents of controversy; new weapons were at hand. "Pamphlets, sir! You may go into a coffee house and see a table of half an acre's length covered with nothing but tobacco pipes and pamphlets."[25] Grub Street was being born, "a street near Moorfields much inhabited by writers of small histories, dictionaries and temporary poems".[26] and, in due course, giving its name to a barely reputable kind of literature which was, however, an essential ingredient in the age that was dawning.

As England grew richer, the country gentlemen, traditional backbone of the nation, were aware that their importance was waning. They might not understand the full sweep and subtlety of the financial revolution that was overtaking them, but they knew enough to fear it and to find something alien and unlikeable in the men who were its most conspicuous agents ("Trade like religion is what everybody talks of but few understand"[27]), the stock jobbers – English, Dutch, Huguenots, Jews – who were undermining old England and her values. Already the country gentlemen had suffered something of a setback in the Civil War; now they saw new catastrophes ahead. They could not be expected to discern that the passing of the old rural society they had known presaged the birth of a vast maritime empire.

I

Le Bel Anglais

The Churchills had come badly out of the Civil War. Winston Churchill, the most conspicuous member of a Royalist family in Dorset, became a cavalry captain at twenty-two and stayed in the fight until 1645, a fact which, in the days after the King's cause had collapsed, was known in the neighbourhood to all too many for convenience. His father, John Churchill, although too old to go to the wars, was also a King's man, for which offence he paid a fine of £440 in order to redeem his estates. It was a heavy penalty, for the Churchills were people of modest means – country gentlemen who were scarcely better than yeomen. So at the end of the war Winston was the unemployed, ex-soldier son of an impoverished Royalist father, and a marked man to Parliamentary officials. However, some time in 1643, he had married a young woman named Elizabeth Drake whose family, socially a cut above the Churchills, was of impeccable loyalty to the Parliamentary cause. Elizabeth, the third daughter of Lady Drake, brought to the marriage a dowry of £1,500. Thus it seemed that, by this marriage across the gulf of war, Winston had insured against the economic penalties of defeat. But not altogether. The Drakes, too, had suffered in the war.

One January day in 1644, Lord Poulett's Royalist troops had descended on Lady Drake's house at Ashe near Axminster, had driven off the Roundhead garrison, looted the house and set it on fire. Shoeless and all but naked, as it was later reported, her ladyship had fled to Lyme Regis. But all was not lost. Later in the year, she was allotted by Parliament a rent-free house in London. In 1650, she was awarded £1,500 compensation for Ashe where, partly roofless and empty as it was, she set up the family home. There she was joined by Winston, her son-in-law, his wife Elizabeth and, in due course, their children. In the meantime, Winston had been fined £446 18s for "his delinquence", a penalty which was roughly equal to three years' income from his property. Awaiting the day when the King would come into his own again, he threw himself into the study of the principle of Divine Right and the genealogy of the Churchills who descended from one Wandrill, Lord of Courcelle, whose youngest son came over with the Conqueror. It was an occupation harmless enough, to be sure, for a frustrated ex-officer with which to while away the years of Oliver's rule in England and the exile of the second Charles.

In the meantime, children came to Winston and Elizabeth, twelve in all, of whom five survived infancy. There was Arabella, born in 1648 and growing up – if the painter Lely does not lie – to be a luscious blonde with heavy-lidded blue eyes and sensual lips. There was John, born on 26 May 1650, a boy of spectacular good looks. While Winston Churchill scanned his pedigrees and polished his laborious prose in the study at Ashe House, his brood were enjoying the healthy, open-air, uneducated life of English farm children in the country where the river Axe meanders between the Devon hills to meet the Channel in Lyme Bay. Two younger sons should be mentioned, Charles and George. They will appear later in the story.[1]

So it went on until that day in 1660 when the world changed and the King enjoyed his own again. In April 1661, Charles II was crowned and in that year Winston Churchill became MP for Weymouth in what is known as the "Cavalier Parliament". Andrew Marvell, one of his fellow-members, had another name for it; he called it the Pensionary Parliament, from the large number of those who sat on its benches and owed gratitude, and therefore votes, for favours received to the Crown or the ministers. Among them, he picked out Sir Winston Churchill – the knighthood came in 1664 – who, he said, had "acted as pimp to his own daughter" in order to advance his political fortunes.

The judgment is severe and is probably unjust. Through the influence of Lord Arlington, Winston was sent to Dublin to serve in the Court of Claims, whose task it was to adjudicate in the question of lands that had been sequestered during the Civil War. It was not a job that could be done with any satisfaction to the judge or the claimant. There was not enough land available in all Ireland to meet the demands of those who had an honest case to put forward, to say nothing of the more

15

numerous dishonest suitors. Very soon Winston was begging Arlington to let him return to London. He and his fellow commissioners had met with "unexpected discouragements". When he came back, he brought with him his son, John, who had been attending the Dublin Free Grammar School – and was now entered as a scholar at St Paul's School. The Churchills settled down in Whitehall, where Winston became Junior Clerk Comptroller to the Board of Green Cloth. After all their setbacks in the war, the Churchills were beginning to move up in the world. While John, aged fourteen, was studying the art of war in Vegetius at St Paul's, his sister, Arabella, three years older, was pursuing a different art in more glamorous surroundings. It was she who gave the family its first real entry into the upper regions of society.

In 1665 she became a maid of honour to the Duchess of York and, some time in the next three years, caught the eye of the Duke himself. This was not an unlikely event, although it was no great compliment to her looks, the Duke being notorious for his poor taste in women. As one of his mistresses* said: "What he saw in any of us, I can't tell. We were all plain and, if any of us had wit, he would not have understood it." The Duke was not the brightest of the Stuarts. Charitably, Charles II suggested that his brother's mistresses were chosen for him by his confessor as a form of penance. They were, however, a commodity for which he had a strong appetite. "I do not believe that there are two men who love women more than you and I do," said Charles to a French ambassador, "but my brother, devout as he is, loves them more."[2] Sinning and repenting, both of them gloomily, James Stuart was an unusual member of his family and a sad contrast to his brother Charles, whose tolerance extended to his own vices. A romantic story is told by the resourceful author of Grammont's Memoirs, that Arabella had a spill in the hunting field which revealed to the enraptured Duke unsuspected beauties of form. Be that as it may, she climbed into his bed and had four children by him, one of whom, her son, James FitzJames, Duke of Berwick, became in due course a Marshal of France. If there is anything in heredity, he did not owe this to his Stuart blood, for his father's family were, through the ages, distinguished for their military incompetence. It seems, then, that it is rather to the Churchill strain that we should look for the secret of Berwick's prowess. As things turned out, he was the second illustrious soldier in the family.

As for the disgrace which Sir Winston was thought by the censorious

* Catherine Sedley.

Marvell to have incurred through Arabella's downfall, too much should not be made of this. After all, it was not compulsory for the Duchess' maids of honour to sleep with the Duke. Some of them did not. And it is reasonable to suppose that Arabella was a young woman who knew very well what she was doing and needed no encouragement from her father. The Heir Presumptive after all was quite a catch. Walking in Whitehall one day, Samuel Pepys met his friend, Mr Pierce, the Duke of York's surgeon, who "told me as a great secret that he was going to his Master's mistress, Mrs Churchill, with some physic, meaning for the pox, I suppose. Or else that she is got with child but I suppose the former, by his manner of speaking it."[3] Whether Pepys' scandalous surmise is correct or not, Arabella lived to a respectable old age, married and raised a second, lawful family.

Meanwhile, Sir Winston, having launched his daughter on her career, busied himself with that of his sons. He set about the task with all the effrontery of a fond father; thus, he sent one boy to carry a letter to his benefactor, Lord Arlington, so that he might "make his first entry into the Court, as I did, under the patronage of your Lordship's favour". John, at sixteen, became a page in the Duke of York's household where his sister was already installed, while his brother, George, went as page to Lord Sandwich on a mission to Madrid. Left far behind were the penurious days in Devon.

For John especially, the prospects were rosy. There he was, sauntering along the galleries of Whitehall, or walking sedately just behind his Royal master, as handsome a boy as any at court, eyed by men with approval; by women with something warmer. This does not of course run counter to the impression that he was probably unpopular with many of his contemporaries, to whom he may have appeared as an odious pretty boy enjoying an unmerited social success. Soon, too, young Churchill changed his page's livery for something more brilliant, the uniform of an ensign in the footguards. He wanted passionately to be a soldier and his master, the Duke, already well disposed to the Churchill family, gave him his commission in the autumn of 1667.

Not long afterwards, as if to prove that he was not content to be a decorative young officer in a fashionable regiment, Churchill went on active service to the Mediterranean, probably to Tangier. This North African town, just outside the Straits of Gibraltar, had come into British ownership as part of the dowry of Catherine of Braganza. It was defended, with some difficulty, against Moorish tribesmen and was used as a base

for several naval operations against the Algerine pirates. Churchill, as it
seems likely, first heard shots fired in anger in a skirmish with the Moors;
took part, it may be, in the naval blockade of Algiers and crossed into
Spain where, at this time, his brother, George, was in the embassy at
Madrid. He did not stay too long among the hard-drinking, grey-clad
Tangier garrison, "soldiers who sought their bread," as Lord Dartmouth
put it, "where finer gentlemen would not vouchsafe to come."[4] Tangier
was stifling, dusty and boring, and it was not the only place where a
young officer could make progress in his profession. There are more ways
than one to climb the ladder of glory. There was London, the court, the
boudoirs of hospitable ladies. It would be lacking in imagination to
underestimate the charm of King Charles' frivolous Whitehall. Consider
its effect on a sober official like Samuel Pepys when first he set eyes on it:
"I followed them up into Whitehall and into the Queen's presence,
where all the ladies walked, talking and fiddling with their hats and
feathers, and changing and trying one another's, but on another's head,
and laughing. But it was the finest sight to me, considering their great
beautys and dress, that ever I did see in all my life."[5]

Above all, there were the apartments of the King's reigning mistress,
Barbara, Duchess of Cleveland. She was beautiful, with red hair and the
volcanic temperament that is sometimes thought to go with it, wild,
fascinating and insatiable, "the lewdest as well as the fairest of King
Charles' concubines".[6] Nowadays she would probably be called a
nymphomaniac. She had been the mistress of the Earl of Chesterfield
when she married Roger Palmer which, however, did not prevent her
continuing as Chesterfield's mistress until he fled to France after killing
a man in a duel. After that, she found another lover. The paternity of her
first child was claimed by Palmer and acknowledged by the King. It is
thought likely, however, that Chesterfield was the father.

Barbara lived in King Street, Westminster, which was the main
thoroughfare of Whitehall. Her apartment was separated by the width
of the street from the principal building of that rambling royal suburb
which, covering twenty-three acres, stretched between St James's Park and
the Thames. For a time she was Lady Castlemaine, Palmer having been
given an Irish peerage by the King. Later, she was Duchess of Cleveland,
with an income suitable to the rank, and an ardour which time and titles
had not diminished.[7]

Her eyes fell greedily upon handsome Ensign Churchill, aged twenty
as compared with her twenty-nine. He was, as it happened, Barbara's

half-cousin. She was a Villiers, one of a clan of famous wantons, male and female, and related to John's mother. That happened which was likely to happen. The siren beckoned, the young man responded and (for the path of concupiscence never does run smooth) the King heard of the affair. Whether it is true that Churchill saved the lady from embarrassment by a dangerous last-minute leap from her bedroom window when the King was about to arrive, or was (through the treachery of another Villiers, Duke of Buckingham) found in Barbara's cupboard by the monarch – ("I forgive you because you do it to get your bread") – these are likely but unimportant scandals of a scandalous court.

A garbled version of the affair was later given by Mrs de la Rivière Manley, a propagandist who abetted Swift in his pamphlet-war on Marlborough forty years later: "The Duchess gave 6,000 crowns for a place in the prince's [Duke of York's] bedchamber for him. She called about her own person his fair and fortunate sister . . . who became the mistress of the prince,"[8] and so on. The narrative has the snigger typical of licentious writing of the period, although whether it did Churchill's reputation much harm may be doubted. On a more prosaic level, it is probable that the Duchess' last child, Barbara (born in 1672) was Churchill's.[9] The baby was educated with English nuns in Paris; later, became the mistress of the Earl of Arran* and mother of Charles Hamilton. She died at Pontoise in 1737, a prioress. In his customary, easy-going way, the King recognized the baby as his ("You may tell my lady that I know the child is not mine, yet I will acknowledge it for old times' sake"). It appears that this matter of paternity did not weigh heavily on Churchill's conscience.

Later, in April 1674, another outcome of the affair appeared. Churchill bought from Lord Halifax an annuity of £500 for which he paid £4,500. Where did the capital sum come from? Shocked or gleeful historians have assumed that it was provided by the amorous and wealthy duchess, and the assumption seems reasonable enough. In rewarding her young paramour, Barbara was gathering one of the purer fruits of adultery, the glow of gratitude in a lover's eyes. As a penniless officer in an expensive regiment, Churchill needed the money; and as a frugal young man he invested it wisely. Five hundred pounds a year, paid by Lord Halifax or his estate for more than forty years – it was a respectable income in days when the average income of a knight in England was about £650. Churchill has been criticized almost as severely for the way he used the

* Later, Duke of Hamilton.

money as for the way he earned it. Behind the smooth exterior of a young man about Whitehall it appeared that a calculating mind was at work. There was something else, too.

In the spring of 1672, England as the ally of Louis XIV went to war with the Dutch. It was one of those moments in time when England's commercial jealousy of Holland had proved stronger than her alarm about French expansion. Unknown to his subjects, King Charles was pursuing a policy at once secretive and consistent. Two years earlier, his adored sister, Henrietta, Duchess of Orléans, had paid a brief visit to England and had made the secret Treaty of Dover: by this, England and France were to attack and partition Holland, Louis was to supply Charles with cash and soldiers and Charles, at a moment he deemed suitable, was to declare himself a Catholic. After the Dutch had been forced to submit, Charles' nephew, William of Orange, was to be allotted a modest role as a French feudatory. At that moment, the Dutch republicans, who were in the ascendant, were refusing to allow William to become a Stadtholder. On a somewhat lower level, Louis sent Charles a dark-eyed Breton lady on whom during his sister's visit to Dover the King's eye had fallen with approval. She was Louise de Keroualle, whom Charles made Duchess of Portsmouth. Between the two Duchesses, Cleveland and Portsmouth, there was, for a time, keen rivalry, although both united in pillaging the King. As a poet, who may have been Dryden,* remarked later:

> Was ever Prince by two at once misled
> False, foolish, old, ill-natured and ill-bred!

When the Dover Treaty was made, William of Orange, the exact contemporary of John Churchill, was only twenty. The allied monarchs, therefore, thought that they were doing him no injustice and that, in any case, he was in no position to resist them. However, things did not work out as they had expected. The French armies swept into Holland. But the Dutch rose against the republicans, murdered their leader, de Witt, and made William their Stadtholder. And William opened the dykes, bringing the French army to a standstill. In addition, there was a naval war in which Ensign Churchill took part.

Leaving the pleasures of London, he shipped with his company of the Guards, on board the *Prince*, flagship of the Duke of York, Lord High Admiral. He was present at the desperate battle of Sole Bay when the Dutch Admiral de Ruyter pinned the English fleet against a lee shore.

---

* The Duchess of Portsmouth, believing that Dryden was the author, hired a gang who beat him up. (Philip Sergeant, *My Lady Castlemaine*.)

Battered for hours by Dutch cannon, attacked by Dutch fireships, the *Prince* was by eleven o'clock so crippled that the Duke was compelled to shift his flag to another ship and, when that in its turn was disabled, to a third. Ensign Churchill and the Guards remained on board the *Prince*. As a baptism of fire, it was sufficiently bloody; a third of the ship's company were killed or wounded. When nightfall brought an end to the fighting, the English fleet was for the time being unable to resume the action and Churchill was put ashore with his company; after which he made his way to London. From Guards' ensign he was promoted captain in the Admiralty Regiment – the Marines – which had suffered heavy losses among its officers. It is thought that his Duchess, benevolently watching over her soldier boy, put up the money which enabled him to take up the captaincy. This seems likely enough. The cost of the promotion would certainly be less than the £1,000 needed for a Guards captaincy and her Grace could well afford it. Not everybody was pleased by the promotion. Churchill's lieutenant, Edward Picks, complained to Lord Arlington's under-secretary that "without Lord Arlington's kindness, I fear I may still continue a lieutenant". He offered to pay the under-secretary four hundred guineas when he received his commission, "confident it may be done by my Lord Arlington".[10]

By the end of the year Churchill was in France wearing the yellow coat of his new regiment. There, with a handful of English volunteers, he joined Monmouth at the siege of the Dutch-held fortress of Maastricht, under the eyes of Louis XIV, who was nominally conducting operations. He took part in a night assault on a demi-lune★ in front of one of the gates of the town. Three times the attack was driven back, after which Monmouth called for support to d'Artagnan, commanding the King's Musketeers, a "gentleman of the greatest reputation in the French army". The musketeers fell on the enemy with fury. Churchill, sword in hand, brought up twelve Lifeguardsmen and (as was reported later) planted the French standard on the parapet. Maastricht surrendered with the honours of war. Churchill, wounded, like hundreds of other less famous soldiers, in the savage hand-to-hand fighting, was praised by Louis, and when he returned to Whitehall was presented to Charles II by Monmouth as "the brave man who saved my life". That autumn he was in the wars once more, this time in Alsace, where he caught the eye of the great Turenne. When one strongpoint was lost, the French Marshal was willing to bet that

★ "An outwork, resembling a bastion, with a crescent-shaped gorge, to protect a bastion" – *OED*.

"the handsome Englishman" would retake it with half the number of men who had lost it.

At the end of 1672, Captain Churchill shared a glamorous mistress with the King; he had a steady income apart from his pay; his exploits as a soldier had caught the eye of authority in London and Paris; his prospects of promotion were bright, especially if war continued – and if he escaped its worst hazards. And at that moment in history, war was one of the future events that a man could count on most confidently. Against whom? Allied with whom? For what purpose? These were questions which did not trouble an ambitious young captain who felt that a colonelcy was already almost within his grasp.

The Churchills, male and female, were doing well out of the Restoration of the English monarchy.

II

The Worst Woman in the World

"You have been the falsest creature upon earth to me."
Sarah Jennings

"Sure she must be the worst woman in the world."
John Churchill

The Jennings – or Jenyns – family of St Albans in Hertfordshire belonged, like the Churchills, to the gentry. They, too, had their roots in the West Country. They, too, had been Royalists during the Civil War, although it does not appear that they suffered in the cause. Perhaps they had kept their heads down, living as they did in a part of England where Parliamentary feeling ran high. Two generations of Jennings had sat in the House of Commons for St Albans. No doubt Richard Jennings, one of the twenty-two children of Sir John Jennings, would have been better-off had his father sired fewer children. But the rentals of his properties in various counties totalled about £4,000.[1] It certainly should have been enough to allow Richard to live in dignity in his St Albans mansion and his manor house at Sandridge, and to make good marriages for his daughters. But apparently Richard mismanaged his affairs for, when he died, his widow, Frances, was left bankrupt with nothing to support her and her two young daughters but her social position as the daughter of a baronet and such kindness as this might bring her in quarters where money was more plentiful. In fact, it brought her sanctuary from her creditors in St James's Palace and a place for her elder daughter, Frances, among the Duchess of York's ladies-in-waiting. As Frances was one of the great beauties in a court where beauty was highly valued and relentlessly pursued, her moral position might have been precarious. But Frances, as unfashionably virtuous as she was fashionably lovely, was able to beat off the customary advances of the Duke, and those of less exalted gallants like Richard Talbot who, however, proposed marriage. A young woman of strong character, Frances introduced into the Duke's household a girl who had a stronger character still, her little sister, Sarah, aged twelve.

Sarah had not the beauty of Frances, although her looks were pleasing, but she had a quality of mind, spirit and temper such as is rarely found in woman – or man either. She was a fascinating child, with soft blonde hair, bright blue eyes and an adorable gift of conversation. She had a mind of her own. A boy or a young man who might be attracted to her was apt to catch a sudden glint in the blue eyes – independence? – a tilt of the chin, suggesting wilfulness, a sharpening of the voice which hinted at asperity, and think that, after all, charming Sarah was not for him. She was an odd little apparition to be found among the higher staff of a royal household – potentially a rebel, possibly a spitfire. One day, no doubt, a youth would come along, more intrepid, or more perceptive, or more deeply enamoured than the rest. Meanwhile, Sarah Jennings, by the time she was sixteen, had shown her mettle in a brief but fierce campaign against that formidable virago, her mother. After a battle in which blows were exchanged, she told the Duchess that if her mother was not expelled from St James's, she would run away. Mrs Jennings retorted that, if she was ordered out, she would take her daughter with her. "Two of the maids," she said, "have had great bellies at court. I shall not leave my child here to have a third." Sarah was annoyed rather than pleased by this maternal solicitude.[2] With all the vehemence of which she was capable, she argued that her mother was a madwoman and, therefore, unsuitable as her guardian. Her case prevailed. She stayed in the Palace. Mrs Jennings was ejected.*

About this time a handsome young colonel returned from the wars and resumed his place in the household of his patron, the Duke of York. After his first campaign in Flanders, John Churchill, aged twenty-four, had been given the command of a composite English battalion in the service of Louis XIV; he had a French colonelcy – an English lieutenant-colonelcy came later. As a mercenary officer, leading mercenary troops, he fought in various actions in the campaign which Turenne was fighting against the Duke of Lorraine in Germany. Probably he was present at Sinzheim, certainly he was at Enzheim in the Vosges in the autumn of

---

* The end of the story is creditable to both ladies. In 1692, Mrs Jennings had a stroke and lingered until May 1693. Sarah sat up night after night with her dying mother in her home at St Albans. Mrs Jennings left Sarah all her money, to the indignation of her daughter, Frances, by that time, Lady Tyrconnel.

1674, when eleven of his twenty-two officers were casualties in a hand-to-hand struggle for the possession of a small wood. On that day, the British cavalry did well at still greater cost – all of the officers who were not killed were wounded; half of the troops were casualties. In a list of unimportant little battles of the world, Sinzheim and Enzheim might well figure. They were bloody and they decided nothing. But, by his part in them, it appears that young Colonel Churchill satisfied his employers and won approbation at home, at least among those who saw no harm in fighting King Louis' battles for him. The report went back to London, "No one in the world could possibly have done better than Mr Churchill." The issue in the war was obscure except to the strategists at Versailles. The glory of defeating generals with names like the Duke of Lorraine or Count Caprara was unlikely to make any British heart beat faster. But, trudging about the upper Rhine valley and among the wooded hills that look down on it, Churchill was learning his trade under the most celebrated of masters. He was also raising the defences between him and the poverty he had at one time known.

Thus, when the fighting was over, he was able to ship back to England, duty-free, two trunkfuls of fine silver. He had collected enough plate in France to furnish a handsome dinner table; in addition, he owned a silver chamberpot. So he was able to set up an establishment in Jermyn Street befitting a young man with a career to make. He danced with the ladies of the court, he partnered the King at tennis. And one day when he was on duty at the Palace he met an extraordinary girl.

Perhaps the encounter occurred at a ball; more likely, he had seen her in her sister's company or in attendance on the Duchess and had scarcely been aware as the pretty child grew up. Then they danced and he found her graceful. They talked and he was surprised by a mind singularly mature and uninhibited. And one day, John Churchill realized that he was deeply, overwhelmingly, irrecoverably, in love. It was a strange accident to befall a cool-headed, self-seeking young man who had already enjoyed – perhaps was at that moment still enjoying – an amorous adventure in more exalted quarters. But it is the part of love to confound the schemer and tempt the wise man to imprudence. It has only to be added that Churchill not only fell in love but stayed in love with that mettlesome girl all his life. And she? And Sarah? She was alive to the young officer's good looks, to his spidery elegance, to his growing reputation as a soldier and a man of affairs. There he was, a smart Guardee, moving through the intricate steps of the dance while on his lips hovered a faint, enigmatic smile. A young man who would go further and was already interesting. It was not at all disagreeable to the girl to feel that she might be stealing something from gorgeous, copper-haired Barbara Cleveland, twice her age and twenty times as rich. That Sarah played her part in the drama of courtship may be assumed. That John's cautious nature was invaded by the turmoil of passion can be gleaned from his letters:

"Let me see you somewhere today, since you will not be at Whitehall . . . Nothing should have persuaded me to have gone abroad but the meeting of you who is much dearer than all the world . . . I fancy by this time that you are awake, which makes me now send to know how you do, and if your foot will permit you to give me the joy of seeing you in the Drawing-room . . . This would be a very long day, if you should be so unkind as not to write . . . I did no sooner know that you were not well, but upon my faith I was also sick . . . I hope you were so wise as to value your own health before your duty to the Duchess, so that you did not walk with her at five this morning . . . I was last night at the ball, in hopes to have seen what I love above my own soul, but I was not so happy . . . Pray see which of these two puppies you like best, and that keep . . . if you give it warm milk it will not die."

Here is the ardour, the tenderness, the breathlessness of true love. And its readiness to be hurt:

"To show you how unreasonable you are in accusing me, I dare swear you yourself will own that your going from me in the Duchess' drawing-room did show as much contempt as was possible. I cannot imagine what you meant by your saying I laughed at you at the Duke's side, for I was so far from that, that had it not been for shame I could have cried. And for being in haste to go to the Park, after you went, I stood near quarter of an hour, I believe, without knowing what I did. Although at Whitehall you told me I should not come, yet I walked twice to the Duke's backstairs . . . when I went away, I did not go to my chair, but made it follow me, because I would see if there was any light in your chamber, but I saw none."

Naturally, the news of the love affair spread over Whitehall and from there, to Paris. The Duke of Monmouth, Charles' favourite bastard, proposed in 1676 to make Churchill lieutenant-colonel of the Royal English, then fighting the Dutch as a component of the French army. Courtin, the French Ambassador in London, passed on the proposal to Louvois, the French Minister for War, along with a full account of Churchill's love affairs. Louvois turned down the idea, saying that

Colonel Churchill would "give more satisfaction to a rich and faded mistress, than to a monarch who did not want to have dishonoured carpet knights in his armies". However, it was agreed that Churchill was the best man available for the post. When it was offered to him, he rejected it. Courtin explained, "Mr Churchill prefers to serve the very pretty sister [Sarah] of Lady Hamilton" – by this time, Frances Jennings had married a needy nobleman named Lord Hamilton – "than be lieutenant-colonel in Monmouth's regiment."[3]

In another quarter, the young man's passion was looked on with dismay. The Churchills thought that their son, from whom they hoped for much, was not taking life seriously enough. The girl was penniless. By all accounts she was a "strange creature" with an even stranger mother. Why could John not be sensible and marry another inmate of the Duke of York's household, Catherine Sedley, the only child of Sir Charles Sedley, one of the richest and also one of the wittiest men in England? The girl was pale and thin but clever. As John Evelyn reported, she was "none of the virtuous, but a wit". Never too prudish where a fortune was in the offing, the Churchills pressed Catherine's charms on their eldest son. With some effect, as it may be, for the French ambassador, that keen observer of the social scene in Whitehall, saw Sarah at a ball, where she "had far more wish to cry than to dance. Churchill, who is her suitor, says that he is attacked by consumption and must take the air in France. I only wish I were as well as he."[4]

It seems likely and, in view of the consummate gift for dissimulation which Churchill displayed later as a soldier, more than likely, that he was deliberately teasing Sarah as she had teased him. Courtin reported that Churchill was being pestered by his father to marry a rich, ugly girl and that he had deserted the Duchess of Cleveland, having plundered her of 100,000 livres.* The Duchess had gone to France "in chagrin" but, if Churchill followed her there, she would be able to patch things up with him. This was in November 1676 at a time when the Frenchman was keeping a sharp eye on the young women of the court. When he gave a party for four of them, Sarah was one of his guests. He reported "there is nothing so dainty as the English woman's *chaussure*. Green stockings are most in vogue with black-velvet garters fastened above the knee by diamond buckles." Apparently, then, while Churchill was making up his mind, Sarah was not pining in solitude.

The inventive Mrs Manley told, years afterwards, a highly coloured

---

* Worth about £7,000 at that time.

story about the ingenious way in which Churchill, having fallen in love "without interest [i.e. a fortune] or the appearance of any", had rid himself of the Duchess by finding for her a handsome new lover and contriving to surprise the pair together. In a well-simulated fit of jealous rage, Churchill then swore he would never see the faithless woman again. It is a preposterous story. Had Churchill done anything of the kind, the Duchess would have dissolved in laughter, and Churchill was far too sophisticated a young man to have risked so clumsy a stratagem. What is true is that this time Barbara, given up by her young lover, went to France, where it was reported "she followeth her old employment very hard, especially with the Archbishop of Paris, who is her principal gallant."[5] The Archbishop, Monseigneur François de Harlay de Champvalon, was well known for his amorous activities, which had already earned him the censure of Mme de Sévigné. However, Barbara was not a girl to be content with one lover, however eminent. In Paris she took the English ambassador, Ralph Montagu, into her bed until Montagu, "as arrant a knave as any in his time",[6] annoyed her by simultaneously making her daughter, Anne, Countess of Sussex, his mistress. This young woman, as wayward as her mother, had formed a schoolgirl passion for the Duchess of Mazarin, an old flame of the King's, whereupon her husband had thrown her out. Barbara then took the girl to France and left her in a nunnery at Conflans while she herself returned to London for a short visit. She had a chilly reception at court because she had taken a new lover in France, the penniless young Marquis de Chatillon, and this had so annoyed Montagu that he told the King of her behaviour. He went further than that, however. Deciding that Anne's morals were in danger at Conflans, he arranged that she be moved to a nunnery at Belle Chase where he could keep an eye on her. Very soon this led to further trouble in which the King was involved. After all, the Countess was his daughter.

Pulled this way and that, is it any wonder that Churchill seemed for a moment to hesitate – or that even the appearance of hesitation on his part touched Sarah to the quick? "Press me no more to see you," she wrote, "since it is what I cannot in honour approve of." One has to guess to what the letter refers – it is not even dated – but if Churchill was being spoken of as Catherine Sedley's suitor then Sarah, proud and touchy as she was, would feel that she could not see him without some loss of respect. He wrote in protest – and again it must be said that the letter is undated: "You say I pretend a passion to you when I have other things in my head. I cannot imagine what you mean . . . I must ever love you as long as I have breath, do what you will. The Duchess goes to a new play today, and afterwards to the Duchess of Monmouth's there to dance. I desire that you will not go thither, but make an excuse and give me leave to come to you."

The dialogue went on: "As for seeing you," she wrote, "I am resolved I never will in private nor in public if I can help it. But surely you must confess that you have been the falsest creature upon earth to me. Too late I see my error." "It is not reasonable," said Churchill in anguish, "that you should have a doubt but that I love you above all expression which by heaven I do." But Sarah was implacable: "I am so little satisfied by this letter as I have been with many others, for I find all you will say is only to answer me and make me think you have a passion for me when in reality there is no such thing." Churchill was in despair. "Yours last night found me so sick that I thought I should have died but that the Duchess has sent me word that the Duke will see me this afternoon so that at night I shall have the happiness to see you in the drawing-room."

Relenting on the main issue, the girl covered her retreat with a shaft of sarcasm: "At four o'clock I would see you but that it would hinder you from seeing the play, which I fear would be a great affliction to you and increase the pain in your head, which would be out of anybody's power to ease until the next new play. Therefore pray consider and send me word if you can come to me without any prejudice to your health." No wonder Churchill, exasperated beyond endurance, wrote to Sarah's maid, Mrs Mowdie: "Your mistress's usage to me is so barbarous that sure she must be the worst woman in the world. I have sent a letter – which I desire you will give her. It is very reasonable for her to take it, because it will then be in her power never to be troubled with me more. I do love her with all my soul, but if I cannot have her love, I shall despise her pity."

Sarah knew how to deal with the crisis. "I have done nothing to deserve such a kind of letter as you have writ to me," she replied, "and therefore I don't know what answer to give; but I find you have a very ill opinion of me and therefore I can't help being angry with myself for having too good a one of you . . . After you are satisfied that I have not broke my word, you shall have it in your power to see me or not – and if you are contented without it I shall be extremely pleased."

The battle was over; the issue was decided. But the war spluttered on for a time, the girl unkind, unreasonable, disbelieving or affecting to disbelieve the man's sincerity; in short, the perfect pattern of the maid who, having been won, must grudge every joy to the victor; the man anxious, prolific in pleas and protests: "You are very unjust in saying that I love you less than I did . . . your unkind, indifferent letter . . ." And so on.

Not by any means unique as a prelude to marriage, although conducted with more than the normal severity of such exchanges. But marriage came. When? In the winter of 1677. Where? Heaven knows. Perhaps in St James's Palace. Marriage against the wishes of the bridegroom's parents. Sir Winston was particularly worried about money just then. He was heavily in debt and wanted his son, John, to sell his share in the entailed family property so as to pay the creditors. To this, marriage to a poor girl might be an obstacle. Besides, was it not the case that Sarah was almost uneducated, that she had not even been taught arithmetic? On this score, at least, the Churchills had no need to worry. As time showed, Sarah had a natural aptitude for arithmetic and required no tuition in it. In the end, neither poverty nor parental frowns prevented the union. John Churchill married on his pay as a colonel and his £500 annuity, plus what he and Sarah had as officials of the court. It was not great affluence; on the other hand, it was far removed from poverty. Churchill had enough money to buy himself promotion to a more lucrative office. He bought the Mastership of the Duke's Robes.[7] He was now quite an important royal servant. He and his young wife were about to play a secondary but not insignificant role on a glittering and tempestuous scene.

War – or peace – was at hand. Nobody in London, apart possibly from the King, was quite sure which. Parliament voted a million pounds on the assumption that war with the French was imminent. And was it not likely? In that year of 1678 King Louis, insatiable for glory and conquest, an autocrat with a superb army, was the enemy, dreaded alike in London, Brussels, Amsterdam, Madrid, Vienna. In England, King Charles had a minister, Lord Danby, who had no doubt that the enemy most to be feared was the French ruler with whom, eight years before, Charles had made the secret Treaty of Dover. Since then, the scene had been radically changed. French armies had swept across the Netherlands and occupied three of the seven Dutch provinces. Dutch East India Company stock had fallen to 25 on the Amsterdam bourse. Holland had been saved from total extinction by the costly expedient of flooding the dykes, and England, in alarm, had withdrawn from the French alliance. But it seemed certain that Louis would one day complete his programme of conquest. Then Danby brought off the coup of marrying the Duke of York's elder daughter, Mary, to William of Orange; the French King heard the news as if it had been the loss of an army.[8] At least, he was highly incensed. While excusing Charles, for whom he was always ready to make cousinly allowances, Louis bore thereafter a lasting grudge against Danby.

For an ambitious young soldier-diplomat like John Churchill, it was a time of intense activity. He was summoned to London by his Royal master, leaving his young wife, Sarah, with his parents at Mintern in Dorset where, at that time, Sir Winston was deep in controversy with Blue Mantle over a new and improved version of the Churchill pedigree. This was something which, it can confidently be assumed, Sarah did not find entertaining. Heraldry was not her passion. Moreover, she knew very well that the Churchills had tried to prevent her marriage to their son; she modulated her behaviour accordingly. At the best of times, she did not get on with her mother-in-law, a woman with a temper as vile as her own. "Since the world began," she wrote long afterwards, "there have not been more than two women who have been good mothers-in-law." John Churchill had at times to use all his diplomatic art to keep the peace between the two.

Now he arrived, weary, in London, changed into his best uniform and presented himself to the Duke of York. He found His Royal Highness in warlike mood. Although James Stuart was a Papist and, in the ordinary way, was pro-French, he was also a militarist who knew that, if war came, he would be commander-in-chief. Moreover, if war was the popular cry, the Duke saw no harm in gaining a little much-needed popularity for himself by joining in it. Finally he wanted the army to be as big as possible since, if he came to the throne, he meant to rule by means of it. As a first instalment, four new regiments of foot were created and Churchill was made colonel of one of them. In the spring he was sent on a mission to Flanders to work out the military details of the alliance against the French. Deal to Flushing and Flushing back to Deal. Churchill made the crossing more than once that year. On one occasion, in July, it was reported that the French had captured him "in a topsail gale at NNW". But there was no truth in the story. He was appalled by what he saw of the Spanish troops in the Netherlands and decided that, while the Spaniards were anxious to be defended, they could do nothing to defend themselves. At The Hague, things were much more encouraging. William of Orange was a young man of brilliant intelligence and fiery spirit. He was ready to put as many soldiers into the field as the English. Churchill was empowered to offer him 20,000 men and an appropriate strength of artillery.

It seemed for a little that Louis would back down without any further ado. His diplomats talked peace. The French ambassador in London promised Charles "wedges of gold in bales of silk sent over in a yacht" if England kept out of war. A fortune in diamonds and pearls was offered to Danby on the same terms.[9] For a time then the war fever in Whitehall abated. After all, it seemed there was going to be no war. "All the fine gentlemen who intended to conquer France are disappointed and this noble army is out-of-hand to be disbanded, to the grief, I think, of none but those who are of it!"[10]

But the whole situation changed once more when the French army, by pouncing on Ghent, was thought to justify every suspicion of their King's intentions. In Whitehall, the war spirit returned with greater intensity than ever. By the end of June, Henry Savile, keeping his sick friend, Lord Rochester, posted about the movements of opinion in town, reported that "whoever is not now in this hot season in a *drap de Berry* coat with enough gold galoon to load a mule is not thought affectionate to the government or the army . . . There are four of our regiments more gone into Flanders upon a certain alarum of war."[11] As part of this mobilization, Churchill was promoted Brigadier of Foot with authority to recruit; in May, he expected to be sent to the Continent. In the meantime, the galleries of Whitehall hummed with rumours of a different kind.

A former friend of Churchill's was once more the centre of scandal. Barbara Cleveland had gone to Paris: "Make the least noise you can," said Charles as she left, "and I care not who you love." From Paris there soon came news of trouble. Henry Savile, now writing from the sweat house in Leather Lane where he was trying to cure an untimely attack of the pox, brought the first tidings to Rochester. "There are terrible doings at Paris betwixt my Lady Cleveland and her daughter, Sussex. As I am a friend to the family, till the story be complete I will not venture at sending you the whole relation." What had happened was this. On 28 May, Barbara had sat down in her Paris apartment and dashed off to the King, in one prolonged effusion of hate, a letter quivering with indignation and dripping with poison. After all, it is not necessary to be virtuous to be morally outraged. Hardly able to write for the tears of grief, "that a child I doted on should join with the worst of men to ruin me", she said that her daughter had not spent two successive days in the monastery where she had been left, but every day had gone out with Montagu and "has often lain for days together in my house, he being always with her till five o'clock in the morning, they two shut up together".

After this creditable display of indignation, the Duchess moved into the attack. Charles would not, she hoped, follow the advice of "this vile man who in his heart hates you and would ruin you if he could. He told me that in his heart he despised you and your brother and that, for his part, he wished with all his heart that the Parliament would send you both to travel – for you are a dull governable fool and the Duke a wilful fool. So that it was always better to have you than him for that you always chose a greater beast than yourself to govern you." Montagu, she went on, had found a fortune-teller who, for money, would write anything that he told him to write. This impostor was going to be sent over to London where he would advise the King to get rid of Lord Danby and the Duchess of Portsmouth, on the grounds that they were ruining him. Thus, room would be made for Montagu, who would become Lord Treasurer in Danby's place and would see that Charles had plenty of money and wenches.

At that moment, Montagu was angling for the post of Secretary of State and had promised the existing incumbent £10,000 to hand it over. While still in Paris, he heard that his reputation was under grave attack in Whitehall. He hurried back to deal with the crisis without obtaining the King's leave to do so. His reception at court was icy. When he proposed to tell the King what had really happened in the Lady Sussex business, Charles told him he had already heard enough about it. And why, pray, was Montagu in London without leave? Henry Savile reported, "His friends and enemies are now struggling at court to support or ruin him. The latter is, I think, the likeliest at every count." This pessimism was well-founded. Montagu was dismissed from his embassy, stripped of all his offices and threatened with the Tower. The jobs he had were distributed among Danby's friends.

While Churchill, who had been assigned to the command of a brigade of five first-class battalions, two of them Guards, was waiting impatiently for his orders to embark for Flanders, the closing months of the year brought important new events. Overshadowing everything else was the Popish Plot. This dangerous canard was invented by a prodigious liar named Titus Oates (with some modest help from facts) and swept the town into a condition of rare hysteria, in which every crime could be confidently attributed to agents of the Pope. To make matters worse, a respectable Protestant London magistrate, Sir Edmund Berry Godfrey, was found murdered on Primrose Hill. But by whom? Was it necessary to look further for the villain than some hireling of the Jesuits?

It is easy enough to be scornful of the credulity of those Londoners of 1678. But this was the age of the Dragonnades in France and the Killing Time in Scotland.★ The Edict of Nantes would very soon be revoked. All the more credit then to the man who kept his head and his scepticism in the crisis of the Plot, King Charles II. One immediate victim of the Plot was Churchill's master, the Duke of York, a Catholic whose household had harboured one of the alleged plotters – the only one against whom any genuine evidence could be adduced – his wife's secretary, Coleman. As for Danby, he might have expected to escape from public fury as one who had carried out a policy of collaboration with the Protestant leader, William of Orange, but at a critical moment his political enemies were powerfully reinforced by money and advice from an unexpected quarter. Their general argument against him was that his real purpose had been not to defeat France but to obtain an excuse to strengthen the army in England. It was not a very impressive case; soon, they had a better one.

The French ambassador was able to tell his Royal master that Ralph Montagu was willing to give Parliament documentary proof that Danby had negotiated for a French subsidy. Naturally the informer would expect to be paid for this service – 100,000 écus was his price. Louis was willing to pay it. In consequence one day the ex-ambassador was led to the bar of the House of Commons where from a black box he produced receipts for French money bearing the signature of the anti-French Lord Treasurer of England, Lord Danby! Dismissal, impeachment, the Tower – these inevitable results were not long in coming. It was true that the King could not afford to have Danby tried before the House of Lords with Montagu as the chief witness for the prosecution. Both men knew too much. Danby was released from the Tower. It was nine years before he again played an important part in politics.

A fortnight earlier, the Duke and Duchess of York had left for Holland on the way to Brussels. They went with bitter reluctance. The Churchills went with them. For months, while the Duke hunted and fidgeted in idleness in Belgium, his Master of the Robes, a young unemployed

---

★ When the extremer sort of Scots Calvinists were hunted down by the dragoons of Claverhouse.

brigadier, spent his time travelling between Brussels, London and Paris on missions designed to further the Duke's interests, both financial and political. In August, a new crisis blew up. The King took ill and his closest associates, who knew best how recklessly he had lived, were the most alarmed. Churchill, by chance in London at the time, was at once dispatched in secret to bring the Duke over. It was essential in this emergency that the field should not be left clear for the Duke of Monmouth, Charles' most ambitious bastard.

Disguised in a black peruke and wearing a plain stuff suit, without his Star and Garter, the Duke rode in haste from Brussels to Calais with Churchill and two other companions. The weather was so bad that their ship took nineteen hours to make the crossing to Dover. There Churchill in full military uniform played the part of the most important person in the party, failing however to deceive the postmaster who swore that, by God, he would be much better pleased to see a better man than he, looking the Duke full in the face. Keeping up the pretence, Churchill took the best available horse but once again the Duke was spotted by a postal official who muttered something to himself as the Duke was mounting. The Duke, however, paid no attention. Riding hard, he and Churchill accompanied by a single footman reached London ahead of the rest of the party. It was seven in the evening when they reined in at an inn at the Barbican. Handing over the horses, they went by hackney coach to a solicitor's office in Lombard Street and thereafter to the home of Sir Allen Apsley, one of the Duke's courtiers. After supper, the Duke rested for a few hours before taking coach for Windsor at three in the morning. There he found the King still in bed but convalescent; the Duke fell on his knees and asked his brother's forgiveness for coming without leave. Charles forgave him gladly enough but could not allow the Duke to remain in England. Public feeling against the Catholic heir-presumptive was too fierce. So James returned to Brussels and Churchill was sent on a new mission to see if he could wheedle more money out of Louis for his master. He did not succeed. When he returned to Brussels he found that the Duke was determined to be an exile no more. He had had enough of foreign travel. He would go to Edinburgh by way of London and Churchill would go on ahead of him and obtain the King's permission. And so it was. The progress from London to Edinburgh took all of thirty-eight days. Sarah stayed in the apartment in Jermyn Street, expecting a baby, which died in infancy.

* * *

"London and Edinburgh are not the same," John Churchill explained, writing to his young wife from the northern city. "For one may find pleasure in being abroad at London, but it is not the same here." It was a mild way of expressing what he thought about an insanitary little city cramped on a ridge of rock and swarming with people who nearly spoke English. He spent more than two years there, part of a foreign body which had established itself in the hastily repaired old palace of the Scottish kings, the court of HRH the Duke of York. The Duke as a Papist, intolerant and stupid, was not at all likely to make a success of his Scottish viceroyalty. Churchill took a gloomy view of the prospects. "Sooner or later," he told a friend, "we must all be undone."[12] As for himself, he was kept busy as a courier linking Edinburgh and Whitehall. He obtained permission for the Duke to come to London to negotiate a deal with Charles' French mistress, the Duchess of Portsmouth. The grasping woman, who probably took a pessimistic view of her lover's expectation of life, wanted £5,000 a year pension from the Post Office revenues, which were the Duke's for life. This money was, presumably, to be in addition to the pension of £17,000 which the King gave her.[13]

In May 1682, while the deal was still being negotiated, the Duke set sail for London in the frigate *Gloucester*. His rule in Scotland had lasted less than two and a half years and had been little short of a reign of terror of which the victims were the more fanatical Protestants. What Churchill thought of it must be guessed; his wife, present at some of the trials, was horrified: "I have cried to see the cruelty that was done to these men." She did not forget what she had seen. On the way south, there was nearly an end of both York and Churchill. The *Gloucester* ran aground on a sandbank off the Norfolk coast, known as the Lemon and Ore. Then she lurched off into deeper water and went down at once. Of the three hundred on board her, only forty were saved. The Duke was one of them and Churchill was another. Various accounts were given of what had happened, some more likely to be true than others. The most convincing was told sixty years later by Sarah, who had it at the time from her husband's lips. First, the Duke refused to take to the one boat which the *Gloucester* carried, although if he had done so not a life would have been lost. When, at last, he was persuaded that the situation was desperate, he handed Churchill his sword to hold back the rush of men who would otherwise have swamped the longboat. So the ship went down with all aboard her "except my Lord Griffin who, when the ship was sinking, threw himself out of a window and saved himself by catching hold of a hen coop". The boat, which, according to one opinion, could have held fifty people, made off to the shore, less than fully laden, but carrying the Duke's dogs and his attendant priests.

Settled in London once more, Churchill – now a peer of Scotland, Baron Churchill of Eyemouth – picked up the strands of his military career. He was colonel of the King's Dragoons and commander of the second troop of Life Guards, both of them well-paid posts. He and Sarah with their growing family – a son and three daughters – could afford to live at Holywell House, St Albans, Sarah's family home which, in due course, they pulled down in order to build a new house in the grounds. Churchill was a devoted and affectionate father. However, it was not likely that either Lord Churchill or his wife would be long absent from the centre of the stage. As it turned out, Sarah was the pivot on whom the next events turned. The Duke of York's younger daughter, Princess Anne, had for long been Sarah's fascinated, passionately loving friend. Anne and her older sister, Mary, both had a tendency to emotional attachments to pleasing members of their own sex. Indeed, at one time, they shared a passion for a beautiful girl named Frances Apsley to whom Mary wrote gushing, romantic letters which began, "My dear husband". Soon, however, Anne centred her love on the tempestuous Sarah Jennings who, for her part, had an altogether cooler approach to the friendship. Later, she said that Anne liked only cards and eating. Now, it was time that Anne married. She was seventeen.

Fortunately, a suitable Protestant husband was available, Prince George of Denmark, blond, plump, stupid and fond of food and drink. It seemed a good match. One of its consequences was that the princess would obviously now need a household of her own. She was, after all, third in the line of succession. She needed at her side an older girl, with more poise, with more knowledge of the world – a girl like darling, clever, beautiful Sarah. If Sarah only would? . . . Sarah would. The Duke consented. And pretty, vivacious, hot-tempered Sarah became Lady of the Bedchamber to her adoring friend, Anne, Princess of Denmark. The salary was not impressive, a mere £200 a year, but the subsidiary emoluments were not to be despised and the opportunities were dazzling. It was the age of Mme de Montespan and, soon, of Mme de Maintenon. In Whitehall, there was that pretty, greedy little Frenchwoman, the Duchess of Portsmouth. All of which went to show what a clever, attractive girl could do. True, Anne was only a princess and was not very likely ever to mount a throne, but one never knew. Besides, there was

John, handily placed if – which God forbid – His Majesty should have a fresh attack of his mysterious illness. The Duke, it was known, leant on John a great deal. Lord and Lady Churchill . . . was it any wonder that looks were already dwelling on them, speculatively, and that tongues were beginning to wag? Already it was being said that John's fault was avarice – a complaint of which more would be heard in days to come. At this stage, what could it be based on, apart from a reported disposition not to stand his round in the tavern? Men have become disliked for lesser reasons. And it must be confessed that, although Churchill had a few close friends, he was not popular.

One day in January 1685 the wind of fortune filled the Churchills' sails. King Charles, who had seemed in good health and spirits, died of a stroke. James Stuart was proclaimed King of England, and a different mood came about at the summit of English life. Nell Gwynne, relic of a looser past, was forbidden to put her house in mourning. The Duchess of Portsmouth, who had asked for protection from unfriendly demonstrators, was told that she would be defended against insolences but not against paying her debts. Catherine Sedley heard from the new king that, "reflecting upon the frailty of mankind by the example of his brother, he had resolved to lead a new course of life and would see her no more."[14] James had been given a scolding by his confessor. Catherine, like a sensible woman, settled for the title of Countess and an annuity of £5,000, a gift which so much annoyed the Queen that for two days she refused food or drink. ("You have made your whore a Countess, why not make her a Queen?") To strengthen him in his struggles with the flesh, James took to the scourge, an instrument of correction, which on his death, his widow gave to the Convent of Chaillot, outside Paris. Catherine was ordered to live in Flanders, but refused to go on the ground that the number of convents there would make the air oppressive to her. She agreed to go to Ireland but, finding Dublin "intolerable" and the Irish "melancholy", she returned to London. James visited her secretly. The scourge had not been enough.

III

No Penny, No Paternoster

"Unblamed of life (ambition set aside),
Not stained with cruelty nor puffed with pride,
How happy had he been, if Destiny
Had higher placed his birth, or not so high!"

Dryden

In the early morning of 13 June 1685, two horsemen rode into Whitehall. They were dusty for they had covered two hundred miles as fast as relays of horses could carry them. They had the perturbed, important look of men who brought serious news. They were carrying a letter from the Mayor of Lyme Regis to Sir Winston Churchill, MP for the borough and an obedient servant of the King. Two days earlier, said the letter, three ships, one of them a frigate of thirty guns, had appeared outside the harbour. They were apparently foreign, although they displayed no colours. It turned out that the frigate was the *Helderenbergh* and that she had sailed from the Texel, under a skipper named Rietvelt, bound for the Canaries. In her hold were 1,500 stand of arms, four small cannons and 200 barrels of gunpowder. More alarming still was the identity of the chief passenger: James, Duke of Monmouth. The Duke, wearing a becoming purple suit, had come ashore with a group of armed companions, and had knelt in prayer on the beach. The local militia, having no powder or bullets, had thereupon disappeared. Monmouth had drawn his sword and led the way to the market-place followed by a green standard on which in gold letters were the words, "Fear Nothing But God".

At the market-place one of his companions, who by this time numbered about a hundred and fifty, read a rousing proclamation explaining that he had come to defend the Protestant religion and the laws, rights and privileges of England from the invasion made upon them by the usurpation and tyranny of James, Duke of York. James, it declared, had instigated the Great Fire of London, had hired men to assassinate the late Earl of Essex in the Tower and was probably responsible for the death of his

39

brother, King Charles. "Now let us play the man for our people and the cities of our God, and the Lord do that which seemeth good to him!" The townspeople of Lyme listened with growing enthusiasm to this summons. Men in the West Country had been prepared by signs and wonders for what was to come: in 1680, a monstrous birth at Ill-Browers in Somerset, and among animals similar instances. In January 1681, an earthquake accompanied by a "whizzing gust of wind". And at the end of 1684, mock-suns were seen on a sharp frosty morning. What did such omens presage?

The Protestant Duke, handsome, gallant, every inch a Stuart, with the star of the Garter glistening on his breast, and, but for one slight disability, a king! And that disability – his bastardy – was denied in the proclamation which had been written for him by Robert Ferguson, son of an Aberdeen-shire laird, a clergyman of sorts and a talented political agitator who had gone hurriedly into exile after the frustrated attempt to assassinate King Charles and the Duke of York in the Rye House Plot. In the proclamation for his arrest issued at that time he was described as tall and lean "with dark brown hair, a great Roman nose, thin-jawed, heat in his face, speaks in the Scotch tone . . . he hath a shuffling gait that differs from all men's, wears his periwig down almost over his eyes." Ferguson was an acrid, intriguing nuisance, more dangerous to his associates than to his enemies. But although his words were wild, they were well-enough attuned to the mood of the hour to bring in fifteen hundred recruits to the army with which Monmouth proposed to rescue Britain from James' popish tyranny.

This was the sensational news which, reaching London in the hands of two hard-riding customs officers from Lyme, sent Sir Winston hurrying to the palace on that fine July morning. The situation was made all the more alarming by the fact that Monmouth's landing had been preceded by a descent on Scotland by the most powerful of all the Highland chiefs, the Earl of Argyll. There were indications that risings were planned in London and Cheshire. The old cavalier was not a man to underrate the gravity of the crisis: the West aflame; rebellion in a region where Dissent was strong and where, at that moment, there was unemployment in the Mendip mines and in clothing towns like Axminster, Taunton and Frome.[1] Sir Winston called on his son, Colonel John, and together they went to the King.

The situation was not, however, quite as dire as Sir Winston thought. The exiled malcontents, English and Scots, who were living in Holland, had been taken by surprise by King Charles' death. They were hard-up.

They had concerted no contingency plan of action. They were men divided in motive and by social class. Argyll, the most notable of the Scotsmen, looked down from a height of pride and prestige on Lowland lairds like Hume of Polwarth or Fletcher of Saltoun. The Scots were suspicious of the motives and good faith of English political conspirators like Wildman, who was proposing to raise London in revolt. Argyll was determined that Monmouth, whose claim to the throne he refused to recognize, should not accompany him to Scotland. So there was a great deal of talk in Utrecht and Rotterdam before it was agreed that there should be simultaneous risings in England, Ireland and Scotland. Then Argyll sailed from the Texel three weeks before Monmouth. The attacks, it seemed, were not going to be co-ordinated. Other misfortunes followed. Wildman failed to light the fires of rebellion in London. A projected revolt in Cheshire came to nothing. Although Monmouth did not know it at the time, his landing at Lyme was already a forlorn adventure.

When the two Churchills told their story to the King, it was probably excitement rather than dismay that made James' habitual stammer worse. Here was an opportunity to test the efficiency of his army – and an excuse to strengthen it. Nor had he any doubts, after the first few minutes, that he could deploy sufficient professional military power to deal with the untrained zealots whom Monmouth might mobilize, even if they were properly armed, which, as it turned out, they were not. Before nightfall, Major-General Churchill (by this time an English peer) left for the West Country with six troops of horse and five companies of infantry. The garrison of Tangier, recently landed in England, was soon on its way to join him. At this moment, the attitude of William of Orange became important. He had, from the beginning, a good idea of what Monmouth and Argyll were up to, yet he had failed to prevent either of the rebels from setting sail. His reasoning seems to have been that, if Monmouth was defeated, it would be one obstacle the fewer between himself and the British crown. On the other hand, if Monmouth looked like winning, King James would be compelled to ask for William's assistance, and the Prince's prestige and bargaining power in Britain would be correspondingly enhanced. Accordingly, when James asked him to send over three Scottish regiments in the service of the United Provinces, William was happy to oblige – without undue speed.

On Monmouth's side, although young men poured in to fill his regiments until they were 4,500 strong, there was a shortage of officers to train and lead them. The gentry of the South-West held aloof. Andrew

Fletcher of Saltoun was an experienced soldier but quarrelsome. In a quarrel over a horse, he shot dead one of Monmouth's most valuable West Country supporters. After that Fletcher took no further part in the rebellion, but went to fight the Turks on the Danube. Then there was the question of arms. Of these, Monmouth had brought over a quite inadequate supply, bought partly by the sale of his mistress' jewels – there was, moreover, an inordinate delay in distributing them. Finally, there was the Duke's own character. He was a professional soldier, who had seen action in Flanders. He was gallant and endowed with his full share of the family's charm. But, as "Captain-General of the Protestant Forces of the Kingdom" he lacked the qualities that make an effective leader of partisans. He was not a Montrose. This, in fact, was the reason Argyll had given for refusing to have him as a partner in his Scottish campaign. Above all, Monmouth had not the instinct which should have told him that, in the adventure on which he had embarked, everything depended on a swift, audacious advance. To falter was dangerous; to retreat, fatal. The English gentry were waiting to see who was going to win.

Meanwhile, the Somerset militia having fled at his approach, he entered Taunton, receiving the welcome of a hero and a liberator. Flowers strewed the streets. His badge, a bow of green ribbon, was seen everywhere. Twenty-seven schoolgirls, aged eight to ten, had for weeks been at work embroidering standards for his army. One, all of cloth-of-gold, bore a crown and the initials J.R. – King James. Monmouth was proclaimed at the Market Cross on 20 June. A Quaker who was present saw him and reported that he looked thoughtful and dejected. He had reason to. If he reached Bristol in time all might yet be saved. There he had friends. There, having crossed the Avon, he might link up with supporters further north. He gave orders for the commandeering of all available scythes and pressed on. After six days of marching, he was a few miles outside Bristol with nine thousand men organized in five infantry regiments, the red (Monmouth's own), white, blue, yellow and green. Nine thousand men! And he had brought to England arms for only 1,500! Monmouth could hardly complain that he was denied the popular support he had expected. At that moment, his insurrection looked dangerous. "The rebels will soon be masters of this country," wrote Lord Fitzharding to a friend. "Where will they stop, God only knows." The fear was soon allayed.

Outside Bristol, with death in his heart, Monmouth learnt that he had lost the race for the city. The day before, Lord Feversham, the King's lieutenant-general, had entered Bristol with the Horse Guards. After a period of drought, the weather had broken. The rain fell pitilessly, deepening the gloom of disheartened men. But, for a moment, Monmouth seemed to toy with the idea of by-passing Bristol and making for Gloucester, a city famous for its heroic resistance to the Cavalier army in the Civil War. His cavalry repaired the bridge over the Avon at Keynsham and crossed over to the north bank. But Gloucester was four days' march away and, in Bristol, the King's generals had by this time collected four thousand men. Accordingly, Monmouth gave the order to retire. Meanwhile, General Churchill had arrived in the area, accompanied by his brother, Charles, who had come from Portsmouth with a train of artillery. The pair joined Feversham at Bath and with no undue haste followed the rebels as they retreated. Churchill was dissatisfied with the way things were going, especially with the fact that Lord Feversham, a middle-aged French Protestant, had been preferred to him as Commander-in-Chief. He knew himself to be the better soldier and felt himself a more deserving servant of the King. But sourly enough, he was forced to content himself with his promotion to Major-General.

Some miles south of Bath, Feversham attacked Monmouth's main force and had the worst of the encounter. Astonishing as it seems, these amateur soldiers from the West Country, without training and scarcely armed, weary and in retreat, could turn and fight. Feversham lost eighty men killed. In spite of this success, the more prudent of Monmouth's soldiers decided that their cause, just though it might be, was hopeless. About then, a pamphlet was distributed among them by Feversham's agents. It promised them pardon if they gave up the fight. Two thousand men slunk away. Next day news arrived at Monmouth's camp; the Earl of Argyll had landed in Scotland bringing with him a stack of swords ready for issue with the words inscribed on their blades, "Gott Bewahr die Aufrechte Schotten". But his enterprise had been shockingly mismanaged from the start and the Scottish government had taken the precaution of throwing his likeliest supporters into gaol. His capital town, Inveraray, was occupied by Frasers. Argyll himself had been captured on the way to Glasgow and had been executed in Edinburgh. Thus, the second prong of the twofold attack on the King was broken. Monmouth had every reason for despondency; the touching thing is, however, that his bedraggled host did not altogether lose its will to fight. They were, let us remember, men of the same stamp as Cromwell had turned into the Ironsides, men who knew what they fought for and loved what they knew. The trouble was that Monmouth had no arms to give them and no time to train them. And he was not Cromwell. On the other hand, those poor weavers and ploughboys had probably some inkling of the fate that was in store for them if they were beaten. It was too late for them to seek the King's pardon.

By this time Churchill had made a wide sweep through Dorset so as to prevent any reinforcements reaching Monmouth from the Channel. He had reported on 19 June to the King, "Unless speedy action be taken, we are like to lose this country to the rebels, for we have those two regiments [i.e. of militia] run away a second time. Half are gone to the rebels. I never saw people so daunted in my life." Now, a fortnight later, the prospect was brighter. Churchill joined forces with Feversham on the wet peat of Sedgemoor. So far the war had, for him, been scarcely more than a police operation with the object of pinning the rebels into a corner where they could be brought to battle. The united Royal army, three thousand regular troops – the First Guards (now the Grenadiers), the Coldstream, the Royal Scots, Kirke's, Trelawny's and Charles Churchill's – with sixteen guns, was in camp half a mile from the hamlet of Weston Zoyland on the edge of the moor. Between them and the enemy was a succession of three broad, marshy ditches, the last of which was called Bussex Rhine, over which there were two crossing places. Some distance away was a force of half-trained militia, in whose loyalty and zeal for action Churchill had little faith. He had seen them blench. He thought that, if things went wrong, they would desert and might even join the rebels.

Monmouth in his quarters at Bridgwater had, for his part, had no clear idea where the Royal army was until a farm labourer named Richard Godfrey brought news. His master, William Sparke, living in the village of Chedzoy on the edge of the moor, had from the tower of the parish church seen the army on the move that morning. He told Godfrey to find out where they had halted and how many there were: after that, Godfrey was to gallop to Bridgwater with the news. The news was that five hundred cavalry were in Weston Zoyland and five regiments of infantry were encamped outside. The Bridgwater road was commanded by cannon. From the church tower of Bridgwater, Monmouth's plan had been to march in the darkness past the Royal army in the direction of Gloucester. This was just what Churchill, on the evidence of his scouts, had expected him to do. He had not been deceived when Monmouth mobilized labourers and made a pretence of fortifying Bridgwater. He knew Monmouth's temperament and heard that he was commandeering horses and saddlery. He would certainly try to break out. But hearing what Godfrey had to say, Monmouth changed his plans. Now that he knew where his enemy lay, a dazzling possibility tempted him: to make a night attack on the Royal camp on the moor. Godfrey would show the way. The plan was approved by his officers.

So, at eleven o'clock that Sunday night, after listening to rousing sermons from their chaplains, Monmouth's army set off towards Sedgemoor, following Godfrey. Deadly silence; no lights. At most, the creaking of wheels was heard as the four cannon were manhandled across the moor. By that time, a heavy mist was rising from the marshy land. Cloud covered the moon. It was not easy for Godfrey to find the way, familiar as he was with the moor. It was far from easy for Monmouth's cavalry commander, Lord Grey, whose task was to turn the left flank of the Royal army. But two strokes of luck had come their way, although they were not aware of it. Feversham had dispatched a troop of horse to watch the roads leading out of Bridgwater to the north. The patrol had returned with the news that Bridgwater was deserted. It seemed that Monmouth had decamped. Hearing this, Feversham had gone to bed. It was just after one in the morning. However, one officer, Captain Mackintosh of the Royal Scots, was unconvinced. In fact, he was willing to bet that Monmouth would attack that night; what was more, he marked out on the ground between the camp and the ditch the lines on which his men were to be stationed in case of trouble. As it turned out, his regiment was on the right flank and took the first shock of Monmouth's attack. Soon after one had struck on Chedzoy parish clock, the attempted surprise of the Royal camp was discovered. A pistol was discharged; a sentry challenged. The alarm was given.

Until Feversham was wakened and emerged from his tent, Churchill took control of things, although in fact there was not much to do in the darkness except to prevent troops firing on one another and to move the cannon from the left flank to the right. Monmouth's cavalry, which were to ride round the flank of the Royal army, missed the vital passage across the Bussex Rhine. Churchill ordered the Scots to open fire on the horsemen, who fled in panic, riding through the infantry that were following them. In consequence, Monmouth's men were out of control by the time they reached the ditch. Trumpets were blaring and drums were beating on the other side. There was no longer any hope of a surprise. Feversham sensibly ordered a stand-to until first light. By that time, the artillery had been brought into position, drawn by coach-horses furnished by the

Bishop of Winchester, "fitter for a bombardier than a bishop". Thus, when daylight came, they could be brought into action, served, in the unexplained absence of gunners, by Sergeant Weems of the Royal Scots. The fight when it came lasted for two hours. The rebels had no effective answer to the Royal cannon: no answer at all after Churchill charged Monmouth's guns and drove off the gunners. Monmouth, pike in hand, fought on foot in the thinning ranks of his doomed but heroic army, until at last it was obvious even to the most desperate that future resistance was useless. Then a charge by the grenadier companies of the Guards and the Royal Scots settled the issue. Monmouth found a horse and rode off across the plain. Feversham sent in his cavalry to break up the stubborn last stand of the men of Somerset and Dorset. Then it was over.

It was over, except for the atrocities of Colonel Kirke's "Lambs", so called from the regiment's badge of a Paschal Lamb, and for the gallows along the roads outside Bridgwater, which Feversham peopled with twitching bodies. In the battle, the Royal army lost two hundred killed; the rebel dead in the fight and the subsequent slaughter numbered about ten times as many. Yet Kirke, brutal as he was, and Feversham, carrying into the English countryside his uncle Turenne's grisly methods in the Palatinate, were soon to be outclassed. A greater man than they was at hand, the appalling Judge Jeffreys, soon to be made Lord Chancellor of England by the King. Jeffreys' score was a hundred and fifty executed and eight hundred sent to work as slaves in the plantations. Public opinion was with the judge. Even Samuel Pepys, whom one would have thought the most humane of men, backed the petition of a sea captain for the grant of a thousand rebels for export to the Indies, "there to be treated according to their deserts".[2] Jeffreys was only an extreme representative of a harsh age. His outstanding triumph, however, was when he ordered that the little girls of Taunton who had sewn Monmouth's standards should be handed over to the Queen's Maids of Honour who could sell them for what they would fetch. The Maids of Honour did not miss this opportunity to punish such dangerous enemies of society.

So ended, in shame and misery, the attempt of the Protestant Duke to defeat his uncle's policy. But it had come nearer to success than, on any reasonable assumption, it should have done. The Reverend Andrew Paschall of Chedzoy parish, who saw the battle from near at hand that morning reported that the rebels "were as near to an entire victory as men could be and miss it".[3] Another man who was there thought that only the great wet ditch had saved the Royal army. He was a young Dissenter from London, the son of a tallow-chandler. He had fought in the ranks of Monmouth's army but was able to escape to safety. This was fortunate for, had he failed, we should not be able to read *Robinson Crusoe*.

Four days after the battle, Churchill wrote from Wells to his wife, "If you are not already come to town, I desire you will, for I hope it will not now be long before I shall be there and I shall be at no ease till I am in your arms." A week later, Monmouth was executed. Churchill would have little doubt what were the main political and military lessons of the rebellion. The Duke of Monmouth had, in the space of three weeks, in two English counties, been able to collect an army nine thousand strong. He had not been able to arm them or to train them; he had been refused the support of the squires. Even so, the meagre remnants of his army, fighting like men possessed, had brought to within a measurable distance of defeat all the soldiers King James could spare to suppress them. To a cool-headed and thoughtful observer, this could have only one meaning; there was another political force in England, apart from the Anglican Tory squires, who could be persuaded to confront the monarch in arms. This was the force of militant popular Protestantism. The national opposition to King James could therefore be estimated, not in thousands, but in hundreds of thousands. How could it be dealt with? Plainly, the militia would not be enough. In Devon, Dorset and Somerset, the militia had shown their unwillingness to die for a king whose policy they disliked. A change of government policy then? From a king like James, whose purpose was rooted in religious conviction, such a change was most unlikely. But if that must be dismissed as impossible, then it was necessary to create a regular army vastly stronger than that on which His Majesty could already call. And such an army could not include those three Scots regiments that William of Orange had sent over from Holland to help the King. They had arrived in the Thames too late for the Sedgemoor campaign. The King had taken one look at them and had decided that they – and especially their officers – were "disaffected". After hanging two soldiers for drinking Monmouth's health, he had sent them back to Holland with all speed.

Early in November Churchill's father, Sir Winston, moved in the House of Commons that supply be granted "for the army"; in the unstable international situation, England needed a standing army of 14,000 or 15,000 men. In the debate that followed, the amount that should be voted was discussed: as much as £1,200,000 or as little as £200,000?[4] Sir Winston argued that the latter sum was far too small.

"Soldiers move not without pay. *No penny, no paternoster.*" In the atmosphere that prevailed – fear of a popish king depending on a popish army – to quote that particular proverb was tactless to say the least. To make matters worse, a few days earlier, Louis XIV had revoked the Edict of Nantes, thus depriving the Protestants of France of their last guarantees of religious liberty. Two hundred thousand Huguenots left France, to the great advantage of neighbouring countries. Aware of these events, the House of Commons settled for a sum of £700,000, to which the Lords agreed, provided there were more tangible guarantees from the King that the soldiers would not be misused. Whereupon the King, in a fury, decided to do without the money. While waiting for a fresh turn in events, he would continue to rely on the secret subsidies he received from his cousin, Louis XIV.

Once back in London, Churchill found that, at court, he was given much of the credit for the victory over Monmouth. He probably deserved it. Although his military advancement was frustrated, as he thought, by the interloping Feversham, in another respect, he had no cause to complain of Royal favour. Three months before leaving for the war in the West Country, he had been elected to succeed the King as Governor of the Hudson's Bay Company.[5] Churchill was now an important figure in big business, for which his talents were eminently suited. He had qualified for the position by buying a share of £300 in the Company, followed later by another £100. Whether he actually paid for the shares is doubtful; it seems possible that he held them as nominal owner for a collaborator named William Yonge. On his return from the field of Sedgemoor, his fellow directors presented him with an address of congratulations and a catskin counterpane. A fort and a river on the Bay were named after him. Because of his connections at Court, Churchill was thought to be very useful to the company, which about that time was involved in a dispute with France over ownership rights.

Financially, he did pretty well out of Hudson's Bay. Three years after he became Governor, he was given a 50 per cent dividend on his holding of £400 stock; in the following years 25 per cent, plus £800 of new stock; in the year after, 25 per cent dividend on his holding, which by that time totalled £1,200. When he sold out in the autumn of 1692, it would probably be at a price of £5,000. On an original investment of £400 (assuming he actually paid for his shares), it was quite a satisfactory result. But by 1692, the world had changed for Churchill, and for England too.

IV

Such Bustle About Religion

"Ho, by my shoul, 'tis a Protestant wind."
Thomas Wharton

The speed of the Catholic Revolution was one of the factors that brought it to ruin. Had King James allowed it to go forward gently as the Pope wished, and not with the impetus and harshness advocated by the French ambassador, Paul Barillon, it is possible that the *coup d'état* of 1688 would not have been delivered. Perhaps it would not have been necessary. But, as things were, almost every day after Sedgemoor brought some fresh evidence of the determination and haste with which James and his secret council of Catholic advisers were carrying out their design of reversing Henry VIII's decisive act a century and a half before. Among these counsellors, more authoritative than any of the others, was a Jesuit named Father Petre. The Society of Jesus has a reputation for intellectual suppleness and political sagacity. Father Petre was an exception to a well-founded rule.

In the two English universities more and more Catholics were admitted, with Judge Jeffreys there to see that the King's will prevailed. Magdalen became a Catholic seminary. In the army, more and more Catholic officers were given commands and – to ensure that the rank and file would obey – the death penalty for desertion was introduced. Judges who hesitated to carry out this policy were replaced by men who had no such scruples. Thus the Chief Justice of the King's Bench and the Recorder of London were replaced. James thought, rightly, that the English and Scottish regiments serving in Holland were likely to be infected by republican and Protestant notions. He proposed to recall them, dismiss the more incorrigible in their ranks, fill up with loyal men – and train the regiments in France. When Churchill asked for the command of these regiments, he was refused: the job was earmarked for a Catholic, in fact for the King's bastard son, Churchill's nephew, the young Duke of

49

Berwick. More and more, Churchill was being looked on with suspicion. In any case, when the time came, William of Orange found a reason not to send the regiments home. Meanwhile, James went as far as he could in changing the religious complexion of the army. He was carrying out the injunction which he later gave to his son, "Never be without a considerable body of Catholic troops, without which you cannot be safe." The Tower, Tilbury, Portsmouth were given Catholic governors. And to every ship in the navy was allotted a Roman Catholic chaplain. The Chapel Royal at St James's became a Catholic church. "I would not have believed," wrote John Evelyn after seeing the priests officiate in Whitehall, "that I should ever have seen such things in the King of England's palace . . . The Lord defend His little flock and preserve this threatened church and nation."[1] Monastic communities and schools were set up. To the scandal of the stricter kind of Protestants, monks were seen in the streets of London. Propaganda went on feverishly. Local administrations, the Privy Council and the City companies were purged of prominent Anglicans although, unfortunately for James, the men who replaced them were often of poor quality. The diplomatic link with Rome was restored, with all ceremonial splendour. Soon it was possible for an intelligent, well-informed observer to estimate with reasonable accuracy the date when England would become a country in which Catholicism had taken the place of the Anglican establishment as the dominant strand in the national ethos. James was following in the footsteps of his cousin, Louis. He was doing so with Louis' money. Louis had written, "He who has given kings to men has desired that they be respected as His lieutenants, reserving to Himself alone the right to examine their conduct."[2] As theology it might be dubious but its appeal to a self-willed monarch was undeniable. To James, it was particularly alluring.

One observer of events was exceptionally well-informed. John Churchill knew about the French money – had he not on several occasions gone to Versailles to ask for more? He knew better than most men that the English army was being infiltrated by Catholic officers and that his own brother-in-law, Lord Tyrconnel, second husband of Sarah's sister, Frances, and now Commander-in-Chief in Ireland, was training an Irish Catholic army which, at a given signal, would be shipped over to England. Meanwhile on Hounslow Heath outside London, fifteen thousand regular troops were encamped. They were – if their loyalty could be counted on – a formidable instrument for the disciplining of Parliament, the subversion of the Church and, if that should be necessary, the browbeating of the judges. Churchill had the best of reasons for knowing what this force could mean in the hands of a ruthless monarch: he had seen a brave but untrained rebel army overwhelmed by fewer than three thousand soldiers at Sedgemoor. He had no doubt what the King was up to but, although he himself disliked the cruelty that followed Sedgemoor and James' ruthless policy in Scotland before he came to the throne, he was not one who gave way easily to moral indignation. But he had a wife of a quite different temperament and more strident opinions on the matter of religion. "The word Church had never any charm for me in the mouths of those who made most noise with it." She wrote that when she was old, but there is no reason to suppose that she thought differently in youth.

Sarah, when she was not looking after her young children at St Albans, was on duty as a lady-in-waiting to Princess Anne. There, she regarded it as one of the most important of her tasks to keep Anne as much as possible away from her father's court where, assuredly, all kinds of pressure would be brought on her to change her religion. A letter of Anne's to her sister, Princess Mary, in Holland gives the clearest picture of what the Churchill couple were thinking at that time. Defending Sarah against the charge of laxity in religion, Anne said, "It is true that she is not so strict as some are, nor does not keep such bustle about religion . . . She has a true sense of the doctrine of our church and abhors all the principles of the Church of Rome. The same thing I will venture to say for her Lord . . . He will always obey the King in all things that are consistent with religion yet, rather than change that, he will lose all his places and all he has." Sarah was too strong-minded a woman to conform easily to a set of doctrines formulated by others and, although outwardly an Anglican, it seems that she had some private reservations. Certainly, she was an anti-clerical.

As for John Churchill, his predicament was complex. He was a Royalist who owed a great deal to the King: Gentleman of the Bedchamber; Peer; Colonel of the second troop of Life Guards; Colonel of the Royal Dragoons when that new regiment was formed; Major-General. Lucrative and splendid appointments. And added to all was the Hudson's Bay governorship, a rich prize, which he certainly owed to the King's favour. But, watching the momentous game that was being played around him in those dangerous eighties of the seventeenth century, he was bound to wonder what were the King's chances of winning – and, should he win, what would be the destiny of John Churchill.

Looking at it as a soldier, Churchill could have no doubt that, with the army growing in strength, a process which through his father he had helped to promote, with it being brought gradually into ideological conformity with the King's purpose, James would very soon be able to govern England as he governed Scotland. There were only two trump cards that could be played against him. If the King's power, concentrated in the army on Hounslow Heath, was neutralized by the defection of any substantial number of its officers, then the situation would be radically altered. By treating every other public institution with contempt, James had made himself dependent on a single element in the nation, the army. And of what did the army consist? Some thousands of men organized in regiments of varying loyalty. Some hundreds of officers, divided into Catholics who would serve a Catholic King with zeal and Protestants who would look sourly on a service where opportunities to men of their religion would dwindle. They knew what had happened to Huguenot officers in the French army. They knew why Lord Feversham was in England. Because there had been no hope of promotion for him in France. But these matters should not be exaggerated.

There were groups of dissatisfied officers in the camp at Hounslow; they were assembled where they could be conveniently reached by agitation – even so, Churchill would see no chance of making out of them a counter-force to James' army. Unless the second trump could be played against the King: military intervention from Europe, which meant William of Orange. However, should William come in on one side, Louis would be likely to intervene on the other . . . An extraordinary, and most improbable, conjunction of events was required to defeat the King's revolution. And this was precisely what came about: the knitting together against James of what Louis called "the greatest conspiracy ever formed". It had its roots in the English aristocracy and in the implacable determination of William of Orange to cut Louis XIV down to size. Churchill was inevitably involved in it. He and his wife, Sarah, might not be among the originators of the enterprise but they held two of the keys to its success, he as a leading army commander, she as the dominant influence on the King's daughter, Anne Stuart. There was, however, a moral obstacle. For Churchill to join the King's enemies would involve him in an act of treachery to a benefactor which could be justified only by pleading that the King was betraying his people, the constitution, and the settled religion of England. It was a good defence, although not altogether impressive for a man who had been as close to the King as Churchill.

In late 1687, James toured the West of England with an imposing escort of cavalry. At Winchester, where he touched for the King's Evil, he was accompanied by Roman Catholic priests, a fact noted by the crowd. Afterwards, strolling in the Deanery Gardens, he had a discussion with Churchill, reported by the anonymous author of *The Lives of the Two Illustrious Generals*.[3] According to this account, which supposedly comes from Churchill himself, Churchill told the King that he intended to live and die a Protestant. James is then reported to have said that for his part he would exercise his own religion as he thought fit. He would show favour to his Catholic subjects and be a father to all his Protestants – but he was the King and must be obeyed. After that somewhat equivocal declaration, he talked no more to Churchill that night. The author of the narrative says that he overheard the King's talk at dinner with the Dean of Winchester, which was on the subject of passive obedience. Later, he was told by Churchill of his discussion with the King before dinner.

Some months before this conversation, the conspiracy against the King had already begun to take shape. William had sent a trusted servant, Everard van Dykevelt, to England to spy out the land. Matters were beginning to move fast. Princess Anne asked her father's permission to visit her sister, Mary, at The Hague but this was prevented by the shrill alarm it aroused in the Catholic party in England, especially in Lord Sunderland, the King's Chief Minister, who, as the climax of a career of ostentatious sycophancy, had delighted James by becoming – or seeming to become – a Catholic. Once a week, the Jesuits were believed to hold private discussions in Sunderland's London house. The King suspected that the Churchills had a hand in Anne's projected visit to Holland. His suspicions would have been sharpened had he read a letter which Anne wrote to her sister: "I have never ventured to speak to [Mr Dykevelt] because I am not used to speak to people about business and [Lord Sunderland] is so much upon the watch that I am afraid of him. So I have desired Lord Churchill, a very honest man and a good Protestant, to speak to Mr Dykevelt for me . . . One dares not write anything by the post."[4]

Two months later, Churchill, who had seen Dykevelt in the interval, wrote to William assuring him that "my places and the King's favour I set at naught in comparison with being true to my religion. In all things but this the King may command me . . . being resolved, although I cannot live the life of a saint, if ever there be occasion for it, to show the resolution of a martyr." Fine words, whatever may be thought of their relevance to the situation in which the writer found himself in 1687! They told William that Churchill was ready, in certain circumstances, to go to the stake for his religion. But William was more concerned to know whether, in less extreme circumstances, he was ready to take the field as a soldier against the King whose commission he held. And this was something about which, reasonably enough, Churchill could hardly be expected to give a clue. All that William could count on was that Churchill would support him if he looked like winning. It was not a great deal.

The months went by: the King persisting in his vigorous pro-Catholic programme in spite of misgivings among the old English Catholic families; Churchill trying and failing to obtain command of the English and Scots regiments in Holland; Lord Halifax, wariest of politicians, turning to William; Lord Sunderland, falsest of proselytes, slyly urging the King to more dangerous measures; William in The Hague hearing all and watching all, and James in Whitehall, blind to all evidence, deaf to all warnings of the storm that was about to break over him. Yet evidence was available in plenty. An eavesdropper had only to listen to the talk of an evening in the Rose Tavern in Covent Garden[5] and he would hear enough to make the hair of the most insouciant monarch rise on his scalp. There the young bloods would meet in the interval between the theatre and the bawdy house and hear the reckless talk of Tom Wharton, rake and agitator. There, officers from crack regiments, with Whig opinions and well-lined pockets, would pick up the latest political whispers and carry them back to the two square miles of tentage on Hounslow Heath,[6] where the King's army was encamped to overawe the capital, or be corrupted by it.

In the spring of 1688, all the town was a-quiver with the rumour that Tyrconnell's popish legions were about to come over from Dublin. Lord Danby, who had been King Charles' minister until Montagu betrayed him, began to gather together the strings of conspiracy among the grandees, Shrewsbury, Devonshire and the rest. Nottingham promised to come in with them and then pulled back. But by that time he was party to a secret which, were it divulged, could hang all of them! They decided to kill him and then, with some misgivings, decided that he could be trusted. And the army? It was necessary to know what James' chosen instrument would do. The conspirators knew enough about Churchill's views to approach him. He talked to Colonel Kirke of the "Lambs", to Trelawny, colonel of the second Tangier regiment, to the Duke of Grafton, Charles' by-blow, Barbara Cleveland's son, commander of the Guards. All of them were ready to join in the treason, and swore that most of their troops would follow them when the time came. Churchill added that Princess Anne and her Danish husband could also be counted on.

James, who must have known something about what was simmering, went on as if he knew nothing. He issued a Declaration of Indulgence relieving Catholics and Dissenters from the penal laws, a liberal act which would be more impressive if it were not known that James had told the French ambassador that he wanted Catholics and only Catholics to be free to practise their religion. Seven bishops who protested were sent to the Tower and tried for sedition; when they were acquitted, all London rang with joy. One event was even more ominous. At Hounslow the King heard cheering and asked what it meant. "Nothing, sire. Only that the soldiers are glad the Bishops are acquitted." But it seemed that nothing in those days could weaken James' conviction that he was sustained by a divine purpose. Had not the Queen given birth to a male child? A Catholic heir to the throne! So much for the hopes of his Protestant daughters, Mary and Anne! So much for the belief of Protestants that time would do their work for them as it had done in Mary Tudor's day! "Now or never," said William of Orange when he heard of the birth.

On the day the Bishops were acquitted, 30 June 1688, the seven leaders of the conspiracy – Shrewsbury, Devonshire, Danby, Lumley, the Bishop of London, Edward Russell and Henry Sidney – met in Lord Shrewsbury's house in London and signed their formal invitation to the Prince of Orange. Then they scattered to carry out their several parts in the great plan. Thus Danby went to take the waters at Knaresborough, while Devonshire paid a visit to his estates in the north. Admiral Herbert, disguised as an ordinary seaman, set off to The Hague with the letter of invitation. Churchill went about his duties with his usual efficiency, serene, composed, unfathomable, although well aware that the edifice of which he was a conspicuous and, apparently, loyal part, was about to be struck by a tornado. On 4 August he wrote again to the Prince: "Mr Sidney" – one of the seven leaders of the conspiracy – "will let you know how I intend to behave myself: I think it is what I owe to God and my country. My honour I take leave to put into your royal highness's hands, in which I think it safe. If you think there is anything else that I ought to do, you have but to command me . . . being resolved to die in that religion that it has pleased God to give you both the will and power to protect." This, although subtly phrased, was a clear indication to a man of the Prince's intelligence that he could count on Churchill's help in the coming crisis. But what exactly would Churchill do? That was left to

Mr Sidney to explain. What is plain is that Churchill had decided William had now a better chance of winning in the coming struggle. But the Prince had still to land, still to circumvent French diplomacy and outwit James' fleet in the Channel. Only then could Churchill be compelled to decide where, on the twisting, narrow, unsure path between gratitude, duty, honour, conscience, religion and – why not? – interest, he should walk.

Suddenly it seemed that everybody in England was singing, whistling or humming the same tune. Some time during 1687 it was first heard, but it was in the year after that it came into its own as one of those rare songs which make history. The air, which was infectious, was attributed, wrongly as it seems, to Henry Purcell, who certainly scored it for the keyboard. The words in a bogus Irish jargon, were highly irreverent and very anti-popish. They emanated from the mind of that versatile Whig propagandist, Tom Wharton. Supposedly sung by an Irish soldier, they told Englishmen of something that Englishmen were only too ready to believe, that Tyrconnel's army of Irish papists was about to descend on England and cut the throats of all the Protestants. Indeed, the only wonder was that this catastrophe had not yet occurred. As the song said:

> O, but why does he stay behind?
> Lilli Burlero Bullen a-la
> Ho, by my shoul, 'tis a Protestant wind!

Never for a hundred years had Englishmen watched the weather-vane so anxiously. If the wind remained in the east then, said the wiseacres, Tyrconnel's ships could not make the crossing from Dublin. And perhaps another fleet might bring another army to England's shores to the defence of "this little flock" and the preservation of "this threatened church and nation". It would need a miracle to bring it about. But in 1688 men were ready to believe in miracles.

One event was dominant in Europe at the time. Far away in the Danube valley the Turks had suffered a shattering defeat. Only a little before, they had stood at the gates of Vienna, a hundred thousand strong. It seemed that the "old imperial city" would fall – and with it, how much of Christendom? And then a Polish army had appeared and very soon the vast Turkish army with its horde of auxiliaries and slaves was streaming away to the East. Buda was won back. At Mohacs, the Turks suffered a second defeat from an army of which the cavalry was commanded by a young man of French-Italian origin named Prince Eugene of Savoy. More would be heard of him later.

Leopold, the chilly Hapsburg who sat on the Imperial throne, made a reasonable settlement with his rebellious Hungarians and turned his mind to the west. More than that. He began to move his troops towards the Rhine. He had heard bad news from Madrid about the health of his half-witted and childless relative, King Charles II of Spain. If anything were to happen to that young man then, beyond all question, there would be a dangerous crisis over the succession to the Spanish throne. Another European monarch, the most powerful and splendid of them all, looked on the situation with a kindling eye, as well aware of its perils and opportunities as Leopold. Louis XIV. Hapsburg or Bourbon? Who would be the next Catholic King to rule the Spanish Empire? As it turned out, however, those rapacious despots were ahead of events. Charles lived, increasingly mad, for another twelve years. In the meantime, Louis had other things to do. By 1688, he had already grabbed most of Lorraine and Flanders. He had incorporated Strasbourg in France. Now he intended to ensure that his candidate – and not Leopold's – became the new Archbishop of Cologne. The Pope backed Leopold's nominee. So much the worse for the Pope! Louis had already solid grounds for grievance against the Holy Father. For example, there was a dispute between them about diplomatic privileges in Rome and another about the use of the revenues of vacant French benefices.

Louis proposed to spend the money to bribe Huguenots to be converted. The Pope was not impressed by this pious enterprise. Looking at the independent tendencies manifest in the Gallican Church, he asked, "What is the good of demolishing all these conventicles if the bishops themselves are schismatic?" James of England, a newcomer to the internecine squabbles in the Roman Church, deplored this disagreement between the two men who, for spiritual and temporal reasons, he most deeply respected. After profound cogitation, the Pope decided that the Emperor's candidate for the see of Cologne, although he had not been ordained, was perfectly eligible for the archbishopric. As the Archbishop was one of the seven Electors of the Holy Roman Emperor, the question was admittedly not one of merely ecclesiastical interest.

As the eldest son of the Church, whose devotion was at that moment being proved anew by countless acts against the Huguenots, Louis professed to be outraged by this turn in events. And, while the Pope might be out of his reach, there were others who could feel the weight of his indignation. He ordered the arrest of all Austrians in Paris and, in the third week of September, invaded Germany with 70,000 men. Before long, Mannheim and Heidelberg were in flames. The Emperor Leopold, still partially involved on the Danube, had not been able to safeguard the western confines of his empire. This, however, was not the last episode in the chain-reaction which followed the Turkish defeat. When Louis decided to march into Germany, it was after a period of hesitation during which he had considered a new attack on Holland. Indeed, he had an army poised to deliver the fatal stroke against her when he had finally settled on the German strategy; the attack on Holland could wait.

Watching those events with an intent, consuming interest was a prematurely aged, asthmatic man of thirty-eight, known to the irreverent as "little hook nose". Strangely enough, he was the son-in-law of James of England. He was William of Orange, Stadtholder of Holland. James disliked him; Louis despised him. James thought that he was not to be trusted, in which opinion James was right. Louis considered that he had neither the resources, the ability nor the prestige to play a leading part in the theatre of affairs. In that respect, Louis was wrong. When he gave the order that spared Holland from attack and, instead, unleashed his armies on the unhappy Palatinate, he made one of the critical blunders of his life – perhaps the most important of all – and he did so partly because he fatally under-rated the qualities of mind and spirit possessed by the Stadtholder. More than anyone else in Europe, William was interested in the commitment by Louis of his armies to the invasion of the Rhineland. For he thought that this would, with a bit of luck, give him time for an enterprise which he himself was contemplating, the invasion of England.

William was one of the most ambitious and single-minded men in Europe; nor was he without means. In addition to the revenues which he drew from thirty territories and jurisdictions, and other income from 102 different sources, he had his salary as Commander-in-Chief of the Dutch army and the dividend from a $3\frac{1}{2}$ per cent holding in the Dutch East India Company.[7] He was, in short, one of the richest men in Europe. In 1688, a long-standing feud between him and the merchants of Amsterdam was interrupted: Louis XIV had upset the city by an anti-Dutch tariff policy. In its annoyance, Amsterdam acquiesced in the prince's ambitious project. William poured out his money in assembling along the Dutch coast a fleet of three hundred vessels of which fifty were warships and the rest transports of shallow draught. By assiduous diplomacy, he persuaded the Elector of Brandenburg to let him hire some of his 30,000 troops, soldiers of the highest quality. By judicious use of money in Scandinavia, he acquired Danish and Finnish regiments. These could now be added to his personal troops, the Dutch Blue Guards, and the English and Scots battalions which James had tried to filch from him. In all, he was ready to put 15,000 troops and 8,000 horses on board the transports when the signal to embark was given. Only 16,000 men were to be left to guard the Dutch frontiers. Naturally, his armada could not be collected without attracting attention. What is extraordinary is that James II, with all the evidence put before him by his agents, could not be persuaded that his son-in-law would do anything so foolhardy as to attack England.

As the months rolled by and the bitterly cold spring of 1688 passed into summer, and autumn arrived with the prospect of stormy weather in the North Sea, the adventure looked more than ever preposterous. But the omens of war multiplied. In alarm, Louis offered to lend James warships for use in the Channel. But James thought that help from the persecutor of the Huguenots and ravager of the Palatinate would do him more harm with his people than it would bring him security at sea. Besides, he had a good fleet of his own – 12,303 sailors in forty-seven warships and twenty fireships.[8] It was as strong as anything the Dutch could put to sea and, recently, it had been brought to a high pitch of seaworthiness by the diligence of his Secretary of the Admiralty, Mr Pepys. He trusted his admiral, Lord Dartmouth, while, as for the rumours which drifted up from Chatham and Portsmouth of subversive propaganda allegedly at work on the lower deck, all that would be blown away the moment an enemy fleet was sighted.

Propaganda. In this word is contained the most powerful weapon of all in William's armoury. When "Their Highnesses the Prince and Princess of Orange" expressed their opinion about "a General Liberty of Conscience", the declaration became a pamphlet of which 50,000 copies were printed, pouring into England by every kind of vessel and distributed up and down the land by eager colporteurs. William thought it was so valuable a statement from a political and strategic point of view – it denied that he and his wife were bent on establishing a severe Calvinism or on persecuting Catholics – that he had it translated into French, Dutch and Latin for reading on the Continent. Working for him, William had a team of writers, in which exiled Scotsmen like Burnet, Johnstone, and Carstares played a disproportionate part. They were enthusiasts and not without a touch of the cynicism that seems to be an occupational hazard of publicists: "The Spirit of a People . . . is often to be entertained by trifles, particularly that of the English who, like all islanders, seem to ebb and flow like the neighbouring sea."[9] More than that, when William's fleet set out on its audacious voyage, it carried with it not only horses and fodder, gunpowder, brandy and tobacco, but also a mobile printing press. The age of modern warfare had arrived.

That autumn James was alarmed enough to reverse his religious policy, restoring Anglicans to the posts in which he had installed papists and seeking to ingratiate himself with the Anglican bishops. The change was all too late and too panicky to be impressive. He brought some regiments of his Scots army across the Border. They amazed people in York by demanding that the landlords should provide fires in their lodgings, "a thing never practised in this garrison".[10] These Scots did not stay long. They were on their way further south.

One day in October, the Dutch fleet set out, only to be scattered by a storm and driven back. The price of Dutch East India Company stock fell heavily on the Amsterdam bourse. Indeed, to anybody but a man of William's iron character, the setback would have been final. As it was, he simply bought new horses to replace the thousand which had been the only casualties of the storm and set out again as soon as the weather improved. He had no time to lose. It was already 1 November when the ships at last left. For a day they sailed north, until a strong east wind, a "Protestant wind", on their starboard quarter forced them to make for the Straits of Dover. Next day, the crowds on Dover cliffs watched the fleet as, for seven hours, it went past in a stately procession in the autumn sunshine, each ship keeping station, each wearing all its flags. On 5 November, anniversary of the Gunpowder Plot, William of Orange stepped ashore at Tor Bay.

His flagship had hoisted a large white flag to signify peace, with a red flag below it meaning that he would fight anyone who opposed him. This display was seen by a priest who was staying in the house of "Mr Carey, a very rigid papist", and chanced to be taking the air on the roof. Seeing the white flags, he came to the wrong conclusion or, as the Reverend John Whittle, one of William's Protestant chaplains, put it, "as well as blinded by Satan in his mind, he presently concludes that it is the French come to land the sons of Belial which should cut off the heretics." Accordingly, he and his companions sang a joyful *Te Deum*. Later, they not only learned their mistake but had the unpleasant experience of sharing the house with William and his headquarters staff.[11] That night it was cold and frosty: the stars twinkled exceedingly.

Two days afterwards, John Churchill was promoted Lieutenant-General and given the command of a brigade at Salisbury. He was on the brink of the most fateful decision of his life, one which has done some damage to his reputation. Yet it may be conceded that he was in a situation of some moral complexity. He owed a great deal to the King and was closer to him perhaps than any other serving officer. On the other hand, he was alarmed by the King's policy and convinced that it must lead to disaster. He was a sincere if undemonstrative Anglican. Moreover, first in Scotland and again after Monmouth's rebellion, James had disclosed a side to his nature which as a Protestant he found alarming. Churchill was aware of what was preparing; he knew that seven magnates had invited William to come over. He knew, it can be assumed, about the wild talk to be heard in the Rose Tavern in Covent Garden, for his brother-in-law, Colonel Charles Godfrey, who had married Arabella Churchill after her affair with the Duke of York came to an end, was one of the habitués of that hotbed. Certainly he knew that the army was in a state of sulky disloyalty, especially the officers, especially the units nearest to the sovereign such as the Life Guards. And what of the navy? There the Duke of Grafton, a former sea officer, had been busy sowing the seeds of disobedience, no impossible task in a service with strong Parliamentary and Protestant traditions. And who knew better about Grafton's activities than Churchill, who had been the first to approach Grafton on behalf of the arch-conspirators? Nor can he have been surprised when he heard that his brother George, commanding the *Newcastle*, a fourth-rate frigate, had entered Plymouth harbour, reporting that his ship was unseaworthy. For the navy's failure to find, follow and attack the invasion fleet various reasons may be advanced: James' hesitations, Dartmouth's incompetence, the wind and the weather. But probably the most substantial is that the hearts of many of its officers were with the other fleet, commanded as it chanced by an English admiral, Arthur Herbert, of whom the navy thought more highly than it did of Dartmouth.

On 14 November the first serious blow fell on the King. Lord Cornbury of the Life Guards had gone over to William, taking with him two hundred cavalry. Cornbury was a man of no outstanding ability. But he was the eldest son of Lord Clarendon, who was the King's brother-in-law by his first marriage to Anne Hyde. Cornbury was also, as the cousin of Princess Anne, one of the frequenters of her circle at The Cockpit. Churchill and his wife Sarah were at the very centre of that circle. When he heard of Cornbury's desertion, Churchill was demonstratively pleased and (it is said) skipped along the gallery at Windsor hand in hand with his friend, Sidney Godolphin.

At the moment the news of William's arrival came by express from Torbay just four days after the landing, James was about to have dinner. He changed his mind, contenting himself with a glass of wine and a piece of bread. Then he set off by horse to Salisbury. Prince George of Denmark, Churchill, the newly made Lieutenant-General, and other officers went with him. On the way the King had a nosebleed. Next day, when he was due to ride to Warminster to inspect the advance guard under Colonel Kirke, he had a return of this trouble. In all likelihood, the nosebleeds, acting as a safety-valve, saved him from a stroke. They were a clear symptom of the intense stress from which the King was suffering at that time. They help to explain the events that followed. On that day, his younger daughter, Anne, wrote to her brother-in-law, William of Orange, telling him that her husband, Prince George of Denmark, had left for Salisbury with the King, meaning to go over to William "as soon as his friends thought proper". It is safe to say that Churchill was one of "his friends" and that he knew – perhaps he even dictated – the form of the letter. It goes on, "I am not yet certain if I shall continue here or remove into the City: that shall depend on the advice my friends will give me." Sarah was one of "my friends" and probably the principal one, as she was the dearest.

The King's sixty-mile ride to Salisbury in that cold, brilliant November weather had a macabre quality. Some of the men who rode with him were already committed to the enemy; others knew what was planned but had not yet made up their minds what they would do; and some, who were faithful, suspected. It was like an episode from the Italy of the High Renaissance, except that, in this case, merely betrayal and not murder was planned. James, who had been amply warned, refused to believe. Churchill was more deeply involved morally than the others, except perhaps for the Prince of Denmark. But the Prince, apart from being unusually obtuse, was bound to follow his wife's lead in these matters and his wife was passionately devoted to Sarah Churchill. Churchill, for his part, was not only the husband of Princess Anne's favourite but was, by general acclaim, the first soldier in England.

On 23 November at a council of war, Churchill urged the King to go forward with his troops towards William. In doing this, his intention was – what? To attack the invader whose army, although hardly as numerous as James', was a great deal more experienced? Surely not. It would have meant a hard and doubtful conflict fought at a time when morale in the Royal camp was beginning to crumble, when the King was swithering from one opinion to another and his Irish and Scottish reinforcements were still on their way to the South. It would have been the opening blow in a bloody civil war, the very thing that Louis of France most wished for at that moment. But if not to fight, what then was Churchill's purpose? He had decided that James, his benefactor, was utterly incompetent, unsuitable, impossible as King of England. With the hard and ruthless intellect which he concealed under layer upon layer of affability and charm, Churchill had arrived at that conclusion.

When he urged the King to march towards the Prince of Orange, was it not perhaps to parley? If there had been a meeting between the two men at that moment, when James' world was crumbling round him, what could have come out of it? Conceivably, James might have been invited to give up the kingly power while retaining the ceremonial title of King. William, as regent, would have the power so long as he stayed in England – and how long would that be? More certainly, James would be compelled to concede that his successor should be a Protestant, either his infant son, suitably brought up in the Church of England, or one or other of his daughters, both of whom were Protestants. In addition, the disabilities of Catholics in England would be re-imposed.

All this would have meant that James would be asked, before a single shot had been fired, to accept the terms that might be given to a defeated monarch. If this was in Churchill's mind when he urged the King to advance, he was expecting the King to do something that no man in his senses would have done: surrender on the enemy's terms at a moment when he was temporarily cut off from his great ally, the King of France. Yet the alternative explanation of Churchill's behaviour is no more creditable: that he was urging the King towards a battle which, in the existing state of his army, he was bound to lose. Feversham argued in favour of retreat, and James agreed. The Frenchman went further, imploring the King to have Churchill placed under arrest as a manifest traitor. This, however, James would not do.

On the night of the council of war (23 November) Churchill, accompanied by the Duke of Grafton and four hundred horsemen, a fair proportion of them officers, rode westwards to join the Prince of Orange at Crewkerne. He left a letter for the King explaining that, while he could never hope to gain as much from William as he had gained from James, yet this was an occasion in which a higher principle than self-interest must prevail – "the inviolable dictates of my conscience and a necessary concern for my religion (which no good man can oppose) and with which I am instructed nothing can come in competition." It was signed, "Your Majesty's most dutiful and most obliged subject and servant." It is not known how the King reacted to this farewell message. A cynical laugh was not in accordance with his nature.

And so, at last, John Churchill had declared his hand and put down on the table the card which, more than any other, lost James the rubber. He could hardly expect to escape criticism for what he did and, indeed, by historians, even those most partial to his cause, he has been severely condemned. His defence would be – what? Anticipating Talleyrand, he might have said, "I was only a conspirator when I had the majority of my countrymen as accomplices and when, in common with them, I sought to save the nation." The plea might not carry complete conviction but, in the circumstances, it was probably the best he could manage. And it was certainly true that the public as a whole was at least not hostile to William. "Neither the gentry nor the common people seemed much afeared, saying The Prince comes only to maintain the Protestant religion. He will do England no harm."[12]

His eyes opened at last, the King sent orders to Whitehall for Lady Churchill to be arrested. He was too late. Either Sarah knew in advance the day on which her husband planned to desert, or she received early news of the event. By way of a ladder built for the disposal of night soil, Sarah and Princess Anne stole out of the Cockpit and made their way to the Bishop of London's house in Suffolk Street, which was ready to receive them. From there they made their way to Nottingham with a mounted escort. The Bishop, booted and spurred and armed with sword and pistol, gave the two ladies the protection of the Church. At Nottingham, they were greeted by Lord Devonshire who now held the city for William. It seemed that all England north of the Trent had gone over to the rebels. Lord Danby had seized York. Lord Delamere had called to arms two hundred of his tenants in Cheshire. Meanwhile, in the West Country, Lord Bath, who had been holding Plymouth for the King, had gone over to William. And Lord Shrewsbury, with two infantry battalions, had taken Bristol from the Duke of Beaufort who had retired in some alarm. The Prince, with no undue haste, advanced towards London. In the towns and villages he passed through, his Finland Dragoons, all in black armour with bearskin caps, made a particularly deep impression. The soldiers paused to admire Stonehenge and speculate what its purpose could be. There were many ideas, none of them convincing. By the time they reached Hungerford, the war, which had not begun, was over.

From the moment he heard of Churchill's defection and his daughter Anne's flight, James Stuart was no longer King of England. He was defeated, bewildered, broken, with no resources left of will or of intellect. Let there be a pause for compassion, then, for one who, whatever his vices as a man and his faults as a ruler, was now only an unhappy human being. His folly had been enormous and his humiliation was painful, but he had never been ignoble. Now he was about to be bundled into the wings of history by men whose patience he had worn out and other men whom he had trusted for too long. He, who had been the pensioner of Louis, was about to become his creature. It was a sad fate for one who, at his worst, had remained steadfastly English in pride and loyalty.

In London, the mob, inconsequential and alarming, had taken to the streets, hounding priests, wrecking chapels, and frightening the Spanish ambassador out of his wits. William gave his terms to the group of politicians who were trying to bring about a negotiated settlement between King and Prince – the settlement Churchill may have wanted to achieve before his desertion: all Papists, said William, must be removed from office; the Tower and the fort at Tilbury must be handed over to the City of London; neither of the two armies was to be stationed within thirty miles of London. At the same time, James was given a strong hint that William would like him to leave the country. First James said that nothing would persuade him to go; then he went. However, his luck was out. The ship that was to take him to France was not ready to sail. While he waited, he was discovered and roughly handled by a gang of fishermen; eventually he was brought back to London. It was 16 December.

The mob, which a little before had been rioting and looting, now went through one of those unpredictable changes of heart to which crowds are liable. They cheered the King in the most friendly manner. James may for a moment have thought that his fortunes had changed. He soon knew better. A message came from William ordering him to leave. Blue-clad Dutch guards, with matches burning, surrounded St James's Palace. On 19 December, the King left in his twelve-oared barge for Gravesend. The officer in command of the Dutch escort, Colonel Wyck, told the King that he had shown such favour to his uncle, Lely, the painter, that he found his present task very unpleasant. That night Samuel Pepys was awakened by a Royal page with the news that the King had fled. After spending the night in a lawyer's house, the King rode next morning to

Rochester. His companion, Lord Ailesbury, who had no riding boots, travelled in the King's coach, troubled when he tried to sleep by the "bloody oaths" of Dixie, the Royal coachman: "God damn Father Petre. But for him we had not been here."[13]

The unspeakable Jeffreys disguised himself by cutting off his eyebrows[14] but was caught at Wapping and taken, not too gently, to the Tower, indignant with the King for not allowing him to join the Royal party leaving for France. He died soon after, of drink or fear. The Secretary of the Admiralty in his office in York Buildings, made a quick shorthand note that day of a request he had received from the Countess of Sussex, whose behaviour in Paris had once caused so much trouble to her mother, the Duchess of Cleveland. The Countess wanted Mr Pepys to arrange to have her belongings shipped over to France. It was no time for a by-blow of the Stuarts to be lingering in London.[15]

Churchill returned to Whitehall. Sarah followed in the company of Princess Anne. For them, it had been a wildly exciting gamble, with one head if not two at stake. Of the pair, Sarah's had probably been the more important role if her strong character and her Whig convictions, as later revealed, are any guide. Consider the evidence. Without her connivance Anne would not have fled from London. Without her influence over him, John Churchill would probably not have deserted the King. Together, these events had almost as much to do with James' psychological collapse as the landing of the Prince of Orange and his army. For these reasons it is hard to deny that young Sarah Churchill was a key figure in what was soon called the Glorious Revolution of 1688.

V

The Cockpit Quarrels with Kensington

"They don't so much value in England who shall be King as whose King he shall be."

George Lockhart, Scottish Jacobite[1]

For the Churchills, life was busy after William had settled in as the effective head of the English state, although not as King yet, because the question of his title was a delicate one and had still to be resolved. When the critical vote came to be taken in the Convention Parliament, John Churchill was too indisposed to attend, which may have been a matter of tact or good taste or caution. It may even have had a medical explanation. Whatever the reason, it resulted in a close vote. William was elected King for life by 51 votes to 49, which meant that, even if Churchill had been well enough to attend, and had voted against William, he could not have reversed the decision. He was, about that time, busy with his professional duties, because William had given him the task of pulling the army together after the traumatic conflict of loyalties it had been through.[2] Some units must be disbanded. Officers who were either Catholics or notorious partisans of the ex-King must be dismissed, and others must be appointed in their place. There was, in particular, trouble in the Royal Scots, a regiment which had always been commanded by a Scots Colonel and, until lately, by a Catholic. William appointed as its new Colonel Marshal Schomberg, a venerable soldier from the Rhineland, and ordered the regiment to embark for Holland. Twenty officers and two hundred men then mutinied and set off to march to Scotland, taking the regiment's pay chest with them. Two regiments of English cavalry and three of Dutch dragoons were sent after the mutineers and coralled them at Sleaford, in Lincolnshire. The regiment was disbanded and re-formed. New recruits of the right quality were not hard to come by in the Scotland of that time.

Churchill's ability was suitably recognized by the King. Not only was he re-instated as Captain and Colonel of the Second Troop of Life Guards, but he received the payments appropriate to one who made lucrative and prestigious appointments to commands from which James' supporters had been expelled. "The harvest my Lord Churchill made by this was vast, for all were sold," Lord Ailesbury noted. Lord Selwyn, who had no obvious qualifications, was given a regiment. On two separate occasions, he gave his footmen a purse of a thousand guineas to hold while he went into Churchill's apartments at The Cockpit. Presumably the first offer had not been thought adequate. Thus, when Churchill was made, as he was at the Coronation, Earl of Marlborough, he was able to support the title with suitable dignity. Naturally, human nature being what it is, envious and spiteful tongues wagged in the drawing-rooms and coffee houses. Sarah, who heard some of the talk, did not allow it to weigh overmuch on her spirits.

"Lord!" she cried to Lord Ailesbury, "they make such a noise at our wealth, I do assure you it doth not exceed £70,000. And what will that come to when laid out in land? And, besides, we have a son and four daughters to provide for." It was, however, a respectable capital sum* although, as it chanced, Sarah would be worth a great deal more before she was finished. She was one of those who, without ever having read it, are by nature obedient to the Eighth Commandment as explained in *The Larger Catechism* of the Church of Scotland which requires "an endeavour, by all just and lawful means, to procure, preserve and further the wealth and outward estate of others, as well as our own". Her own personal share in the blessings of the change of monarch had to wait a little longer until Parliament had voted an increase in Princess Anne's income. But when it came, it was substantial. If Churchill had really thought that their last-minute espousal of William's cause involved a sacrifice of their interests, he was being proved too pessimistic.

Churchill was not, however, the only member of his family who was accused of sharp practice just then. His brother George, a captain in the navy, was in trouble with a group of London merchants who complained about him to the House of Commons, of which George was a member. They said that he had demanded money for protecting their ships on convoy and that, if they did not pay, he threatened to take their best seamen for service on his ship. Needless to say, George denied the charge, but admitted that he had been given a hundred and fifty guineas as a

* It may be multiplied by twelve or fifteen to give an approximate idea of its value in modern terms.

"voluntary gift". The House sent him to the Tower of London for three days. A little later, John's other brother, Charles, fell under the suspicion of embezzling military stores at Kinsale in Ireland. His explanation that they had been given him by the governor, appointed by James while he was still King, was not accepted by everyone. Like George, Charles spent some time in the Tower.

John was, however, operating on an altogether higher and more dignified level of affairs than his brothers. And now he was transferred from the business of building an army to one of using it in the field. By the summer of 1689, William faced danger from two quarters. While he was dressing for the Coronation, he heard bad news. James had landed in Kinsale and all Ireland, except the Protestant north, was in revolt! At the same time, the French were threatening Flanders with a powerful army. In this crisis, William went to Ireland, Marlborough to the Netherlands to join the army of the Prince of Waldeck, an elderly general much respected by William. With Marlborough went eleven regiments of infantry and two troops (i.e. regiments) of Life Guards, in all about 7,000 men. In the opinion of those who saw them leave for Flanders, the soldiers were not of the highest quality: "ill-paid officers, ill-conducted colonels, and sickly, listless, undisciplined and disorderly men."[3] However, very soon, as a result of Marlborough's endeavours, they were being regarded as the best troops in Waldeck's army. He had demonstrated that, like Cromwell, he had the necessary first gift of a good general: he could train soldiers. The first clash with the French came some miles south of Charleroi outside the old fortified town of Walcourt. The Dutch and the English were in a strong position which only a rash general would have attacked. This, however, Marshal d'Humières did. While the French guards tried to batter their way into the town, the Dutch general Slangenberg attacked one of their flanks and Marlborough, leading the Life Guards and the Blues, charged the other. The French pulled back with the loss of two thousand of their best infantry. The French Marshal was relieved of his command while Marlborough was highly praised by Waldeck ("the English did marvels and the Earl of Marlborough is assuredly one of the most gallant men I know"). William, whose affairs in Ireland had gone badly, appointed him colonel of the Royal Fusiliers, a newly formed regiment under the Master-General of the Ordnance, the function of which was to defend the artillery in battle. Its colonel's emoluments were lucrative, especially when added to Marlborough's other colonelcies. In another direction, however, matters did not go so smoothly.

A cloud appeared in his relations with the Royal couple. A storm was blowing up. It was over money and, needless to say, Sarah was at the heart of it. Queen Mary was tall (five feet eleven, one inch shorter than her ancestress, Mary Queen of Scots, and four and a half inches taller than her husband, William); she was elegant, clever and devout. She disliked Sarah and distrusted Marlborough. Now a delicate question arose. How much should Princess Anne receive to maintain herself and her household? Seventy thousand pounds a year was thought by Anne to be a reasonable sum, in which opinion she was loyally supported by Sarah – who had probably been the first to think of the amount. William and Mary, for their part, thought that £30,000 would be enough. But if they imagined that no more would be heard of Anne's demand, they underestimated her zest for battle – or, rather, Sarah's. They were particularly offended by Anne's insistence that she wished the money to be voted by Parliament instead of being granted her by the favour of her sister and brother-in-law. Sarah went to work, lobbying Tory MPs who were only too pleased to annoy the King. After some ill-tempered bargaining, a Parliamentary grant of £50,000 a year was agreed. At the end of the dispute, Mary and Anne were friends no more and Mary was confirmed in her original view that Sarah was an evil influence on her sister. "The quarrel is great between the Cockpit and Kensington," Robert Harley reported.[4] As for Marlborough, the Queen had never trusted him. In one respect, the incident ended well. In gratitude to her beloved friend, Anne settled on Sarah ("my dear, adored Mrs Freeman") an annuity of £1,000.

Later, Sarah found a new ground for annoyance with the Queen who had, most vexatiously, intervened when Sarah sold for £1,200 two posts as pages in Anne's household. Mary told Anne that the nominees were Catholics and so in consequence Anne was forced to dismiss them. More annoying, the Churchills had to hand back £800 of their commission on the deal. Nothing was better calculated to rouse Sarah's animosity against the Queen.[5]

One day at the end of August 1690, Marlborough, while waiting impatiently at Portsmouth, wrote a letter to Sarah. He was impatient because he was engaged in an enterprise which demanded speed and he thought that some people who ought to be helping him were dragging their feet. And, when he had made all due allowance for Sarah's state of health – she had just had her fifth and, as it turned out, her last child – her letter which provoked Marlborough's reply had been unkind. Her power to hurt him was, after all these years of marriage, after all his painfully acquired knowledge of her strange, wild character, as potent as ever. She had accused him, for the hundredth time, of a failure to love her, of preferring other company, other interests, to her. He wrote defending himself. "As ambitious as you sometimes think me, I do assure you I would not live in this place to be emperor of it – I shall have no time satisfactory till I see you again."

When Sarah taunted him with ambition, she was touching one of the mainsprings of his character. Inordinately ambitious and intensely secretive, Marlborough knew himself to be something more, much more, than a capable officer who had so far been denied the chance to show his real stature. He was conscious of unusual talents, perhaps of genius, certainly of a superiority to poor, battered James whom he had deserted and even to this Dutch prince whom he had helped to a throne. A man of destiny? It was a century too soon to use such a romantic expression, but it is certain that Marlborough felt in himself the stirrings of greatness. He was aware, too, that the years were passing at none too slow a pace: he was on the eve of forty. Meanwhile, he waited in Portsmouth for wind, weather and the leaden-footed bureaucracies of War and Admiralty to release him on the important, secret expedition which had from the beginning been his idea. The objective was Ireland.

In that island, the military situation was far from satisfactory. True, William had defeated James in the Battle of the Boyne. Weary and profoundly discouraged by the defeat, James had fled to Dublin, exclaiming bitterly to Lady Tyrconnel, Sarah's sister and the Lord Deputy's wife, "Madam, your countrymen have run away!" She had answered, as Sarah might have done in the same circumstances, "Sire, Your Majesty seems to have won the race." Then the Tyrconnels left for France. James had done the same. But there were still 5,000 French troops in the South of Ireland. Limerick still held out for James, although William was besieging it. Cork and Kinsale, strategical harbours on the South Irish coast, had garrisons loyal to James. To crown all, the Anglo-Dutch fleet under Lord Torrington had been resoundingly defeated by the French navy in the battle of Beachy Head. It seemed that France had it in her power to invade England or pour reinforcements into Ireland through Cork or Kinsale. Marlborough, who had been left by William as Commander-in-Chief in England, now presented a bold plan to the Council of State which advised Queen Mary in her husband's absence. It was this. An expeditionary force should be gathered at Portsmouth and, with all possible secrecy, sent to seize Cork and Kinsale, thus cutting the line of communications between France and Ireland. It was an audacious project, because to carry it out would mean stripping England of most of its regular troops. The Council of State vetoed it. The Dutch generals who surrounded William were against it. But William was as great a gambler and almost as astute a strategist as Marlborough. He accepted it.

Plans went forward behind a thick veil of secrecy pierced only by false reports. The ordnance stores were searched for weapons. Battalions brought from Holland were ordered to Portsmouth. Finally, eight infantry battalions and two of marines were embarked, with victuals for forty days. The favourite explanation, encouraged by Blathwayt, the Secretary at War, was that "some revenge upon the French" was contemplated. August was far advanced before the Admiralty was told what it was all about; the Queen signed Marlborough's instructions on 25 August, naming Cork and Kinsale as the objectives. Three weeks later, after a false start due to contrary winds, Marlborough sailed from Portsmouth with a fleet of eighty ships, men o' war and transports. After an unpleasant voyage during which he suffered terribly from sea-sickness, he ran into Cork Harbour and summoned the governor, Colonel McElligot, to surrender. The governor replied by hoisting a red flag of defiance. But, if Marlborough had hoped to have an independent command, he was disappointed. He was joined by 5,000 Danish, Dutch and Huguenot troops from the main Williamite army in Ireland, which was under the leadership of the Duke of Würtemberg. As a Serene Highness, the duke claimed the right of overall command. In vain, Marlborough produced his instructions bearing the Queen's signature. After some talk, it was agreed that the generals should command on alternate days. The siege opened with a bombardment by heavy guns landed from the ships, after which the Danish infantry crossed the river Lee from the north, while the English crossed another branch of the estuary breast-high in water. While the joint force was preparing for the final assault, McElligot raised the white flag. The siege of Cork was over.

In the storming of the town, the Duke of Grafton, Barbara Cleveland's son by Charles II, was mortally wounded. He had deserted King James but had voted in the Lords that William should be regent and not King. For this offence his regiment, the Grenadier Guards, was taken from him by King William and, instead, he was given a naval command. He was not the only Royal bastard in the neighbourhood of Cork that day. James' son by Arabella Churchill, the Duke of Berwick, arrived with

4,000 Irish troops. Berwick was, of course, on the Jacobite side. But when he saw that he was too late to affect the issue, he withdrew.

Marlborough, without delay, moved on to Kinsale seventeen miles to the west. It was a little fishing town but its two forts commanded a fine harbour, at the point where the River Bandon meets the sea. Here he was compelled to wait for his siege guns to come from Cork. They could not be sent by sea owing to contrary winds and, after the rainy weather, the roads could scarcely be used by heavy vehicles. To add to his troubles, there was sickness in the army. Food was hard to come by and the legendary terrors of an Irish winter were at hand. There was no time to lose. In the darkness one night he put 800 men into some boats which the Irish had carelessly failed to destroy. He intended them to attack the Old Fort to the west of the harbour entrance. When they did so, the garrison was completely surprised. Half of them were killed and the other half surrendered. It was now the turn of the second and more powerful fort on the east shore of the harbour. Against it, Marlborough organized a twofold attack – Danish troops on the east, English to the north – which, however, had to wait until his siege guns had arrived and been sited. After three days of continuous bombardment, the garrison asked for terms. Marlborough allowed them to leave with their arms and baggage, and arranged that they should be escorted to Limerick where he knew they would add to the supply difficulties of the local Irish garrison. It was just six weeks after the capture of Cork.

He sailed for England at the end of a campaign which had transformed in England's favour the face of the Irish war. The French troops had, to their own great relief, left Ireland and it was unlikely that a new French expeditionary force could be landed. Marlborough dined with the Constable of the Tower in January 1691, and gave orders that £100 should be distributed among the Irish taken prisoners at Cork and Kinsale. He felt that he had done well in the little war.

He was, however, far from satisfied with the way he was being treated.

No person in the world is so unlikely to be contented with his lot as a rising officer; every day that he is denied a brilliant command he feels that he is surrounded by jealous and hostile intrigue; every day brings peace nearer with all its dangers of unemployment, retirement and poverty. This applies even to a commander-in-chief, like Marlborough. It applies with all the greater force when he serves a king whom he has helped to the throne and who, ungratefully, surrounds himself with foreign officers. William, however, should not be blamed too much if he looked on Marlborough with a coolly appraising eye. The general had deserted one king and might therefore desert another. When, in due course, whisper reached William that Marlborough, like others of his kind, was in correspondence with the exiled James, the King was neither surprised nor disillusioned. He was a man who had started in life without many illusions. And if Marlborough and the others thought that they could "re-insure" by apologizing to James for an act of betrayal, then he, William, probably thought that they were adding a tincture of naïveté to their original crime.

Strangely enough, he gave more of his trust to Sunderland than to any other Englishman. Yet Sunderland had been James' closest lay adviser, had even turned papist to please him, had left his George and Garter with Marlborough when he fled to Holland in 1688 and now came back, as the final twist in a career of versatile treachery, to enjoy the favour of the new monarch. But naturally William's closest trust was given to the Dutchmen he had brought over with him and who were soon loaded with British titles and incomes. His praetorian guard was Dutch: tough, businesslike soldiers whose blue uniform was thought to be less soldierly and was certainly less gorgeous than the scarlet of the Grenadiers and Coldstream. Anyone who saw them in Whitehall was thus reminded every day of the subordinate status to which England was reduced in the new reign.

Subordinate it might be but it was essential to William's vast design which aimed at the defeat and, if possible, the destruction of Louis XIV. Nine years before, Louis had levelled the walls of Orange, the French principality from which William derived his title, had fined its inhabitants and forbidden any more Protestants to settle in it. For that affront, William was determined to be avenged. There was bitter personal animus as well as larger arguments drawn from religion and politics behind the assiduity with which, year after year, through every danger and discouragement, he whittled away at the French colossus. For this reason above all he had come to England, a country lamentably lacking as he thought in an understanding of how its interests were involved with European affairs. This blindness he considered nothing less than a punishment from Heaven.[6] For this reason, now that the tiresome Irish diversion seemed to be over, he gathered the leaders of his allies at The Hague in the spring of 1691 so that together they could fashion a lever strong enough to overthrow the Great Monarch. Marlborough had been left in

Whitehall to recruit and train soldiers for the war that lay ahead. He was in a disgruntled mood. He had not been given the Garter which he regarded as his by right. Worse still, the post of Master-General of the Ordnance, most lucrative of all military appointments, with almost unlimited perquisites, had been given to Henry Sidney who did not know one end of a gun from the other. The disappointment was particularly galling because, had he possessed the Master-General's revenues and opportunities, Marlborough could have afforded to be made a duke at a time when William was scattering titles like confetti among his supporters. To put the cap on his irritations, he was having an endless squabble with the Lord President, Lord Danby, who was forever carping and sneering, forever making odious jokes about the too grasping, too clannish Churchill family.

Usually so equable, Marlborough was driven to write a letter of testy complaint to the King. By that time, however, William had other things on his mind. A few days after Marlborough's letter was sent and while William was still busy with his diplomatic manoeuvres, a French army, a hundred thousand strong, loomed up before the fortress of Mons. It was led by the Duke of Luxembourg, "le nain bossu aux illuminations soudaines" (the hunchback dwarf with sudden flashes of genius), who was the best of a new generation of French commanders. Mons surrendered before William could relieve it.

Thirsting for vengeance, William summoned Marlborough to Flanders and gave him command of the British component of the Allied army. However, he was not involved in any serious fighting. The French kept the initiative, specializing in surprise cavalry raids and avoiding any excessive involvement. They had decidedly the best of the exchanges. Thus, when the time came for the armies to go into winter quarters, neither William nor Marlborough was in the most amiable of moods. Not long afterwards, the relations between them grew spectacularly worse. It was not simply that the King had discovered that the general was in correspondence with the ex-king James. This William had known for some time – as he knew the same about other courtiers like Godolphin and serving officers like Admiral Russell, in command of the fleet. He probably knew that Marlborough had inspired Princess Anne to write a daughterly letter to her father. To all this double-dealing, William, as an immigrant King, with his own guards and his own cronies round him, turned a blind eye. Men like Marlborough were, he knew, bound to him not by loyalty but by interest. From James they had nothing to gain as, when it came to the point, they were bound to see. Marlborough's subversive talk among his fellow officers was certainly irritating and even offensive to the King. But it was one of the burdens he had to bear.

It was different, however, when word reached him through his friend Bentinck of a conspiracy, in which Marlborough was involved, to remove him and Mary from the throne and put Anne there in their place. He recalled how much he owed to Marlborough for Anne's placid, if sulky, acquiescence in their succession three years earlier. He was likely to be well-informed about the sayings and doings in The Cockpit. He probably knew that Anne in her letters to Sarah called him Caliban, the monster, the abortion. His close friend and supposed mistress, Elizabeth Villiers, disliked Sarah Marlborough but was on friendly terms with Lady Fitzharding who, like Sarah, was a lady-in-waiting to Princess Anne. What the King learnt through these channels was alarming enough to make him act. On his orders, the Queen summoned Anne to her presence and bade her dismiss Sarah. There was a loud and furious quarrel between the sisters. Anne left the palace, persisting in her refusal to part with her beloved Mrs Freeman.

Next morning, Marlborough was dismissed from all his offices and forbidden the court. It was not the end of the trouble. After three weeks' absence Anne went to court. She took Sarah with her. It was an insufferable insult to the Queen which only Sarah could have devised and only Sarah would have had the impudence to carry out. By the Lord Chamberlain's command, she was ordered to leave The Cockpit. Anne went too. Anne borrowed Syon House from the Duke of Somerset and, quitting Whitehall, set up her household there.

Naturally, news of a scandal so outrageous spread quickly from the court to the coffee houses and so to the country at large: "This ungrateful man . . ." wrote an unknown correspondent to an unknown recipient, "has spoken insultingly of the King in terms that would merit between gentlemen the last vengeance. He thought by making himself feared was the infallible way to be a Duc and Master of Ordnance so the King was obliged to strip him of his six offices. Everyone detests his ingratitude and avarice."[7] What was this intolerable insult of which the writer spoke? Robert Harley, who as Tory leader in the Commons was likely to hear all the whispers of Whitehall, reported that Marlborough was alleged to have said that William "had not virtue enough to value high ends or courage to punish his enemies". While conceding that even an insensitive man might be annoyed by such contemptuous language, it must be added that the reason for Marlborough's dismissal remains conjectural. As for his avarice, instances of it abounded in the gossip of London. Marlborough had only three suits, one of which he kept for Royal birthdays. He did not entertain, which made him unpopular with his fellow-officers. He spent as if he had an income of a thousand a year "although he has eight thousand plus his big ordinary revenue and the sale of the smallest jobs by himself and his wife".[8]

One day in May 1692, a worse fate than hostile whispering befell Marlborough. He was arrested and taken to the Tower.

VI

Prisoner of State

"Wherever you are, whilst I have life, my soul will follow you, my ever
dear Lord M., and wherever I am, I shall only kill the time until the night
that I may sleep and hope the next day to hear from you."
Sarah, Countess of Marlborough, 1692

The Tower of London. The jewels, the traitors, the cannon – the keys of
the Kingdom, sitting there on its riverbank, unimpressive, almost
domestic, in its aspect belying its sinister reputation; at the point where
the river stretches out its arm towards the labyrinth of mud beyond which
the grey sea opens. On the way down towards that sea, either bank is
punctuated by waterside settlements making up, when one is added to
another, a long naval town, on this side Tilbury, Benfleet, Southend; on
the other, Greenwich, Chatham, Margate. As the wind chooses for him, a
traveller would take one route or the other to, north or south, the foreign
cities lurking behind their sandbanks. To one prisoner, treated with the
deference which, through centuries of practice, the Tower knew how to
measure out to its lodgers, those cities already meant something and
would soon mean more. In the meantime, he had the leisure and the
comfort to think a great deal about them.

As state prisons went, the Tower of London was not so bad. The
prisoner could have his meals sent in, to be served by his own footmen.
He might even be allowed as a special favour to be visited by his friends
as John was visited by Sarah, his wife, and Arabella, his sister. There was,
of course, the disgrace of it all. But that was not so grave after all. Danby
had been there before him, so had the seven bishops, so, for that matter,
had Samuel Pepys; Robert Walpole was to follow him. And none of
them was any the worse for the experience. In the early part of his
imprisonment, however, Marlborough was rather strictly supervised.
When Sarah was allowed to see him, it was "for this time only"; he was
not allowed to dine with his fellow-captives, fellow-peers who had been

arrested at the same time. There was a reason for all this. The government was in a state of alarm. A French privateer had been wrecked on the Goodwin Sands: on board were found letters from Tourville, Admiral of the French fleet, to his agents in England. These revealed that the French were about to invade. They had three hundred transports tucked away in harbours in Normandy and had assembled an expeditionary force of 20,000 men, half of them French, half Irish, all ready to sail as soon as the French Mediterranean and Channel fleets, steering into battle together, had won control of the Straits of Dover.

Furious last-minute preparations were being made in Britain, above all in the naval dockyards. Because the grim fact was that only a few thousand regular troops were left in the country. If the French landed at Dover they could almost certainly march to London, where they would find willing hands to help them. One of the Council's first decisions then was to order all Roman Catholics to leave the town. In addition, two companies of the trained bands were to be on guard in the City every night. The arrest of Marlborough was part of the defence system improvised by the Queen and her Council in the King's absence. It was a strange turn of the wheel for a man who, only a few weeks before, had been the Commander-in-Chief in England and, on his return from Ireland as victor a year earlier, had been entertained to dinner here in the Tower by the Constable. True, he had been in treasonable correspondence with the exiled King James but so had other Ministers, so for that matter had the man who was at that moment commanding the Channel fleet on which the safety of the realm primarily and, in fact, wholly depended, Admiral Russell. But against Marlborough there was a more specific charge.

A gaolbird named Robert Young swore that the earl's name was on a bond of association by which the signatories pledged themselves to seize the Prince of Orange and restore King James. This document was said to be hidden in a flowerpot in the Bishop of Rochester's house. And so it was. For Young had forged it and one of his accomplices had put it in the pot. It was the kind of story which, in more tranquil times, would have been quickly investigated and its falsity exposed. But the times were far from tranquil. There was the French fleet assembling sixty miles from the coast of Dorset. There was the evidence of a vast and dangerous French design. It was a time when the Queen was burning her private journal, when the air was electric with rumours of Jacobite preparations, when the price of a loaf of bread in London rose from 9d to a shilling. And when the flimsiest canard could be credited.

Then, even more suddenly than it had blown up, the panic died away. The English and Dutch fleets, sixty-three ships of war and thirty-six respectively, with 7,144 guns between them, came together while Tourville, weather-bound for six weeks, was still waiting to be joined by the Toulon squadron. Although outnumbered two to one, the French gave battle off Cape de la Hogue. There they were mauled by the Allied gunpower and hunted into their harbours. After that day (19 May) there was no danger that England would be invaded. Indeed, all through the rest of the era of Louis XIV, the English fleet had command of the sea. This did not mean, however, that the naval war came to an end. It only changed its character. The great age of the French corsairs was opening, men like Jean Bart and Duguay-Trouin, who have much the same stature in France's naval history as Drake has in Britain's. These freebooters took up the struggle where the French regular navy was compelled to break it off. In the fighting off La Hogue Marlborough's fat – and dishonest – brother, George, distinguished himself. So for that matter did the admirals most suspected of Jacobite leanings. Watching from the Norman cliffs, King James had the pain of witnessing the navy he had helped to build, led by men whom he thought were his supporters, demolish his hopes of restoration. For Marlborough, too, the day was fateful, although in a different sense. The naval victory had, in all possibility, saved him from the scaffold. In the calmer months that followed, the Privy Council examined the flowerpot fiction and, without much difficulty, found it to be a tissue of lies. Four days after that decision, Marlborough asked to be released on bail of £6,000 which his friends Shrewsbury and Halifax helped to provide, to the fury of the Queen. On 19 June he left the Tower. It had been a narrow squeak.

In the first days of August, the French, by a brilliant victory on land, compensated for their disaster at sea. In the palace of St Cloud, the Duchess of Orléans[1] – second wife of King Louis' brother, Monsieur – was awakened at midnight. "Monsieur was holding an open letter in his hand and said, 'Don't be alarmed, Madame. Your son is wounded but only slightly. There has been a great battle in Flanders, the King's infantry has beaten that of the Prince of Orange.' "[2] The battle was at Steenkirk. British infantry, commanded by a Dutchman, Count Solms, who was highly unpopular in the British army, had there been overwhelmed by the French Household troops, with the loss of half of their numbers including two generals. The British blamed Count Solms. With a brother, Charles, and a brother-in-law, Colonel Godfrey, present on that day,

Marlborough heard all about the battle from the British army's point of view. He passed on their opinions to his fellow-peers. He was now spending most of his time with Princess Anne at Berkeley House in Piccadilly, to which she had moved from Syon House. So was Sarah, whom Anne, to her sister's annoyance, refused to give up. Occasionally, however, Marlborough went down to their country house at St Albans. On the way by coach, one August night, he had a rude reminder of the lawless England in which he lived. He was held up by highwaymen who robbed him of five hundred guineas. It may be assumed that the news of this mishap aroused laughter at court and chuckles in the messes; his avarice was fast becoming one of the accepted truths of English life.

Now he was an out-of-work officer, in disgrace at court and still not cleared by Parliament. Clearance came, however, in November, after which he became a spokesman in the Lords for the general proposition that British generals should not be put under Dutchmen. He expressed a sense of grievance in the army which had a substantial foundation. Under the King, the British infantry was commanded in 1691 by one Dutchman and the cavalry by another; of the six lieutenant-generals, only two were English and one of them, Marlborough, was in disgrace; of the five major-generals only two were English.[3] The Lords agreed with Marlborough but, in the Commons, King William's influence was stronger. They voted money for another campaign without making it a condition that the grievances of the army should be removed.

Although Marlborough continued to be idle, he can hardly have been short of money. When he was forced to sell his offices in 1691, he received a sum which cannot have come to less than £8,000. After his six weeks in the Tower, he resigned as Governor of the Hudson's Bay Company having already, as we know, disposed of his stock at an estimated price of £5,000. He did not mean the money to lie idle. There were, as it chanced, no lack of opportunities in London about that time for a man with funds to invest. The Bank of England was about to be founded, "revolutionary in its own way",[4] not only a deposit and clearing bank but an issuing house which offered credit in notes and was about to preside over an astonishing increase in the scale and tempo of English commerce. Marlborough was occupied at the time with high politics, particularly with making the peace, if it could be made, between the Queen and her sister, Anne, on terms acceptable to Sarah. He was not one of the original subscribers to the Bank. However, on 28 November 1694, during the first few months of its existence, he bought £4,000 of its stock at 10 per cent above the par value. This he sold at 14 per cent over par in the following year, having in the meantime received the first year's dividend of 6 per cent.[5] In addition, there was £1,000 a year which Sarah received from Anne plus the perquisites of her office which, it was said, included her card-table winnings from the princess, rumoured to be enormous.* However, money is not everything.

It was galling for Marlborough to be an idle general during years when the army was involved in one defeat after another in Flanders. After Steenkirk came Landen where William's army lost 20,000 men and Marlborough's nephew, the Duke of Berwick, was captured by Marlborough's brother, Charles, and ransomed for 30,000 florins. There was a deplorable incident at sea when an Anglo-Dutch convoy of four hundred ships outward bound for Smyrna was, through incompetence, caught by the French fleet and mercilessly punished with the loss of a hundred merchantmen worth a million pounds. Naturally there was uproar in the House of Commons over this disaster in which Marlborough's brother, George, took part. But when George said, tactlessly, that too many "brewers' clerks" had been given naval commands, he was sharply reminded of the occasion when he had taken money for giving naval protection to merchant vessels. One way and another, the Churchills were contriving to keep in the public eye.

In the summer of 1694 there came another military failure from which the reputation of Marlborough in history has suffered. Brigadier Tollemache commanded a force of seven thousand men who were given the task of landing in Camaret Bay on the south coast of the great natural harbour of Brest. After making a reconnaissance by yacht, Tollemache decided to go in with his assault force. There was no question of a surprise, for the French had seen the fleet and all the area had been alarmed by firing cannon and lighting beacons. Tollemache found that his fleet of assault boats came under the fire of five batteries of mortars. Musketry fire from troops in well-sited trenches swept the beaches. Early in the operation Tollemache was mortally wounded. The fire was so hot that sailors had to be bribed with five pounds before they would agree to bring off the stricken officer. Before retreating, the British lost five hundred dead or prisoners. In short, Camaret Bay was a disaster. But could it have been anything else? The French had known for a month or more that the British meant to attack the port of Brest. There had been no precautions

---

* A figure of £5,000 was mentioned. "She thought only of eating and playing cards," said Sarah later when she had quarrelled with her friend.

comparable to the elaborate concealment and deception which preceded Marlborough's attack on Cork. The French had not been idle. Vauban, their great expert on fortifications, had hurried down to prepare defences. Cavalry and six battalions of coastal defence troops were moved to the area. Of all these counter-measures, the British government was well aware. They were aware, too, that the French knew the purpose of the ships the British were assembling in Portsmouth and of the battalions encamped on the hills above the naval base.

Finally, a delay of a month between the departure of the ships from Portsmouth and their arrival off Camaret Bay had obviously given the French time to prepare their counter-measures. Instead of calling the whole thing off, however, the Cabinet, once committed to the expedition, took the cowardly way out by leaving the final decision to Tollemache, who was simply told to consult with the Admiral, Lord Berkeley, as to how the forces could best be used to annoy the enemy. To write such an order was to invite a brave and ambitious officer to err on the side of audacity, which was exactly what Tollemache did.

But what had all this to do with Marlborough? Nothing whatever at the time; indeed, nothing until many years later. Long after Marlborough's death, however, documents were published which purported to come from the archives of the exiled Jacobite court. Major-General Sackville, a Jacobite agent in England, sent a letter to King James enclosing a letter from Marlborough, dated 3 May 1694, in which he told the King that he had just learned that the ketches and regiments at Portsmouth would sail next day to burn the port of Brest and destroy the men o' war that were in it. In other words, Marlborough was, according to this story, telling James something that the French had known for at least a month. Given the fact that Marlborough was in touch with the Jacobite court, why should he trouble it with old news? There are several features in his letter and in the note from Sackville which accompanied it that should be mentioned. Each repeats expressions that are used in the other, e.g. the paramount need for secrecy; each makes an attack on the good faith of Admiral Russell. Why the repetitions? Marlborough is alleged to say "no consideration can prevent, or ever shall prevent me from informing you of all that I believe can be for your service." Why should a protestation as artless and dangerous as this be made in an urgent intelligence report?

There is, too, the fact that neither Sackville's letter nor Marlborough's now exists. Each of them purports to be a re-translation from a French original which, of course, was sent in cypher. The whole affair is complicated and puzzling. However, it must also be said that in King James' Memoirs the letter was duly minuted: "May 4, Lord Churchill informed the King of the design on Brest." The question of date is another difficulty. Sackville's letter from England is dated 3 May which will certainly be Old Style, corresponding to 13 May New Style in the Continental usage which King James employed. Making allowance for the time an express courier would need to reach Saint Germain from London, the King could not have been "informed" by Lord Churchill before 18 or 19 May. How, then, did he come to say in his Memoirs (supposing that he wrote them himself) that the information reached him a fortnight earlier?

Clearly – if one can use such a term in this context – the incident is wrapped in confusion and doubt. The Jacobite papers, long since destroyed, were first tampered with and then worked over by Jacobite exiles anxious to prove their own importance and by editors like James Macpherson, inventor of *Ossian*, who wished to make their story more exciting. At the end of it all, however, the impression remains that, in Jacobite circles, Marlborough was believed to have given away the secret of the Brest raid – although at a time when it was no longer a secret. It was, to say the least, a strange thing for a cautious man to have done. But human nature is capable of odd quirks. If Marlborough's good name in history has suffered more than it deserves from the Camaret Bay episode, can anyone wonder? It is a natural consequence of his record of double-dealing towards two kings, the King he had deserted, the King he had helped to the crown.

On another occasion, Marlborough was in difficulty. In June 1696, a Jacobite named Sir John Fenwick was arrested for treason; he offered, on condition of pardon, to give a full account of Jacobite plotting. He named Shrewsbury, Godolphin, Russell and Marlborough as James' leading supporters in England. The House of Commons, pondering the evidence, decided that the allegations were false. Fenwick was attainted and executed. Marlborough took an active part against him in the debates in the Lords.

One consequence of the Camaret Bay disaster had a direct bearing on Marlborough's affairs. The death of Tollemache led, naturally enough, to increased pressure on William to recall Marlborough to active duty. But William would not yield. To him, Marlborough was "a vile man", a traitor. He declared that although he had profited by the treason he abhorred the traitor. This he had told Bishop Burnet three years earlier,

John Churchill, 1st Duke of Marlborough
(*National Portrait Gallery*)

Barbara Villiers,
Duchess of Cleveland
(*National Portrait Gallery*)

Arabella Churchill
(*Radio Times Hulton Picture Library*)

William III, King of England
(*Radio Times Hulton Picture Library*)

King Louis XIV of France
(*Radio Times Hulton
Picture Library*)

Sidney, 1st Earl of Godolphin
(*National Portrait Gallery*)

Elizabeth Charlotte, Princess
Palatine, Duchess of Orléans
(*Radio Times Hulton Picture Library*)

at the time when Marlborough was leading the outcry against the Dutch officers in British service. He had not changed his mind since. Yet it may be doubted whether William's resentment, so violent and so lasting, had a purely political motive. There was a personal wound which had not healed. At this, Lord Shrewsbury, the Secretary of State, hinted when he asked William to forgive Marlborough and admitted that "some points remained of a nature too tender for me to pretend to advise upon and of which your Majesty is the only and best judge."[6]

A few months after the Camaret Bay disaster, there came a sudden turn in events. Queen Mary caught smallpox; on 28 December she died. To William, whom she had loved dearly and selflessly ("I live like a nun," she had said) it came as a heavy blow. Perhaps heavier than he had dreamt of, although all that can be said is that his feelings about his wife were one of the deepest secrets of this secretive man. Mary had disliked his friend-ship with Elizabeth Villiers, Sarah's enemy, of whom Swift said that she was the wisest woman he knew and that "she squints like a dragon". Now William gave her a grant of land in Ireland expropriated from adherents of James and married her off to Lord George Hamilton, a soldier from a Scottish ducal house, whom he created Earl of Orkney.

With the Queen's passing, it might have been thought that William's position would be weakened and that the way would be open for Marlborough's return to office. Neither event occurred, although Marlborough was received at court once more. The Revolution Settle-ment seemed as firmly established as ever; Anne's succession seemed assured. When William began to negotiate the Peace of Ryswick with Louis, he offered a pension of £50,000 to James' wife, Mary of Modena. It was exactly the amount that Parliament had granted Princess Anne. Further, he offered to recognize James' son as his successor provided he could bring the boy up as a Protestant. This would have excluded Anne from the throne and the Churchills from influence. James declined both offers.

Peace came in October 1697. After three bad harvests ("the great misery and want of bread in France" was duly noted in the English newsletters of that summer)[7] Louis decided that for the time being he had done enough for the glory of France. William obtained the right to be called King of Britain "by the grace of God"; Louis gave his Royal word not to help William's enemies nor to assist anyone who sought to trouble him in the possession of his kingdoms. On the other hand, Louis refused to expel James from France or to abandon his right to control the entry of

French subjects to the principality of Orange. At the end of all the talk
Louis had kept many of his gains but had conceded enough to make men
realize that the complex and fragile web of alliances which William had
woven against him had been worthwhile. And of course nobody believed
that the struggle was over. The combatants had reeled back, panting, from
one another; soon, with strength restored, they would be at one another's
throats again. "There seems a strange curse on this peace," wrote the
Duchess of Orléans to her half-sister. "The news of it was received without
any joy, although everyone here wanted it for so long. Even the people
of Paris weren't pleased."[8]

VII

A War to Plan

"The art of war, however, as it is certainly the noblest of all arts, so in the progress of improvement, it necessarily becomes one of the most complicated among them."

Adam Smith, Wealth of Nations, *Book V, Chap. 1, Part 1*

One day in June 1698 the clouds, which had covered his sky for six years, parted and the sun of Royal favour shone again on Marlborough. He was appointed governor of Princess Anne's young son, the Duke of Gloucester, with a salary of £2,000 plus £1,200 "for his table". More important still as a sign of his restored prestige, he was not long afterwards named one of the Lords Justices who acted as a council of regency when the King was out of the country. His son, Lord Churchill, was made Master of the Horse to the young Duke (salary £500). Even this was not the end of the benefactions to the Churchills. The past forgotten, Marlborough's brother, George, was appointed to the Board of Admiralty (£1,000 a year).

These appointments did not come by chance. There had been a significant change in the influences nearest to the King. His boyhood companion, Bentinck, now Earl of Portland, had lost to a younger man, his fellow-Dutchman Arnold Joost van Keppel, the first place in William's affections. Keppel was handsome, light-hearted and without any particular ability. He was just the companion for a lonely and often melancholy widower. Besides, Portland was in distant Paris on an important and, it seemed, successful embassy. Portland had, for a long time, been Marlborough's enemy, perhaps because he was married to a Villiers and the Villiers women were the sworn enemies of their relatives the Churchills. At any rate, anyone whom Portland disliked, Keppel – later, Earl of Albemarle – was bound to like. He liked Marlborough and, with all due tact, pressed on the King his qualifications to supervise the up-bringing of the boy Duke. This did not mean that all was peace and harmony between

Marlborough and the King. Marlborough was still a loyal member of Princess Anne's faction, causing annoyance to the King when he argued that Anne's husband, Prince George, should be paid the mortgage of £85,000 on Danish properties which the Prince had surrendered in 1689. In the end, the King reluctantly paid and blamed Marlborough for it. Then there was also a dispute about grants of Irish lands formerly belonging to Jacobites which Marlborough thought should be restored to their original owners in spite of the fact that his own sister, Arabella, had a pension of £1,000 a year from those forfeited lands. Once again the King and he were at loggerheads. But these proved to be differences of minor consequence. Marlborough was drawn more and more closely into the King's councils by an immense crisis which, long threatening, at last broke upon Europe.

Charles II of Spain succumbed to a multiplicity of disorders, physical and mental. From this moment it was obvious that a renewal of war would not be long delayed. Should the Austrian Hapsburgs or the French Bourbons succeed to the throne of Spain? Should the Spanish Empire be split up and, if so, how? The question was not simply one of dynastic right and privilege. Far from it. If the French claimant were given the Spanish throne, then all the trade with the Spanish Empire, the biggest colonial commerce in the world, would belong to France or would be hers to concede on suitable terms to a dependant. It was a prospect on which neither England nor Holland, the two leading maritime powers of the West, could look with equanimity. Nor could the Emperor Leopold who, as head of the Hapsburg family, regarded Spain as part of the domains that belonged rightfully to his relatives. While waiting for the Spanish king to die, Louis XIV had been neither idle nor pessimistic. He thought that England did not want to fight and that, if she were forced to do so, she lacked the necessary resources for a war. Not long before, the English Parliament had cut down the standing army from the 30,000 figure which William thought was the minimum necessary to 8,000 plus Scottish and Irish garrisons.

"A deadness and want of spirit in the nation" was reported to William by one of his ministers. However, Louis was quite mistaken in thinking that England could not afford to fight. He underestimated the speed with which a commercial nation could recover. In all the circumstances, he thought that he could safely risk a technical breach of his Royal word. His wife, Maria Theresa, had, on her marriage, renounced all claim to the Spanish throne but the condition of the renunciation had not been fulfilled: her dowry had not been paid. Louis therefore claimed the Spanish throne for his son. The Hapsburg claim was put forward by the Emperor Leopold on behalf of his son, Charles. Leopold's daughter had been persuaded to give up any right she may have had. But as this daughter, married to the Elector of Bavaria, now produced a son and as the Spanish government refused to recognize her renunciation, it looked as if the little Bavarian prince had a good claim to the succession when the wretched Charles II died. Deprived of his army by Parliament, furious above all that his Dutch Guards were ordered to leave England, William did what he could by diplomacy. He suggested that in a carve-up of the Spanish Empire England should be given naval bases in the Mediterranean and that the Spanish possessions in Italy should go to the Emperor. Louis said that England could not legally obtain any concessions at all. A new complication arose when the Bavarian prince died and a new secret partition treaty was agreed, allotting Spain, the Indies and the Low Countries to the Austrian candidate, while the French prince was to obtain the Italian possessions plus Lorraine. Whether Louis would ever have kept this bargain may be doubted; soon it was obsolete.

The Latin sisters, France and Spain, dwelt side by side, sharing a civilization and a religion, divided by mutual incomprehension and the Pyrenees. Spain was as proud as France was intelligent: for different reasons, the one felt for the other an antipathy which verged on hatred. France was the impatient executor itching to get her hands on the property, Spain was the moribund body that would not lie down and be buried. Her Golden Age was over; it had ended nearly sixty years earlier at Rocroi. After that decisive battle, Philip IV of Spain reigned on as "The Great King" but, as a contemporary said, his was a greatness "only as a hole becomes great as more and more earth is taken from it". When he died, surrounded by the corpses of saints assembled to make sure of his spiritual welfare, he was succeeded by his son, a child of four, Charles II, who, as has already been stressed, was a grotesque and tragic figure, the end-product of a long process of in-breeding.

Through converging channels of maleficent destiny the child inherited in concentrated form the poisons of his tainted blood, the prognathous jaw and melancholia of one strain, the insanity of the other. His physique was wretched. At four, he could not stand; at six, he could not walk; owing to the malformation of his jaw, he could not masticate. He could speak with some difficulty. He could write if an attendant steadied his hand on the pen. Most of the time, his mind was clouded. He grew up to be sensual but impotent.[1] Naturally enough, his relatives in Paris and Vienna expected him to die at any moment. In the meantime, they arranged marriages for him, first to a French princess, then to a German. He could give neither a child. He believed the Devil was responsible for his misfortune and in this belief the Inquisitor General and Charles' confessor concurred. Through a village priest who had some reputation as an exorcist, they sought the Devil's advice on the problem. The Devil was unco-operative. Where religion failed, could science succeed? Medical treatment went on at the same time as spiritual. Charles was put on a diet of hens and capons fed on vipers' flesh; a plaster on his stomach seemed for a little to improve his digestion but the English ambassador was not optimistic: "The King looks like a ghost and moves like a clockwork image." But, defying all the probabilities, he held on to life until the summer of 1700 when he – or, more likely, someone acting in his name – summoned the Council of State and asked its opinion about the future. He was advised that the Empire should go to the prince best able to defend it, i.e. to one of the grandsons of Louis XIV.

That monarch was now put in an awkward position. If he rejected the offer, King Charles would make the Austrian Archduke Charles his heir; on the other hand, if Louis accepted, he would be committing perjury since he had signed a secret treaty with William of Orange to divide the Spanish Empire. In perplexity, Louis refrained from giving an answer. But the moment of decision was not long delayed. In September, the corpses of two saints were urgently brought to the palace in Madrid in the hope of a miracle. On 3 October, Charles added the decisive clause to his will by which the undivided Empire was left to the Duc d'Anjou; after him to his brother, the Duc de Berry; and then to the Austrian Archduke. On 1 November Charles died, aged thirty-nine. And so the lamentable story came to an end and another story began.

As could have been expected, Louis, a patriotic Frenchman, committed perjury. Summoning the Duc d'Anjou to his closet, he told him, "You are the King of Spain." The Spanish ambassador, Castel des Rios, was so overcome by the emotion of the occasion that he made a most un-Spanish remark: "There are no more Pyrenees!" This, it may be assumed, was the very last thing his fellow-countrymen wished. Aristocrats or peasants, they were Spanish and meant to remain so. Looking at the matter more coolly than her in-laws, the Duchess of Orléans thought that the Duc d'Anjou was a very suitable King for Spain: "He looks rather Austrian and always has his mouth open. When he is told to close his mouth, he closes it; as soon as he stops concentrating, he opens it again."[2] Thus one trait of the Hapsburg family was perpetuated in the new Bourbon King. When Charles V first went to Spain a peasant had said to him, "Your Majesty, shut your mouth. The flies in this country are very insolent."[3]

At first, it seemed that Louis' *coup* had succeeded. In England, a Tory Parliament was ready to believe that France would not unite her crown with Spain's. To show their willingness to think the best of their powerful neighbour – and to annoy King William – they had just cut the British armed forces to the bone. They had no intention of building them up again. Without England's help, Holland could not stand against France. The Emperor had troubles enough of his own without challenging Louis to battle. So for a time, all went as smoothly as could be wished in Versailles. The House of Commons even decided that it preferred the Spanish King's will to the treaty of Partition which it blamed Portland for negotiating. Portland defended himself by saying that the government as a whole was responsible. He added Marlborough's name to those of the ministers who had been in the secret. In the House of Lords, Marlborough retorted that the treaty had been shown to him as an accomplished fact. Other ministers said the same. So far, then, Louis had succeeded in throwing into confusion his enemies in England. Now, however, something happened which disturbed the equanimity of the English public.

Somehow, a letter written by Lord Melfort, one of James II's ministers in Paris, addressed to his brother in Saint-Germain, turned up at the General Post Office in London. It spoke of a coming French invasion of Scotland in support of the Jacobites in that country. Naturally there was a sensation when the document was revealed to Parliament. Louis was furious. Melfort swore that he had addressed the letter to Saint-Germain and argued that someone must have put the letter in the wrong mail-bag. He was ordered to leave Paris. The most probable explanation of a disclosure so shrewd and so well-timed is that it was the work of an agent in William's pay. The hangers-on of the Jacobite court were a fertile recruiting ground for every kind of mischief, from murder upwards. Very soon there was more substantial evidence that Louis could not be trusted.

He had promised that the crowns of France and Spain should be forever separate. Now he obtained from the Parlement of Paris a declaration that his grandson, the new King of Spain, could inherit the French throne if his other grandson were to die. Moreover, he set up a French company to manage the monopoly of the *Asiento*, the concession to supply Negro slaves to the Spanish plantations. This vastly lucrative trade was, at that time, in the hands of the Royal Africa Company of London. Finally and most unmistakable of all as a sign of French perfidy, Louis sent an army into the Netherlands and expelled the Dutch garrisons from the fortresses which they occupied by right of treaty and which the Dutch regarded as essential to their defence. Down went the forts like so many ninepins without a shot being fired – Antwerp, Mons, Namur, Venloo, Liège, Huy. With one exception – Maastricht – the whole defence system covering the approaches to Holland melted away in a matter of days. And this at the very moment when Holland and Britain were hopefully agreeing that the young Duc d'Anjou was the rightful King of Spain!

In the early summer of 1701, the English peace-party was losing its self-confidence and the nation's doubts about Louis were growing into something like alarm. Daniel Defoe presented a Memorial to Parliament signed "Legion – for we are many", condemning the deserting of the Dutch and demanding that Louis be ordered to quit Flanders, that William should declare war on him and that Parliament should vote money for the purpose. This remarkable journalistic intervention, from which Defoe was lucky to escape without arrest, was followed by a dinner in Mercers' Hall at which the main dish was calf's head. This item on the menu had a political significance as an oblique reference to the execution of Charles I. It was a custom that, in Calf's Head Clubs all over the country, the anniversary of the Royal martyrdom was celebrated by unrepentant republicans with coarse buffoonery. At the Mercers' Hall dinner its appearance on the menu emphasized the anti-Jacobite character of the proceedings.

In the space of a few months, the wind of opinion in Britain had swung round dramatically from peace to war, from placid acceptance of France's predominance in Europe to something resembling determination to resist it. On 5 June, the Act of Settlement was passed, ensuring that the monarchy should remain Protestant. The Duchess of Orléans welcomed the news in a letter to her aunt, Sophie, Electress of Hanover, "I assured you that you and your sons would be called to the English throne. The Princess of Denmark [Anne] is said to drink so heavily that her body is quite burnt up. She will never have any living children, and King William's health is so delicate that he can't live long. So you will soon sit on your grandfather's throne."[4] The Princess was right in her gloomy prognostications about William. The hand of death was already on the King when, on the last day of May 1701, he made Marlborough Commander-in-Chief of the English forces in Holland, and a month later, Ambassador Extraordinary to the United Provinces. On 1 July, the two men left in the Royal yacht for The Hague. They were going on important business of state.

Marlborough had suddenly become the second man in England, supplied with resources adequate to support his exalted station. His salary was £10 a day, in addition to which his brother-in-law, Colonel Godfrey, Master of the Jewel House, was ordered to provide him with 5893 *oz.* of silver plate and 1066 *oz.* gilt plate. He had £1,500 for his equipage and £100 a week for "entertainment". In addition, he could spend any amount he thought necessary on the secret service. One way and another, Marlborough was going to enjoy the income of a prince. When King William and he set off from the Thames to the Dutch coast, it was just eight months since the King of Spain died, and just eight days before the first battle was fought (in Italy) in the great war that his death had made inevitable. Inevitable? It is hard at first to see why the death of a mad King and the succession of one who was little more than a cypher should lead to bloody battles, vast devastations, a prodigal squandering of treasure and the perturbation of states:

> "And what they fought each other for
> I could not well make out."

In fact, under the guise of a dynastic quarrel, Europe was about to witness a conflict between rival social systems for the mastery of half the world. What was coming was, in truth, an ideological war with the maritime commercial powers, the forerunners of capitalism, ranged against a state ruled by a supervising and directing autocracy, the logical end of which would have been a monarchical form of State Socialism. Old Kaspar, as he is described in Southey's poem,★ could hardly be expected to discern the deeper reason for the conflict.

Once arrived at The Hague, William established Marlborough in semi-regal splendour in the Mauritzhuis. There the Englishman collaborated with the ailing King in a diplomatic task of enormous scope and incredible intricacy: the creation, from large states and small states, wealthy and needy, advanced and backward, independent and venal, of a network of political and military agreements which – were it finished in

★ "The Battle of Blenheim".

time – would stand between Europe and the ambitions of the French King. There was a need for urgency, for the time available was short: already the French armies were in action in Italy, already they were massing just beyond the Dutch frontiers, waiting the signal from Versailles which would certainly be given as soon as the spring sun began to dry the earth. There was another factor; men were mortal. If William had not known it from warnings given him by his own frail body, events of the next few months would tell him. It was a bad time for the Royal families of Europe.

The Duchess of Orléans, recently widowed by the death of her husband, Monsieur, noticed that James II's stutter was getting worse that autumn: "Good King James," she reported, "will do himself a mischief with his boundless piety. The day before yesterday he spent so long kneeling and praying that he fainted clean away!"[5] Twelve days later he was dead. Louis at once acknowledged his son as James III, King of Great Britain. This was a disavowal of his promise to William given in the Treaty of Ryswick and it deepened English suspicions of the French King's good faith. More changes were to come. Lenox's *Almanack*, published in Paris, predicted at the end of the year: "March 20, 1702. A potentate goes to his grave. This pleases not a few." On 8 March, William of Orange died at Hampton Court after a riding accident. Lenox was just twelve days out. William had been at work to the last constructing the Grand Alliance system round France. Now the task must be completed by others, above all by the man whose character he had distrusted for so long, whose abilities he had at last reluctantly acknowledged. Six days after the King's death, Marlborough's commission as Captain-General of the British land forces was issued. His era was opening.

Louis was in a position of extraordinary strength. Not only was he the master of the greatest military power in Europe, however it might be measured, in strategic geography, in gun-power, or in the 400,000 soldiers who marched at his orders. He had just added Spain to the realms owned by the family of which he was head. And Spain meant the Indies, South America and half of Italy. He had, by a month of bullying, elbowed the Dutch out of almost all their outworks in Belgium. Bavaria was about to become his ally. A new Pope looked on him with approval. When he moved against Holland, who would withstand him? The Dutch with forts and inundations and an army of 40,000 soldiers, native or hired? The English? Superior at sea, no doubt, but without a base in the Mediterranean. On land weak, with a peace-loving Parliament. Moreover, their King, Louis' arch-enemy, was dead and who was to say what path would be followed by the new Queen, a Stuart, daughter of the dead James and – it was said – repentant for her part in bringing him down? It seemed that she was a churchwoman, one of the High Church party – a term which probably meant little to Louis – and a Tory, detesting the clique of Whigs who were, if truth be told, little better than republicans. She was reported to be much addicted to food – or was it drink? – and much under the sway of Lady Marlborough who, by all accounts, was a clever and domineering woman and very much of a Whig. Louis knew that sort of woman well; he had one at his own elbow although she was not, God be thanked, a Whig. No, the English picture as it was presented to Louis in his closet at Versailles was not quite as clear as he would like it to be, but, with the realistic respect for his army that existed in England and the equally realistic readiness there to take his money, he was confident that he would achieve his purpose by an adroit mixture of war and diplomacy.

Meanwhile, there sat in the Mauritzhuis at The Hague this English milord whom Louis had met years before – was it after some battle in Alsace, or was it when James, the King's unfortunate cousin, had sent the man to ask him for a subsidy? Louis remembered a man of exceptional good looks, one who might have fluttered the heart of his brother Monsieur, poor dead Monsieur, with his huge flashing ear-rings, and his languishing eyes. With the striking appearance, Louis recalled, there had gone a polish, an address that came through the man's halting French. Since then, Marlborough had risen far. He was no longer a trusted servant – wrongly trusted, as it had turned out – but a minister, nay, more than a minister, an ambassador and a commander-in-chief, one who was something greater than a pawn on the chess-board of power.

And before the new reign in England was many days old, Marlborough had risen still higher. He had the Garter. He was Master-General of the Ordnance (salary £1,500), the coveted appointment controlling supplies and munitions for the army which William had given to Henry Sidney. He was Captain-General of the English forces on the Continent. Small wonder that John Evelyn shook his head over "the excess of honours" conferred on him.[6] Nor was Sarah omitted in the distribution of places. She became Groom of the Stole, Mistress of the Robes and Comptroller of the Privy Purse while the married daughters of the Churchills became Ladies of the Bedchamber. The Earl of Portland, William's former favourite, had been Ranger of Windsor Park. Anne now gave the post to her dear friend, Sarah, who had often admired Windsor Lodge, the Ranger's official resident. It became Sarah's for life.

Naturally, in a land where the nobility was jealous and powerful, where political feelings ran high and political talk ran free, these extraordinary marks of Royal favour for one family did not go without being noticed and disliked. There was, too, a solid financial aspect to all this grandeur. Soon it was being estimated that Marlborough's income from offices and pensions was £54,825 while Sarah's was £9,500, figures which excluded what their investments were bringing them.* Nor were other members of the clan in a state of penury. One Churchill brother, Charles, became a general and commanded the infantry; another, George, was an admiral and a favourite drinking-companion of Prince George of Denmark, the Queen's adored husband. Needless to say, neither George's past nor Charles' was forgotten when talk grew loud and careless in the London coffee houses. Upon all these minor matters the new Captain-General turned his back when, with all decent speed, he left once more for The Hague. There, complex and urgent business awaited him, a coalition to make, a war to plan.

* For an estimate of the income in detail see Appendix A.

VIII

God Has Sent Our Heart's Desire

Over the hills and over the main
To Flanders, Portugal and Spain
Queen Anne commands and we'll obey,
Over the hills and far away.

D'Urfey

At the age of fifty-one, Marlborough had apparently reached the climax of a long, chequered, but, on the whole, successful career in war and diplomacy. He was, in fact, on the brink of his real destiny. He had served with credit in a few minor engagements, he had some reputation as an adroit intriguer, one who was none too scrupulous; he had been busy in the corridors of Whitehall and, in spite of a high-pitched voice, was an effective debater in the House of Lords. Among many doubts about his character there was universal agreement on one score: Marlborough was grasping and close-fisted. Altogether, he appeared to be a secondary figure on the stage, a man of real talent who had, for some reason, failed to impress himself as deeply on his time as he might have done. Now opportunity beckoned. But, at fifty-one, had it not come on the scene too late? Was not Marlborough fated to go down in the story simply as one who had made a great deal of money, who had climbed a rung or two higher on the social ladder than his starting-point; and who had in difficult times shown a notable gift for self-preservation? What else was there?

He was a too indulgent master, so it was said.[1] In consequence, his servants robbed him, according to his wife. His compliant nature might well be evidence of weakness of character. His opinions were conventional and, for the most part, were well concealed. He shrank from displays of anger with a genuine horror. To an extent remarkable in one who lived in the most passionate and stormy circles of the world of his time, he had preserved an outer coolness which seemed to correspond to an inner tranquillity. Was it inborn or was it imposed by an unusual power of self-

97

discipline inculcated during the long years of his service in the courts of one monarch after another? There was something about him which mystified and did not always please, if the rare judgments of his contemporaries may be trusted.

One portrait of Marlborough painted at that stage in his life is lucid and unflattering, "very handsome, proper, well-spoken and affable . . . supplies his want of acquired knowledge by keeping good company".[2] The implication is that he was lacking in intellectual ballast although not in social graces. It is true that his spelling was, throughout his life, too casual even for that libertine age. "Timorous in council and cunning in politics" was the verdict of the Earl of Ailesbury, "obliging words but no performance."[3] Another man who described his character was a Friesian nobleman, who knew Marlborough better than Evelyn or Ailesbury did and liked him even less. Sicco van Goslinga brushes aside as matters of common knowledge the manner in which Marlborough founded his fortune, his behaviour towards James II and the Duchess of Cleveland; then he goes on: "born a gentleman; height above average; a perfectly handsome face; beautiful, sparkling eyes, an admirable complexion, pink and white, able to compete with the more beautiful sex; fine teeth; apart from his legs, which are too thin, one of the handsomest of men . . . Talks very agreeably even in French which he speaks badly . . . He is of a profound dissimulation, all the more dangerous in that he covers it with manners and modes of speech which seem to express complete frankness. He has limitless ambition and a sordid avarice which influences all his conduct."[4] The picture, painted by an enemy, vivid with dislike, is that of a person of formidable brilliance and seductive charm. It is reminiscent of the portrait of a woman drawn by a lover whom she has betrayed.

Clearly, the Captain-General on his momentous crossing from Harwich to The Hague was taking with him not only the military and financial power of Britain, but something of his own, an ability still masked and unmeasured but which men could sense as something exceptional. Before his arrival at The Hague, he had told the Dutch that the Queen would be faithful to the promises King William had given. Soon after he landed, he had an interview with Goes, the Imperial ambassador, assuring him that if the people of the Indies declared for the Emperor, England would have no more to say. On the other hand, if the Caribbean islands did not avow themselves to be pro-Hapsburg, then England would insist on her right to keep any of them she might take in the course of the coming war. But she conceded that the Emperor should have a free hand in Italy.

However, more immediate and more delicate problems faced Marlborough than those relating to the ultimate peace settlement: who should command the Allied army? Queen Anne wanted the post for her husband, Prince George. Four German princelings had pretensions. The Dutch looked with disapproval on any Royal commander-in-chief; they were republican in outlook, qualified only by their sentimental attachment to the House of Orange. Their candidate for the post was an elderly Dutch general named Ginkel. A stodgy old soldier? So much the better thought the anti-war party, which was strong in commercial circles in Amsterdam. Such a man would be less likely to embark on dangerous adventures. Marlborough pressed the claim of Prince George with all the vehemence which loyalty to the Queen demanded. However, he visited the States-General in full ceremonial splendour as an ambassador-extraordinary. He was also, as his costume showed, Captain-General of the English army. Marlborough's appearance on that day was in itself an unstated and impressive claim. The English army might not be as strong as the Dutch army – 30,000 men (English and foreign) as against 45,000 – but it was likely to grow and, in any case, without England at her back, the Republic must make peace with Louis.

By the time Marlborough went back to London for the funeral of William III, he had brought about a secret re-statement of the terms of the Coalition: the allies would attack France on 4 May. In addition, he had won the approval of the leading Dutch officials, above all of Heinsius, the Grand Pensionary, that is to say, Foreign Secretary. Heinsius was the most important official of the United Provinces, a patriot burningly aware of the danger Louis offered to his country. He and Marlborough formed a close alliance in trust and friendship.

Even closer was the association between Marlborough and Queen Anne's new Lord Treasurer, Sidney Godolphin, whose son had recently married Marlborough's daughter. Godolphin was a circumspect minister and a wild gambler, who served four English monarchs yet is best known in history as the man who imported the Godolphin Arabian, and is therefore venerated as one of the founders of English bloodstock. He and John Churchill had been boys together at the Duke of York's court; they had been friends ever since. About to undertake an unprecedented political and military task on the Continent, Marlborough said he could not serve unless Godolphin was appointed to manage the money in Whitehall. So Godolphin was lured away from his adored Newmarket and, not without groans, set to work making a ministry and organizing the finances of a country which, in a day or two, would be at war. He became the Queen's first Minister.

On 23 April, Queen Anne was crowned, having been carried into the Abbey, poor invalid lady, by four yeomen of the guard. The coronation favours bore the motto, "God has sent our heart's desire." In the crush, several ladies lost jewellery of great value. The by-play of ceremonial occasions has not changed very much with the passing of time. A week later, Marlborough was at Margate, waiting impatiently for "the first wind" for Holland. The Dutch had reached a decision of crucial importance: Marlborough was to be commander of the Dutch as well as the English troops. It was a bold, indeed a remarkable choice, for Marlborough had no experience as a director of major operations of war. It had been made basically because Marlborough had completely won the heart and confidence of Heinsius, the strange, lonely, dedicated public servant who was the most powerful statesman in his country and, by that fact, one of the key figures in European politics. There was a great deal he could teach Marlborough about the difficult world he was entering. All one can say is that the Englishman learnt fast.

By recognizing the "Old Pretender", James III, as King of Britain, Louis had made it certain that the anti-Jacobite Tories would support the war, hoping that it would not be waged too fiercely or too much on land. This, Marlborough thought, was a thoroughly dangerous line of criticism of his policies – "if they can once be strong enough to declare which way the war shall be managed, they may ruin England and Holland at their pleasure."[5] At the same time, in a sharp debate in the Commons, the old attack on the foreign, i.e. Huguenot, officers in the army was revived and beaten off, not without difficulty. The old suspicions of a regular army remained alive, although Parliament had voted to raise an army of 40,000, of which, however, only 18,000 were to be British; and the problem of filling the ranks was a difficult one: £4 bounties were offered; the prisons were emptied; paupers and poachers were roped in; political opponents of the magistrates were not overlooked. "Half-hanged Smith"[6] who had, by accident, escaped the gallows, did valuable service in the cause of patriotism by betraying 350 pickpockets to the authorities who forthwith drafted them into the Guards. Generally speaking, it was a difficult time for recruiting officers: the country was too prosperous. Daniel Defoe wrote when it was all over: " 'Tis poverty and starving that fills armies, not trade and manufacturing . . . In the late war few English could be had without the utmost violence and compulsion; even the Scots were not able to supply any sufficient numbers; the reason was plain: trade flourished."[7] However, "trade and manufacturing" could perform one military function. They could provide the funds to hire armies abroad.

The naval press-gangs which, by established right, could lawfully find men for the fleet, were called into use to help the recruiting campaign. A thousand English deserters, who gave themselves up to the French, swore that they had been pressed for the navy, then blindfolded and taken to Flanders.

To find officers was an easier matter. In the taverns of Covent Garden and Drury Lane there lounged a breed of shabby, quarrelsome and hungry idlers who had been living on half-pay since the Peace of Ryswick. They were soon given work to do. While he lay dying William III signed two hundred commissions of half-pay officers in a single day. Parliament debated a Bill to encourage farmers to own arms and to shoot at the butts. One way and another, an unmilitary nation was accustoming itself to the idea of war.

When Marlborough, in the middle of May, said an emotional goodbye to Sarah, who was watching from the cliffs at Margate ("I could have given my life to come back"), he knew very well the immensity of his task: Louis had 400,000 men to whom very soon 45,000 Bavarians would be added: against him, the English, well-trained but untried in battle, made, with the Dutch, an army of 60,000; in addition was the Emperor's army which fell short of the 82,000 which he had undertaken to put into the field against France. Moreover, the Imperial troops were far away from the lower Rhine where, it seemed, the issue would be decided. In addition, there were soldiers which England or Holland had paid for – Prussians, Hanoverians, Palatines and Danes. But who was to say how such a polyglot gathering would behave in the field? One could only hope, and record the impression that they were hardy and well-disciplined. Whether they would earn the subsidies which had been paid to their princely masters remained to be seen. Already while Marlborough was still on his way to the great camp at Nijmegen and the army was commanded by his deputy, the Dutchman, Ginkel, there had been a narrow escape from total disaster. The French Marshal Boufflers had by a sudden lunge threatened Ginkel's communications with his base. Only by hard marching had the army been saved from destruction. "If Boufflers had won the race not a man of our small army would have escaped; all must either have been killed or taken."[8] From the beginning, then, there could be no doubt about the quality of the enemy. A few days later, the Prussians, Palatines and Dutch captured Kaiserswerth on the east bank of the Rhine which, while it was in French hands, had barred the way to Southern Germany. However, there was still a French army 60,000 strong in the country between the Lower Meuse and the Rhine and while that was so, Marlborough's first task was obvious. He must, if he could, winkle Boufflers out of that area for, until he did so, the Dutch would never allow him to move south into the Spanish Netherlands.

The question was, would the Dutch let him do what was necessary? It was apparent that he should cross to the west bank of the Meuse and march southwards. By doing so, he would compel Boufflers to hurry in the same direction so as to protect the roads over which his convoys came, bringing him supplies from Brabant. Day after day Marlborough spent reasoning and pleading with Ginkel and the States General who were terrified that, were he to do as he proposed, the French Marshal would make another grab at Nijmegen. When at last the Dutch consented to his southward advance, Marlborough moved quickly on Liège and Boufflers did what Marlborough had predicted he would do. He retreated, fast. In fact, the French army escaped from a major disaster only by an extraordinary stroke of luck. In heath country, Boufflers was hurrying in some confusion across the front of Marlborough's advance. Taken thus in flank, his army ought to have been destroyed. But the Dutch field deputies, political "commissars" acting on behalf of the States-General, whose veto Marlborough was bound to heed, first agreed to an attack and then forbade it. It was the first of several occasions on which Dutch caution and lack of imagination came between the Captain-General and victory.

Allowance must be made here for the difference between the situations of the two countries: England, protected by the Channel in which the French fleet could not challenge her; Holland with the war on her doorstep, conscious that one major defeat could mean annihilation. Beyond this, there was the contrast between a military genius seeking to express himself in decisive action and the defensive outlook proper to a small power threatened by a great one. Naturally, Marlborough was annoyed by the inconvenient turn of events. In addition, his professional pride was hurt. He sent a messenger to the French commanders (one of whom was his own nephew, Berwick) saying that the failure to give them battle was through no fault of his. His officers, not all of whom had his evenness of temper, were even more annoyed; ill-feeling in the English camp was only appeased by a series of successful sieges in the Meuse valley, in particular by the capture of the St Michael fort at Venloo. This was an audacious feat of arms carried out by an Anglo-Irish brigade commanded by Lord Cutts, known for sufficient reasons as "The Salamander" ("as brave and brainless as the sword at his side," said Jonathan Swift, who did not like him). Before the fighting had ended that year, Liège had fallen to Marlborough's assault but the Grand Alliance had suffered a setback in diplomacy more important by far than the capture of any fortress on the Meuse.

In September, the Elector of Bavaria, after a long session of horse-trading, decided to throw in his lot with France. His price was not small: the promise that Bavarian territory would be enlarged and that he, a Wittelsbach, would replace the Hapsburg Leopold as Emperor. In effect, it meant that Louis, already controlling all the Spanish Empire through his grandson, Philip V, could now hope to achieve the mastery of Germany through his creature, Max Emanuel, at that time Elector of Bavaria and, with any reasonable luck, about to march down the Danube to Vienna at the head of a Franco-Bavarian army. It seemed that Europe was on the threshold of an extraordinary new era and that a new super-power was about to come into being, mightier even than Charles V's empire had been a century and a half before. The superpower of France. It seemed that little stood between the union of the French troops and the Bavarians but the thin shield of the south German states. That shield was pierced before autumn ended: by a daring *coup de main*, the Bavarians seized Ulm, a Protestant city on the Danube between the Bavarian frontier and the French outposts in Alsace. Thus, by the time that the regiments went into winter quarters that year, the balance of military power in Europe had swung even further in favour of Louis. And Marlborough's task in the coming year would be that much greater.

At sea, too, matters had gone less than brilliantly for the Allies. The Grand Fleet, as it was called, under Sir George Rooke, carried the Duke of Ormonde and 14,000 soldiers to take Cadiz. Rooke was against the whole strategy behind the expedition which was designed to seize a base for future operations in the Mediterranean. Ormonde, recognized head of the Irish Protestants, was weak but popular. Between them, the two commanders made a shameful failure of the enterprise; worse still, the troops they put ashore at Port St Mary, at some distance from Cadiz, ran riot, looting, burning and raping. In this disgraceful orgy, the officers took the lead. On its way home, the fleet had an undeserved stroke of luck. The chaplain of one of the ships was a French-speaking Jerseyman who, in talk with the French consul at Lagos in the Algarve, picked up the news that the Spanish treasure fleet was unloading in Vigo Bay. It had crossed the Atlantic from Vera Cruz under an escort of French warships which timid British naval captains had refused to attack in spite of the heroic example set them by Admiral Benbow. The morale of the officer corps of the navy was, in those days, a patchy business. It had suffered too long from too much politics.

At the thought of the treasure in Vigo Bay, Rooke, Ormonde and their men marvellously recovered their fighting spirit. The fleet sailed to the Bay and broke the boom protecting the treasure ships, while Marines stormed the Fort which guarded one end of the boom. For the loss of two hundred men, the whole Spanish fleet was destroyed in a day's fighting. Although most of the treasure had been carried away by pack-mules before the fleet arrived, the haul was satisfactory; probably about a million sterling, a great deal of which belonged to Dutch merchants carrying on trade between Spain and her colonies. But that did not prevent rejoicings when the news reached London. Rooke was delighted with this ironic outcome of the expedition. His name was associated with Marlborough's in the gratitude of Parliament. But he had not secured – as he had not wished to secure – a Mediterranean base for the navy, an aim which Marlborough's strategy required and which the High Tories disliked.

As it was now necessary for Marlborough to return to England for urgent political consultations, he set off in a yacht down the Meuse from Maastricht accompanied by another boat in which sixty armed men were travelling. On the river bank a cavalry escort rode alongside the vessels. The Captain-General should have been safe enough from enemy raiders. However, before Marlborough in his little boat reached safety in Dutch territory, there was a small town held by a French garrison in which was an Irish deserter from the Dutch army with the evocative name – or *nom de guerre* – of Lieutenant Farewell. He had got wind of the river trip. He and a band of fellow-desperadoes waylaid and seized the yacht on its way down the river. Marlborough's companions had safe-conducts signed by the Duc de Bourgogne, one of the French commanders. Marlborough had not. But a quick-witted clerk on his staff, a man named Stephen Gell, slipped him an out-of-date pass made out in the name of his brother,

General Churchill, and with this Marlborough was able to argue his way out of danger. After five hours of discussion, he went on his way downstream. Farewell vanished, with the silver and plate he had seized on the yacht, and when he turned up in Holland later on, was pardoned for his desertion and (a suspicious circumstance) promoted to a captaincy.

Meanwhile, news of Marlborough's capture had reached Versailles and The Hague. Louis gave orders that he should be well treated. The Dutch were plunged into gloom. The State-General sent a courier to Vienna telling the Emperor not to release Marshal Villeroi, recently captured in Italy, but to hold him in exchange for the Captain-General. In consequence, when Marlborough reached The Hague a vast wave of relief and emotion swept over the town. "That which moved me most," he told Godolphin, "was to see a great many of both sexes cry for joy . . . From five in the afternoon till after ten at night there was perpetual firing in the streets, which is their way of rejoicing." Stephen Gell was given, by the man he had saved, £50 a year for life. He had certainly earned it by his part in ensuring that the Marlborough story did not end in a sorry anti-climax.

After that Marlborough crossed to London where, at Anne's insistence, he was given the dukedom disliked by most people and, in particular, by Sarah, whose irritation with the title lasted through her life. "I mortally hate 'Madam' and 'Your Grace'," she said as an old woman. John Evelyn frowned over it as he wrote in the last week of December – "a duke for the success of one campaign!"[9] When Sarah had received the Queen's letter announcing the honour that was to come, she was as one who has "received the news of the death of one of her dear friends". The burdens of ducal rank! The expense! Marlborough was inclined to agree ("we ought not to wish for a greater title till we have a better estate"). Before leaving Holland he had discussed the matter with the Grand Pensionary, who thought it would be better if the honour were given quickly when everyone was pleased with what Marlborough had done. Besides, the Dutchman had said, he might never have such success again. When Marlborough reached London the worrying question of how he was to support his new dignity had still not been settled. But the Queen's bounty was not exhausted.

More embarrassing news was to come. The Queen proposed to give him a pension of £5,000 a year during her lifetime from the revenues of the Post Office; she told Parliament that she would like this pension to be, like the dukedom, in perpetuity. This suggestion did not go down at all well with the House of Commons, where it was thought that the new duke was doing quite well enough already out of the public purse. It was, thought John Evelyn, "a bold and unadvised request from one who besides his own estate had £30,000 a year in places and £50,000 at interest".[10] In all probability, Marlborough had about twice as much as Evelyn thought. Without any loss of time or any undue loss of dignity, the proposal was withdrawn. Desperately anxious to please her temperamental friend, the Queen offered Sarah £2,000 a year out of the privy purse – "This can draw no envy for nobody need know it" – in addition to her life pension from the Post Office. The offer was declined.

This disagreeable imbroglio, into which the Marlboroughs had plunged through cupidity, was followed by a family tragedy. Their only son, Lord Blandford, aged sixteen, fell ill at Cambridge of malignant smallpox. Sarah nursed him. Marlborough wrote to her: "For God's sake, if there be any hope of recovery, let me know it." He arrived in time to be present at the boy's death-bed. It was a brutal reminder of the vanity of human wishes and fell with particular weight on one who, by nature a dynast, had just founded a ducal dynasty. Sarah's grief was so wild that for a time her reason was thought to be in danger. Marlborough altered his will, leaving his property on trust to Sarah for their eldest daughter's husband, Mr Godolphin. Later on, at The Hague, he told his Jacobite friend, Lord Ailesbury: "It is fit for me to retire and not toil and labour for I know not who." Fortunately for him, he had many worries to take the edge off his grief.

IX

Malbrouk S'en Va-t-en Guerre

"This world is made more for trouble than for happiness. I am hagged out of my life."

Marlborough to Sarah, 17/28 April 1704

In the jungle of Europe some of the beasts were wilder than others. None was so fierce as Charles XII of Sweden. He had come to the throne at fourteen and found himself surrounded by enemies dedicated to his destruction. It seemed likely that before he came of age, the boy would be stripped of his wide possessions south and east of the Baltic. Sweden would become what it had been before Gustavus Adolphus, a remote northern kingdom lost among its vast forests. Unfriendly neighbours in Russia, Saxony and Denmark agreed in 1699 that the time had arrived to divide up the boy's Swedish Empire among them. They reckoned that the task would not be too difficult. Nothing could have been more mistaken.

They had roused in his lair a teenage ruler who was one of the most ferocious and almost ungovernable warriors in history. In 1701, helped by an Anglo-Dutch fleet, he had compelled Denmark to sue for peace. Before the year was out, he had confronted Tsar Peter at Narva on the Gulf of Finland and shattered his army. Since then, he had been devoting himself to driving Augustus, Elector of Saxony, from the throne of Poland. Charles' doings were watched with admiration and alarm by both parties in the war in Western Europe, by Louis, although Sweden was traditionally the ally of France; by Marlborough, although England and Holland, acting together, had saved Sweden from defeat by the Danes. Nobody could be sure what Charles was going to do next. The young man was an unpredictable element in a Europe which already contained too many unstable factors; he was a soldier of genius, and a monarch of volcanic temperament. While Marlborough was on his way to The Hague, Charles had taken Warsaw and installed a puppet king on the Polish throne. Emperor Leopold looked on this disturbance at his back door with an anxious eye. As if he did not have enough to worry about with his Hungarian rebels! To say nothing of the French who, as it seemed, would at any moment when the weather improved, march down the Danube valley to Vienna.

For the Western States, the war in the North could not be dismissed as a barbarous conflict involving savages, Slavs and serfs, with which civilized men need not concern themselves. Alas, no. So far as England and Holland were concerned, the Baltic was the main source of the masts, timber, tar and sailcloth without which their fleets could not be put to sea. In addition, although it might be annoying that Denmark, claiming neutral rights, insisted on trading with France, it had to be borne in mind that Denmark, while maintaining her neutrality as a state, hired out to the Allies some of the best troops money could buy. The consequence was that Denmark was allowed to sell anything she liked to the French, horse alone excepted. Horses were, rightly, regarded as contraband of war and France, self-sufficient as she was in most things, needed to import 30,000 horses a year to keep her farms, her wagons and her armies moving.[1]

The criss-cross of military and commercial interests led to a great deal of ill-feeling, especially between the English and the Dutch. In these commercial matters there was not much to choose between the two, except that the Dutch were more blatant in doing business with the enemy. But smuggling – "owling" – of wool from Sussex ports to Normandy went on vigorously through the war. The Scots, who could argue that they were neutral while they provided excellent regiments to Holland and England, had no compunction about lending the use of their flag to English vessels out on business which the London government had banned. English privateers, for their part, were delighted when they fell in with Dutch ships carrying goods to Spanish ports in South America. These ships were, of course, instantly plundered. In the summer of 1703, the three allies, England, Holland and Austria, promised to stop all trade with the enemy. The promise could not be kept.

By that time, Portugal and Savoy had decided to throw in their lot with the two sea powers. It was cynically said that Savoy had never finished a war on the same side as she had entered it. It was still to be seen if that pattern would hold good. The Duke of Savoy had close family ties with the French Royal family; one of his daughters was the wife of the grandson of Louis, the Duc de Bourgogne, who would, in the natural course of things, one day inherit the French throne; another daughter was married to Louis' grandson, Philip, whom he had made King of Spain.

However, family ties are not the only factor in deciding a ruler's policy.

The Duke of Savoy looked with dislike on the prospect of having the Bourbon power established in Italy and encircling his duchy. In consequence, when Godolphin promised him an English subsidy of 800,000 crowns a year to join the anti-French coalition, he was seriously tempted. The news of the offer reached Louis who, in reply, promptly arrested all the Duke's subjects then serving in the French army. For the Duke, this was the last straw. Without further ado, he declared war on Louis. It was a suicidal step, as it seemed to the English envoy in Paris: "The Duke will lose his country or we shall lose the Duke." However, in the meantime Savoy, situated as it was at the crossing of important routes into Italy and Austria, might be useful in Marlborough's plans.

Portugal, as owner of the great port of Lisbon, certainly was. By treaty, Portugal gave a market to English wool and, in return, the drinking classes in England became partial to port, which now paid a lower duty than claret or burgundy. But the price paid for Lisbon was heavier still. England, Holland and the Empire agreed to keep 12,000 soldiers in Portugal and provide arms and pay for 28,000 Portuguese troops. Without that help, the King of Portugal thought that he would not be able to enter the war against France and Spain. A remote and, in the end, more serious consequence of the Portuguese treaty was that it shifted the preponderance of allied policy from the Low Countries to Spain. It became a fixed aim of statesmen – Tory first and later, more stridently, Whig – that the French King of Spain, Philip, should be replaced, by an Austrian, the Archduke Charles.

For Marlborough, the immediate problems in the spring of 1703 were caused not by his enemies but by his allies. He found the Dutch at their most stubborn and unco-operative. He was not idle, however; he captured Bonn and, by doing so, cleared the Rhine waterway all the way from the Dutch frontier. But an elaborate plan which he evolved to seize Antwerp collapsed when one of the Dutch generals upset the arrangements by going off on a plundering raid into West Flanders. What made this all the more frustrating was that Marshal Villars, most unconventional and daring of the French generals, in the meantime had captured Kehl on the east bank of the Rhine near Strasbourg and was about to cross the Black Forest into Bavaria. As it turned out, however, Marlborough was not the only general to have trouble with his allies.

Villars, a hot-tempered Provençal who had no aptitude for courtly behaviour, no respect for most of his fellow-marshals and no patience at

all with slow-motion warfare, quarrelled with Max Emanuel, Elector of
Bavaria, whose idea of the next move in the war was to seize the Tyrol.
And this at a time when the road to Vienna was open, the road down
the Danube! And on the west, the supply-route to France was safe-
guarded! The obvious, commonsense course was to march on Vienna and
do so without delay. Villars estimated that the job would be completed in
a matter of days, eight at most, as he told King Louis. But common sense
does not always speak with the loudest voice in the council chamber. So
Max Emanuel took his army off to the Tyrol, having argued Villars into
a reluctant acquiescence with his plan. At first, all went so well with the
campaign in the Tyrol that it seemed the Elector would very soon be
crowned Emperor. In their alarm, the Council at Vienna made preparations to move the imperial court to Graz. For the French and Bavarians
were not the only danger to the Emperor. On the eastern outskirts of
Vienna hovered the Hungarian insurgents, Protestant landowners and
Catholic peasants, united in indignation that their country had become the
prey of Austrian tax-gatherers. It seemed that Hapsburg rule in the
Empire would soon be ended. Villars himself was for a little caught up in
the general euphoria and wrote Max Emanuel a humorous letter asking
him for a duchy when he mounted the imperial throne. However, a
surprise lay ahead.

The Tyrolese mountaineers, both peasant and gentry, remembered
that, by tradition, they were first-class soldiers; now they fought like
tigers for the house of Hapsburg. The Bavarians retreated in a hurry to
Munich. And Villars quarrelled with the Elector so furiously that Louis
recalled him to France to lead the campaign against the Huguenot
insurgents in the Cevennes. There were only a few thousand of those
Protestant die-hards, but Louis regarded them as an intolerable stain on
the shining religious uniformity of his realm. The Camisards, as they were
called, fought on fanatically, savagely, desperately, encouraged by English
sympathy but not supported by English arms.

For Marlborough, pondering the war maps in his tent, the important
thing about these developments was that Vienna, against all odds, was
going to be safe until the campaigning season of 1704 opened. In that case
there would be time to carry out the fantastic operation which was
forming in his imagination. To nobody had he breathed a word of it at
that time, although William Cadogan, soldier son of a Dublin lawyer,
Marlborough's Quartermaster-General and, as we should now say,
chief-of-staff, may have gleaned some vague notion of what was in his

master's mind. Marlborough had an unmatched gift of secrecy; Cadogan knew how his mind worked better perhaps than any man in Europe.

When the war slowed down to a standstill in the autumn of 1703, it was plain to Marlborough that some new and surprising initiative was called for. The Dutch generals had made his life so difficult that on several occasions he had been on the verge of throwing in his hand. They had, for example, frustrated "The Great Design" of a surprise attack on Antwerp in the autumn of 1703. This had been planned as an operation of the highest complexity, involving the movement of twenty battalions from Bonn to Bergen-op-Zoom by barge down the Rhine, an attack on Ostend by a Dutch army and fleet for the purpose of dispersing the French forces. After that there was to be a concentric drive against Antwerp by three armies. For success, the plan called for meticulous timing and co-ordination; above all, it required the will to carry it through to success, which the Dutch generals did not have. In consequence the Great Design was a great fiasco.

The sorry anti-climax in which the year's campaigning had ended made the political situation in England more confused and troubled.The Whig grandees, by attacking the government for incompetence, thought to escape the odium of supporting a war which was going badly and was likely to go worse. The Tories were not to be allowed a monopoly of criticism of the men who were directing strategy. Marlborough, in particular, was attacked as a weak general. At the same time there was even louder grumbling among the Tories, who now had solid grounds for their dislike of the Dutch. Marlborough understood very well how they felt; after all, he was himself a Tory, although a moderate one, with no liking for party labels. At that time, however, the Tories were in process of dividing into two factions: the first supported Marlborough's war policy; the second, composed of High Churchmen, was chiefly intent on harrying the Dissenters. Either faction was liable to act independently of Godolphin and Marlborough. Thus, Lord Nottingham, the Secretary of State, had, at a time when Marlborough was still in the Low Countries, removed 2,000 English troops from the Netherlands and sent them to the Peninsula. The decision to do this he took without warning the Captain-General, whose indignation when he found out can be imagined. It could only have happened in a time when party feeling ran high.

Jonathan Swift watched these scuffles with a sardonic eye: "the very ladies are split asunder into High Church and Low and, out of zeal for religion, have hardly time to say their prayers!"[2] Even Marlborough was tempted to think ill of the Tories ("we are bound not to wish for any-body's death but should Sir Edward Seymour die it would be no great loss" – as he confided to Sarah), although he refused to go over to the Whigs. "I can by no means allow that all the Tory party are for King James," he protested to his wife. The Queen could use both parties in the nation's interest. So he argued. But it could not be denied that, on the whole, the Whigs, the party of the Revolution which had brought in the Dutch King, were more reliable as supporters of the war than the Tories were. It was a moment when Marlborough needed to be sure of loyal support at home if he were going to carry out his plan for the next campaigning year. He had decided that, as a theatre of war, the Nether-lands was ill-chosen. As he pointed out to the Dutch, the belt of fortresses in the Low Countries between the Allied army and the French frontier was so deep and so dense that, at the rate of two major sieges a year, it would require another Thirty Years' War to break through it. This was an exaggeration, but the exaggeration of a truth. The French possessed eighteen major fortresses in the Netherlands in addition to those on their own territory. They had constructed a more or less continuous line of field fortifications which ran from the sea to Antwerp and then south-wards to the Meuse. To break through the fortress zone called for some prolonged and tedious siege warfare which would inevitably have grave political repercussions in England. If the war went on long enough, sooner or later the anti-war party there would gain the ascendancy. But the changed face of the war now offered better prospects in other quarters. For example, Savoy was now an ally and might be persuaded to attack Toulon if an Anglo-Dutch fleet entered the Mediterranean and, with its cannon and marines, menaced the Riviera coast. Another change had occurred in the European scene which Marlborough was bound to observe with interest. The Emperor, in his danger, had called back to Vienna from Italy the most famous soldier in Christendom, Prince Eugene of Savoy. If any commander had a record as impetuous and daring as Charles of Sweden, it was he.

While Marlborough was directing operations in "the old prize-fighting stage of Flanders",[3] Eugene was fighting the French in Italy where, at Luzzara, he met Marshal Vendôme in a bitterly contested battle which ended in a draw. But, east and west, the strategic situation was grim for the Emperor. Finance was equally gloomy. His banker and principal army contractor, Samuel Oppenheimer, died, bankrupt. "This is so deadly a blow," said an observer, "that France herself could not have contrived anything more harmful to the Emperor." The overall picture was ominous in the extreme.

Marlborough could not believe, however, that so fiery a spirit as Eugene would for long be chained to a desk in the Hof burg. In the new, grave situation in the European war, Eugene would be sure to play a part. As for himself, he was beginning to prepare for the campaign of 1704. In letters to the German princes who sent their contingents to his army, he aired the notion of an invasion of France up the valley of the Moselle, the most direct route to Paris. The mere thought of so bold a move filled the Dutch politicians with apprehension: the "foreign commander-in-chief" and his bizarre theories of warfare were severely frowned on. Had they known the secret that Marlborough still concealed, their alarm would have been even more acute. In his mind there was maturing an operation so far-reaching and breathtaking that he knew better than to spring it on his allies. They must be persuaded, lured, even cheated into it. This process was going to take time. He did not even disclose it to Sarah, knowing that, with all her virtues, she was not a woman who could be relied on to keep a secret. It is probable that the first man to be allowed to share it was his old friend since 1698, the father-in-law of his daughter Henrietta, Sidney Godolphin, the Lord Treasurer. Maybe the second confidant was that strange, untypical Dutchman, the Grand Pensionary, Heinsius. In the meantime, the idea gained currency that the Duke of Marlborough was fascinated by the project of a campaign in the Moselle Valley.

Naturally, echoes of this rumour reached Versailles, the centre of the most efficient intelligence network in Europe. Marlborough talked to Cadogan, the tall Irishman who was his chief-of-staff and trusted personal friend. He dictated a stream of letters to Adam Cardonnel, his secretary, the son of a Huguenot refugee. And he spoke more and more openly to Heinsius. The project for a campaign in the valley of the Moselle went forward. Amid the storms of that winter, Marlborough crossed to The Hague and in the strictest secrecy, told the Dutch government of his Moselle plan. With some difficulty, Heinsius won the consent of the States-General for the project. By the time he came back to England, Marlborough knew that the first and easiest part of his task was over. He had gained reluctant permission for an undertaking which he had no intention of carrying out.

In the spring of 1704 when Marlborough was on the eve of embarking for the Continent, he was assailed by a particularly painful domestic trouble. Sarah accused him – not for the first time – of being unfaithful to her. Apparently, the seeds of this suspicion had been sown by their son-in-law, Lord Sunderland, a Whig and a political trouble-maker, whom Marlborough had never trusted and to whom he had given his prettiest daughter, Anne, with some reluctance. What had Sunderland said? Who was the woman who was alleged to have tempted one who had in youth been a successful rake? These questions remain without answers. There would be no lack of ladies in – and out of – London society who would be ready to cast an approving and speculative eye on the Captain-General, a good-looking man of fifty-four with an elegant figure, agreeable manners, considerable wealth and immense patronage. All that is certain is that Sarah believed the story and made her husband's life a misery to him. His letters to her make that quite clear.

"As I know your temper, I am very sensible that what I say signifies nothing! I did little expect to have had anybody put you in so ill-humour as to make me so miserable as I am at this time. Your suspicion of me as to this woman will vanish, but it can never go out of my mind the opinion you must have of me." "I do from my soul curse that hour in which I gave my poor dear child to a man that has made of me of all mankind the most unhappiest." To Godolphin he wrote: "You know the tender concern I have for Lady Marl., so that I need not tell you how unhappy her unkindness makes me. I would have seen you this morning, but that I am not fit for any company." Soon the rift in the Marlborough household was known to others besides the parties most concerned. Sarah was not likely to keep her discontent to herself. Not everybody took her part. For instance, Lady Southwell wrote to her, "You proclaim your lord an ill husband as I often hear you do everywhere . . . Give me leave to tell you that what you call your misfortunes have proceeded wholly from yourself."[4] It is unlikely that Sarah allowed herself to be influenced by this frank opinion. For her it had been a year of suffering, her only son dead, and the thought, hardening soon into certainty, that she would not have another child, so that the dukedom and, even more important, the fortune would go to the offspring of one of her daughters, none of whom she really loved. In these circumstances, Sarah went to see her distrusted, guilty (as she had no doubt) and beloved husband off at Harwich Quay.

New battalions and drafts to fill up the ranks of regiments already overseas were boarding the transports. Men o' war lying at anchor offshore were ready to give protection to the convoy. All the daunting pageantry of war was present. On the quay there was a glittering array of senior officers, grim-looking gentlemen in feathered hats, gold lace, full-bottomed wigs and scarlet coats. At their side, they trailed clanking swords. At the centre of the assembly, covertly or openly eyed by all, was John Churchill, pink-cheeked as a girl but less cheerful than usual. For Sarah was there to say farewell to her husband, but implacable woman that she was, not willing to embrace him. Instead, she handed him a note containing who knows what of accusation or reproof. It seemed that she was not ready to forgive; not ready to do that even harder thing: admit that she might be mistaken.

Thus, in gloom and unhappiness the Captain-General left England on 8 April on his most adventurous and, as it turned out, most famous campaign.

X

The Glorious Interview

"Love me as you do now and no hurt can come to me."
Marlborough to Sarah, April 1704 – 5 May 1704

At length the fame of England's Heroe drew
Eugenio to the glorious interview.
Addison, The Campaign, *1704*

But all was changed when in a field on the outskirts of a sad little German town, the general inspected the troops he was about to lead on a long and adventurous march. His heart swelled with pride and confidence at the sight of them: robust, weatherbeaten, resolute men, obviously well-trained, well-equipped, well-fed, well-mounted – look at those gleaming horses, the alignment of those sabres and muskets, the timing of the evolutions – it was the second time in a week he had felt that a weight had been lifted from his mind. The first time had been when a letter arrived at The Hague to say that Sarah had forgiven him and he had answered that she had "made me so happy that I do from my very soul wish we could retire and not be blamed". He had burnt that terrible letter she had handed him on the quay at Harwich. But could he keep this new letter? She had said she wanted to be with him. There was nothing he would like more, but unfortunately he was about to go up into Germany where she would not follow – "but love me as you do now no harm can come to me".

He had been troubled by headaches and "the spleen", i.e. depression, to which he was subject. Could she send him by Lord Cutts some liquorice and rhubarb for his digestion? He would also be grateful for two Stars of the Garter to wear with his uniform coats. There were occasions when he wanted to look his best. Like this one in the meadow at Bedburg when his little army passed in review order: the squadrons, nineteen British and twenty foreign, the fourteen battalions of British infantry, the sixty English cannon. In all, not far short of twenty thousand men. Not many when he thought of the armies the King of France could put in the field

Sarah, Duchess of Marlborough
(*National Portrait Gallery*)

A. S. A. Le Duc de Marlborough.
B. S. A. le Prince Eugene de Savoye.
C. S. A. le Prince Hereditaire De
Heſse Caſsel Genl. de La Cavall. de
L'H.P. Les Etats Generaux. &c.

The Battle of Blenheim
(*British Library*)

Prince Eugene of Savoy
(*Radio Times Hulton
Picture Library*)

James FitzJames,
1st Duke of Berwick
(*Radio Times Hulton Picture
Library*)

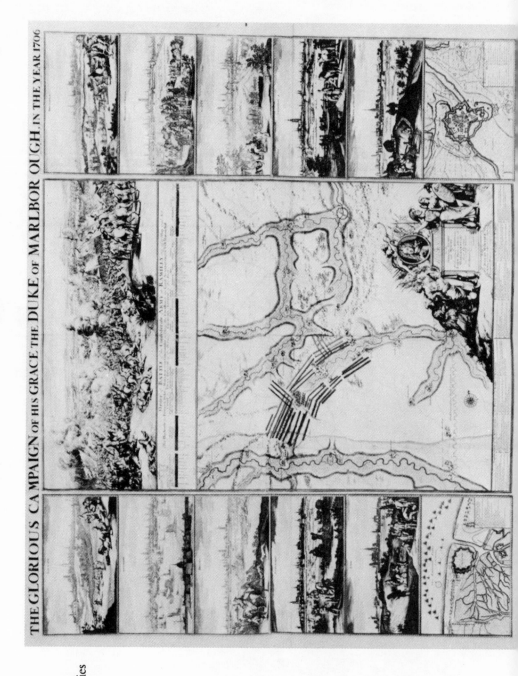

The Battle of Ramillies
(*British Library*)

but, looking at them now, likely to be enough to do the job. And before many days were past, before the end of the march which he was about to begin, the army was certain to be more numerous. That was something he had already arranged. Most important of all, the men were under his sole, unfettered command, to lead where he willed according to the secret design which he had formed in his heart and which probably nobody – not even the faithful Cadogan, that pearl among chiefs-of-staff – had divined in all its breath-taking scope and detail. Certainly, he had kept it hidden from the Dutch, who paid £10,000 of his salary and with whom, in his splendid quarters at The Hague, he had just concluded a week of tiresome negotiations.

He thought that the Dutch were altogether too cautious in their approach to the war besides being altogether too apt to meddle with his notions of how it should be fought. There is, however, something to be said on the Dutch side: the France of Louis XIV hung as a huge, constant, permanent threat over Europe, rather like the threat from Russia towards the end of the twentieth century. Spain was in advanced decay. The Empire was a clutter of states, some big and some larger but, of the larger, Hungary was in rebellion, Bavaria was an ally of France and Prussia unreliable. Holland was impoverishing herself by keeping as many as 100,000 troops in her service, most of them mercenaries. England, hiring soldiers abroad and impressing them at home, was able to support an effort roughly as great as the Dutch. But France, with nineteen million people under a centralized government and an ambitious monarch, was able to challenge all the rest of Europe with a military force that was growing all the time in strength and would soon number 400,000 men. It seemed not at all impossible that her King cherished the design of making himself Emperor one day or of seating some obedient satrap on the imperial throne.

At this moment when Marlborough was discussing the future of the war at The Hague, King Louis had eight separate armies in being which moved according to his supreme will: one was in Spain, another was dealing with the Camisard rising in the Cevennes, a third in Lombardy, a fourth in Piedmont and a fifth in Savoy. Finally, there were three French armies north of the Alps, each poised, ready to march when the rains ceased, the floods subsided and the mud dried on the roads. Above all, Marshal Villeroi's army was stationed in Flanders, 46,000 strong, with the manifest task of bringing the Dutch Republic to heel. It was hardly surprising then that Marlborough found his friends at The Hague in a cautious frame of mind, thinking in terms of a defensive strategy, of shortening the line, of pulling out of Germany the troops that were in their pay, and not at all in the mood to listen to the extraordinary proposals he had brought with him. These were as follows: He was going to have no more interference from the Field Deputies. Further, and more alarming, he was going to march up the Rhine valley as far as Coblenz, a city which was a hundred miles from the Dutch border. He would take with him the troops in English pay; if more could come, so much the better. And after Coblenz? Then the valley of the Moselle would lie open to him, the gateway into Alsace, the most direct route to Paris. But that – a glance at the map told anyone who cared to think – would lay Holland open to Villeroi's offensive! When the Dutchmen pointed out this objection to the project, Marlborough retorted that when he began to move up the Rhine the French marshal would give up any idea of an attack on Holland. It might indeed be so. But to men who, a few years before, had seen their country flooded to save it from French invasion, the thought of any weakening in their defence was a reason to shudder. However, when Marlborough insisted on having his way, the Dutch opposition collapsed. After all, the Duke was the voice of England and England was the ally that Holland must have. England, even if her policies were rash almost to the point of madness, was better than no ally at all.

During a few hectic days at The Hague these matters were thrashed out. Then Marlborough drove off in his coach and six to join the twenty thousand soldiers he had assembled on the plain not far from Cologne. Better than anyone else he realized how dangerous was the adventure he was embarked on, for he and only he knew its real nature. Had the closest of his friends at The Hague known what was in his mind their hair would have turned white with anxiety. But, driving along those German roads, Marlborough's heart was lighter than it had been for a long time. He was a happy husband. He was, at last, a commander free from the trammels of politicians and allies. As for the future, it would depend more than anything else on the quality of the men drawn up to meet him. He saw them that day at Bedburg and was content. The army was not large but it was good. He thought he could count on it to do what he wanted.

Their bearing betrayed nothing of the difficulty that the recruiting officers had experienced in putting them into the Queen's uniform. Already, with the war hardly begun, England was running short of soldiers. One of the last things Marlborough had done before leaving home was to tighten the laws on impressment so that any vagabond between sixteen and forty, provided he was reasonably healthy and had four limbs, could be put into a scarlet coat and shipped across the sea to shoulder a musket for Queen Anne. After that, he would be fed fairly well on bread and boiled beef, burdened on the march with sixty pounds' weight of equipment, paid a net sixpence a day and savagely punished for breaches of the Articles of War. It was hardly surprising if sometimes the recruit sought refuge in desertion and stowed away on one of the packet boats for England. However, once there his troubles might not be over. The Mayor of Dover was making a good thing out of spotting deserters as they came ashore and handing them over to the government for a suitable reward. There had sprung up a class of professional deserters who left one regiment and enlisted in another, thus wrongfully obtaining the bounty of £2 given to a new recruit. This practice made reliable statistics of recruiting more difficult to obtain but, broadly speaking, it could be said that in a season without a battle the army lost as many men by desertion as it would suffer by casualties in a year of fighting. The British army or, more exactly, the English and Scots armies, were a compendium of the nation's unsolved social problems and ought to have looked like it. But, strange to say, Marlborough thought as he passed along the ranks, that his soldiers looked fit and confident. Discipline, training, regular rations and a dormant strain of national pride; these had worked something like a miracle on the ne'er-do-wells and vagabonds. In one of his letters to Sarah, John Churchill wrote of the joy he took in his army.

The march to the south began on 5 May.

Meanwhile, in Munich, soldiers serving on the other side turned more or less reluctantly from the peaceful occupations on which they had spent the winter. As Colonel de la Colonie, commanding a regiment of French grenadiers in the Bavarian service, remembered, "The opening of the campaign of 1704 caused a truce to love-making." He bade a tearful farewell to his mistress and applied himself to improving the discipline of his soldiers. This, however, turned out to be an impossible task. There was no provost-marshal. Looting was a settled habit of any French formation in Germany and the army butchers were in collusion with the cattle-thieves who wore the uniform of King Louis. The French were carrying out the preliminaries essential to their main project, the capture of Vienna. At Strasbourg, Marshal Tallard had gathered 10,000 new troops which he proposed to dispatch to join the forces of the Elector of Bavaria and Marshal Marsin. This task of reinforcement was not without risk for, not far to the north of the route which the new levies must take, some-where beyond the Black Forest, lay Imperial forces under the Margrave of Baden, fifty thousand strong. However, as it turned out, with luck on the one side and negligence on the other, the operation of reinforcing Marsin was duly completed. Tallard returned in safety to Strasbourg with the troops he had used to cover the movement, while Marsin and the Elector of Bavaria fell back on Ulm on the Danube, where they had set up a strong fortified camp. As soon as the new drafts, for the most part raw conscripts, had been smartened up and worked into their units, the Franco-Bavarian army could begin the march on Vienna.

However, just then something happened that perplexed the King of France and his generals. They heard on the word of reliable witnesses that Marlborough was on the move to the south with twenty thousand men, marching parallel with the Rhine on which, as if by coincidence, a large collection of boats began to move up-river. Almost as impressive, two bridges of boats were being thrown across the river at Coblenz. Marshal Villeroi did not doubt what was the likeliest explanation of all this activity. Where Marlborough went, there was the point of danger! Accordingly, he divided the Flanders army into two: leaving one-half to watch the Dutch, with the other, he marched into the Ardennes. If, as he thought probable, Marlborough was going to invade France by way of the Moselle, he, Villeroi, would be well placed there to fend the invader off. It was not yet certain, though, what the Englishman was up to. Watching anxiously, Villeroi remembered the boats which were coming up the river from Holland. If Marlborough decided to double back on his tracks, these craft could carry his army downstream to the Low Countries far more quickly than Villeroi could march there. In that case, there was the disagreeable possibility that the half of his army which Villeroi had left to watch the Dutch would be overwhelmed before he could arrive to the rescue with the other half. This was only one of the problems that Marlborough's march posed to the French High Command.

Meanwhile, the British march went on at a steady pace, the cavalry a day's march ahead of the foot. At three o'clock each morning the tents were packed up and the columns moved off in the cool dawn. At nine in the morning, they halted, pitched their tents and boiled their kettles, having covered twelve or fourteen miles. "As we marched through the country of our allies, commissaries were appointed to furnish us with all manner of necessaries for man and horse . . . Surely never was such a

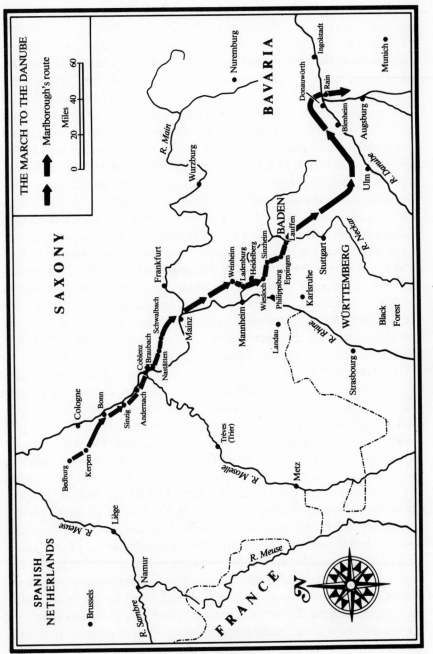

SPANISH
NETHERLANDS

• Brussels

R. Sambre

Namur

Liège

R. Meuse

SAXONY

Cologne
Bonn
Kerpen
Bedburg

Sinzig
Andernach
Coblenz
Braubach
Nastätten
Schwalbach

Mainz

Frankfurt

R. Main

Wurzburg

Nuremburg •

BAVARIA

Ingolstadt •

Munich •

Donauwörth
Rain

Blenheim
Augsburg

R. Danube

Ulm

BADEN

Weinheim
Ladenburg
Heidelberg
Sinzheim
Wiesloch
Philippsburg
Eppingen
Mannheim

Lauffen

R. Neckar

Stuttgart

WÜRTTEMBERG

Karlsruhe

Landau

R. Rhine

Black
Forest

Strasbourg

Trèves
(Trier)

R. Moselle

Metz

FRANCE

R. Meuse

2 The Long March

march carried out with more order and regularity and less fatigue both to man and horse."

Every three or four days they rested for a day while bricks were unloaded from their carts, ovens were built and a fresh batch of bread was baked. Each oven required 500 bricks, the load of one cart; twenty thousand men needed 30,000 rations a day, the output of eighty bakers working one day to supply bread for the next three.[1] Although Marlborough worked closely – some people thought too closely – with bread contractors like Mynheer Hecop and the brothers Solomon and Moses Medina,[2] whom he had known ever since they had helped to finance William of Orange's descent on England in 1688, the final responsibility for ensuring that the men and the bread arrived together at the right time was on his shoulders. To feed an army on the march, especially one made up for the most part of soldiers as notoriously hard to please in their diet as the British, was a delicate business. And what if the march was of exceptional length, over terrain of varying fertility? What if it would probably be necessary – as it was – to switch from one source of supply to another? What if the general in command had no large staff to organize matters but only a quartermaster-general, a secretary and a financial agent? To carry out the operation that Marlborough had in mind called for an extraordinary degree of professional competence.

Five days after the review at Bedburg, Marlborough and his cavalry had arrived at Bonn. They had marched into open, rolling country of spacious vistas and prosperous looking villages. It was for the general, as well as the troopers, an exhilarating experience. The news that had reached him there at Bonn was both good and bad. He was told that Tallard had been able to reinforce the Bavarians with twenty thousand men. (It was, in fact, half that number.) The move against Vienna on which the fate of the Empire would depend could not long be delayed. On the other hand, Villeroi had given up the idea of an attack on the Dutch and was on his way to the south. This was exactly what Marlborough had expected. Finally, the Dutch generals had asked the States-General if they could send Danish troops in their pay, both infantry and cavalry – eight battalions of one and twenty-one squadrons of the other – to join Marlborough. This was a magnificent offer. Evidently, although the Captain-General had his critics, military and civilian, some of the men at the head of the Dutch army were in favour of his strategy. If the Danes, stalwart soldiers with good equipment, were allowed to come, his cavalry would be half as strong again as it was at Bedburg.

It was now essential to waste no time in reaching Coblenz where the Moselle, flowing out of Alsace, pours into the Rhine. Mackenheim, Sinzig – where he saw the first vineyard on the hills – Andernach, the woods were beautiful and the view immense on his right, through one pleasant Rhineland village after another he rode with the British columns clattering after him, until at last he caught sight of the broad stream coming from the south-west to meet the still broader river majestically flowing from the south. At that point the old Hessian city of Coblenz fills the angle of land where the two rivers meet and the dramatic fortress of Ehrenbreitstein sits squarely on top of a rocky slope above the further bank, dominating the scene.

It was a moment in history, as he knew better than anyone. The more sensitive spirits in the trudging battalions behind him may have realized it, too, although for them it held a surprise. As Captain Parker of the Royal Irish said, "now when we expected to march up the Moselle, to our surprise we passed that river over a stone bridge and the Rhine over two bridges of boats." The two bridges, a mile beyond the confluence of the two rivers, were there because Marlborough had providently arranged that they should be. After the river was crossed, he passed ahead with the horse up the valley of the Lahn, leaving his brother, Charles, to bring along the infantry with the guns. There was no time to be lost, for just then it seemed that the French and the Bavarians were about to deliver the assault on Vienna which might decide the future of the Grand Alliance.

For the French commanders and their Royal master, one question had now been given its answer: Marlborough did not mean to attack along the valley of the Moselle. This still left unanswered the question of what his ultimate intention was. The evidence was confusing. At Mannheim, the Landgrave of Hesse, a member of the Alliance, had gathered his artillery together. When he did so, he believed that Marlborough was bent on a campaign on the Moselle. At the same time, a hundred miles to the south of Coblenz, bridges of boats were appearing across the Rhine at Philippsburg. Plainly, they were meant for the Englishman to use. If that were so, it would signify that he was going to invade Alsace. Meanwhile, he and his army made their way through the winding valley looked down on by the medieval castle of Marksburg, and passed through a walled town of half-timbered houses, named Braubach. The woods above the river were of exceptional beauty. At length they met the Rhine again at Mainz, just three days' march beyond Coblenz. By taking this route, they had by-passed the finest vineyards of the Rhine. Rudesheim and Johannisberg, for example, were a few miles to their right as they marched.

At one point during this stage of the journey Marlborough met his agent, Henry Davenant, who had driven over from Frankfurt and with whom he arranged to have a month's money to pay the army. This was important but even more so was a supply of new shoes for the infantry, all fourteen battalions of them. Weeks before, he had arranged that this should be done, but it was Davenant's part to see that the shoes arrived in time. This he did. From Mainz the army, in high spirits, marched due south for fifty miles or so to the Neckar. At Weinheim, not far from Mannheim, Marlborough spent the night in a house belonging to the Elector Palatine from which he had a view over "the finest country that is possible to be seen. I see out of my chamber window the Rhine and Neckar but would be much better pleased with the prospect of St Albans which is not very famous for seeing far." Thus, he wrote to Sarah who, repentant for her recent behaviour, persisted in wanting to join him, which was out of the question. Next day, 3 June, the cavalry, swollen now by German reinforcements to eighty squadrons from the nineteen that had set out from Bedburg, crossed the Neckar at Ladenburg. The time had come when he could tell the anxious States-General and his brother, Charles, marching behind him at the head of the British infantry, what was his real objective. *He was going to the Danube.* He was going to deal, if he could, with the threat to Vienna. Now, nobody could stop him. Now the French marshals and their Royal master at Versailles knew the exact astonishing nature of the task that faced them.

While the army rested beside the Neckar, one of the officers, a sombre Scot of the Cameronian battalion, spent the afternoon alone on the banks of the river. There, as was his custom, he communed with God. John Blackader was somewhat different from most of his service companions. He was a soldier dourly bent on his duty although marching was, he thought, not proper work for the Sabbath, especially when nothing was to be heard around him but oaths and profane language. Often he trembled to think on the wickedness of the army and its probable punishment from a just God. "Marching all day in the middle of an English army," he wrote in his diary. "I need say no more!" It was Blackader's idea of a foretaste of hell. He took refuge in his own thoughts, "frequent in ejaculatory prayer". Blackader was, in fact, a throwback to the old Covenanting wars and a man who badly missed the "quickening and reviving sermons" on which, as a son of the manse, he had been brought up. Of a more cheerful temperament was Captain Richard Pope of the cavalry, who wrote home from the Neckar to say that the Electors of Treves and Mainz had watched them pass as also had "at least two hundred ladies, some of them much handsomer than we expected to find". The march might be tedious at times but apparently it had its more agreeable moments. The Elector of Mainz, for his part, was impressed by the spick-and-span turn-out of the Guards. "All these gentlemen are dressed for the ball," he exclaimed.

After weeks of hesitation, the French High Command, at last, were no longer in doubt what was in Marlborough's mind. Not to double back to Flanders, not to march along the Moselle, not to besiege the fortress of Landau and invade Alsace. He was going further east to try conclusions with Marshal Marsin and the Elector of Bavaria. He commanded an army which fresh German contingents were joining all the time and which would soon be 50,000 strong. The Danish troops had still to arrive. But they were on their way. To the south of him, and already in contact by courier were the Margrave of Baden's forces, also 50,000 men. Thus, two Allied armies lay between the Villeroi and Tallard army at Landau and the Marsin-Elector army a hundred miles to the south-east at Ulm. By watching and hesitating, the French had brought one of their armies into dire peril. Now what should they do? Louis asked his marshals to submit ideas.

Villeroi replied, "Your Majesty understands war better than those who have the honour to serve you." Tallard was no more helpful. Saint-Simon said acidly of Villeroi that he was "a man formed expressly to preside at a ball and, if he had a voice, to sing at the Opera . . . very well suited to lead the fashions and for nothing else." Tallard, no doubt, remembered how Louvois, the King's great war minister, had warned generals not to upset the monarch by imprudently losing battles. At a moment when speed and decision were needed, Louis was offered only obsequious timidity. Speed above all! For now came word that Prince Eugene had been released from his desk in Vienna and had taken the field. And from Marsin came a warning that the Elector of Bavaria might be forced to flee with his family and take refuge with the Hungarian rebels. A general, riding all the way from Marsin's camp, brought even graver tidings to Versailles. Bavaria was defenceless, he reported. The Elector's health was bad. If he died, his soldiers would go over to the enemy on the following day. In this crisis, what should the King do? The general had no doubt. Send an army through the Black Forest to reinforce the Elector. On this advice,

Louis acted within the day: Tallard was ordered to advance over the mountains into Bavaria with forty battalions and fifty squadrons – the regiments were chosen by the King himself and included some of the best units in his army. Meanwhile, Villeroi was to watch the enemy from Offenburg, a town not many miles south-east of Strasbourg. A third French army, smaller than the other two, was to guard Alsace. Thus, in haste, Louis improvised his answer to the Englishman's thrust.

Tallard protested that he was being given a task beyond the strength of the force assigned to him. But he obeyed. With 35,000 men he crossed the Rhine at Kehl on 1 July and set off through the passes of the Black Forest to join Marsin and the Elector. It was a long march on bad roads and it was carried out in haste. The horses suffered terribly on the way. Worse still, they caught a serious infection and many of them had to be destroyed. The soldiers looted the peasants as they went along, and the peasants took their revenge by murdering any stragglers that fell into their hands. One who was there reckoned that, through this cause alone, the French lost a thousand men.[3] It was probably an exaggeration.

What was certain was that Tallard must hurry if he was going to save the Elector, for Marlborough had altered the direction of his march a day beyond Ladenburg. He had turned almost due east, travelling through heavy rain. On 10 June at Mündelsheim, a small village south of Heilbronn, he met the man whom above all others in the world he had been longing to meet, the most illustrious soldier in Christendom, Prince Eugene of Savoy. The contrast between the two men was remarkable: the pink, dandified Englishman, the half-Italian, half-Frenchman with the swarthy, pock-marked skin and the long pointed nose. "His nose spoils his face," the Duchess of Orléans, known as Liselotte, had noticed. "He is always dirty and has lanky hair which he never curls."[4] But it was some years since she had seen Eugene, who had been a boy at the time. She had not noticed his fierce, darting eyes; she knew nothing of the passionate energy with which he could stir councils of war or inflame soldiers in battle.

Eugene's life had been sufficiently extraordinary. He was born in Paris in 1663, the youngest son of Olympia Mancini, one of the three nieces whom Cardinal Mazarin had brought to France to help him amuse and rule the young Louis XIV. Eugene was also a cousin of the Duke of Savoy. Louis had wanted to marry the voluptuous Olympia. "Marry her and be damned to them," had been the advice of Christina, the lesbian Queen of Sweden. But Mazarin had said "No" and Olympia had married the Comte de Soissons instead. Her house became famous for its gaiety and above all for its cooking – Olympia's chef had invented an olive salad (olives, buried in quail, quail in partridge, partridge in pigeon, pigeon in chicken, chicken in suckling pig, pig in veal) which was highly thought of. Even more bizarre, however, was Olympia's interest in the black arts.

Nothing was more fashionable in Paris just then than magic unless it were poisoning and abortion. When the Affair of the Poisons broke, horrifying all Paris and shaking Louis with its revelations of murders and blasphemies in which some of those who were dearest to him were involved, Olympia was among those on whom suspicion fell. Saint-Simon thought her guilty: the Duchess of Orléans thought not. But in January 1680 she was ordered to leave France. Her children, among them Eugene, were put under the care of the Princess de Carignan. As it turned out, the princess' care was rather lax. The two younger daughters turned the Hotel de Soissons into a sort of brothel. One of them ran off to Geneva with a renegade priest. Eugene grew up as one of a small coterie of young homosexuals, among whom he was known as "Madame l'Ancienne". Louis had the idea, born of ignorance or malice, of making a priest of the boy, but Eugene had other notions. He altered his ways, practised riding and fencing, took up the study of war and applied for a commission in the French army. "The request," said Louis, "was modest but the applicant was not – like an angry sparrow-hawk." The application was refused.

In July 1683, Eugene fled from Paris with the Prince de Conti; both wore women's clothing as a disguise. It was probably not the first time they had done so. Eugene took his sword to the Emperor at Vienna; with it went an implacable resolve to be avenged on Louis. His commander on his first campaign said, when presenting him to the Emperor, "This young Savoyard will in due course emulate all those whom the world regards as great generals." Eugene, after a brilliant display in his first battle when the Turks were defeated just outside Vienna, was made colonel of the Kufstein Dragoons. His mother, who was in Madrid, wanted him to join the Spanish service. The King of Spain made him a Grandee, first class. But Eugene stayed loyal to the Emperor and, as it happened, his mother was forced to leave Spain in a hurry, being suspected of having murdered the Queen. Ever since the Affair of the Poisons, a sinister cloud had hung over her reputation. Two years later, Eugene was a major-general. The skinny, swarthy little boy with the long up-turned nose had proved to be a tremendous fighting soldier, a heroic figure in the wars against the Turks. An admiring poet said later on,

"Ce fut en apprenant à se vaincre soi-même
Qu'il apprit à dompter ses plus fiers ennemis"

In 1697 at Zenta, some distance to the north of Belgrade, he carried out an astonishing forced march at the end of which he caught the Turkish army divided into two on either side of a river. In the battle that followed, thirty thousand Turks lost their lives; the Janissaries mutinied and the Sultan fled. Among Eugene's booty were 30,000 camels. The victory was, in fact, the beginning of the gradual withdrawal of the Turks from Europe. By the Treaty of Karlowitz, the Sultan was forced to surrender Hungary to the Emperor and the Dalmatian coast to Venice. With the scars of sixteen wounds, Eugene was soon the hero of all Germany. He was hated at the Hofburg, especially by the Empress Eleanora. Said the French Marshal Villars who had fought against him, "Where are Eugene's enemies? At Vienna, as mine are at Versailles." Eugene, who had arrived penniless in Vienna, became very rich, built a palace employing the choicest architects – Fischer von Erlach, Lucas von Hildebrandt – bought pictures by the score and books which he had no time to read.

Marlborough, meeting him that day, saw a little man who looked more like a monk than a soldier in a shabby brown coat with brass buttons. As the conversation went on between them, he took lavish pinches of Spanish snuff from the supply that he kept loose in his pocket. Eugene was captivated by Marlborough's charm. Marlborough was reminded by Eugene's ingratiating ways of "my Lord Shrewsbury, with the advantage of seeming franker". It seems that from the beginning they felt that they could be open with one another. And as it happened, Marlborough had something to tell, indeed he had news of the highest moment. Somewhere on the line of march he had received a letter from a secret agent of his at Celle. It contained a copy of the French plan of campaign in the form of a memorial written by the French Minister of War himself, Chamillart. Marlborough's intelligence service had brought off one of its most spectacular *coups*.

Of the man who was about to complete their triumvirate, Eugene spoke frankly. The Margrave of Baden, the Emperor's Lieutenant-General, was, he said, a prickly individual, apt to be on the lookout for any slight to his dignity. Worse, although he was an experienced general he was without daring. Marlborough was warned to be on his guard. If the worst came to the worst, Eugene had the Emperor's authority, imparted to him in secret, to remove the Margrave from his command. However, this was a step which would only be taken in the direst emergency, for the Margrave was not only an imperial general; he was a ruling prince. It seemed then that a time lay ahead which would test the diplomatic as well as the strategic talent of both Eugene and Marlborough. Meanwhile, Eugene reviewed the cavalry and made the polite remarks usual from an inspecting officer. The Emperor offered to make Marlborough a prince of the Empire. This, however, he modestly declined. Three days later the Margrave arrived.

XI

"The Enemy Have Marched"

"We marched from Bois-le-Duc here in twenty days. . . The troops are in very good condition."

Captain Richard Pope

By the time the Margrave arrived on 14 June, Marlborough had a good general picture of the man and his intentions. He knew, for example, that the Margrave had already been in touch with his old friend, the Elector of Bavaria, whom he hoped to wean from his allegiance to the French. On this matter, both Marlborough and Eugene were profoundly sceptical. They thought that the Elector had everything to gain by spinning out negotiations with the Margrave until Tallard could reach him with reinforcements from the Rhine. Besides, the Imperial diadem which Louis had held out to the Elector still shone with a lustre which it would be hard for the Allies to match.

Eugene had agreed to a general plan by which he would hold the Rhine front while the Margrave invaded Bavaria. It was a sensible enough idea although both Eugene and Marlborough suspected that the Margrave was keeping a substantial army under his own command in order to use it as a bargaining counter in negotiations which might come. In short, when the three generals met, in front of the Lamb Inn at Gross Heppach, there was something less than complete trust behind the gracious smiles and the elaborate courtesies. Marlborough, the oldest of the three and the youngest in military experience, received the Margrave with the show of deference due to a general who had fought twenty-five campaigns, besieged twenty-four fortresses and been present at twenty-nine battles. Eugene, a fighting soldier with an even more impressive record, knew the Margrave of old. When Eugene's mother had been compelled to leave Paris hurriedly all those years ago, the Margrave's mother had looked after the boy. She was the Princess de Carignan. Later, the Margrave had been Eugene's commander in his first campaign.

Eventually, the trio got down to the business of planning the next phase of the war. Eugene needed more soldiers; the Margrave agreed to furnish them. His own proposal was that there should be a dual attack on Bavaria, Marlborough to invade from the north, the Margrave from the south. The Englishman pointed out that he was still waiting for a substantial force of Danish cavalry to join him under the Duke of Würtemberg. Until they arrived – and they were twelve days' march distant – his army would not be strong enough to operate as an independent force. It was agreed that, in the meantime, he and the Margrave should share the control of a combined army, each of the two being in command on alternate days. And so the conference ended and the generals parted: Eugene, with many misgivings, on his way westwards to the Rhine, which with 30,000 men he was to hold against a French army which was reckoned at 60,000; the Margrave, to his army which was quartered somewhere north of Ulm; Marlborough, to march south-east and cross the Swabian mountains to the Danube. This proved to be a difficult and disagreeable journey through desolate country. Nor was it without danger, for it involved a near approach to Ulm, where Marsin and the Elector of Bavaria were concentrated. The road over the mountains narrowed in one place to a steep pass through which the wagons and the guns were worked with difficulty. And, although it was by this time the end of June, the weather was cold and the rain incessant. "I am forced to have a fire in the stove in my room," wrote Marlborough to Sarah. Not everyone was so fortunate. "The poor men, I am afraid, will suffer from these continual rains."

He was aware that he had embarked on the greatest gamble of his career. At home, in England, the march to the Danube had produced an intense political crisis. Already, the High Tories had broken with the government; now they waited impatiently for the moment when they could settle accounts with Marlborough, whom they regarded as the arch-traitor to the party and who was now leading his army deeper and deeper into Europe, further and further from England. His conduct was rash to a degree. Was it not even treasonable? One day, sooner or later, his mad strategy would surely end in disaster. That would be the moment for a reckoning. Waiting confidently for the event, the Tories formed their plans. A defeat for the Duke would, undoubtedly, lead to a complete reversal of the political scene in England; and, in Europe, to the collapse of the Grand Alliance against Louis XIV. In that case, there might well be a Jacobite insurrection in Britain supported by the victorious French army. Nothing seemed more probable. And who was to say what would be the outcome?

All this was clear enough to Marlborough, who was the most political of generals and was being kept well posted by Godolphin and Sarah on the movement of opinion in Britain. Meanwhile he and his army had reached and crossed the Danube, at this point a mere muddy brook. Now he marched alongside a stretch of boggy land through which the river trickled, before he turned eastwards along its north bank at a respectful distance from the widening river. The river line was held by French or Bavarian garrisons for sixty or seventy miles to the east of Ulm. He was making for a walled town named Donauwörth where he intended to establish a base and bridgehead which he could use for an invasion of Bavaria. There was one difficulty, however. In order to take possession of Donauwörth, he must seize the height of Schellenberg overlooking the town. This was a military necessity of which the enemy high command was already aware. The Bavarian general, Count D'Arco, was given the task of defending Donauwörth. To do it, he had 12,000 troops, both Bavarian and French, infantry, cavalry and cannon. Helped by French engineers, D'Arco set to work repairing the earthworks on the summit of the Schellenberg, which dated from the Thirty Years' War. He meant to combine the hill above and the town below in a single system of defence. However, it is likely that he did not believe Marlborough would attempt to carry the height by assault. In consequence, at the time Marlborough's attack was launched, although the fortifications of the Schellenberg on the east side had been restored and a section of earthworks had been improvised to the west of the hill, on the steep slope, where the hill defences joined the town wall below, nothing was ready. Reasonably enough, Count D'Arco thought he could hold the Schellenberg long enough for relief to come from the main Franco-Bavarian army which was already on its way to Donauwörth.

On 1 July, Marlborough had a greater reason for haste than D'Arco. Next day, it would be his turn to take command. In these twenty-four hours he meant to reach and seize the Schellenberg. Before dawn on 2 July, word reached him from Eugene which gave an additional spur to urgency; the Prince's courier, Baron Moltenburg, rode from the Rhine with the news that Tallard was about to march through the Black Forest to join the Elector. And, on the south bank of the Danube, the main Franco-Bavarian army was now only a day's march from Donauwörth. At three o'clock that morning, Marlborough set off with 6,000 picked

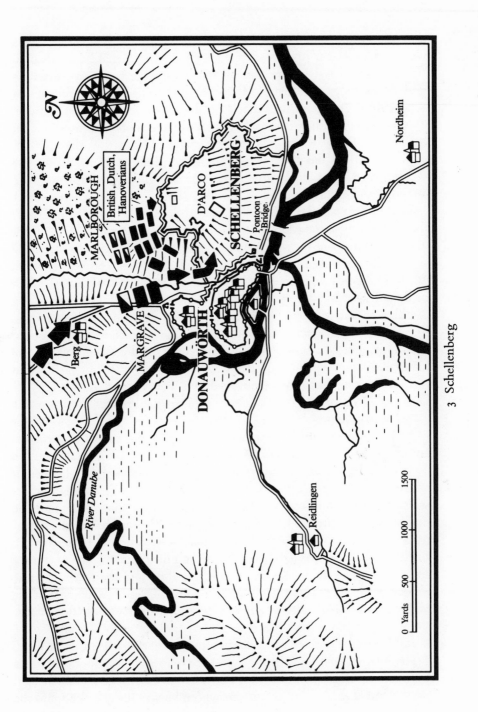

3 Schellenberg

troops over the muddy roads that led to the Schellenberg. In advance went a detachment of engineers whose job was to make sure that the artillery would not be held up on the way by bad roads or defective bridges. Riding on ahead, Marlborough came within sight of the Schellenberg at nine o'clock that morning. It was impressive, a shoulder of hill covered with cornfields, rising above the roofs and towers of the old town of Donauwörth. The hill was encircled by earthworks on which parties of soldiers and peasants could be seen furiously at work. Its summit was crowned by an old square fort built by the great Gustavus Adolphus. Where it shelved away towards the north, the hill ran into a dense wood.

When he surveyed the scene that morning, Marlborough knew already the dimensions of the problem that faced him. The fortified camp on the hilltop was manned by a garrison of fourteen thousand good French and Bavarian troops. To storm it would call for a major and costly assault which could only be carried out by troops of exceptional quality. Could it be done by soldiers weary after a fifteen miles' tramp over the shocking Swabian roads? Most of the generals thought not. The Margrave, who had ridden up to join Marlborough in the reconnaissance, was not optimistic. But Marlborough said that it must be done and done before nightfall. Donauwörth, he declared, was worth the lives of ten thousand men. And the Margrave acquiesced. He even passed over to Marlborough's command three battalions of Imperial grenadiers to join the storming columns.

There followed hours of impatient waiting for the rest of the army to come up and for the artillery to be dragged into position. Marlborough estimated that he would have two hours of daylight in which to fight and win the battle. He set the waiting cavalry to work cutting fascines which the assault troops would throw into any ditches that might be holding up their attack. It was agreed between the two commanders that Marlborough should supervise the attack – which was to be mainly British – on the completed entrenchments on the hill, while the Margrave aimed his assault at the gap between the hilltop and the town. By five o'clock in the afternoon everything was ready. The northern angle of the earthworks nearest to the woods was to bear the brunt of the first attack, although there was little room to deploy and the troops as they were assembled were subjected to a fierce bombardment from the Bavarian guns.

The infantry had been issued with the fascines cut by the cavalry and now used to fill the ditch in front of the earthworks. The Dutch General Goor stood at the head of the troops whom he was about to lead into the desperate enterprise. Out in front was the "forlorn hope" – *les enfants perdus* – fifty English guardsmen, led by Lord Mordaunt, a young dare-devil whom Marlborough had, not long before, rejected as a prospective son-in-law. The English and Austrian guns, sited less than a mile away, inflicted losses on the Bavarians massed on the hill awaiting the attack. Just after six o'clock the guns fell silent; drums beat the charge and, in three columns, the attack opened – Grenadier Guards, Royal Welch, Royal Scots, Hampshires. The Bavarian fire, case-shot and musketry, was deadly. Goor was killed. Hundreds of others fell. The British sent up a cheer so alarming to the defenders that La Colonie, who was in the eye of the storm with his grenadiers, ordered his drummers to drown the noise. For a time, the battle was undecided, while hand-to-hand fighting of exceptional savagery continued on the crowded hilltop. A Bavarian counter-attack drove back the British and the Dutch, the redcoats and the blue. Having rallied in a stretch of dead ground where they were safe from enemy fire, the assailants came on a second time led by generals fighting on foot. Once again they were thrown back. The Bavarians recovered a great deal of the ground they had lost until the English cavalry was brought in by General Lumley to drive them off. Now the moment of decision had arrived.

For, while this fierce struggle in the north-west corner had drawn more and more of Count D'Arco's troops into its bloody turmoil, the Margrave and his infantry had arrived before the unfinished and half-deserted entrenchments which joined the hilltop camp to the town. With the Margrave leading the way on horseback, they swung to the left and mounted the hill. La Colonie, desperately engaged in holding off the British and the Dutch, suddenly saw a mass of grey-white uniforms approaching behind him and thought they were French come to his rescue. A minute later, he realized that he was being attacked in the rear. Count D'Arco threw in his cavalry in an attempt to stem the Margrave's advance. Just then, the British and the Dutch surged forward in their third onslaught. Lord John Hay's Scots Greys leapt from their horses and joined the infantry in the attack. Taken on two sides, the Bavarians broke and made off down the slope in some disorder. Marlborough, at the head of the British cavalry, rode forward to the southern brow of the hill. He looked down on a scene of pursuit and slaughter. The broad Danube glittered beyond the town and, far off across a vast stretch of plain bathed in the evening light, was a beautiful line of mountains.

He had won, but for the victory the Allied army had paid a heavy price. After an hour and twenty minutes of continuous musket fire, the corpses of fourteen hundred Allied soldiers lay on the small space of the hilltop. Four thousand more were wounded. One out of every three British soldiers engaged in the battle was a casualty. Seven Allied generals were killed and nine were wounded. The Margrave was one of the latter. Count D'Arco's losses were not so heavy, but, in addition to the casualties in the hand-to-hand fighting for the hill, he lost two thousand men as prisoners and an unknown number in the pursuit. Marlborough had captured his artillery and stores. Donauwörth, the town below the hill, was Marlborough's. His troops poured into its streets and searched its gabled houses for Bavarian fugitives or for plunder. More important, the defeated Bavarians had failed to destroy the bridge over the Danube. On the other hand, the pontoon bridge which the Bavarian engineers had thrown across the river collapsed under the fleeing wagon-trains. But, with one good bridge in his possession, Marlborough could now operate on either bank of the Danube. He sent his cavalry, all thirty-five squadrons of them, British and Prussian, to ride down the disordered fugitives.

In the opposing army, La Colonie had been hit in the jaw by a spent bullet during the desperate fighting on the hill-top. Dazed and in pain, he tried to escape but was hampered by a heavy uniform and long, tight boots. The wife of a Bavarian soldier came to his aid and helped him out of boots and tunic. He lay, exhausted, among the standing corn not too far from the river's edge, wondering whether it would not be best to stand in the water up to his chin until darkness came and he could escape. Just then a patrol of English cavalry approached. Throwing away hat, wig, pistols and sword, La Colonie plunged into the Danube and, while bullets whizzed about his head, reached the further bank. There a friendly quartermaster gave him a horse and a cloak. He spent the night in the little town of Rain, not many miles away, kept awake by the rumbling of baggage wagons as they hurried back to escape Marlborough's victorious cavalry. Next day, La Colonie was ordered to organize the defence of the town. Weeks passed before La Colonie saw his mistress again and even then his misfortunes were not over; he found her "enjoying the society of a noble bumpkin of the most uncouth appearance" who had, moreover, the bad manners to be furious at the idea of her receiving a Frenchman.

Marlborough had won his first major battle in the war. But had it been worth the price that was paid, the lives of 1,400 men? He had no doubt himself. For now he and the Margrave stood between the French army and Vienna. The Empire was not yet safe, but it was in a less immediate danger than it had been. Moreover, he could obtain fresh supplies for the army by way of the route now open to him that led northwards from Donauwörth through Franconia to Nuremberg.

When the storming of the Schellenberg became known, the whole of Europe was electrified by the news that a new military factor had entered the field, a spirited army, well-trained, well-equipped and led by an able and ruthless general. The British troops were regarded with a respect to which they had not been accustomed. It is true that this favourable opinion of the event was not shared by all. In Hanover, which had supplied a large contingent to the battle and suffered a thousand casualties, it was thought that the cost had been too high. The Elector of Hanover blamed Marlborough for the losses and gave the credit for the victory to the Margrave. The Dutch did likewise. The old anti-war wing of the Tory party in England shook their heads over the price of victory. And what had it achieved? They wanted to know. Crack regiments had been badly mauled. The English had suffered worst of all the nationalities involved. An obscure hill among the many hills in central Germany had been taken. And that was all! What they would have said had Marlborough lost the battle can be guessed.

More impressive was the criticism that came from the fighting men. Captain Richard Pope, who had his horse shot under him in battle, wrote, "It appeared to me with a different face to what it did over all Europe, it being in my opinion a considerable advantage purchased at a dear cost." The Margrave of Baden was less than enthusiastic about the aftermath of the battle. He had done his full share in the fighting; he had been wounded; his horse had been killed. Now he thought that Marlborough was given too much of the credit for the result.

For Marlborough the urgent problem was the re-organization of supplies: "our greater difficulty is making our bread follow us, for the troops I have the honour to command cannot subsist without it and the Germans that are used to starve cannot advance without us." However, English credit was still good at the bank and, with its help, the Duke of Würtemberg was persuaded to send two hundred wagonloads of stores from his own country. Beer was another difficulty, until a disused local brewery was brought back into production.

The immediate objective now was to persuade the Elector of Bavaria to change sides. At first, it seemed that talk would be sufficient. But on the day before the Schellenberg was stormed, Tallard had crossed the

Rhine. Now he was hurrying through the Black Forest to join the
Bavarians. There was nothing for it, then, as Marlborough saw it, but to
do so much damage in Bavaria that the Elector would hear the lamenta-
tions of his people and give in. It was a deplorable strategy, as he admitted.
"You will, I hope, believe me," he wrote to Sarah, "that my nature
suffers when I see so many fine places burnt." Finally, it met with the
failure it deserved. But, during the early days of July it had some preliminary success; the Elector negotiated: he was offered forgiveness by
the Emperor, compensation in cash for the damage done to his country
and even some minor addition to his territory. He agreed to go to a
rendezvous with Wratislaw, the imperial envoy, and sign an agreement.
But at this moment, Marsin intervened to dissuade him, pointing out that
the Allies might kidnap him and threatening, if he went on with the talks,
to retreat from Bavaria with all the French troops. The French generals
insisted loudly that their chief concern was to quit Bavaria. While the
Elector, in anguish, was trying to make up his mind, word reached him
which decided the issue: Tallard was on his way to Bavaria with thirty-
five thousand men. The Elector decided to remain true to his alliance.
As Captain Parker put it: "he would serve as a dragoon under the King of
France rather than as general of the Emperor's forces." A few Bavarian
villages given up to the flames by Allied marauders were a sorrow that
could be borne when so much was at stake. According to Parker, the
devastation was by no means trifling: 372 towns, villages and farmhouses
laid in ashes. Even so, the Elector was prepared to endure the sufferings
of his people.

Marching for a month and a week, threading the mountain passes of
the Black Forest while vengeful peasants hovered all about them, Tallard
and his army met Marsin and the Elector on 7 August at Biberbach near
Augsburg. The united Franco-Bavarian army would now be stronger
than that of Marlborough and the Margrave. But very soon the balance
of forces was about to be altered once more. For a month, Prince Eugene
had been aware of Tallard's move from the Rhine. Now he had taken the
risk of leaving his Palatine troops to watch Villeroi on the Rhine while he
set off with 18,000 men to join Marlborough on the Danube. Somewhere
on the banks of that river, a battle would be fought which would decide
everything. "The old Italian prince", who was, in fact, twelve years
younger than Marlborough, rode into the Englishman's camp at
Schrobenhausen on 6 August.

Eugene might be an unimpressive figure at first, but when he talked, he changed. The words poured out in a torrent, supremely confident and inspiring, matched to an hour of crisis. And crisis it certainly was. The Hungarian rebels were within thirty miles of Vienna. The French and the Bavarians, reinforced by Tallard's army, had by this time crossed the Danube and were on their way eastwards along its northern bank. From Turin came piteous pleas for military help from the Duke of Savoy, Eugene's cousin. It was an ill-chosen moment to ask for help and Savoy was given little comfort by the English minister at his court. "I am afraid," said the minister, "that Marlborough and Eugene will say, Our own child is first to be christened." Marlborough and Eugene had reason during those early days of August to be worried about the health of that child.

Victory in a pitched battle was their best hope of extricating themselves from a dangerous situation. But the Margrave, either out of caution or because he was a personal friend of the Elector, could not agree to risking an encounter with the main strength of the enemy. Instead, he proposed to besiege Ingolstadt, an important fortress on the Danube in enemy hands. He was all the more eager to conduct the siege in person when it was clear that Eugene himself was willing to do so. To this proposal of the Margrave's, Marlborough agreed: it meant depriving himself of the Margrave's 15,000 troops, but, on the other hand, Eugene was bringing 18,000 men from the Rhine. And so the generals parted: the Margrave to march to Ingolstadt, Eugene to join his army on the north bank of the Danube at Hochstädt, Marlborough to move twenty miles west to Rain where, a few weeks before, La Colonie had spent a sleepless night. In Vienna, the air was heavy with the sense of crisis; the Emperor Leopold ordered three days of solemn intercession, saying repeatedly, "In these three days the fate of the House of Austria will be decided." Later, it was thought that he had received some supernatural information. The English ambassador, George Stepney, took the more prosaic view that "the pious emperor" had gleaned, by messenger, some hint of the generals' intentions.

At dusk on 10 August a horseman rode into Marlborough's camp at Rain with a letter for the Captain-General from Eugene:

Camp of Münster, two hours from Donauwörth.

August 10, 1704

Monsieur,

The enemy have marched. . . .

Everything, milord, depends on speed and that you put yourself in movement forthwith to join me tomorrow, without which I fear it will be too late.

XII

A Long, Hot Summer's Day

The Battle was Bloody
The woods were pierced.
The Fortifications trampled down.
The Enemy fled.
The Town was taken.

Henry St John, Viscount Bolingbroke.
Proposed inscription for the Column at Blenheim Palace

The plain of Dillingen, about thirteen miles west of Eugene's camp at Münster, was filled with French. This was the report brought back to the Prince by an officer he had sent to reconnoitre the country bordering the Danube. Moreover, the white-clad French regiments, among which some Bavarian formations were mingled, were pushing forward. Very soon, it seemed, Eugene would be compelled to pull out of his camp and fall back on Donauwörth where, six weeks before, the bloody fight for the Schellenberg had taken place. But he was anxious to retreat as short a distance as possible, because further east the mountains closed in on the river and there would be no room to stage the major trial of strength that he sought. So he urged Marlborough to risk taking a short-cut across a small tributary of the Danube called the Lech – "one must not allow oneself to be shut in between these mountains and the Danube." Before receiving Eugene's letter, Marlborough had already dispatched his brother, Charles, across the Danube by a pontoon bridge. At midnight, he himself set out by the route Eugene had suggested. Eugene, as soon as he knew that Marlborough was on his way to join him, ordered his infantry, already in retreat, to turn about and march back to Münster where his cavalry patrols were keeping an eye on the enemy.

In the opposite camp, there had been some ill-feeling between the French generals and the Elector. They had been annoyed that he had split up his garrisons in Bavaria into penny packets so as to protect his private properties from Allied marauders – "instead of what they should have

140

guarded, his frontiers". But now that Tallard had arrived all these minor disputes were forgotten, the Elector was eager to give battle and it was Tallard who wanted to stand on the defensive. He even accused the Elector of gambling with a French army while keeping many of his own troops out of the battle. However, his colleague, Marsin, thought that honour demanded an immediate attack on the enemy, and Marsin's generals were so much of the same opinion that they said fifty denunciations of Tallard would reach Versailles if there was no attack on the Allies. Reason was on Tallard's side: if Marlborough and Eugene had been denied an immediate decision, the consequences, to Marlborough at least, might have been grave. He could hardly have survived the winter as Captain-General unless he were able to silence his enemies in Parliament with the trophies of a victorious battle. But Tallard lost the argument. When he proposed to strengthen the Franco-Bavarian camp with redoubts, the Elector would have no truck with such timidity. The Allies must be attacked. Then captured deserters, when compelled to talk, brought the tidings that Marlborough had joined Eugene and that the Allied army was about to move off to the north. It seemed that the Englishman was pulling out of his adventure on the Danube. The truth was otherwise.

Marlborough had met the Prince in his camp at Münster and together they rode out, heavily escorted, to look at the enemy. From the tall church tower of Tapfheim they had an excellent view of the French and Bavarian camp less than five miles to the west. On their left, as they looked towards their enemy, was the Danube, a hundred yards wide, running fast between steep banks. It was fringed by reeds and its course was broken by shoals and small islands. On the other flank the ground rose gradually into low hills clothed with pine woods. In front, the open plain was traversed by a marshy stream, the Nebel, which ran into the Danube beside the village which the British have come to call Blenheim, but which was known to its inhabitants as Blindheim. It consisted of a cluster of white buildings, with red-tiled roofs. From its centre rose the steeple of the village church like a narrow white pencil with a sharp black point. Its churchyard was ringed by a wall eight or ten feet high. Needless to say, Blenheim, acting as anchor of the French position on the river, was barricaded for defence. Between the woods on the one hand and the great river on the other was a plain about four miles across. The cornfields were stubble; the reapers had been at work. The earth, where it showed, was a deep and beautiful brown. It was a fine stretch of arable land and an ideal site for an important battle. The two generals decided to attack next morning, although their subordinate commanders thought that this was bold to the point of rashness.

Before daybreak, Marlborough was up and dressed. For three days he had suffered from a violent headache; now, suddenly, it had lifted. His chaplain, Dr Hare (who had been his son's tutor at Cambridge), gave him communion. A day when so much was at stake – his military, political and possibly, even, his physical life – demanded a solemn opening. It was not a question of Victory or Westminster Abbey, but of Victory or Tower Hill. Of this the Captain-General had no doubt at all. By the time his prayers were ended the drums had roused the soldiers in their tents. They donned their uniform and equipment (the total weight of which was, on an average, sixty pounds) and set off, horse and foot, in nine columns along the riverside meadows to the chosen battleground. On their left, the flank nearest to the Danube, marched two British brigades, those of Rowe and Ferguson under the fire-eating Lord Cutts. In all they comprised twenty battalions and fifteen squadrons of cavalry. In the left half of the army, Captain Blackader marched with his battalion of Cameronians. He combined, in the manner of a bygone age, religious fervour and a zest for battle. "While marching towards the enemy," he reported, "I was enabled to exercise a lively faith." On the right of the advancing columns were the blue-clad formations of Prussians and Danes, and the Imperialist cavalry in grey. They were under Eugene who had taken command of the right half of the army. Far behind were the cannon, fifty-two in all, an arm in which the Allies were notably weaker than the French, who had ninety guns. In other respects, the two forces were roughly equal, each about 52,000 strong. The British contingent numbered 9,000 men.

For a time the riverside mist hid one army from the other. Then the sun broke through and the curtain rose on a military spectacle splendid and exciting beyond belief. Better placed than most to see it was a young Fleming, Count de Mérode-Westerloo who, with his regiment of Spanish cavalry, was serving with the French. The night before he had made a cautious reconnaissance beyond Blenheim village. When he rode back he had sat down to a good hot plate of soup in the village with his fellow-officers. Food and wine were plentiful and good, and, by the time he went to bed in a neighbouring barn he felt that he had never been in better form. At six he was roughly woken by his head groom, Lefranc, who had taken the horses out to grass and had been alarmed by what he saw: "The enemy are here!" When Mérode, incredulous, laughed at him, "Where? There?"

Lefranc threw the barn door open: "Yes, there!"

Mérode saw the whole sunlit plain before him, alive with colour and sparkling with points of light. A magnificent sight which, however, he had no time to admire. This was an army marching towards him! He threw on his uniform and gulped down a cup of chocolate while his fourteen horses were being saddled.[1] Then he mounted and rode to the camp where his regiment was quartered. There all was quiet, the troopers still snoring in their tents, utterly unaware of what was about to happen although by this time the enemy were so near that their standards could easily be counted. The French outposts had been neglectful; the mist had lifted suddenly. With shouts and kicks, Mérode ordered the men to mount. Only after that did he see the first signs of movement in Blenheim village. Tallard galloped up and ordered him to sound "To horse", and to send word to the artillery so that the 24-pounders might fire two salvoes to recall the foragers. Watching the Allies, Mérode saw them moving along the woods that bordered the plain to the north. The French officers decided that this meant that Eugene and Marlborough were pulling out of Bavaria. Just about this time, Tallard was finishing a letter to Versailles in which he told the King that this was likely to happen.

Soon after, the two armies were exchanging their mutual defiance by trumpet and drum. With these musical accompaniments the prelude to the battle was a stirring pageant of war at its most picturesque. Not long afterwards, about ten o'clock, the first abrupt notes of the artillery overture were heard. Cannon fire was different at that time from what it became later. A cannonball could be seen approaching almost immediately after it had left the gun. Its flight was too slow to be invisible. Sometimes, with luck, the projectile could be evaded.[2] An artillery duel had therefore some rough resemblance to the "knock-up" before a tennis match. However, it was deadlier. In the preliminary bombardment, Mérode lost two horses killed and a third badly wounded. By this time, the nine columns of the Allied army had come so near that he could pick out the details of uniforms.

The French generals realized that, unbelievable as it might seem, they were about to be attacked in their strong, prepared position. They acted as the situation seemed to demand. On their right the baggage wagons could be seen scurrying away from Blenheim village while the defences were being hastily completed. Holes were being punched in the walls of barns and farmhouses to provide firing-points for sharpshooters, and the ground between the village and the Danube was blocked by overturned wagons behind which were drawn up dismounted troopers of Tallard's cavalry – whose horses had been abandoned because, on the forced march from the Rhine, they had been infected by glanders. It seemed, then, that the right flank of the French army was reasonably secure. In front was a stretch of low-lying ground through which the Nebel brook flowed on its way to join the river. The green of the vegetation, the occasional glint of water, the glimpses of gleaming wet soil, disclosed the fact that here was marshland, a serious obstacle to an attacking force. Further to the left, where Tallard's command joined that of Marsin and the Elector, the ground rose gently, the trees began and there were the villages of Unterglau, Oberglau and Wellheim, two of which were set on fire by the French foragers before they fell back on the main army. The smoke drifted across the plain.

While Eugene's troops, Austrians, Danes, Prussians and Hanoverians, trudged onwards to take up their appointed position in the grassy country below the pinewoods, Marlborough watched the scene in front of him where the pioneers were at work improving the boggy crossings of the Nebel with brushwood and pontoons. As they did so, they were interrupted by French gunfire and occasional raids by horsemen. Eventually, five new crossing places were prepared and one which had existed before was repaired. Marlborough took some care over the siting of the British cannon. It might have been a review in Hyde Park. Mounted on a white horse, wearing a scarlet coat, with the blue ribbon of the Garter, he was visible to all, especially to the French gunners. Once a cannonball fell near him and covered him with dust. Then, while he waited for the message from Eugene that the Prince was ready to attack, he sat down to lunch with his officers. The display of nonchalance was impressive and calculated.

By this time, Rowe's brigade had established itself on the far side of the Nebel immediately in front of Blenheim. They were severely harassed by fire from a battery of heavy guns sited not far from the village. The French artillery, handled by a Swiss infantry officer named Zurlauben, was far more deadly at this stage than the British, crashing into the dense masses of the Allied infantry and causing more than a thousand casualties before battle was joined. Marlborough's chief anxiety while he and his soldiers waited in the hot sunshine of that August day was to know when Eugene would send his signal that all was ready. At length the Englishman sent his chief-of-staff to enquire. Time was getting on. Cadogan came

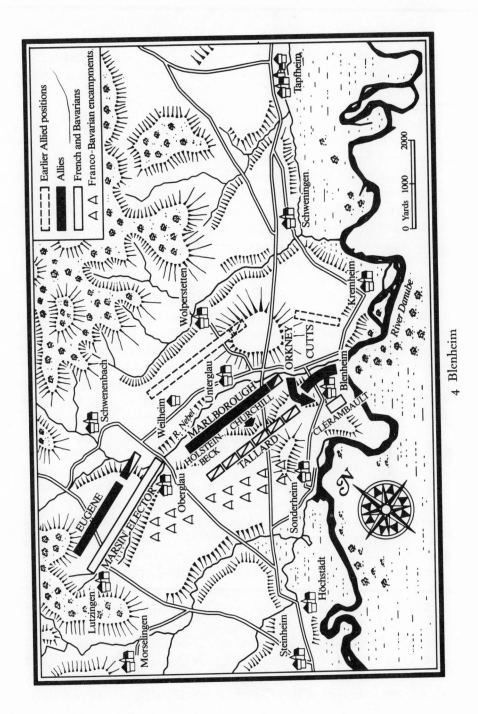

4 Blenheim

back with the word that Eugene would soon be ready. Soon after, an aide-de-camp arrived at the gallop bringing more precise information: at half-past twelve the Prince would attack. The Duke mounted his horse. "Gentlemen, to your posts!"

The moment had come.

Lord Cutts' troops – the brigades of Rowe and Ferguson with an equal number of Hanoverian and Hessian foot – rose from their damp shelter in the Nebel marshes and advanced on Blenheim village. To their right in the centre of the line, Charles Churchill's infantry began to make their way, sometimes walking, more often wading, across the stream. Thanks to the recent spell of dry weather it was not so deep as they had expected. Thanks to bad judgment on Tallard's part, or to his bad eyesight – he could see only ten paces in front of him[3] – they were allowed to reach the dry ground on the further bank without serious opposition. Perhaps Tallard had the notion that he would allow some to cross and then drive them back into the marshes. The first clash came on the extreme left of the Allied line when Rowe's brigade tried to carry by storm the barriers outside Blenheim. Not a shot was to be fired by a British musket until Rowe had driven his sword into the woodwork of the palisade. These were his orders. The moment his sword entered the palisade Rowe fell dead. The assaulting troops reeled back – losses were heavy, amounting to as many as a third of the attacking force. But, in one respect, their action had altered the face of the battle. They had diverted the attention of the French artillery and enabled the infantry, moving forward on their right, to cross the Nebel. This was Lord Orkney's brigade, five battalions strong. Somewhere in the midst of them came the skirl of bagpipes. This would be the piper of the Royal Scots, the only piper on the strength of the army.

About this time, Tallard seems to have decided that his flank on the Danube was secure for the time being. Further north, where Marsin and the Elector were directing operations, there were the roar and the thunder and the smoke of heavy fighting. Tallard galloped off to see how matters stood there. This was, as it turned out, a misfortune, for, in his absence, a major blunder was made. The commander of the Blenheim defence, the Marquis de Clérambault, was alarmed by the pertinacity of the Allied attacks on the village, where Ferguson's brigade had come into the fighting alongside Rowe's. A Scots battalion – the 21st – lost its colours to the French Gendarmerie, but now more and more regiments were splashing their way across the brook, among them the Cameronians who had been in the second line. Captain Blackader, who was in front of his company, thought, reasonably enough, "Lord it were easy for Thee to cause Thy angel to lay all these men low."[4] Later he was wounded, one of twenty officers in his battalion who became casualties that day. Lord Orkney, whose brigade linked the troops attacking Blenheim with the centre of the line, counted nine battalions already on the further side of the brook and hoped, vainly as it proved, to bring over four field guns.

It was at this moment that Clérambault made his disastrous decision. He ordered first, seven support battalions, then eleven reserve battalions, to march forward into the village and help to defend it. If his idea was to draw more of the Allies towards Blenheim so that they could conveniently be mown down before it, it was an error of judgment. Twelve thousand French troops, including regiments that bore historic names, Navarre, Artois, Provence, Languedoc, Rohan and La Reine, were penned up in the crowded lanes and farmyards of Blenheim, unable to attack and for the most part unable to use their weapons in defence. But what Clérambault thought and why, will never be known. While the battle was still raging, the poor devil realized the consequences of what he had done. In horror, or despair, he rode his horse into the Danube and was swept away. But that was later.

At the moment of Clérambault's blunder, it did not seem at all certain that its consequences would be so grave. The Allies were far from winning the battle. Indeed, it seemed that they were about to lose it. Fighting to break into Blenheim, their losses were frightful. A second attack had been made and had failed. Eugene's Austrians, Prussians and Danes were held up at Oberglau in bloody fighting. And now Tallard could see – if his eyesight allowed – the beginning of a cavalry clash which held great promise. Squadrons of Gendarmerie, in brilliant scarlet coats, had appeared on one flank of the Blenheim position. No, there they were on the other flank as well! Eight squadrons in all, the most cherished, the most formidable heavy cavalry in the King's Household, there they rode downhill where a line of English dragoons was drawn up ready to meet them. Already they had captured the colours of the 21st Foot (later retrieved by the Hessians). Now they were fanning out as they rode towards the line of English dragoons.

These were five squadrons of British horse commanded by Colonel Palmes. Without waiting to receive the shock of the French charge, the colonel ordered his two majors to attack to left and right, while he launched his own squadrons head-on against the front of the Gendarmerie. The result was surprising to good military judges who knew, as all

147

Europe knew, the reputation of these French regiments. The Gendarmerie paused, turned and left the field in some disorder, followed for three hundred yards by the English cavalry. The Elector saw the collision of the two bodies of horse and its outcome. "What! The Gendarmerie fleeing! Go, tell them I am here in person. Lead them back to the charge!" The officer entrusted with this message was, however, wounded and made prisoner. There is no evidence that the Gendarmerie ever heard the Elector's rallying cry.

Meanwhile, Tallard was appalled by what he had seen and, later on, regarded it as the turning-point in the battle. He was at last aware of the build-up across the Nebel of Marlborough's central force, cavalry supported by infantry. Against this threat he delivered a cavalry attack which had some success against Allied horse but was quelled by the musket fire of the Allied foot. While this was going on, General Lumley pushed more Danish and Hanoverian squadrons over the stream. The storm-centre of the battle now shifted to the right of the Allied line.

There, the Prince of Holstein-Beck was leading two battalions against the village of Oberglau where the Marquis de Blainville met them with an onset of nine battalions, in the forefront of which was the Irish Brigade, the "Wild Geese". This impetuous counter-attack was supported on the flank by French cavalry thrown into the battle by Marshal Marsin. Holstein-Beck was mortally wounded. It was a crisis of extreme gravity; as it turned out, the supreme crisis of the battle. Marlborough's troops, assembling on the far side of the Nebel, were now in danger of being rolled up from the flank and destroyed. At this juncture, he galloped to the spot and took over local command. In addition, he sent an officer to Eugene to ask him for the brigade of Imperial cuirassiers that was under the Prince's orders. The Prince himself was, at that moment, desperately involved and was fighting, sword in hand, in the front line. But he agreed immediately to give the English general the help he called for. In the meantime, Marlborough had brought three Hanoverian battalions and a field battery across the Nebel. The Irish were driven back. But the crisis was not over. Marsin's cavalry, sixty squadrons strong, went forward at the charge against the flank of the Allied centre. At that moment, Tallard thought the battle was his. Not so! The Imperial cuirassiers struck the French squadrons on the left flank, the English artillery brought into play by Marlborough pounded them with caseshot and, in front, the German troops which Holstein-Beck had commanded drove the enemy back on Oberglau.

Mérode-Westerloo, writing long afterwards, gives a vivid impression of the battle at that moment: "From a church tower you would have seen the enemy repulsed on one flank and we on the other, the battle rippling to and fro like the waves of the sea, with the entire line engaged in hand-to-hand combat from one end to the other – a rare enough occurrence... This spectacle, lit by bright sunshine, must have been magnificent for any spectator in a position to view it with sangfroid."[5] He was himself too busy in the confused fighting in the centre to appreciate the scene from an aesthetic point of view. He had already had his own horse killed under him by musket fire fifteen yards from the Nebel, and was indignant that none of the Allied grenadiers on the other bank had the chivalry to help him to his feet. When a groom brought him another horse, he set about trying to form a new line out of his battered squadrons. He rode over to Blenheim intent on pulling a dozen battalions out of the village where they were doing no good. But, "shouting and swearing", Clérambault drove the men back into Blenheim. He was in an excited state; a little later it was to end in tragedy.

Mérode then turned his attention to the centre where matters were going badly for the French. He had wanted to follow when the Gendarmerie charged, now he attacked the troops that were still pouring over the Nebel. One line he and his squadrons had driven back, then a second. But the appearance of a third line of fresh horsemen was too much for Mérode's men. In some disorder they retired across the Nebel where they were joined by troopers of the Gendarmerie who had rallied after their defeat by Colonel Palmes' squadrons. At this time Mérode realized that the cavalry force that had been on his left were pulling out of the fight while the Allies were continuing to come over the stream. The French cavalry were reforming somewhat to the rear with the Duc d'Humières in command, an imposing figure in a gilt cuirass.

By this time Marlborough had completed his preparations. He had drawn up his main force on the distant bank of the Nebel – the bank on which Mérode's cavalry was being marshalled. Marlborough's troops were in four lines, two lines of cavalry sandwiched between two lines of infantry: in all, ninety squadrons and twenty-three battalions against the fifty squadrons and nine battalions that Tallard could employ on this sector. In other words, Marlborough had roughly twice the weight of the French at what had become the vital sector of the battle. He was sure that he would win. An aide-de-camp was sent at the gallop to reassure Eugene: all was well! Nor was it possible for the French marshal to reinforce his infantry in the emergency. Too many men were pinned down, uselessly, in Blenheim. On the other flank, Marsin's divisions, like Eugene's, were weary after five hours of bitter and bloody fighting round Oberglau. Some of them were disheartened. Imperial cavalry units bolted. In a fury, Eugene shot two fugitives with his pistol. Then he joined the Brandenburgers: "I wish to fight among brave men and not among cowards."

At half-past five, Marlborough judged that the time had come to unleash against the depleted French centre the whole weight of the force he had saved for this moment. The trumpets blared. The drums beat in the tempo of the charge. The Allied attack faced a gentle upward slope. As they mounted it – eight thousand horses and fifteen thousand men on foot on a front a mile across – their pace gradually quickened. On the hard earth of the stubble fields the drumming grew louder; the momentum increased. It was measured, controlled, formidable, a fast trot and never a gallop, a deep thunder above which waved thin rags of sound, orders, shouts, cheers, trumpet-notes. And the Captain-General was where he had to be, riding on his white horse in front, the star of the Garter sparkling on his coat, his sword ready to strike. It was – and this as a soldier he must have known – the pinnacle of his life.

And so at last on the crest of the slope, the incoming tide of animals and men crashed into the squares of French infantry – young soldiers who were cut down as they stood and were found next morning in their straight, unbroken ranks, dead. Tallard's cavalry halted to meet the onset – halted, turned and then, for retreat can be as infectious as attack, broke in flight. The Maison du Roi, the King's Household troops, the cream of French chivalry, gave ground to the west. This was the climax of the battle – the instant which, in truth, can only have been of a few minutes' duration, when the battle was lost and won. But it was not over.

A gap had been torn in Tallard's centre. Confused formations of horse and foot were streaming to the rear. Tallard himself was taken prisoner along with some of his officers. Mérode, surveying his horsemen, saw that they were men now instead of squadrons and that only two of them still kept their standards and kettledrums. More serious, the nine raw French battalions, deserted by their cavalry, were being cut to pieces by the Allied horsemen and died "right out in the open plain, supported by nobody".

Just then his own troops were engulfed by a tide of Allied cavalry. Marlborough's decisive charge swept over him: "We were borne back on top of one another. So tight was the press that my horse was carried along some three hundred paces without putting hoof to ground right to the edge of a deep ravine." Marlborough's horsemen were now close to the Danube and Mérode was closer: "down we plunged a good twenty feet into a swampy meadow; my horse stumbled and fell . . . Men and horses fell on top of me, as the remains of my cavalry swept by . . . I spent several minutes trapped beneath my horse."

While Mérode was extricating himself from the heap of living men and dead horses that had fallen on top of him, the British and Dutch infantry brigades of Lord Orkney had swung round Blenheim and reached the Danube, sealing the village off. By this time Clérambault in despair had plunged into the river while Tallard, who had been trying to enter Blenheim, was captured by Hessians. Marlborough recognized the captive marshal from the insignia of the Saint-Esprit he was wearing and went forward to greet him politely. He brought up his coach and six and placed it at the Frenchman's disposal. Then, pulling out a tavern bill, he scribbled in pencil a note to Sarah: "I have not time to say more but to beg you will give my duty to the Queen and let her know her army has had a glorious victory. Monsieur Tallard and two other generals are in my coach . . . The bearer will give Her an account of what has happened." The bearer was Colonel Parke, a tall, burly Virginian who, having run through his fortune, had joined the army as a volunteer.[6] Marlborough had made him an aide-de-camp. Without loss of time Parke swung his horse's head to the north and set off on the long ride to Windsor.

Outside Blenheim, Lord Orkney, a heavily built, ungainly member of the ducal family of Hamilton, took over the management of operations on the west side of the village. He had been engaged in fighting in the centre and, when that issue seemed to be decided, had moved battalions to the left which cut off the garrison in Blenheim. Twice, he and his infantry had reached the heart of the village in an effort to gain possession of the churchyard. It was an objective of the first importance, with its high stone wall. But twice Orkney had been driven out. Now, seeing his troops in an exhausted state, he tried what could be accomplished by diplomacy. On his orders, the drums beat a parley. Then he made an offer to the French: if they laid down their arms he would see that they were not plundered. His aide-de-camp, Sir James Abercrombie, boldly rode up to an ensign who was carrying the colours of the Regiment Royal, and tried to snatch the flag from him. In the ensuing scuffle, Abercrombie was slightly wounded.

By this means, Orkney had already persuaded two brigades to capitulate, now he asked Dénonville, colonel of the Royal, how many battalions were still in the village. He was told twenty, and twelve squadrons of dragoons. Orkney concealed his dismay: at that moment, the total Allied strength outside the village was only a third as many. He invited Comte de Blanzac, who had taken over the command from Clérambault, to come and talk to him. Blanzac arrived, along with Hautefeuille, *maître-de-camp* of the dragoons. Orkney invited him to see for himself how hopeless his situation was: the village ringed by Allied troops; the French centre driven from the field in confusion; Tallard a prisoner of war. Blanzac retired to confer with his officers. But the task of convincing the regiments to surrender was left to Dénonville, a young man who owed his promotion to the fact that his father was responsible for the upbringing of the heir to the French throne. Dénonville, who had a ready tongue and a good opinion of himself, harangued the troops, telling them that they should give themselves up so that they could serve the King later on.[7] They listened to him in silence, all except the Navarre regiment* who protested indignantly at the disgrace and burnt their colours rather than hand them over. While negotiations were going on, Orkney remarked to Blanzac that Marlborough had promised to reinforce him with twenty battalions and all the artillery. "To tell the truth," as Orkney confessed in a letter to Lord Bristol, "it was a little gasconade in me." And so, with a little bluff and some Scots cunning, Blenheim was persuaded to capitulate.

When Abercrombie made his way through the village and brought the news to Lord Cutts, commanding on the other front, the Salamander was incredulous, knowing that his troops, having been repelled five times already, were incapable of making another attack. But capitulation it was. "Oh, que dira le roi?" cried the French officers. They blamed the generals. The soldiers swore that they had been betrayed. Their dismay was not unreasonable, since with determined leadership they might have fought their way out. This opinion was held by many, but Lord Orkney was not one of them. Long afterwards, he told Voltaire that no troops emerging from the alleyways of Blenheim into the converging musket-fire outside could have escaped from the village.

By the time Marlborough reached the scene, he realized that he had a problem on his hands: thousands of French prisoners, all of them angry, some of them rebellious, and about as many Allied troops to look after them. He ordered that the captives should be closely guarded until

* One of the four "old" French regiments raised before 1575.

morning, which meant hard and tiresome work for soldiers whose day had begun sixteen hours before. They formed a lane in which the prisoners stood all night.[8] Orkney summed the business up in his dry vernacular. "Without vanity, I think we did oor pairts."[9] Meanwhile, the booty was being assembled and counted: thirty-four coaches; 5,300 draught horses; 330 mules; 117 cannon and twenty-four mortars; 300 flags and standards.

To return to another victim of the débacle. Mérode dragged himself free of his heap of men and horses: a passing hussar missed him with a pistol shot; a tall English horse grenadier approached with sword uplifted. The Flemish Count ran the Englishman through so hard that his blade snapped off in the soft earth. While Mérode lay panting on the ground his valet rode up and hoisted him on his horse. He refused to get up behind his master, who asked, "But what will you do, Leblond?" At that moment, some passing soldiers emptied their muskets into the poor fellow. Mérode rode off, removing the badges that would identify him. Being a good linguist, he was able to ride through the Allied patrols and reach the town square of Hochstädt, "where I found some French generals who had the nerve to tell me I was pretty late. I retorted that they, for their part, had arrived too soon. We then all had a drink at the fountain."

It had been a long, hot summer's day.

XIII

Principalities and Powers

"As we were sitting down to dinner came a copy of my lord Marlborough's letter to the Duchess."
William Stratford writing to Thomas Coke, MP, 10 August 1704

Eight days after parting from Marlborough, Colonel Parke rode up to Sarah's apartment in St James's and handed her the note from her husband. Then, with a fresh horse, the Virginian rode on to Windsor where he found Queen Anne sitting in the long gallery overlooking the Terrace. The Queen gave him a thousand guineas and a miniature of herself.[1] By that time, the news of the victory was spreading across southern England. John Evelyn, who had been able to bring in all his crops in "the very seasonable harvest weather", indeed "excessive hot", heard that the French had suffered "such a defeat as never was given in Europe these thousand years".[2] The church bells rang, the guns of the Tower boomed, the taverns were packed with exhilarated crowds, even the High Tories, frustrated though they were in their political hopes, could not refrain from admitting that Marlborough had done well, although they kept their enthusiasm within bounds. The Jacobites disappeared from the streets. It was not their day. In her waspish way, Sarah said that, from the behaviour of the Tories, one would think Blenheim had been gained over the Church of England and not over the French. Party feeling in London was soon back to its normal level of pettiness and ill-feeling. In the countryside, people said that at last they had received some return for their taxes. As usual, the farmers complained about the weather, "all sadly burnt up".[3]

On the same day that Parke brought the news to London, King Louis learnt it in Versailles, where it arrived along with a packet of letters for the families of French prisoners of war. The King who knew, better than most men, what it meant to his prestige and his plans, had the pride and good sense to insist that in Paris and at Marly, where he was staying, things went on as if nothing had happened. So magnificent firework

154

displays celebrated the birth of a baby to the Duchesse de Bourgogne. For different reasons, then, the two countries rejoiced.

Marlborough did the little he could for the wounded. There were thousands of them and there was only one surgeon to each battalion. By this time he had been seventeen hours in the saddle. He fell asleep, exhausted and exultant, in a millhouse near Hochstädt, a few miles from the battlefield. It was full of barrels of gunpowder left by the French. Not far away, a French garrison had not yet decided to surrender. But he slept soundly enough for three hours. The day after the battle, he arranged for the wounded to be taken to Nordlingen, a walled town eighteen miles to the north, where he established his general hospital. Captain Blackader, who had been wounded in the second attack on Blenheim, in which the Cameronians lost twenty officers killed and wounded, walked over the battlefield as was his custom "to get a preaching from the silent dead".[4] Stripped and laid out ready for the gravediggers, the silent dead numbered something over twenty thousand. As they lay in a stretch of land about four square miles in area, like a vast open-air morgue, they were a sight ghastly enough to satisfy the sombre taste of the Scottish officer.

The dead horses could be counted in thousands. In the British and British-paid regiments alone there were three or four thousand of them.[5] At any rate, when the bounty came to be paid, £31,292 was for horses and the usual allowance for a remount was £8 (80 guilders). The carcases were left to rot where they had fallen; no soldier was allowed to touch them for fear of infection. As a result, the stench very soon became insufferable. The slaughter of horses in battle; the epidemic of glanders which soon spread from the French to the Allied army; in Spain, thousands of French army mounts dying for lack of forage – 1704 was a bad year for horses. This holocaust had one certain result. By October, Henry St John, just made Secretary at War, was writing a characteristic letter to his boon companion, Thomas Coke: "The Jews are publicly buying horses in Germany for the King of France who, without this recruit, could not remount his cavalry . . . As to whores, dear friend, I am very unable to help thee. I have heard of a certain housemaid that is very handsome; if she can be got ready against your arrival, she shall serve for your first meal."[6] The King found it less simple to find horses for his cavalry; the Jewish dealers complained that they were watched too closely by the Allies to send him the horses that they had bought. Louis was driven to take saddle and coach horses from the nobility.[7] By that time, the King had other worries.

"We were not accustomed to misfortune," wrote Saint-Simon, "and that one was unexpected . . . This prodigy of mistakes and blindness, so gross, so unbelievable. One can judge what was the general consternation in which each illustrious family, to say nothing of the others, had dead, wounded and prisoners and what was the King's sorrow who had held the fate of the Emperor in his hands and now saw himself reduced to defending his own possessions on the banks of the Rhine."[8] Saint-Simon went on to complain that Dénonville alone was dishonourably cashiered and, after he had served a prison sentence, did not dare to show his face in public. But Tallard, to the general scandal, was appointed Governor of Franche-Comté. The King's nephew, the Duke of Orléans (Monsieur's son), commented that it was necessary to give something to a man who had lost everything, a remark which greatly displeased the King when it came to his ears.[9]

Marlborough behaved with extreme courtesy to his defeated opponent. He sent a messenger to the French camp to fetch Tallard's coach; more than that, he arranged that the Marshal's own account of the battle should be carried to Versailles by a French officer who was given parole for the purpose. Reluctantly, Tallard attended a review of the Allied army at which Marlborough invited the Frenchman to admire the troops. "They have just beaten the best troops in the world," said Tallard. "What then must be said of the troops who have beaten *them*?" asked Marlborough. He had split the haul of prisoners fifty-fifty with Eugene, whose Germans and Danes had borne their full share of the fighting without the consolation of a *coup* like Orkney's at Blenheim. Tallard was later brought to England along with the trophies of Blenheim; he spent nine years, in comfortable captivity, at Nottingham, where he is credited with having introduced the growing of celery.* In his gratitude for the victory, the Emperor freed Eugene's Stadtpalais in Vienna from rates and taxes. He also made Marlborough Prince of Mündelheim in the Holy Roman Empire. The Emperor at first tried to fob him off with the mere title of prince but Marlborough and, above all, Sarah were not interested in empty honours. They wanted something solid such as lands and revenues. The trouble was that the imperial domains were not of unlimited extent so that the Emperor, having originally promised Marlborough a principality, tried to slip out of the full implications of the offer. The House of Hapsburg in a time of dire peril was one thing, but quite another when the peril had passed.

* But this tradition is no longer believed.

"Most illustrious Cousin and most dear Prince" – his letter dripped with flattering honorifics, but Marlborough was not so easily caught. He told Count Wratislaw of his astonishment that no imperial fief had been specified, no seat in the Diet of the Empire. In London, Godolphin heard of his colleague's pained dissatisfaction. Meanwhile, Wratislaw undertook the task of persuading his Imperial Majesty that, on this occasion, it would be prudent to be generous: "this man will be indispensable to you for many years." So, while the victor of Blenheim continued to insist that the whole business was a great inconvenience to him, the imperial bureaucracy creaked into action and the small town of Mündelheim in Swabia was solemnly proclaimed a principality and assigned to "your Delection . . . in consideration of your personal merit, and your great deserts towards me, my August House and the Holy Roman Empire." While the process of bargaining was still going on, the Emperor died and his successor carried out the deal.

The Prince of Mündelheim then became Lord of a pleasant little domain about fifteen miles square in extent which had been confiscated from the Elector of Bavaria; all that remained were the feudal ceremonies needed to set up the new dignity in proper form. These would be tedious and, which was worse, expensive, likely to swallow up in one way or another, many years' revenue of the principality. Sarah's opinion of the business can be imagined. In the end, the costs of installation were cut down from twelve thousand pounds to £4,500, which Marlborough thought a fair price for a princedom. An attempt by the King of Prussia to have the dignity made heritable by all Marlborough's heirs was, however, defeated by the other princes of the Empire. As things turned out, he did not enjoy many years of the income from Mündelheim which was reckoned at about £2,000 a year. It is doubtful if he did better than cover the initial expenses. It may be wondered whether Sarah would have given a warmer welcome to Eugene's tax- and rate-free palace in Vienna. But principalities and palaces were not the only rewards of victory. There was also the Bounty to the victorious army from a grateful government. This amounted to £64,013, of which Marlborough as Captain-General received £600 plus £117 as colonel of his regiment. Although the sums were modest when compared with his total earned income, which exceeded £50,000, they were certainly well-earned. (So, for that matter, was the £1 bounty allotted to privates.[10])

In London, the Queen drove in a coach and eight to the unfinished cathedral of St Paul's with the duchess at her side. The City livery companies lined the streets. But until Marlborough returned with his captives and his trophies, no adequate celebration of the event could be held. And Marlborough was for four months detained in Europe. For that there were reasons good and not so good. The vast haul of prisoners needed to be guarded and fed, which raised serious problems of manpower and supply. There was also the question of what were going to be the political consequences of the battle, above all what would the Elector of Bavaria do? "What the devil do I do now?" he had asked Count D'Arco. He wrote asking Marlborough if he could still have the terms that were offered him before Blenheim was fought. On this matter, it was necessary to consult the Emperor, who was, with difficulty, persuaded to give him any terms at all, far less those of a few months earlier. His wife, the Electress, who was in favour of making it up with the Emperor, set off from Munich in the hope of reaching him. She was turned back by Allied patrols. The Elector decided to stand by France.

While his wife stayed in Munich, he set off to the west with the 4,000 Bavarian troops who had survived the battle. After all, he was one of those fortunate beings who, as the expression goes, "wear two hats". Not only was he the Elector of Bavaria but also the Vicar-General (Governor-General) of the Spanish Netherlands, a post which brought him a salary of £60,000 a year. In his capital of Brussels he would be conveniently placed to negotiate with the Allies should misfortune still pursue King Louis. Meanwhile Marsin's army, reduced to 13,000 men, marched from the Danube through the Black Forest to the Rhine at Strasbourg losing, on the way, many stragglers and deserters who "gave themselves up rather than be knocked on the head by the boors of the country". Marlborough estimated that, in consequence of these defections, the total French losses in the Blenheim campaign amounted to 40,000 men. To make things worse, the horses of the cavalry and transport were decimated by the glanders that had attacked Tallard's dragoons on the way to Blenheim.

Following the enemy, Marlborough crossed the Rhine at Phillipsburg in the early days of September and provided cover for the Margrave of Baden's troops besieging the fortress of Landau. The Margrave, who considered that he had been tricked out of the glory of Blenheim by Marlborough and Eugene, was in the worst of humours. The siege dragged slowly on. Lack of forage and a pestilential distemper attacked the horses. "The left wing is entirely ruined. We have not above twenty horses or troops left," reported Captain Pope, "and probably not ten of these able to march to Holland.''[11] He blamed the disaster on the Margrave who was taking his revenge for Blenheim. A more certain reason for the length of the siege was that the Allies had no siege guns available until they had reduced the fortress of Ulm on the Danube. Landau held out until 28 November and with its fall ended "the tedious but ever glorious, memorable and victorious campaign of 1704 which was in length thirty weeks and one day," as Sergeant Millner of the Royal Regiment of Ireland calculated, "of which our corps in the Grand Army marched 91 days and therein 392 leagues or 1176 miles English."[12]

It was time for the Captain-General to go home. His health had for weeks been bad, the symptoms being fever and what seems to have been hypertension, the cause nervous exhaustion. He thought passionately of home and Sarah. "You will find me ten years older than when I left England . . . I am so very lean that it is extreme uneasy to me, so that your care must nurse me this winter or I shall certainly be in a consumption." Sarah and Godolphin begged him to drop everything and hurry back. Sarah told him about the work that had been going on at Holywell House, knowing his interest in the property. She was also careful to pass on spiteful Tory remarks about Blenheim which had, according to their version, scarcely been a victory at all, apart from the losses of the French. He replied, "I will endeavour to leave a good name behind me in countries which have hardly any blessing but that of not knowing the detested names of Whig and Tory." It is unlikely that the woman who read this letter, and was the most vehement Whig in England, was unaware of the rebuke that its words contained.

But Marlborough would not go to England until he had put the army in a favourable position for the next campaign. This involved establishing himself in the valley of the Moselle. He marched through "very terrible mountains" (the Hunsrück) to Treves. On the way he wrote in philo-sophic mood, "How very unaccountable a creature man is, to be seeking for honour in so barren a country as this, when he is very sure that the greater part of mankind, and even his best friends, would be apt to think ill of him."[13] Even then his task was not over. He must be sure of the help of Prussia and Hanover for the coming year. Above all, he must try to prevent Prussia from embarking on a war in the east against that dynamic young man, the King of Sweden.

So by coach and six, with an escort of clattering squadrons before and behind, Marlborough set off on the verge of winter along the roads that led first to Berlin and then to Hanover. In the first capital, his manner was flattering, his arguments were powerful; in the foreground, warm praise of the Prussian infantry and, less ostentatious, a hint of how disagreeable a British fleet could be in the Baltic. Even more persuasive, although inaudible to all but the alertest ear, was the chink of English guineas and Dutch guilders. In all, the promise of a sack of three hundred thousand thalers was dangled before the Prussian King, provided he would send eight thousand of his soldiers to help the Duke of Savoy against the French. Then the King saw which way German patriotism, glory and interest beckoned him, and Marlborough drove away from Berlin having accomplished his mission. Safe in the coach with him were various pieces of jewellery worth thirty thousand crowns and following him were two fine saddle horses for his stables, where they would be housed with the eight carriage horses which the Duke-Regent of Würtemberg had given him two months before. In Hanover, he made a profound impression on the Electoral court by the extraordinary deference he showed to the Electress Sophie, who at that time was heiress to the English throne and therefore an object of intense dislike and suspicion to Queen Anne. For her part, this shrewd and formidable old lady had been prejudiced against Marlborough ever since the Schellenberg battle in which she thought too many Hanoverian soldiers had lost their lives. He knelt to kiss her hand and refused to sit in her presence, by such simple arts winning her approval while giving her no encouragement at all in her hope of an invitation to London. This, he knew, the Queen would never grant.

When he left Hanover, he was the richer by a piece of tapestry from the Electress and a jewel worth 25,000 thalers from her son the Elector. After Hanover came a brief visit to Amsterdam and The Hague: the Dutch were ready to forgive everything and to forget that he had made off with part of their army into the depths of Germany and had caused them the acutest anxiety. All this was lost in the dazzling sunshine of Blenheim. They presented him with basins and ewers of gold. After that, he took ship for England. He landed at Greenwich on 14 December, accompanied by Marshal Tallard and sixteen French generals. On the same day there was published the most lasting and the most successful poem about his victory.

Months before, the Chancellor of the Exchequer, Henry Boyle, had climbed to a third floor garret in Haymarket to call on that distinguished man of letters, Joseph Addison.[14] The English government was about to make one of its rare excursions into patronage of literature. Whether Lord Halifax or Lord Godolphin had the idea first is not important; the project, which did credit to either nobleman, was for a poem in celebration of the victory at Blenheim. Addison, in his garret, agreed to supply the required article and prepared a draft which the Lord Treasurer, Godolphin, read and approved. Should it be a Tory poem, likely to please the Queen or, as it were, a coalition poem favouring all parties? Addison opted for the latter and produced a set of verses in which the name of only one living Englishman occurred, Marlborough. As a reward, he was appointed a Commissioner of Appeal in Excise with a salary of £200 a year. Addison's poem arrived at the London booksellers at the time Marlborough set foot on English soil. It was called "The Campaign". Addison became an under-secretary.

Blenheim, of course, was a famous victory for which, when every allowance has been made for good luck and the exceptional incompetence of the French high command, the chief credit must be given to Marlborough. By cool, harsh and ruthless judgment, he had taken the battle while it was still fluid and had shaped it according to his will. He had taken more risks with his own life than his officers thought proper but, in his eyes, no risk was comparable with the risk of defeat which for him would certainly have meant disgrace. The march into Germany was in itself an extraordinary adventure for one who was not a ruling prince, who had, indeed, begun life as plain Mr Churchill, and who commanded an army composed mainly of non-British troops. Strategically, it had been a gamble, however refined the calculations behind it, however brilliant the staffwork it had required. Morally, it was open to the gravest criticism: his duty was to defend Holland and by doing so to defend England, and there he was, two hundred and fifty miles from the Dutch border, defending the Emperor while three French armies lay between him and Holland. Only victory of the most resounding kind could possibly justify a course of action which some would regard as madness and others as betrayal, and which was certainly secretive and wilful, if not downright dishonest.

The gamble had succeeded, the battle was won, and not merely won – which would hardly have been enough – but won in a manner that rang through all the Continent and ensured that, when Marlborough came ashore at Greenwich, he was at that moment the most famous man in Europe: "Ce nouveau Turenne à été le premier mobile de l'affaire."[15] Some of the praise for the success must go to Orkney: if those twenty-four French battalions had not been corralled in Blenheim, it would still have

been a victory, but shorn of the toll of prisoners – and such prisoners!
the flower of the French army – it would have lacked its special *éclat*.

A French army had been destroyed, but there were other French
armies in the field, seven of them, and King Louis was not yet short of
manpower in reserve. But something else had been shaken – the legend of
French supremacy in arms. A card of real, if intangible, value had been
snatched from Louis while the game was still in progress. However, this
should not be exaggerated: a battle had been won, the war was by no
means over. In London they had the weightiest of reasons for knowing it.
The army in Flanders was to be reinforced to fifty thousand men; ten
thousand were needed in Portugal; five thousand men – seamen – were to
be taken for the fleet. The cost would be £9,000,000, a sum voted by the
House of Commons in a glow which would in time die down. The public,
especially those sturdy churchmen who paid so much of the cost of the
war by the operation of the Land Tax, would before long begin to
grumble about the high cost of military glory. In the St James's Coffee
House, the Whigs might continue to be warlike, but in Ozinda's, the
Tories would be asking in ever louder voices why our gallant redcoats
were shedding their blood in this obscure struggle on the Rhine; the
Jacobites, in the Cocoa Tree over against the Palace Gates, would as usual
be muttering treason; only the men of fashion in White's Chocolate
House would keep their thoughts firmly fixed on cards and women.

In the early days of 1705, all this lay in the future. Just then all was
national pride and military excitement, heartfelt speeches in the House of
Lords to the returned hero, patriotic drinking in the City. John Evelyn
ran into the Duke one day in town and saw that he was wearing "a most
rich George" set in diamonds of inestimable value.[16] Were they possibly
the King of Prussia's diamonds in a new setting? Very soon Evelyn, who
thought that Marlborough had gained quite enough from the generosity
of the Queen and nation, had fresh reason to raise his eyebrows. The
Queen made the Duke Colonel of the First Regiment of Foot Guards,
a lucrative appointment. Parliament made permanent his Civil List grant
of £5,000 a year. And, most striking of all, the Queen sent a message to
the House of Commons, announcing that she was going to give the Duke
the Royal manor of Woodstock, 15,000 acres of land with a rental of
£6,000 a year. There she proposed to build a palace which would
worthily commemorate her general's victory.

XIV

"As Emphatic as an Oath"

Behold the glorious pile ascending!
Columns swelling, arches bending,
Domes in awful pomp arising,
Art in curious stroke surprising!

Addison, Rosamund

It seems that the first choice of a man to design the palace was the obvious one, Sir Christopher Wren. But by that time the architect of St Paul's was getting on in years. Was he not becoming too cautious? When he visited Woodstock and saw what was contemplated, he reported that the Queen's munificence would be likely to cost her all of £100,000. The estimate shocked Anne. And Sarah cried out against the madness of the whole scheme, which she saw as the one serious weakness in her husband's character. Wren did not get the job. Why?

It may have been his estimate of the cost, which was, in fact, conservative. Five years later, when the palace was still unfinished, its cost was put at a quarter of a million. It may have been politics. At that time there was a versatile member of the Kit-Cat Club – and therefore a Whig – named John Vanbrugh who was designing a mansion at Castle Howard for Lord Carlisle. Vanbrugh had been a captain in the 13th Foot who had spent some time in the Bastille after he had been accused of travelling in France without a passport, in other words, of being a suspected spy. After spending some time there not too disagreeably, in the Tour de Liberté, he had been exchanged for an important French agent. Five years later, with a rapid change of setting and profession, Vanbrugh was the author of a highly successful comedy in Drury Lane Theatre, *The Relapse*, in which Colley Cibber played his most famous part, Lord Foppington. But all did not go smoothly for Vanbrugh.

A moral revolution was bent upon transforming the character of the stage. Loose-living courtiers no longer set the tone; middle-class outlook and respectability were creeping in. "Venomed priests", as Vanbrugh

163

called them, attacked the morals of the theatre and The Society for the Reform of Manners singled him out for special denunciation as "a man who has debauched the stage beyond the looseness of all former times". Vanbrugh named the little house he had built for himself at Greenwich The Bastille, expecting, as he said, to end his life as he had begun it. Further flouting Puritan opinion, he brought the Italian Opera to London. Castrati! What could be more degenerate! The novelty, which in time became a popular craze, was not immediately successful and Vanbrugh lost a great deal of money over the venture. However, all was not lost. Lord Carlisle used his influence to have him made Clarenceux King of Arms, although he knew nothing about heraldry; moreover, his lordship engaged him as an architect, a profession for which he had received a modicum of training, but enough for the time! It was the age of the inspired amateur. Then, all of a sudden, in June 1705, the Queen, the most conventional woman in her three realms, appointed the man who had debauched the stage to be the architect and surveyor of Blenheim. The retired captain, the ex-spy, the successful dramatist, the failed impresario, had arrived. And, through Vanbrugh's talent, Marlborough was about to become, like Eugene in Vienna and the Margrave of Baden at Rastadt, a soldier whose fame was commemorated by an imposing edifice.

Would it be grand enough, however, to please the Royal donor and her general? Vanbrugh produced drawings, plans, and a model which conjured up the vision of a building which would, it seemed, be magnificent enough to satisfy the most exacting megalomaniac. Marlborough met the architect one evening at the theatre, liked the man and was captivated by his drawings. This palace, which Vanbrugh insisted on calling a castle, exactly expressed his mood. It was male, military, heroic, baroque, "as emphatic as an oath", in the phrase of its architect. The scale was vast, the drama of the roof and the façade was spectacular. "Although the building was to be calculated for and adapted to a private habitation," Vanbrugh explained later, "yet it ought to be considered as both a Royal and national monument with the appropriate qualities viz. Beauty, magnificence, duration."[1] It was a monument rather than a dwelling. But the Queen inspected the wooden model which Vanbrugh had prepared and was satisfied. What Sarah thought of it all was not immediately disclosed: it was probably enough for her at that stage that the architect was a Whig of unimpeachable credentials. The time had not yet come when she would call him "this wretch" and condemn the building as "Vanbrugh's madness".

At a time when the war was in a particularly frustrating and tiresome phase – the German princes quarrelling with one another, the Dutch obstructive of their English Captain-General, the campaign in the Peninsula going badly, and, at home, the usual political backbiting – Marlborough's letters from the Continent dwelt frequently on the house which was being built for him among the Oxford fields. A "draught" of the house and gardens fell into French hands but, it being the age of gentlemen's war, was sent on to him unopened. He hoped that Sarah would go down to Woodstock for three or four days and find out if Henry Wise, the gardener, still thought that he would be able to finish the plantations in the following season. The gardener was soon aware of the Duchess' "extremely prying-into habits" which, in this case, were encouraged by the Duke.

Marlborough wished to see the walks planted when he returned for, as he said to Wise, "I am an old man" – he was fifty-five – and he wanted to see the 2,000 acres of gardens before he died. So Wise supplied from "that inexhaustible magazine" (Evelyn), his nursery at Brampton Park, thousands of full-grown trees. They were brought to Blenheim, each swaddled in moss, in an osier basket, in the hope that they would take root and flourish. Godolphin was thanked in a letter from Marlborough at Coblenz for forwarding the building "for I own my heart is very much set upon the ending my days quietly in that place". He always wrote about his palace as if it were a modest country retreat in which an old soldier, weary of the wars, could pass the evening of his days pruning the roses. But Blenheim was something different.

On the day when, with all appropriate ceremony, the foundation stone was laid, Marlborough was at Trier, plagued by the anxieties of his mission. He wrote to Sarah, "Pray press on my house and garden for I think I shall never stir from my own home." Some fifteen hundred men were at work on the foundations; a ha-ha was being made to keep rabbits and deer out of the garden; 1,220 yards of dung were dug into the parterres; and stone from twenty quarries was needed for the house. As it chanced, there were political difficulties over the stone: some of it came from a quarry at Cornbury owned by Marlborough's High Tory opponent, Lord Rochester, who, however, put politics aside and gave the stone free "with compliments to Your Grace"; some from Glympton, owned by a Whig, Sir John Wheate. In due course, Wheate, by Sarah's influence, became MP for Woodstock.

Watching from afar, Marlborough kept a jealous eye on his new property. When he heard that some people had keys and could come into the estate, he sent a sharp word home that the keys were to be altered. His new palace and its gardens fascinated him. In the marshalling of stone and the disposition of parterres, the weary soldier could find happiness and occupation in old age. Blenheim still kept in concealment its potentialities for embarrassment and trouble. For the present, all was excitement and a strange new beauty. Beauty? Not everybody thought so, but it was undeniably impressive, heroic, a fitting memorial of a great moment in history. The day was still distant when Sarah would be enquiring if it was really necessary that the grand bridge should contain thirty-three rooms. And why was there a covered way for the servants in the kitchen court? "Painters, poets and builders have very high flights, but they must be kept down," said Sarah. There was another and more important issue. The palace, so arrogant, so costly, with a thousand workmen swarming all over it, was visible nourishment for that fertile but unlovely passion, envy.

XV

"See What a Happy Man He Is!"

"I believe this pleases him as much as Hochstädt."
Lord Orkney[1]

At the close of the campaigning season, the new Prince's troubles were far from ended. He faced difficulties with the Dutch generals, who were, most of them, jealous and obstructive. In Vienna, now that danger was past, sloth and bad faith flourished. Eugene was out of favour. The German princes sulked and reneged on their commitments to furnish soldiers. The Margrave of Baden treated his wound with Schlangenbad water and made it worse by doing so. Many thought that the wound was fictitious, but those who saw it pronounced it real and even serious. Meanwhile, logistical problems multiplied. Bread was in short supply. Bakers were elusive. Magazines to supply the coming campaign were half-empty. The commissary responsible absconded to the French, taking with him the money he had stolen. Horses for the gun-teams were hard to come by, which was in a way just as well because forage was scarce. It had been a cold, dry spring.

While the campaign faltered, Marlborough's post-bags were swollen by letters from a multitude of sources. Colonel John Seymour sent his congratulations from Maryland.[2] Amiable exchanges between the rival camps flourished. Sarah's Jacobite sister Frances, Duchess of Tyrconnel, turned up at The Hague where she was entertained by her brother-in-law. They talked of everything but politics. Sarah asked him to send tea to her in London, but in Holland Marlborough could not find any fit to drink. A breath from the vanished, raffish past blew in the form of a letter from the Duchess of Portsmouth, Louise de Keroualle, now living in Paris. The letter was difficult to read, for the duchess left no space at top or bottom of the paper and no space between the lines. But the meaning of its large, energetic script was clear enough. Louise, who had once for her greed been the most detested woman at Charles II's court, asked if her old friend could send her sherry or Madeira of which she could get no supplies owing to the English blockade. Marlborough would have been delighted to oblige. The best he could do, however, was to send the lady a little palm wine from his private store.

Marshal Villars, who blocked his path into France with 100,000 men, wrote apologizing for the military necessity which had compelled him to open intercepted letters. In acknowledging this courtesy, Marlborough sent him a case of palm wine and cider. Such were the amenities of warfare in the century of good manners. Behind all these exchanges was there some more serious diplomatic purpose? It is likely enough. War flagged; alliances were frayed; the King of France had suffered a bad spill on the path to glory. Perhaps the time had come for a change of policy.

Marlborough dreamed of his palace and fretted when Vanbrugh was slow in sending on some promised drawings. In April 1705, he was inspecting pictures in Madame Schepers' gallery in Rotterdam.[3] The palace which was being built at Woodstock was never far from his thoughts. The pictures would hang on its walls.

He had planned to invade France along the Moselle by way of Thionville and Metz, a project which, were it successful, would certainly have brought Louis to sue for peace. Now it was clear that nothing of the sort was going to happen. He had only half as many soldiers as he had reason to expect. He was pinned down to the Lower Rhine, in a part of Germany which he found disagreeable, limited to operations which could only be of minor importance however brilliantly they were executed, suffering from ague and the nervous headaches which plagued him all his life. Then, after a time, a French offensive move against the Dutch compelled him to leave the area. He did so with disgust, telling the Queen that he would like to resign. Before leaving, he sent Villars a verbal apology for his failure to attack him; it was an act of politeness which produced raised eyebrows at Versailles. Among the most respected judges of good manners, Marlborough's action was thought to be excessive.

Already he was aware that his enemies at home and in Europe were gleefully at work. French propaganda spread the opinion that the victory at Blenheim had been a pure fluke, an undeserved stroke of luck for a general of modest abilities, "a mortified adventurer", as Villeroi called him. This taunt the peace party in London took up with enthusiasm. As a variant on the general theme, it was said that Marlborough's success was entirely due to his brilliant staff. More dangerous politically was the anti-Dutch campaign in London which alleged that the splendid energies of the Captain-General were being frustrated – if not betrayed – by the timidity of high Dutch officers. Should not the alliance be brought to an end? How else account for the weak and uncertain conduct of the war? This argument would have been insidious enough at any time but it came at a moment when Louis was launching in The Hague a peace offer of exceptional subtlety, a most skilful product of French diplomacy, calculated to appeal to a business-like people like the Dutch. For the basic economic fact of the war, from the point of view of Holland, was that she was fighting far beyond her means, maintaining year by year armies, her own and those she subsidized, which could only be financed by borrowing more and more money. She had started the war as the equal partner of England. If it went on long enough, she would be England's puppet. There was a strong case then for Holland to make peace on any reasonable terms.

It is true that she was not alone in feeling the pinch. Austria's coat was threadbare; the Sun King was aware that the shadows of want were lengthening behind his magnificence. It seemed that only England, soon to be Britain, was a land of plenty where men grumbled but ate heartily.

When Louis proposed to the Dutch that the Spanish Netherlands should be independent and that the Austrian Archduke Charles should be given Naples and Sicily in return for renouncing the rest of the Spanish Empire, the moderate party in Holland were tempted by the proposal. On reflection, it was not, however, as attractive as at first it seemed. So long as French troops were stationed at Milan, they could reach Southern Italy whenever they chose to do so. Austria could do nothing to prevent it. In other words, she would hold Naples only at France's pleasure. Marlborough pleaded with his friend, Heinsius, not to heed the beguilements of Versailles. Among other things, he told the Dutchman that England would never accept a peace which did not establish a Hapsburg on the Spanish throne.

Here was an extraordinary new extension of the war! What had begun as the defence of the small Protestant country of Holland against French aggression had swelled into a European coalition the main beneficiary of which had become the Emperor who, among other things, was oppressing the Hungarian Protestants! And now, it appeared, an indispensable purpose of the Alliance was to put an Austrian prince on the throne of Spain! But what had Austria done to deserve such a favour? It was a reasonable question and one that was difficult to answer at a time when

Austria's ability to hold her own in Italy depended – apart from the genius of Prince Eugene – on the Prussian and Danish contingents that reached there thanks to Marlborough's diplomacy and to Dutch and English money.

In the Low Countries, the war went on in a minor key. The French had built a line of earthworks and other obstacles stretching over sixty miles from the sea at Antwerp to the Meuse at Namur. It was called the Lines of Brabant. To pass this barrier was thought to be difficult and was likely to be expensive, especially as the French and Bavarians who would man the Lines slightly out-numbered the troops under Marlborough's orders. But this was exactly the kind of military problem that he revelled in. Secrecy, duplicity, cunning – these were among his virtues as a commander. In the first place, the Dutch generals, among whom he had a particular antagonist, a veteran named Slangenberg, must be deceived about his intentions. At the same time, the French marshal who commanded on the other side of the Lines, Villeroi, must also be deluded. Marlborough's plan was simple enough.

One Dutchman, Overkirk, an elderly field-marshal, was taken into his confidence; he played his part to perfection in the elaborate deception plan. Marlborough let it be known that, after making a feint attack to the north, he was going to attack the Lines at their weakest point, further south near the river Meuse. It seemed a sensible idea. Accordingly, therefore, Overkirk marched to the south, crossing a tributary of the Meuse by four bridges and building seven more as if in readiness to serve a much bigger army; to make quite sure that nobody could fail to realize what was intended, Marlborough ordered twenty additional bridges to be built. Responding to the warning signs, Villeroi duly sent 40,000 men to the threatened point in the south. Then, after dark on 18 July 1705, Overkirk turned to the right about and marched at speed to the north. At ten o'clock that night, Marlborough set off in the same direction.

By this time, Villeroi realized that something was afoot but, when he heard that cavalry were moving to the north, he supposed that the Allies were on their way to a favourite camping ground. At dawn, English infantry appeared before the Lines at Elixem, one of the strongest points in the whole defensive system and, for that very reason, thinly manned. The English attacked and in a short time, and for the loss of a handful of men, the Lines of Brabant had been passed. When the Bavarian cuirassiers arrived on the scene, all in black armour, a blood-chilling sight, they were too late. With French, Spanish and Belgian cavalry supporting them, they were assailed by British squadrons. In a little, Marlborough himself was where no commander-in-chief should be, in the thick of a fierce cavalry battle. A Bavarian lunged at him with his sabre, missed, and fell off his horse. "See what a happy man he is!" wrote Lord Orkney of the encounter. "I believe this pleases him as much as Hochstädt [Blenheim] does." In another part of the battle, Lord John Hay, leading the charge of the Scots Greys on the right flank of six dragoon regiments, captured the enemy general. All told, the British took 3,000 prisoners in a fight that lasted two hours. Then the enemy withdrew and the sweating troopers, waving their bloody swords, acclaimed their fighting general. Before settling down to rest, he wrote an exhilarated letter to Sarah: "My blood is so hot that I can hardly hold my pen and my heart is so full of joy for the great success that, should I write more, I should say a great many follies." In the sedate, middle-aged commander, with so many grave matters of state on his mind, there still lived the young officer who had fought under Turenne all those years ago. Later, he apologized for this outburst but "the kindness of the troops had transported me". To Godolphin, he sent a more sober report by courier. "This day has given me a great deal of pleasure, however" – now came a characteristic touch – "I think £500 is enough for the bearer." The Lines of Brabant were, after all, not Blenheim. Naturally enough, Sarah wrote a wifely letter reproving him for risking his life. He denied that he had done so out of vanity; if he was to keep the affection of the army, he must share the dangers.

What followed was an anti-climax: first, Marlborough failed to exploit his success to the full. The British troops were eager to press on. Even Marlborough's bête-noir among the Dutch, General Slangenberg, believed that they could take Louvain, seven miles away. But word came that Overkirk's regiments were exhausted after their march of twenty-seven miles, without which the great manoeuvre could not have succeeded. In these circumstances, the Duke decided to halt. The next contretemps was on a more familiar pattern. By adroit and daring handling of his army, he worked Villeroi into a position near Brussels which was unfavourable and, indeed, dangerous. Villeroi found that he must sacrifice either Louvain or Brussels; he chose Louvain. Marlborough was eager to launch an attack on the French but, on this occasion, the Dutch imposed their veto. Convinced that a God-sent chance to conquer all the Spanish Netherlands had been lost, Marlborough felt that even a course of Spa water would not be enough to restore his equilibrium. He longed to go home but – "if any misfortune should happen to the army after I were gone, I should never forgive myself". He wrote to the States-General a letter complaining bitterly of the weakening of his authority; and took care that the letter was leaked to the public before their High Mightinesses had time to discuss it.

In London the government planned to send Lord Pembroke as a special envoy to protest to the Dutch. In the meantime, there was an explosion of popular fury in the Dutch cities. The crowds were on Marlborough's side, even in Amsterdam where, for commercial reasons, the peace party had always been strong. Brigadier Palmes, who had led a cavalry charge at the crisis of the Blenheim battle, called on Slangenberg on behalf of Marl-borough's brother, General Churchill. He demanded satisfaction for remarks which Slangenberg was alleged to have made about Marl-borough's "impudent" attack at Blenheim. Slangenberg denied that he had spoken disrespectfully of Marlborough and, afraid that he might be lynched, left for Aix-la-Chapelle.

Not all was acrimony, however. Lord Ailesbury, who had lived in exile since the day he left England at the time of the Revolution, went to dinner with Lord Orkney at Tirlemont. The entertainment was splendid – excel-lent wines and the hautbois of the First Guards to supply music. And who should appear but the Captain-General himself in his most genial mood. He ate heartily and, like the others, became "perfectly merry". For him it was an unusual outbreak of frivolity.

Next day, at Lord Albemarle's, he and Ailesbury met again. Marl-borough was about to drive off in his chaise when he recalled that Ailesbury had not seen the plan of the house he was building at Wood-stock. This was produced, to Ailesbury's thinking, "one mass of stone without taste or relish". Ailesbury asked who the architect was and when he was told, said, "I suppose you chose him because he is a Whig." Marlborough did not think it amusing.

The campaigning months of 1705 had been frittered away. Clouds had spread over the sun of Blenheim. The forcing of the Brabant Lines had been a fine achievement, which had led to nothing of any importance. Marlborough, in a tetchy mood, quarrelled with his own government because they had edited one of his bulletins in a way that concealed the responsibility of the Dutch deputies for the failure of the campaign. "I must be madder than anybody in Bedlam," he told Godolphin, "if I should be desirous of serving when I am sure my enemies seek my destruction and that my friends sacrifice my honour to their wisdom."

Here indeed was an outburst from a man usually equable to the point of suavity! But when it was a matter of criticism of his conduct as a soldier, Marlborough was always sensitive. Protestations, apologies, cajolings were needed to soothe the resentful warrior. Lord Shrewsbury wrote from Augsburg, "weak through incessant haemorrhages", to warn Marl- borough of the dangers that come from envy.[4] The warning was not needed.

For the King of France, the campaign had one lesson: to stand on the defensive was not only unsuitable to the national genius, it imposed on a general the need to spread his forces too thinly over too wide an area. So he wrote: "Do not expose yourself to a general engagement without need, but do not avoid it with too much precaution." It was a typically ambivalent directive from a sovereign to a commander in the field, an incitement to battle with a word of caution to blunt its spur. All would depend on how Villeroi interpreted it. And that was something which another battle in another year would reveal.

XVI

Consternation at Versailles

"It needs more cleverness than is generally supposed to draw up a bad plan of battle: but one has got to be able to change it into a good one at a moment's notice: nothing so disconcerts the enemy."
Maurice de Saxe, Lettres et Documents Inédits

All over Europe diplomatic couriers sped hither and thither: ambassadors had grave and complicated talks with foreign ministers. Before a new campaigning season opened, it was necessary to see whether the war could not be brought to an end, or whether, by persuasion, cajolery, blackmail or some other means, the balance of forces could not be altered. In this game of international politics, the French King was the most assiduous player, and probably the most skilful. But others, too, were at the tables.

In the dashing little cavalry action on that July day in 1705 when the Lines of Brabant were pierced, the Marquis d'Alègre was captured by Lord John Hay. Marlborough, conspicuously humane to prisoners of war, an aspect of his character which Louis had already noted with approval, gave the marquis two months' parole to settle his affairs in France. At the same time d'Alègre was to give his King a respectful greeting from the English commander-in-chief. Not unreasonably, the French government regarded this as a hint which they lost no time in taking. D'Alègre came back to Holland in October with a message in which Marlborough was loaded with the most flattering compliments. The message went on to stress the King's longing for peace. How richly he would reward the man who would bring that blessing to a troubled world! The pity was that Marlborough already possessed every honour that a subject could be given by his sovereign, and there was left to an intending benefactor only that less splendid, but no less honourable, token of esteem – hard cash. The sum of two million livres was mentioned, which had a value of about £150,000 in the money of that time. A respectable sum it must be admitted; sufficient, as the French pointed out, to raise a man above the embarrassments that envy may put in the path of the famous. Naturally, the proffered reward did not come unaccompanied. There were also suggestions for a new division of Europe. What were the political proposals, which emanated from the Royal cabinet at Versailles? They were definite enough.

Louis' grandson, Philip, was to remain as King of Spain and the Indies, with the possession of Milan as well. The Hapsburg Archduke, Charles, who was at that moment fighting to assert his claim to the Spanish throne, was to become Elector of Bavaria and Max Emanuel, the Elector who had been defeated at Blenheim, was in compensation to reign in Naples as King of the Two Sicilies, i.e. of Sicily and all Italy south of the Papal States. The Dutch were to be appeased with the Barrier fortresses in Belgium which they believed were essential to their security. France was, however, to hold the Rhine bridgeheads, and thus would keep a foot in the door that led to Germany. Finally, the Duke of Lorraine, who would be sure to resent the proposed French gains on the Rhine, was to be bought off with that rich prize, the Vicar-generalship of the Netherlands.

It was an ingenious and comprehensive sketch of a European settlement but one did not need to be a political genius to see that Louis was keeping all the plums for himself. For instance, he proposed to keep the Spanish Empire in his family. He would dominate Italy through the army he would keep at Milan, and he would stand on the Rhine as a perpetual threat to Germany. If he were to obtain Marlborough's collaboration in this project, his two million livres would have been an excellent investment. However, Marlborough failed to succumb. Not only so, but he argued against the terms when he talked to the Dutch. Then he trundled off in his great coach to Vienna, Berlin and Hanover in a new round of diplomatic visits, a fresh attempt to glue together the rickety structure that had the pompous title of the Grand Alliance. It was, without a doubt, in urgent need of rehabilitation.

Austria had lapsed into her perennial state of bankruptcy. The King of Prussia sulked in his palace in Berlin, strongly of the opinion that the Emperor was not showing enough gratitude for the Prussian soldiers who had gone to fight his battles in Italy. King Frederick was displaying – or, which was more alarming, was concealing – a disconcerting willingness to listen to various seductive murmurs which reached him from Versailles. In Hanover, there was continuing trouble of a different kind, which of course had its origin in the fact that the Dowager-Electress Sophie was

Queen Anne's heiress. And Anne felt the same antipathy towards her most likely successor as Queen Elizabeth had done towards hers a century before. The English Tories, who for the most part had no affection for the House of Hanover, sought at this moment to make mischief between Godolphin and the Queen by pretending to espouse the Hanoverian cause. They played the hand clumsily. Sitting in the gallery of the House of Lords, the Queen, scarcely able to believe her ears, heard the Duke of Buckingham urge that Sophie must be invited to England because the Queen might fall into her dotage, leaving the state without a head. Such arguments were not calculated to endear her Hanoverian relations to the Queen. In Hanover her dislike of her German kin was duly reported and resented.

For more reasons than one, then, Marlborough had plenty to occupy his mind when he mounted his coach for Vienna on 26 October 1705. Twelve days earlier, an event in Spain had changed the face of the war. Lord Peterborough had captured Barcelona for the Hapsburg Archduke who was the Allies' nominee as King of Spain. It was likely, therefore, that Marlborough would find the atmosphere in Vienna more genial than had once seemed likely although, the Hofburg being what it was, this could not be taken for granted. Pausing at Frankfurt on his way through Germany, Marlborough had an apparently friendly meeting with the Margrave of Baden; more important, he talked business with the British financial agent, Davenant, and with various bankers in the city, whose services he would probably need before long. By 12 November, he reached Vienna after a tedious voyage down the Danube in a yacht belonging to the Emperor.

At this stage, he supplemented his prestige and charm with a more reliable diplomatic weapon: his personal credit with the Viennese bankers was pledged to the tune of 100,000 crowns* so that the more pressing embarrassments of the Imperial court could be removed. In addition, he undertook to arrange that a loan of a quarter of a million pounds be raised in England and Holland to pay the wages of Eugene's army in Italy. He was careful, however, to arrange that the money was to be paid into Eugene's account in Venice and would not pass through Vienna where it would certainly be lost in the general chaos of the Imperial finances. By the end of the month, he arrived in Berlin, after travelling for eight days in great discomfort over deplorable roads. In a busy week of discussions he persuaded King Frederick that England could be relied on to look after

* £25,000 in money of that time.

his interests in the final peace settlement; in return for which Prussia would maintain the strength of her mercenary troops with the Allied forces. When Marlborough set off on the drive to Hanover, he was the richer by a jewelled sword.

He found the Hanoverian court highly indignant because Queen Anne's government had rejected the Tory proposal that the Electress Sophie should be invited to visit London. He was able to calm things down, however, by bringing news of a bill, shortly to be introduced in the English Parliament, for the purpose of naturalizing the Electoral family. More than that, it would be arranged that, on the death of Queen Anne, a regency of seven "Lords Justices" would automatically come into being who would ensure a smooth transfer of the crown. Leaving Hanover somewhat appeased by these tidings, Marlborough drove to The Hague where he found the government by no means eager to carry out the financial obligations he had assumed on their behalf in Vienna. While he waited in freezing weather for a wind to bring the convoy in which he would sail to England, he worked hard to show the Dutch where their true interest lay. It was no easy task. "The truth is," he groaned to Godolphin, "everything here is in such distraction that there is no government." The war was dragging on, the national burden of debt was growing and French diplomacy was skilful. At last, at some time between 22 December and Christmas Day, the States-General agreed to pay their share of the cost of Eugene's ragged army in Italy. A few days later, they were willing to supply funds for the war in Catalonia. Marlborough returned to London well pleased with the outcome of his mission. In the course of one weekend in the city he floated the loan for Prince Eugene. He and Queen Anne's husband headed the subscription lists;[1] the Bank of England managed the issue. The financial climate was favourable. "The Kingdom was blessed with plenty," says Smollett of that halcyon time, "the Queen was universally beloved; the people in general were zealous for the prosecution of the war; the forces were well paid; the treasury was punctual." A rosy picture. Too rosy to last, as it turned out. For the time being, Queen Anne, in her annoyance with the Tories, was smiling on the Whigs. Parliament was willing to vote funds for armies bigger than had ever been contemplated before. All this was just as well because, in spite of all Marlborough's diplomacy, it seemed before long that the Grand Alliance was, once more, disintegrating.

In addition, it was apparent that Louis had made up his mind to win Barcelona back from the Allies in spite of the pessimism of his commander on the spot, Marshal Tessé. The French army in Catalonia was brought up to a strength of 20,000 by reinforcements sent from France and, in April 1706, a new siege of Barcelona began. In Italy, Marshal Vendôme, an energetic and unconventional soldier whose habits were as deplorable as his morals, gave the Imperialists a thrashing at Calcinato and, what was worse, massacred the Prussian and Danish contingents. Thus, King Frederick in Berlin was given a fresh grievance against the Austrians, a new excuse for falling down on his military commitments. But when Marlborough returned to The Hague at the end of April, his mind was filled with a dazzling new idea. He would march to Italy; there he would join Eugene and, with him, relieve the Duke of Savoy who was beleaguered by the French in his capital, Turin. After that, the two generals would attack Toulon in conjunction with the English Mediterranean fleet. The conception was imaginative and audacious to the point of rashness; to carry it out, elaborate and meticulous staffwork would be needed, for, before Marlborough's troops could fire a shot in Italy, they would need to complete a march twice as long as the march to the Danube. Before leaving London, he obtained Cabinet approval for the project. Godolphin was uneasy but could not resist Marlborough's enthusiastic advocacy. Queen Anne set her seal on his instructions which, among other provisions, enabled him to act independently of the Dutch if need be. With him on the crossing to Holland travelled Lord Halifax who was on his way to Hanover, bearing the Garter for the Electoral Prince.

On arrival at The Hague, he found that Their High Mightinesses were quite willing to let him go on the great adventure to Italy provided only that he did not take the Dutch army with him. However, all these dreams of an Italian campaign were shattered when, on 3 May, Marshal Villars, with brutal suddenness, attacked the Margrave of Baden's troops near Landau and sent them flying helter-skelter over the Rhine. After that, there could be no question of a "fine jaunt"[2] up the Rhine and over the Alps. Marlborough was going to find that all his fighting would be confined to Flanders. But this could only happen if the French were willing to come out and fight which, as he told Sarah, he was certain they would not do: "I have the curse at my age of being in a foreign country from you, and at the same time very little prospect of being able to do any considerable service for my country or the common cause." In a mood of deep depression, he went to join the army assembling for the new campaign. "God knows," he told Godolphin, "I go with a heavy heart . . .

unless the French would do what I am very confident they will not, namely, come out and fight."

There was one possibility. The French knew how weak his forces were and how poor were his chances of getting reinforcements. The Prussians were apparently not going to join him. Their King was more sullen than ever because he had learnt, by means of an intercepted dispatch, about the Italian project, of which Marlborough had told him nothing. The Hanoverian troops were several days' march from Marlborough's camp. The Danish King refused to allow his cavalry, twenty squadrons strong, to join the main force until they had received their arrears of pay, which the Dutch were withholding. But there was a chance that Marlborough in his weakness might be able to lure Marshal Villeroi out of his safe position south of the Dyle river. He set about the task with some cunning. A man named Pasquier, a well-known inhabitant of Namur, was apparently willing to betray the city to the Allies. With alacrity, Marlborough conspired with him. By accident or design, some inkling of the plot reached Villeroi. Then, on 19 May, the whole picture changed.

One day, Richard Hill, the British agent in Turin, said in a letter to Godolphin, "The French King's treasury begins to fail him. He is already bankrupt for twenty-five millions." By the first week of May, the inglorious financial aspect of the war had been brought home to Louis. In alarm, he told Villeroi that he needed an early peace, which his enemies would grant on his terms only if they were sufficiently impressed with his military strength and resolution. For that reason, France must take the offensive on all fronts. Villeroi must sally out across the Dyle, the Flemish river behind which he had been standing on the defensive. He must not shrink from challenging Marlborough to battle. The King's instructions were peremptory and Villeroi did what he was told. With sixty thousand men he left his defensive position and marched towards the Allies. He had some reason to feel confident, for in his army were the best soldiers in the French service, including the aristocratic regiments of the Maison du Roi – the Household Cavalry. All the soldiers had been fitted out with brand new uniforms and the Maison, gorgeous in gold and silver braid, were naturally the most resplendent of all. If anyone had imagined that the defeat at Blenheim had rung the death-knell of France's military might, he was answered by the glittering columns that were pouring across the fields of Flanders in those days of early summer. And the spirit of those soldiers of the Sun-King matched their bearing. This was, it seemed, the most warlike army in the world as well as the most spectacular. It was the firm resolve of the troops to wipe out the misfortune – one could even say the disgrace – of Blenheim.

With what delight did Marlborough hear from his spies that the French were advancing! An end to frustration! An end to dreary diplomatic exchanges with whimpering princes or cheeseparing burgomasters! Here was the prospect of a momentous clash, and a swift decision. Here was a problem which he approached with quickened spirit. Within two days of the news of Villeroi's advance being brought to him, he had united the British troops and the Dutch. The Prussians were still held back in Germany by their touchy King. But the Danish cavalry were close at hand and were coming to join him by forced marches, Marlborough having appealed to their fighting spirit – and having personally guaranteed that their arrears of pay would be forthcoming. In consequence, the Danes arrived on the day before the battle – a battle in which, as it turned out, they were going to play a notable part.

In the early hours of Whit Sunday morning, when the countryside was covered by a thick fog, Marlborough, in camp at Corswaren, gave the order to march. He was intending to occupy a plateau at Ramillies, twelve miles to the west. Ahead, he had sent Cadogan, whose task it would be to find suitable ground and mark out a camp. At eight o'clock, when the mist was beginning to rise from the fields, Cadogan and his escort of cavalry stumbled on the first French patrols. He saw that the enemy was in possession of the high ground near Ramillies. So far as he could make out, they were in great strength. He sent his aide-de-camp galloping back to Marlborough with the news. Two hours later, the Duke himself had arrived on the spot, while the army marching in eight columns still toiled behind along roads muddy after a heavy downpour of rain. "I never saw roads or the weather worse," Blackader wrote to his wife. She, God-fearing woman, was staying in Rotterdam where, a few weeks earlier, before the campaigning had begun, Blackader had been too frivolous for his conscience to be easy: "I often stay out in company too late at night: I must keep at a great distance from the world." Now, on the march, he felt much better: "The nearer I come to action, the more cheerful and vigorous I am and grace more lively."[3]

Riding far ahead of the Scottish soldier, Marlborough had seen the French army. The sight were inspiring to the warrior, daunting to the timid. Before him was four miles of open country, bounded by the river Mehaigne on his left, and crossed by a smaller stream, the Geete, which grew out of marshy ground in the middle of the scene. Several small villages were dotted here and there, in particular Ramillies in the centre with Taviers to the south of it, set among the marshes of the Mehaigne, and Autre Église about the same distance to the north. Between those two hamlets stretched the might of Villeroi's army. It was almost exactly the same strength as Marlborough's except that on this occasion, unlike Blenheim, the Englishman had a superior weight of artillery – a hundred twenty-four pounders.

La Colonie, who had had such a narrow squeak at the Schellenberg, was present once again with his Franco-Bavarian grenadiers. "There being nothing to impede the view," he wrote later, "the whole force was seen in such a fine array that it would be impossible to view a grander sight. The army had but just entered on the campaign, weather and fatigue had hardly yet had time to dim its brilliance . . . The late Marquis de Goudrin, with whom I had the honour to ride during the march, remarked to me that France had surpassed herself in the quality of these troops; the enemy had no chance whatever of breaking them."[4]

Marlborough, when he set eyes on them that May morning, had no doubt that he was looking at a French army "the best of any he had ever seen". He also saw that his opponent had picked a good position: the bulk of his infantry faced Marlborough's right, on ground which rose steeply above the marshy land in which the Little Geete took its origin. Ramillies in the centre was held by twenty French battalions. Marlborough was told that no attack on the northern part of the front was likely to succeed. On the other wing, facing open country, ideal for the operations of horse, the mass of the French cavalry was drawn up with, in the forefront, the gorgeous squadrons of the Maison du Roi, the Bodyguard, the Musketeers, the Horse Grenadiers, the Gendarmerie in their red coats. Opposite these warriors, Marlborough placed the Dutch cavalry with infantry in the rear, and behind that, the regiments of Danish horse. This southern half of the army was under the command of that admirable Dutch general, Overkirk. To the north, facing the boggy valley of the Little Geete, were the British and Danish infantry led by Lord Orkney. In the centre of the line was the Scots Brigade in the service of Holland. On this occasion, it was commanded by a cantankerous, Whiggish but undoubtedly valiant young nobleman who was chief of the most powerful Highland clan, Red John of the Battles, otherwise known as the Duke of Argyll.

About one o'clock on that Sabbath day, as Blackader called it – it was Whit Sunday – the regimental bands stopped playing and the guns took over. The Elector, who had been to mass, arrived just in time, having galloped most of the way. The British infantry on the right of the line, Guards, Royal Scots, the 16th Foot and so on, moved down into the marshy valley in front of them and climbed the slope which led to the villages of Offuz and Autre Église. Behind them came the cavalry. Villeroi, obeying a directive he had received from the King, had already strengthened the flank that was about to receive the first shock of the British attack. The French defence was obstinate, but Lord Orkney was confident that his men, who were, after all, the cream of the British army, would hold their own. However, a surprise was coming to that seasoned general.

At the other end of the Allied line, the extreme left flank, Dutch Guards had brought off an important *coup*. They had driven a French garrison out of the village of Taviers and had beaten off a counter-attack by French and Swiss troops. Taviers was set amidst the marshes of the river Mehaigne and, to reach it, a storming party must wade up to the knees in boggy water. Once they had taken the hamlet, the Dutch were able to harass the French extreme flank with the fire of their field guns. More important still, there was a space between that flank and the river into which a wedge of resolute cavalry could drive. Twenty-one squadrons of Danes were conveniently placed for just such a task. Already General Overkirk had successfully set them on the dismounted dragoons composing the French counter-attack. At this point Marlborough made an unexpected and puzzling change of plan. One young man in scarlet, splendidly mounted, listened to the general's words, saluted and, putting spurs to his horse, made off. One galloper, then another. A few minutes later they reached Lord Orkney with an extraordinary message. He was to break off his attack on the northern villages. Orkney received the order at first with incredulity. There must be some mistake. The Commander-in-Chief could not know how well the battle was going on his sector. Then Orkney's face darkened with fury, as rider after rider came up at the gallop repeating the order to withdraw. At last, the Chief-of-Staff, Cadogan himself, arrived to explain: Marlborough could not spare any cavalry for the right wing: they were needed elsewhere. And without the support of mounted men, Orkney's attack could not succeed. Orkney's infantry – Guards, Royal Scots, Royal Welch, Cameronians and the rest – fell back to their starting line in the worst of humours, convinced that some dreadful misunderstanding had snatched victory from them. What had happened?

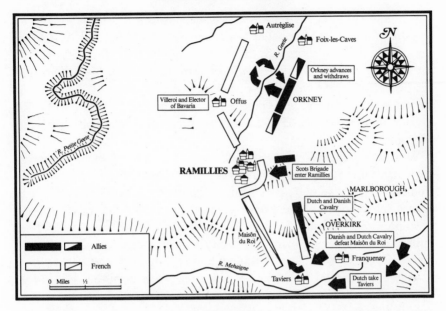

5 Ramillies

It has been supposed that, from the beginning, Marlborough intended
Orkney's attack to be no more than a feint in order to draw French
strength away from the place which he intended to make the crux of
the battle. And that he concealed this from Orkney, who might not have
pressed the attack with convincing force. It may be so; it seems more
likely, however, that Marlborough's mind was responding to the unexpected Dutch success at Taviers and the chance that the Danes would be
able to exploit it. In this case, Marlborough would be able to use all his
cavalry to better advantage further south. A battle may be planned but it
is apt to grow after some pattern of its own shaping. The good general
encourages it to grow in the most favourable direction. Whatever the
reason, eighteen squadrons of cavalry were transferred from Orkney's
wing to the centre. There, as it chanced, they arrived too late to influence
the issue. By this time, Overkirk had launched his cavalry in one crowded
mass at the French – forty-eight squadrons of Dutch horse. The Maison
du Roi did not wait passively to receive the shock. They rode forward to
meet it. Part of the French line forced the Dutch squadrons to give ground.
The Gendarmerie and the Light Horse, led by Prince Rohan, gained five
hundred yards. Then they were struck in the flank by the Danish cavalry
who, in the meantime, had come into play. For a time the turmoil was

violent and confused, as squadrons advanced to the attack, pulled out to re-form and went into the attack once more. Shouts, the clash of steel on steel, the rumble of thousands of hooves. The cream of the horsemen of three nations were locked in a confused, desperate action. Then it became clear that the incredible was happening. The Maison du Roi, caught in front and on one flank, was faltering. At that moment, the second line of cavalry in the pay of King Louis, Bavarians and Walloons, gave up the fight.

While this tremendous cavalry action was going on, Dutch infantry in the centre of the line had advanced into Ramillies village. In their fore-front was the Duke of Argyll, leading the veterans of the Scots Brigade against the senior of all the French regiments, Picardy, and driving it out of its positions. Fighting his way into the village, Argyll was hit by three bullets, none of which had the velocity to pierce his coat. The effective range of a musket was at that time a modest thing.

Villeroi now faced a situation in which the centre of his line had lost its strong point, the hinge on which it could be re-aligned. It had done so at the very moment he was trying to wheel his right wing into a new line at right angles to the one it had originally held. He was too late. Somewhere in the faltering line, the fatal cry went up, "Sauve qui peut!" Seeing what was happening, Marlborough knew that the moment had come. He gave the order, taken up at once by all the trumpets, for a general advance of the whole line – and rode forward with his men.

Orkney's resentful battalions started vengefully forward. Villeroi's army, half of which had not been in the fight, was beaten. Shielded by Spanish and Bavarian horse, a long train of artillery was leaving the field when Allied cavalry, Dutch and German for the most part, interrupted the retreat. The escort scampered off. The guns were taken. Further to the north, Lord John Hay's Scots Greys overtook the Regiment du Roi – a French infantry regiment which the King used to train future officers – and made prisoners of all its men who did not throw down their arms. Lumley, at the head of a British cavalry brigade, begged Orkney to send him some foot so that he could mop up eight or nine enemy battalions who were ready to surrender. Orkney obliged but did so too late. The birds had flown. There were three hours of daylight left. They were devoted to converting Villeroi's retreat into a rout. The English cavalry, galloping, wheeling, wildly excited, did not stop until it had reached the approaches of Louvain.

While the cavalry action in the centre was at its hottest, Marlborough had a narrow escape. He had put himself at the head of the Dutch Guards when they ran into a wing of the Maison. Ten Dutch squadrons were routed and Marlborough was carried along with the crowd. In leaping a ditch, his horse threw him and some fugitives rode over him. Without hat and wig, he ran off as fast as he could in his heavy boots. He was pursued. Luckily, General Murray saw there was a danger that the Commander-in-Chief would be captured, and sent two Swiss battalions to rescue him. Another horse was found for him and, while he was mounting, his aide-de-camp, Colonel Bringfield, who held his stirrup, was beheaded by a cannon ball. Before resting, Marlborough rode after the routed enemy for twelve miles to the north and west. Then, hopelessly lost in the darkness, he slept on the ground, sharing his cloak with Sicco Van Goslinga, a Frisian civilian who was one of the Dutch deputies and one of Marlborough's bitterest critics. By that time, Marlborough had been twenty-eight hours in the saddle. He had fallen heavily and narrowly escaped death or capture. He had been supreme commander in a great battle.

Altogether, it had been a heavy ordeal for a man of fifty-six who paid a price in constant nervous headaches for the mental burden he carried: anxiety about politics at home, where the delicate balance of forces could at any moment change disastrously; anxiety about the situation in Europe where, so often, a happy turn of fortune had been followed by unexpected and disagreeable sequels. Even the extraordinary triumph of the past few hours might, on the pattern of recent events, be followed by slackened loyalties, failure to carry out obligations, changes of heart, suspicions and ingratitude. But a triumph it had been: a French army, the *best* French army, routed, destroyed as a fighting force: 13,000 men lost, plus an untold number of deserters, at a cost of 1,066 killed and 2,500 wounded ... After three hours' rest, Marlborough rose and called for his groom. Dawn was approaching. A busy day lay ahead, in which he must find time to write to his "dearest soul" and to Godolphin.

The Elector of Bavaria had been seen weeping as he rode from the battlefield: "the effect is so great, the terror among the troops so horrible." In the market-place of Louvain he consulted with Villeroi. The light of torches hollowed the cheeks of the weary officers but the strain of battle hardly showed on the fine new white uniforms. The tale of disaster was grim: all the artillery lost; all the baggage; eighty standards. An army of nearly seventy thousand men turned into a panic-stricken rabble fleeing across the Flemish fields from the sabres of the Dutch, the British and,

most ruthless of all, the Danes who remembered the massacre of their
compatriots at Calcinato in Italy. There was nothing for it but to give up
the Spanish Netherlands. Villars, hearing of the day's outcome in his
headquarters on the Rhine, called it "the most shameful, humiliating and
disastrous of defeats". If only he had been allowed to advise Villeroi! But
Villeroi had been advised by the King.

The first ominous news of the defeat reached the King when he woke
on 26 May. "I was at Versailles," writes Saint-Simon. "Never was seen
such consternation. What was worst was that for six days there was no
mail. The King was reduced to ask news here and there."[5] Then in his
extreme anxiety, Michel de Chamillart, the Minister of War, drove
in a post-chaise to Lille to seek the truth. There he found Villeroi,
who was convinced that he had acted for the best. After a cool interview
with the marshal, Chamillart reported he "is full of zeal and good intentions but has not the gift of being liked by the soldiers." By this time, the
marshal had abandoned the whole of Spanish Flanders. Louvain, Brussels,
Antwerp, Ghent – all had gone. These losses Villeroi accepted as reasonable enough in the circumstances, while conceding that "good reasons
are no explanation for catastrophe". The whole of Belgium was falling
into Marlborough's hands. By 21 June, Cadogan, pursuing the French at
the head of the cavalry, had reached the Bridge of Erps over the Dendre
near Alost: "Your Grace will please to pardon the haste this is writt in:
the detachment of the enemy being still drawn up on the other side of the
bridge. It is growing now dark. I suppose they will hardly think of doing
anything."[6] As it turned out, Cadogan was right. Ramillies, in its different
way, was a disaster as complete as Blenheim had been. "As fatal as
Hochstädt [Blenheim]," the Elector of Bavaria told Louis. But, in this
crisis, the King behaved as a man of honour should: he wrote to his
grandson, Philip of Spain, "we have not been fortunate in Flanders." It
was some time before he was ready to acknowledge that Villeroi must
be dismissed.

When the news reached London, the rejoicings were like those that
followed Blenheim. The Queen drove to St Paul's: the choir sang a
Te Deum by Purcell, and the Dean of Canterbury preached from the text,
"Happy art thou, O Israel. Who is like unto thee, O people saved by
the Lord?" As there was no room in Westminster Hall for more trophies,
the captured French standards were hung in the Guildhall. Sarah called on
"poor Mr Bringfield's widow", whom the Queen, on Marlborough's
appeal, had undertaken to look after.

"This morning," wrote James Craggs to the Duke, "we have renewed our transports with more ecstasy, for the streets are now in a flame and the cellars in a flood." From Dublin, Lord Cutts, who had fought at Blenheim, reported rejoicings "in my own house with Trumpets and Hoboys".[7] The general impression – which was also the correct one – was that the casualties had been light. Certainly that was true of the British regiments. The Dutch and the Danes, who had done the bulk of the fighting, had, however, suffered more heavily.

On the day after the battle, the mood of the Marlborough story changed for a moment from drama to something more like musical comedy. In Swabia, Mr George Stepney, British envoy in Vienna, deputizing for Marlborough, was installed as Prince of Mündelheim. The ceremonies were long and, at a guess, tedious. The dignitaries of the little town did homage; the civil accounts were gone into, a local convent of English nuns were confirmed in their pensions and a Jesuit college performed a "sort of opera" in Latin which extolled Marlborough's heroic virtues. In this entertainment a young Count Fugger played the leading part. Stepney was presented with a basin and ewer worth six hundred florins. He reported that the new principality was agreeably situated, the air healthy and the soil fertile; the inhabitants were industrious and would be in good circumstances had they not been exhausted by frequent wars.

The new Prince, who was receiving those honours *in absentia*, was engaged in gathering the fruits of victory in Belgium. In Brussels, he was given the honours paid to the Duke of Burgundy in former times. A *vin d'honneur* was brought in a gilded tun painted with the Marlborough arms, borne on a carriage drawn by six horses, with an escort of drums, trumpets and mounted students. The cost of the wine, music and escort was borne on the Duke's account: 122 guilders, 4 stivers.[8] The Princess Palatine, Duchess of Orléans, writing from Versailles to her aunt, the Electress of Hanover, summed it all up. They were both old ladies and they had inherited more good sense and humour than most of their Stuart forebears. "The upheavals of the last twenty years are unbelievable," said the Princess. "The Kingdoms of England, Holland and Spain have been transformed as fast as the scenery in a theatre. When later generations come to read about our history, they will think they are reading a romance and not believe a word of it."

But the romance was not yet ended.

XVII

The Bonny Blue Caps

"Our letters today from Scotland are full of hopes."
Godolphin to Sarah, 18 October 1706

One day in late September 1706, Marlborough wrote a jubilant letter to Sarah. He had just heard that, a fortnight earlier, Eugene had relieved Turin and that the French were pulling out of Italy. It was as extraordinary a turn of fortune as could be imagined. Only two months before, Turin had been encircled by one French army, 60,000 strong, while another army held Eugene at bay in the country at the mouth of the Brenner Pass two hundred miles to the east.

It seemed impossible that the Prince, brilliant soldier as he was, could influence the fate of the city, especially as he had just taken over the command of an army which had suffered a demoralizing defeat in March with a loss of ten thousand men. However, several things happened which changed the picture. Eugene pulled the beaten army together. Reinforcements poured in from Germany, the fruits of Marlborough's diplomacy and money. Louis decided that Vendôme was needed in the Netherlands and that Marsin, a lesser man, should take his place. And, one day in early July, Eugene began a long and devious march.

Using the river system of Northern Italy to confuse and mystify his opponents, as Marlborough had used the Rhine two years before, he made his way towards Turin. The march was, roughly, as long as Marlborough's march to the Danube and lasted about as many weeks. For most of the time the army moved by night, avoiding the oppressive heat of the summer days in the Po valley. Meanwhile, the French siege of Turin went on with such a dignified lack of haste or alacrity that one day the Duke of Savoy was able to slip out of his capital and take to the hills. In the first week of September, he joined his cousin, Eugene. Without wasting any time – for by now the situation in Turin was desperate – the two set about the task of relieving the city. Fetching a wide circle round Turin, they launched an attack from the west, having noticed that in that quarter the

188

trenches of the besieging army were weak. Eugene attacked at daybreak on 7 September; not long after midday, the French gave way. Marsin, who had for weeks been haunted by a premonition of death, fell mortally wounded. Then the young Duke of Orléans, twice wounded and now Marsin's successor in command, ordered that the siege should be raised. In good order the French army marched home over the Alps. And so Turin was saved by the bold strategy of Eugene and the stamina of his German troops. "It is impossible for me to express the joy it has given me," wrote Marlborough to Sarah. "I really love that Prince."

He stayed on in Flanders reducing one by one the fortresses that were still in enemy hands, receiving the welcome of city after city which had returned to their allegiance to the Hapsburg "King of Spain". By the time Vendôme arrived from Italy to take over the command against Marlborough, he found the army dispersed and the morale of his officers at a low ebb. "Everyone is ready to doff his hat when one mentions the name of Marlborough." They thought of the English general very much as the Eighth Army thought of Rommel before Montgomery arrived in the Desert. The French rank and file were, however, in better heart. It was the kind of emergency which suited Vendôme's temperament. As Eugene told Marlborough, "He is beloved by the common soldiers." He pieced together a new army and was careful to avoid any major collision with the Allies. In one skirmish he had the good luck to capture Cadogan, Marlborough's beloved Quartermaster General. Marlborough heard at first that his friend had been killed and, in distress, sent a trumpet to the Governor of Tournai to find out the truth. With no waste of time, Vendôme sent Cadogan back on parole; Marlborough exchanged him for a French general captured at Ramillies.

In the first week of October, the fortress of Ath fell and the fighting season was over. The Allied army was only twenty miles from the French frontier but the rain, falling steadily on the Flemish fields, blotted out any hope of further campaigning. Another year's campaign would probably be needed before a peace could be made that "would give ease to Christendom for many years". So Marlborough told Godolphin, as his army made ready to go into winter quarters. A few days later, he mounted his coach and drove to the ship that would later take him to England. In London once more the pageantry of triumph was unfolded: the captured standards and colours borne in procession; the congratulations from Parliament; the banquet in the Vintners' Hall. There were, too, more substantial rewards: already his pension of £5,000 was perpetual, now his ducal title could descend through the female line – which to him, without an heir and with a strong sense of family, was a matter of some importance. And so, with fitting marks of favour, ended a year of martial triumph; ahead, guessed by him more clearly perhaps than anyone else, lay enterprises less glorious than the campaign of Ramillies but scarcely less wearisome.

A spectacular victory in Flanders had been followed, three months later, by one even more remarkable south of the Alps. The French had pulled out of Belgium and had abandoned Italy. In Spain, it was true, they had done better. Although Barcelona had been saved from French besiegers by the last-minute arrival of an English fleet, a march on Madrid by the Allies had ended in disaster. A bitter feud broke out between the Archduke Charles – "King of Spain" according to Allied policy – and the Earl of Galway, the French Huguenot soldier who commanded the English army in Madrid. Louis sent a new general to lead his troops, Marlborough's nephew, the Marshal-Duke of Berwick, who proved to be more than a match for Galway. Lord Peterborough, the other British commander in the country, clever, witty, essentially untrustworthy, "the ramblingest, lying rogue on earth", as Swift said, left Spain when he saw things were going to turn out badly. But the decisive factor was that the people of Spain turned against the Austrian candidate and his heretic allies. They fought their own furtive, pitiless war against the intruding redcoats. On the other hand, the English held Gibraltar, their fleet was established in the Mediterranean Sea, and had captured Minorca. So long as that was so, the French base at Toulon was neutralized and King Louis could not control Naples and Sicily.

The time had come to take a new look at the war. Perhaps the time had come to explore ways of ending it. However, this was not a thought that occurred to the Captain-General. In his judgment, one more year of fortunate war was needed to bring the French King to the frame of mind in which he would be prepared to contemplate peace on tolerable terms. One more year . . . it was the first of what were to become annual visitations of this delusion. So Marlborough laboured and schemed to keep the Grand Alliance in being, in a world that was shifting all the time under his feet.

While Belgian delegations waited on him with obsequious addresses, the victor of Ramillies heard a scrap of news from London which brought back to him the carefree days of thirty years before when he was a young spark on the prowl in Whitehall. Barbara Villiers, aged sixty-four plus and admitting to fifty, the Duchess of Cleveland who had been Queen of the revels at King Charles' court, poor Barbara who had long since lost her looks but had kept her money and her appetite, now fell wildly, unsuitably, disastrously in love. The object of her passion? A Jacobite, a notorious gambler named Beau Fielding who was as stupid as he was beautiful and a scoundrel to boot.[1] "She only begs he will be civil to her . . . Wedding clothes are making," old Lady Wentworth reported gleefully to her son, Lord Raby, who was the Queen's ambassador in Berlin.[2] The inevitable sequel was not long in coming.

After the marriage, Fielding broke into Barbara's closet and stole four hundred pounds. More than that, he beat her up and, when she screamed "Murder" out of the window, he fired a blunderbuss at the crowd she had attracted. Then it was discovered that the Beau was already married to a woman whom he had been duped into thinking was an heiress – and whom he had promptly deserted. He was tried for bigamy and convicted. Round the messroom tables in Flanders the story, like the plot of a sardonic comedy by Wycherley, was greeted with coarse laughter. Even the boldest officer would, however, take care to let no echo of this merriment reach the ears of the prim, illustrious general who was, incredible as it might seem, the father of Barbara Cleveland's daughter, Barbara, by this time a nun at Pontoise.

The year ended well.

"Our letters today from Scotland," wrote Godolphin to Sarah on 18 October 1706, "are full of hopes to carry the Union." Hopes, yes, but not yet certainties. "The bonny blue caps",[3] as Harley called them, were in a highly volatile state of mind. "They are a people," as one of his correspondents told him, "unaccountable, differ from all the world . . . They are proud, lazy and envious."[4] The young Duke of Argyll had been the second man to enter the village of Ramillies at the head of the hardy mercenaries of the Scots Brigade. Five months later he was riding down from Edinburgh Castle with the Scots Horse Guards behind him on a different and hardly less important military mission: to clear the High Street and Parliament Close of Edinburgh of the mob who, when their blood was up, were as savage and dangerous as any riotous crowd in Europe. "Certainly," said Daniel Defoe, "a Scots rabble is the worst of its kind." In the autumn days of 1706, the temper of those men was close to flash-point. Wherever he went in the wynds and closes of the old town,

Daniel Defoe could hear them growling at his heels as they detected his English accent. Had they known he was an under-cover agent of the English government – freed from Newgate Gaol only three years earlier to become the most valuable informer of the Secretary of State about the trends of opinion in Britain – they would undoubtedly have set upon him and left his dead body on the causeway. Most sinister sign of all, there were more Highlanders in the city than usual, "formidable fellows, I only wish Her Majesty had 25,000 of them in Spain, a nation equally proud and barbarous like themselves." For, incredibly enough, "they are all gentlemen. The absurdity is ridiculous to see a man in his mountain habit armed with broadsword, target, pistol or perhaps two, a dagger and staff, walking down the street as haughty as if he were a lord and withal driving a cow, bless me!" Defoe was not Harley's only informant in Scotland. On the payroll also were William Paterson, founder of the Bank of England, and by this time very hard up; David Fearn, a Cameronian;* William Gregg, who was later executed in London for betraying official secrets to the French; and Captain John Ogilvie, who moved in the best of Jacobite circles and, in addition to his work for Harley, took money from the French. With such helpers as these, Harley, during critical months, knew more than any other man about the situation north of the Tweed.

In such a country, at such a time, anything might happen. Most likely there would be an explosion shattering the whole elaborate political edifice laboriously pieced together in London and Edinburgh. The extreme Covenanters of the south-western shires were "full of tumult". "Glasgow is mad," and Defoe was advised not to go there. The Jacobites of Aberdeenshire waited the order to march. And who would give the order? Could it be in doubt? The Duke of Hamilton, first Scottish peer, looked round the assembled Parliament. "Where," he asked, "are the Douglases and the Campbells? Where are the peers, where are the barons, once the bulwark of the nation?" He had only to give the signal and the country would have been ablaze. The plain people would have taken to the streets. The better-off would have barricaded themselves in their houses. The regiments Marlborough had sent north would have crossed the Tweed. Whether Argyll's troopers could have held the mob at bay is doubtful. Could they be trusted? Half of them were Jacobites. But would the match be put to the train? There were respectable reasons why it should not – and others not so respectable.

* i.e. member of an extreme Protestant sect.

The supreme argument for the Union was that, at any moment, the Queen might die. The English Parliament would then opt for the Hanoverian Succession; the Scots, in their prevailing Anglophobe temper, would perhaps incline towards the male Stuart line. In that case the Union of the Crowns would be broken. And a Catholic King would reign in Holyroodhouse! A Catholic! It was hardly a prospect to fill the bosom of any Covenanter with holy joy.

Nor, for that matter, was the Duke of Hamilton, leader of the National-ists, any more enthusiastic. Did he not think his family had a better right than the Stuarts to the Scottish throne? "The bonnet is mine and I'll wear it," so he was heard to say. To exert himself to bring in a moth-eaten prince from Saint-Germain did not make sense. Besides, his Grace had rich estates in Lancashire. Other motives operated with other people. The shareholders in the disastrous Darien scheme, who blamed the English government for the loss of their capital, were appeased with a promise that the money would be paid back, with interest. Then, too, there was the undoubted fact that Marlborough's victories, in which Scottish soldiers had played their part, had raised the prestige of England all over Europe. This inevitably had an influence on events in Scotland where the public felt that, whatever they might be losing by Union, they were about to join a thriving concern. So order was kept in Edinburgh. Clause by clause, the Treaty was approved by Parliament. And, protesting, resenting, but in the end half-willing, Scotland was dragged into the eighteenth century.

All things considered, it was the greatest achievement of Godolphin's ministry and, for that matter, of the Queen's reign.

XVIII

"The Wigths and the Thorys"

"L'aigreur était alors très vive entre les deux partis des Wigths et des Thorys."

M. de Torcy[1]

In April 1707, Marlborough set off from The Hague in his great coach on yet another diplomatic foray into Europe, the most delicate and momentous of them all. He was going to call upon the violent and unpredictable young warrior of twenty-five who sat on the throne of Sweden, or rather, sat in the saddle at the head of the powerful Swedish army. He had defeated Tsar Peter and driven Augustus of Saxony from the Polish throne. Now he and forty thousand Swedes sat at Altranstadt outside Leipzig. There the young King was receiving tempting political proposals from the French. Why did he not invade Austria, for example, and force the Emperor to yield on various matters in dispute, such as the ill-treatment of the Protestants in Silesia? A successful Swedish attack on Austria, which the Allies could do little to prevent, would be a grave, perhaps a fatal, development. Already, with the laurels of Ramillies still unfaded, the war was going badly for them.

In Flanders, Louis had brought together a new army, a hundred thousand strong, and put Marshal Vendôme at its head. Vendôme's habits might be unsavoury but his energy and talent were not to be doubted. Besides, at his back was Vauban's string of fortresses. On the Rhine was another French army, that of Villars, about which Marlborough's spies brought him disquieting rumours. From Spain came ominous sounds presaging defeat. If there was to be a happy reversal of fortune, Marlborough could only imagine it as coming about through Prince Eugene. In his mind the germ of a plan had formed. It depended on the Empire being able to play its part in the Alliance. And this was something that Charles of Sweden, crouching only a hundred miles from the Bohemian frontier, would be able to prevent.

Could Marlborough divert the young man's furious energy to another direction? He found Charles hatless, wigless, in a plain coat and top boots, living like a military monk, and privately rather scornful of the Englishman's scarlet and Garter star. "Why do you think it necessary to charge at the head of your troops?" asked Charles. Marlborough replied that if he failed to do so, they would not think so much of him. He noticed that the Swede's blue eyes lit up when he spoke of the Tsar. He saw on the table a map of Russia. He drew his own conclusions. Charles dreamt of forming a League of Protestant German Princes, hostile to the Emperor. Marlborough showed how this would weaken the coalition against Louis, the arch-enemy of Protestant Europe, the man who had revoked the Edict of Nantes. The Emperor must certainly treat his Protestants better. That was essential. He, Marlborough, would do what he could to bring it about. But he hoped greatly that, in the meantime, Charles would do no more to disturb the Empire. Charles was already doing quite a lot in that way, being settled in Saxony with forty thousand men. But he fell in with Marlborough's views. He even promised to help him with some Swedish troops, as soon as he could do so. The two soldiers dined together; the food was wretched. Then the kettledrums beat for the King's prayers. They had talked for four hours.

Next day, Marlborough took his leave, having summed up the strange, alarming young man against whom – but on the whole, he thought it unlikely – he might yet find himself pitted, and having bestowed handsome "pensions" on the young man's ministers. He thought he knew what the Swede was likely to do. Not at once, but later, when the Emperor had, at last, decided to be sensible. In fact, it was September before the Swedish army began its trek into the forests and swamps of Russia. Marlborough discussed the question with Eugene when the two of them met. Let the boy do what he wants to do, he argued; he will ruin himself and we shall be rid of him. Eugene thought otherwise. An invasion of Russia might be too successful, after which the King of Sweden, victorious at the head of 40,000 soldiers, would be able to overrun the Empire. In the end, the question was resolved in the snow at Poltava.

Meanwhile Marlborough drove back to The Hague by way of the court in Berlin. There he had some talk with the British ambassador, Lord Raby, a pushful young man who wanted an earldom, pointing out that he could well afford the title, having a net income of £4,000.[2] Marlborough had seen four monarchs[3] in as many days. Later he told

Sarah, "If I were obliged to make a choice, it should be the youngest, the Swede." As it turned out, the need did not arise. In his three-week tour of Germany, he had brought off a diplomatic *coup* of some importance, saved the Empire, which hardly deserved to be saved, and frustrated the King of France. He had also, although this was no part of his plan, given Swedish policy a nudge towards Russia and total catastrophe.

But while Marlborough was trundling across Europe to his interview with Charles, the Emperor was betraying his Allies. Secretly, he was making a treaty with Louis which would "neutralize" Italy and allow twelve thousand French troops, until then pinned down in Milan, to march back to France. This was the first of several setbacks to Marlborough. The second occurred three days before he met the Swedish King. At Almanza in Spain, an Anglo–Dutch–Portuguese army, commanded by Lord Galway, was destroyed by the French, led by Marlborough's nephew, the Duke of Berwick. Five English, six Dutch and three Portuguese regiments were captured, all the cannon and, incredibly, the colours. The news reached Marlborough in Brussels. It was a shattering blow after which there was no real hope of putting the Austrian Archduke, who was Britain's candidate, on the Spanish throne. But this painful truth was not immediately realized. Indeed, it seemed that Spain was, for English politicians, a more important theatre of war than ever. Lord Peterborough might say, "We are all great fools to get ourselves killed for two such boobies" (as the French and Austrian candidates for the Spanish throne). But most people disagreed with his lordship.

The blame for the Almanza disaster was put on Galway who, in spite of his Irish title, was a French Huguenot, one of William of Orange's men and was for that reason anathema to the High Tories. To them Berwick became the "brave English general who has beaten the French". Marlborough heard with disgust that in the City of London glasses were being drained "to the confusion of generals"; "Were it not for the concern I have for the Queen and England, I could wish they had Peterborough and such-like favourite generals and that the Lord Treasurer and I were at quiet." He agreed that Galway must be dismissed. The trouble was to find a general to replace him. That the defeat gave Britain an opportunity to be rid of the Spanish incubus was something that neither he nor any of the politicians would recognize. After the humiliation of Almanza the national temper was roused.

And what, in all this, had become of Marlborough's "Great Design"? This was that there should be an attack on Toulon by Eugene marching from Turin to the Mediterranean coast when he would link up with the English fleet, commanded by Sir Cloudesley Shovell. Toulon was France's great naval base in the Mediterranean. Were it threatened, she would be compelled to hurry reinforcements from Spain, and Madrid would, once again, fall into Allied hands. Were Toulon to fall, then Louis must surely sue for peace. Pinned down in Flanders by Vendôme's army and by the caution of the Dutch deputies, the stroke against Toulon seemed to Marlborough the most hopeful project open to him. A few weeks after his return from Germany the picture had changed once more for the worse.

On 22 May, there was a splendid ball at Strasbourg. Music; scores of ravishing women; French officers in resplendent ceremonial uniforms. The host of the evening was the commander-in-chief, Marshal Villars, whose Gascon temperament was marvellously attuned to a festive occasion of which the news had, as if by chance, reached the Imperialists in their prepared defences on the other bank of the Rhine. Villars' lively eye darted here and there inciting the dancers to fresh exertions, until, at a moment which he seemed to have pre-determined, it caught the glance of certain generals and summoned them to his side. To one and then another, he gave orders which sent them hurrying to their horses. Their battalions were already on the march. Villars was about to deliver a surprise attack on the Stollhofen Lines, a powerful system of defence which barred the way between the Black Forest and the Rhine and guarded the crossings of the great river for fifty miles to the north. As fortifications they were magnificent. The trouble was that they were thinly manned, especially as the Emperor, pursuing some purely Hapsburg purpose, had lately dispatched an Austrian army to march through Italy and capture Naples from the Spaniards. However that may be, the French achieved total surprise on the Rhine and over-ran the famous Lines without the loss of a man. On 23 May, Villars slept in the magnificent palace at Rastadt, the pride and joy of the late Margrave of Baden, the man who had thought, not without some excuse, that Marlborough had cheated him of his share of the glory of Blenheim. Germany was open to a French invasion. And Villars was not the man to lose so brilliant an opportunity for loot and levy. Marlborough, warned by his secret service that the French marshal ought to be watched, had passed the word to the Germans, who had paid no heed. Spies seem to have been exceptionally busy at this time, as a letter in his files indicates.[4] Needless to say, French diplomacy was now hard at work, urging Charles of Sweden to make an end of the Hapsburg Empire. It was touch and go for a time.

While the French ravaged Swabia and Franconia almost as far as the battlefield of Blenheim, Marlborough continued to urge his Toulon project on Vienna where it was greeted with something a good deal short of enthusiasm. If Toulon were taken from the French, it would certainly strengthen the position of the maritime powers in the Mediterranean; moreover, as the war went on and the Dutch fleet wasted away, the "Maritime Powers" was becoming simply another name for Britain. But what would be the advantage to Austria, or to Savoy for that matter, of the capture of Toulon? It would merely mean that the British navy was firmly established between the Hapsburg Emperor in Vienna and his relative, the King of Spain, assuming for a moment that, against the odds, a Hapsburg prince and not a Bourbon ruled in Madrid. There was always the danger, too, that a success at Toulon might give the British a chance to make a separate peace with France to the detriment of Austria.

In due course, with no excessive haste and no great hopes of success, Prince Eugene moved down to the coast road which led to Toulon. He had 35,000 men. Turning westwards along the shore, the army was supplied by Shovell's fleet. "If the siege of Toulon prospers," Marlborough wrote to Godolphin, "I shall be cured of all diseases but old age."[5] By that time, it was past midsummer; the sun was hot; the local peasants were unfriendly and, when given a chance, hostile to the invaders. And Toulon, which had been without a garrison, was quickly put into a state of defence by its commander Marshal Tessé. The French fleet was sunk in the shallow water of the harbour; its guns and gunners were brought ashore to help ward off an attack by land. Twenty thousand infantry, pulled in from the Alpine passes, arrived in time to man the entrenchments Tessé had prepared. When Eugene arrived, he found Toulon ready to receive him. To Shovell's annoyance, he proposed to withdraw and, when argued out of that course, set about siege operations with no great energy. Probably the Prince was acting against his own instincts and in conformity to some directive from Vienna. Before the end of August the enterprise was abandoned. The "Great Design" had ended in fiasco.

Only one gain had emerged from Marlborough's strategy. The French fleet had committed suicide and would play no further substantial part in the war. This was an advantage not to be despised, but it was far short of the decision that had been hoped for. Watching the situation from his camp in Flanders, Marlborough was naturally depressed. It seemed that the French recovery was complete: Southern Germany was at the mercy

of their marauders; Spain was – after Almanza – theirs; the attempt on
Toulon had failed. Most galling of all, he himself was unable to bring
Vendôme to battle. First, the Dutch imposed their veto; then, the
weather broke with spectacular fury. Rain fell without let or pity;
Flanders became a morass, "the mud up to the horses' bellies which is
very extraordinary in this month", as Marlborough wrote to Sarah on
4 August 1707. Thus a whole campaigning season passed without a major
battle being fought. Among the Dutch, who were mainly responsible
for this ineffectual defensive strategy, the rumour spread that the Captain-
General did not really want to end the war which, while it lasted, brought
him such magnificent emoluments. Needless to say, this was an opinion
which found many willing believers in London.

The Duke changed into his winter underclothing and had the fire lit in
his room. But even in that bitter season, when the climate of Europe
seemed to be changing for the worse, hard-won comfort was not everything. Compelled to stay indoors, he was all the more at the mercy of
that relentless bore, Lord Peterborough, full of his grievances, busy with
his intrigues and loaded with debts. Marlborough's mind dwelt a great
deal on his age and the prospect of retirement. From Sarah he had warnings that the work at Blenheim was far behind schedule. No matter, if
they had only half a house for their old age, it would be enough. Enough?
There was, after all, the house at St Albans, Sarah's mansion in London
and her life-tenancy of Windsor Lodge. Their retreat from the world
would be dignified enough. And anything was better, he thought, than to
go on being the victim of ungrateful fate and scheming politicians: "I am
at an age and a humour," he told Sarah, "that I would not be bound to
make my court to either party for all that this world could give me."
Whigs and Tories. One party as bad as the other. If it were not for his
duty to the Queen and England! The Queen? "I owe to you my apprehensions," he wrote to Sarah, "that somebody or other, I know not who,
has got so much credit with the Queen that they will be able to persuade
her to do more hurt to herself than we can do good."[6]

Somebody or other, I know not who . . .

One man in England had begun to play with the notion of peace. He was
Robert Harley, the Secretary of State and ex-Speaker of the House of
Commons, a man whose character was distrusted but whose ability was
regarded with a wary respect. Men thought that one who looked so
crafty and deceitful could hardly help being a master of plots and wiles.

"Robin the Trickster", they called him. What was certain was that Harley knew more about the state of opinion in the country than any other member of the government. He knew because he had taken the trouble to find out through a network of secret agents, of whom the most reliable and most diligent was Daniel Defoe. Through such reporters, men who listened in tap-rooms and gossiped in market-places, Harley followed the trend of thinking in the country.

He was a whole-time politician in the modern sense of the term. A House of Commons man who had studied Parliamentary procedure diligently, and, having mastered it, moved on to study the passions and motives of the men who sat on the benches in Westminster. From that, he would move still further. But at present life was "Parliament, eat and sleep" for him. He was a political manager of exceptional assiduity and skill. In party allegiance he was, as Marlborough had been, a Tory and, like Marlborough, he believed that it was best if government were carried on by loyal servants of the Queen, whatever their party colour. With a proviso: in Harley's opinion ministers should be country gentlemen. That was not only natural and traditional; it was an indispensable condition of good government.

He himself came of respectable Dissenting stock. His grandfather, during the early, exuberant days of the Civil War, had led a pious mob which destroyed many of "the relics of medieval superstition" in Canterbury Cathedral. His father, sharing the outlook of the grave nonconformists, thought of life as a journey through the valley of the shadow "towards that unchangeable state to which every minute hastens". On the other hand, neither his grandfather nor his father had approved of the execution of Charles I. For that reason, they had lived under the shadow of official disfavour during the Commonwealth but had returned to the sunshine at the Restoration. Robert Harley, who was brought up as a Dissenter, whose wife and children attended a Presbyterian church, nevertheless became a Member of Parliament in 1689, when he was twenty-eight. He was made Speaker in 1701, which in effect meant that he was Leader of the House. Although he was sly and secretive in manner, his knowledge of the eddies of opinion in politics, instinctive to begin with and improved by study, was so great that he became indispensable in government. While Marlborough ran the war and diplomacy and Godolphin looked after finance and home affairs, Harley became the necessary third man who managed Parliament with consummate skill. His political success was in one way surprising, because he had no gifts at all as an orator. However, this deficiency was amply supplied by a man seventeen years younger, who became his closest ally in the House of Commons.

Henry St John's family background was curiously similar to Harley's; he was brought up as a Presbyterian although he took communion occasionally in order to qualify for office; he was probably a deist. In his case, the Puritan ancestry was balanced by a more flamboyant strain; his father was a rake and a duellist. Inheriting one of these interests, Henry kept the most expensive tart in London, Miss Gumley. When he was appointed a minister, the piazza at Covent Garden rang with the jubilation of the ladies of the town: "Seven thousand guineas a year, girls and all for us!"* As Secretary at War, St John's salary was £1,356. In addition, however, he received one day's pay for every officer he registered on the muster rolls. A clever man, if not too prudish, could certainly squeeze a substantial secret revenue from the army contracts he distributed. And nobody could deny that young Mr St John, aged twenty-six, had the finesse and aptitude which the post demanded. Rake, gambler and spendthrift, he was vivacious and shallow, energetic and quite unscrupulous, with caressing ways which had an appeal for both sexes. He wrote well and talked better. He was just the man to shine in the half-honest, wholly savage guerrilla wars of Westminster. Brazen, unstable, sensitive, with a streak of cruelty, he was also a natural ideologue, which is a rare thing in British public life, and an extremist, which is not. Extreme. But on which side? The Dissenting strain had produced a deist, and the deist had become a leader of the Tory churchmen at war with Dissent! In view of his family's record, this called for some impudence. This necessary talent St John possessed.

What was not so certain was whether St John had the moral fibre needed to carry a man through a life-or-death crisis. In 1704, when he became a minister, the question could not be answered. He was known simply as an ambitious young politician of unusual talent, a spirited and elegant debater, popular in the coffee houses and the brothels, living on his wife's money and rewarding her with consistent infidelity. His heroes were Harley and Marlborough, in the latter of whom he had "a faith which comes near to superstition". How long would that faith last? He was not the most constant of mortals. He said once of his relations with women, "I never loved long, but was inconstant to them all for the sake of all." Unaware of this aspect of the young man's character, Marlborough assured Godolphin. "You may rely on him. He will never deceive you."

* So Voltaire reports.

A percipient spectator of the British political scene in the year of Ramillies would detect that a subtle change was coming over it. Behind the team of Marlborough and Godolphin there was forming – for those who had the vision to see it – the shadow of another team with a different aim: Harley and St John. It was still no more than a shadow. Harley, whatever his inner doubts might be, insisted that the war in Spain, now costing so much and going so badly, must be fought to a victorious end. St John's letters to the Captain-General were flattering to the point of adulation. The High Tories were grumbling but there was nothing novel about that. If there was in the air an uncomfortable, indefinable feeling of transience, it was without any solid evidence to support it. Yet Ramillies, brilliant victory as it was, lacked the surprising glory of Blenheim. It was possible to look with a cooler eye on the war and notice, for example, that no Allied soldier had yet set foot on French soil, that the chain of Vauban's fortresses had still to be pierced, that the Dutch were weakening in finance and in enthusiasm for the struggle, that the Emperor seemed to be more interested in crushing his Hungarian rebels than in supporting the Western Allies without whose help and financial aid he could not make war anywhere. One day, something might happen which would produce a decisive change.

There would be a bad harvest; it was all the more likely since there had been a remarkable succession of good ones. Or Marlborough's diabolical luck would desert him. Or there would be some change at the palace, some alteration in the relations between Anne and Sarah. Both women had reached an age that is hard on women. Anne was Stuart enough to know that she was Queen of England and that she was owed the respect that Sarah did not always give her. Mrs Morley no longer had the evenness of temper which had enabled her for so long to put up with Mrs Freeman's tantrums. As for Sarah, she was more strident than ever; worst of all, she had become more of a Whig as Anne, with the years, became more of a churchwoman and, therefore, more of a Tory. But she still had charm and magnetism for some: Lord Hervey wrote, "Did you know her but half as well as I have the happiness to do, she would make you think of her as one said of the sea, that it infinitely surprised him the first time he saw it, but that the last sight of it made always as wonderful an impression as if he had never observed it before."[7] Finally, and most important of all, the little female cabal of two women had become a trio.

The human race is divided into two classes: those who are poor relations and those who have them. Sarah belonged to the second category. She had a family of cousins named Hill, the orphan children of a bankrupt London merchant. She exerted herself to help those unfortunate relations: one of the girls, Abigail, was, by Sarah's influence, given a post as dresser and, later, as bedchamber woman to the Queen; another girl was brought into the palace laundry; the boy, "four-bottle Jack", was a more difficult case, but Sarah pestered her husband to obtain a commission for the young man. This the Duke did, while continuing to insist that Jack was "good for nothing". The case of Abigail was more interesting.

If an elderly, ailing woman were looking for a companion, she might insert in the *Lady* an advertisement reading something like this: "Wanted: Person of good upbringing and appearance; discreet, sympathetic, orderly; sound Christian principles. Proficiency at the harpsichord an advantage . . ." So far as it goes, this would have been a reasonably accurate description of Abigail Hill.★ That there was more in her than those qualifications implied was in due course apparent. Obviously she was very different from her cousin, the Duchess.

One day in 1703, before Abigail was promoted to the bedchamber, the Queen wrote Sarah a letter in which she envied her ability to go to the opera but, "my fever is not quite gone and I am still so lame, I cannot go without limping". Anne continued, "I hope Mrs Freeman has no thoughts of going to the opera with Mrs Hill, and will have a care of engaging herself too much in her company, for, if you give way to that, it is a thing that will insensibly grow upon you . . . For your own sake, as well as poor Mrs Morley's, have as little to do with that enchantress as 'tis possible." A letter which showed that already the Queen was falling under the spell of Abigail Hill. The duo was turning into a triangle which, as is notorious, is only an intermediate stage in the formation of a new duo. But this was something that Sarah was too self-assured and self-centred to suspect. It was later that the revelation came to her and by that time it was too late for her to restore the situation.

Then she found that Anne was discussing state business with her bedchamber woman, the ungrateful creature whom she, Sarah, had brought up from nothing, who without Sarah's charity would be still the nobody she had been. Sarah, in this unexpected and alarming situation, made every possible blunder. She wrote in panic to Marlborough and in ill-temper to the Queen. Anne's answer was a little gem of insight and

★ "Good appearance"? Abigail was thought to have a red nose, a blemish on which not only the Whig pamphleteers commented.

provocation: "I believe that others that have been in her station in former times have been tattling and very impertinent, but she is not at all of that temper, and as for the company she keeps, it is with her as with most other people. I fancy that their lot in the world makes them move with some sort of civility, rather than choice."

A few weeks after reading these words, Sarah recognized, in one flash of truth, how far she was excluded from the Queen's confidence, how completely she had been superseded. Abigail, the waif she had rescued (although mostly at the public expense, it may be observed), had married some months before, in secret, Colonel Masham, a gentleman of the Prince Consort's household. Worse still, the Queen had been present at the wedding! Here, indeed, was occasion for resentment, for rage, for the most drastic re-appraisal of Sarah's position at court and, therefore, in the ruling coterie. It was also a matter for her husband to consider with as much gravity as if, at the crisis of a battle, a force of indeterminate loyalty had appeared in a vital sector. The political danger, which Marlborough had sensed a few months earlier, was now defined and bore a formidable shape. Mrs Masham, who was Sarah's cousin on one side of her family, was, on the other, the cousin of Robert Harley, the Secretary of State, the third man in the government.

In the late summer of 1707 when all was going badly abroad, politics in Britain moved towards a crisis. Harley had the ear of the Queen through Mrs Masham. His probable aim was to take Godolphin's place as Lord Treasurer and form a government which would rely on the support of moderate Tories. Sarah, raging against Abigail ("the black ingratitude of Mrs Masham, a woman that I took out of a garret and saved from starving"), did all she could to influence Marlborough and Godolphin against the Queen and the new favourite. Watching the situation with apprehension from his headquarters in the Low Countries, Marlborough sometimes suspected that his wife might be distorting the picture; he was unwilling to take part in a struggle in which, he felt, he could win nothing but grief: "If you think that she [Abigail] is a good weathercock, it is high time to leave off struggling. Nothing is worth rowing against wind and tide, at least when you come to my age." But these bouts of dejection, although growing in frequency ("I have often had the spleen but never with so much reason as now"[8]), were interruptions in a lasting conviction that the war against France must be won and that he alone could win it. "The English do not know their happiness, but if they oblige the Queen to a peace, they will be sensible in a very little time of their error...

But God's will must be done. I have prepared myself for the worst."

While waiting for the new campaigning season to open, he spent some time looking at pictures in the dealers' galleries at The Hague. Occasionally, he bought; for instance, two Rubens portraits from Haensberge for 500 florins*; six pictures by Lucas Jordaens (330 pistoles). The prices were reasonable. In addition, he imported looking-glasses from Paris which were a little more expensive at 3,673 guilders and a tapestry which he meant for Blenheim† – Episodes in the life of Alexander the Great, 2,800 guilders. Interests like these took his mind off politics in England where the situation was made worse when Anne, without consulting her ministers, appointed two Tories to bishoprics. Harley had told her she had a perfect right to do so. But Godolphin and Marlborough looked with alarm at the prospect of the Whigs, outraged by the Queen's action, quitting the government. If that were to happen, how could the war be carried on? As autumn passed into winter, the crisis deepened. The attack on the administration was aimed at their conduct of the war at sea and, in particular, at the apparent failure of the convoy system to protect merchant shipping against French privateers. But here was a political complication.

Although the Queen's husband was nominal head of the Admiralty, the effective chief was Marlborough's brother, George, who was a "very indiscreet Tory" with "little judgment", as Marlborough said. When George Churchill was attacked by the Whigs in the House of Lords, Marlborough, who had come over from the Low Countries a fortnight before, was indignant. On another issue, he lost his temper more publicly. Lord Rochester, speaking for the High Tories, proposed to divert twenty thousand troops from the Flanders theatre of war to Spain. This was an old manoeuvre which the general's Tory enemies had tried to use against him once before. It would have meant the complete paralysis of his campaign in the Low Countries. In beating off the Parliamentary attack, Marlborough claimed that preparations were being made to send an Imperial army to Spain, probably under the command of Prince Eugene. This disclosure turned the tide. Marlborough had won the Parliamentary battle. But he had done so by deceiving the House. There was no plan to send a substantial army to Spain. Eugene would not take the command there unless he were given an army capable of taking the offensive, and Marlborough was determined to keep the military centre of gravity in

* Say £50.
† Where it hangs today.

his own theatre of war which, at that moment, he was planning to reinforce. But Spain, which, to begin with, had been a Tory obsession, was now the concern of both parties.

After that, the storm which had threatened to drive the government on the rocks blew itself out: the Queen gave the See of Norwich to a Whig and promised to appoint no more Tory bishops. She appointed a protégé of Marlborough's to a Regius Professorship at Oxford, to the chagrin of the University. In short, she showed a spirit of compromise. The Whigs, for their part, agreed that there could be no peace while Spain remained a Bourbon possession. How to achieve this, how to undo the consequences of the defeat at Almanza was, however, another matter. Meanwhile, the rumpus over the Admiralty died down. A commodore who had made merchants pay him blackmail to protect their ships from enemy attack was disgraced; but George Churchill stayed in office. At the same time, Godolphin had decided that he could no longer trust Harley to rally the Tories behind the government. Harley was engaged in political plans of his own which would involve the removal of Godolphin. Marlborough, forced to make a choice, decided that he must stand by his old friend, the Lord Treasurer.

At this point, Harley had a series of misfortunes. A Scotsman called Gregg, a clerk in his office whom he had used as a secret agent, was found to have sent copies of important official letters to the French Minister of War. On the last day of December 1707, Gregg was arrested. He was found guilty and sentenced to death. About the same time, two smugglers, Vallière and Bera, whom Harley had employed to bring secret information over from France, were proved to have supplied intelligence to the French government. They were what would now be called double agents. It seemed that Harley's office had been careless, if it had not been something worse. When the political crisis broke, Harley was, therefore, under a cloud although, in fact, as Gregg insisted to the end, the minister was innocent of any part in the treason. In the first week of February, Godolphin accused Harley of treachery to him which "I am very far from having deserved of you. God forgive you." Harley's intention seems to have been that Godolphin should be dismissed while Marlborough should continue to serve as Captain-General under a Tory administration.

The weakness of the scheme was that Marlborough would have nothing to do with it. He told the Queen bluntly, "no consideration can make me serve any longer with that man Harley." He and Godolphin resigned. England was without a government. It was a crisis, but one in which the Secretary of State kept his head, knowing he could count on the backing of the Queen. As was customary, she presided over the Cabinet on 9 February, when Harley, proceeding as if nothing had happened, was interrupted by the Duke of Somerset. Said his Grace, "I cannot imagine what business can be done as neither the General nor the Lord Treasurer is here." For a moment, Harley was disconcerted and the Queen, embarrassed, adjourned the meeting. Next day, Harley resigned, taking with him St John and two other Tories. Marlborough and Godolphin were back in power. Henry Boyle, a moderate Whig, took Harley's place. Robert Walpole took St John's.

The Queen had been humiliated but she was not isolated; Mrs Masham was still at her side and still able to control those who came and went by the back stairs to the Queen's closet. So, at least, said Sarah, who at the height of the crisis had a stormy interview with Anne: "As Lord Marlborough is now about to be forced from your majesty's service, I cannot, in honour, remain any longer at court." However, the Queen persuaded her to stay. If the political crisis of 1708 has a quality of tension, not to say hysteria, all its own, the reason must be sought in the emotional lightning which flashed from one to another of a trio of women; one, angry and jealous; another taking her revenge for years of humiliation; the third, a queen. "I had a very low curtsey from Lady Marlborough, which I returned in the same manner and, as for looks, indeed, they are not to be described by any mortal but her own self." Abigail wrote thus four months before the storm but it admirably sums up the particular kind of poison in which these events were steeped.

A few days after Harley's resignation, Britain had something to think about more serious than a change in the Cabinet. On 4 March, Henry Boyle, the new Secretary of State, told the Commons that the man known to the Jacobites as "James VIII of Scotland", the Stuart Pretender, aged twenty, at that moment travelling as the Chevalier de St George, was about to embark at Dunkirk with twelve battalions of French troops, 17,000 stands of arm, ample military stores and all the paraphernalia of a Royal court. The colours and standards of the expedition had been blessed by the Pope. It was to be a crusade. The fleet sailed on 6 March: its destination was the Firth of Forth. Marlborough knew what the French meant to do. "My man in Mons" (as Sunderland called his almost daily correspondent in that town)* told him about the movement of

* "Mon homme de Mons."

French battalions towards Dunkirk, of the thirty English warships lying in wait off Gravelines, of the Duke of Hamilton, who was believed to have made a treaty with the King of France and the Pretender – "tout assuré-ment, toute l'Écosse est pour lui."

In the new crisis, everybody behaved much as might have been expected. Both Houses of Parliament pledged life and fortune to the Queen. The Duke of Hamilton left Scotland to visit his estates in Lanca-shire; in due course he was lodged, comfortably enough, in the Tower. Thus, his Grace was saved from having to make the embarrassing choice between supporting a Stuart claimant or opposing what might turn out to be a nationalist movement. Lord Leven, who commanded the troops in Scotland, occupied Edinburgh Castle where he found "not one farthing of money, few troops and naked". The Scottish army, three thousand strong, was for the greater part Jacobite in sympathy; Leven proposed to pull out of Scotland and retreat to Berwick if there was a French landing. Marlborough, whose spies were as usual keeping him well-informed about French intentions, had arranged with Cadogan to send ten English battalions from Ostend to Tynemouth. He dispatched other reinforce-ments to the north by land. As it turned out, the threatened invasion was prevented by the weather, which was shocking, and the timely arrival of a British flotilla which outgunned the French.

The invasion fleet was commanded by the Comte de Forbin, a seaman in the great tradition of the Dunkirk privateers. Forbin thought the whole expedition a piece of nonsense: "As for me, I risk nothing. I can swim": he looked with contempt on his Jacobite passengers and was delighted when bad weather in the North Sea made them sea-sick. In the end, he narrowly escaped being bottled up in the Firth of Forth by the British fleet and, when he found it impossible to land at Inverness, made his way home by the same route as the Armada had taken. His passengers suffered greatly on the way. One of the French ships was captured with a few Irish and Scottish Jacobites aboard. And the Pretender's proclamation to "the good people of his ancient kingdom of Scotland" was never read. The allegiance of the Scottish people was not put to the test, although the castles of Edinburgh and Stirling were crowded with Jacobite lairds who were no doubt as relieved to be imprisoned there as Hamilton was to be in the Tower. Defoe, reporting from Edinburgh, said that the "poor, honest, but ill-natured" people of Scotland were willing to let the French and the English fight it out. In London, the Funds fell fifteen points and there was a run on the Bank. There was a call on the shareholders to pay in 20 per cent of their capital; Godolphin furnished all the money available at the Treasury. Marlborough and the big money interests in the Whig party rallied in support. The popular alarm subsided with the news that the expedition had failed.

In Paris the King behaved with the courage he usually displayed in adversity. Marlborough's agent* reported that Louis had shown himself very jovial while reviewing the Guards in the Avenue de Versailles. The colonel of the regiment, the Duc de Guiche, had put all the best-looking soldiers on the right, knowing that the King usually inspected the right-hand line. So as to tease him that day, the little man in the high-heeled shoes and the fantastic feathered hat inspected the left line. Guiche was embarrassed; everybody else found it hilarious. Not for nothing was Louis the grandson of Henri Quatre! But in private – the agent was told by one of the first valets de chambre – the King was very thoughtful (très rêveur).† When the British general election came, as it did in May 1708, the Whigs floated to victory on a surge of patriotism. Jonathan Swift reported from Leicester, "there is a universal love of the present government." The result of the voting was, as Lord Sunderland told the Duke of Newcastle, "the most Whig Parliament there has been since the Revolution."

At the end of March, Marlborough left for The Hague, where Eugene was waiting to talk business.

* But see Appendix B.
† Blenheim MSS. DI-7.

XIX

The Mines are Worked Out

"I wish," quoth my uncle Toby, "you had seen what prodigious armies
we had in Flanders."

Laurence Sterne, Tristram Shandy, *Ch. 18*

That summer Marlborough's health caused him to be anxious. He had a
nervous collapse, a seizure, perhaps a slight stroke: it is hard to say what
it was. The symptoms were psychological as well as physical. The origins,
too, were probably complex. To begin with, there was the military
situation. The Flemish cities, round which his army was quartered, were
seething with disaffection and hatred for the Dutch officials who occupied
the country. Flemish aristocrats were secretly in touch with the French,
who had mobilized an army of 110,000 men at Lille under the Dauphin's
son, the young Duc de Bourgogne, and Marshal Vendôme. They were
ready to march over the border into the Netherlands and pluck whatever
might be the fruits of the conspiracy. In a few days the fruits were ripe.
Ghent and Bruges were surrendered to the French. In the meantime,
Marlborough had summoned Prince Eugene to make a forced march
from Coblenz, 150 miles away, so that they could make a surprise
combined attack on the French. Was such an attack now possible? He was
doubtful. But, losing no time, Eugene was already on the way. He had
started to move on 29 June. Four days ahead of his army, he drove in his
coach, with an escort of hussars, wild-looking horsemen from the
Hungarian *puzta*. The "old Italian prince" – who was thirteen years
younger than Marlborough – slouched into Marlborough's quarters to
find the Duke in the depths of gloom.

A Prussian officer who was at the Duke's headquarters gave an alarming
report of his health: "The day before yesterday I believed he would
succumb to his grief; he was so seized by it that he was afraid of being
suffocated." Eugene was surprised at such despondency over a minor
mishap: the loss, through treachery, of two Flemish towns. The Duke's

exhaustion was, he thought, quite incomprehensible in any rational terms; moreover, his depression was spreading to the whole army. However, Eugene had just the temperament to deal with a psychological crisis of this kind. He was the soul of energy, overwhelming in argument, irresistible in confidence that the enemy could be attacked and beaten even before his own troops had arrived. He was one of those happy mortals who are at their best when things are at their worst. Marlborough was comforted and convinced. And then he collapsed. His physical troubles came to a head in a high fever for which the doctor gave him medicine. Next day, 9 July, he was well enough to mount his horse, and insisted on doing so. Behind his seizure was something more difficult to deal with than the military mishaps which Eugene was right in thinking were of secondary importance.

There had been letters from England, from Sarah, from the Queen which reminded him that he might win battle after battle and yet have it all undone by some tiff in the Bedchamber. Marlborough felt the ground moving under his feet... He spent the night of 10 July sleeping in the open with the troops at Lessine, fifteen miles from Oudenarde. By that time he knew that a major battle was at hand. He also knew that Sarah had not simply lost the Queen's love but had earned her antipathy. That was abundantly clear. The friendship between the two women had been the small, sure point on which was poised the whole delicate structure of English politics. And now it was no more.

Cadogan, riding ahead with the vanguard, had at nine o'clock on the morning of 12 July reached the hills above the marshes of the Scheldt at Oudenarde. There he intended to throw pontoon bridges across the stream for the main army. Just then, six miles to the north, he was amazed to see the French army which at that moment was crossing parallel to him. At once he dispatched a courier at the gallop. An hour later the news startled Marlborough. He, with Eugene, and twenty squadrons of Prussian cavalry, galloped to the spot. By the time they arrived, Cadogan had laid five pontoon bridges over the Scheldt. His troops – British infantry and Hanoverian dragoons – were posted on the other side to defend the crossing.

The French were surprisingly dilatory in attacking Cadogan's bridge-head. First, they were incredulous at the speed of the Allied advance. They had some reason to be. Two days before Marlborough had been at Asshe, fifty miles away. Then Vendôme and the royal Duc de Bourgogne, who was the nominal commander-in-chief, disagreed on what should be done. The two men were hardly on speaking terms. Bourgogne, a pious prince who loved his wife (who loved the Prince de Conti), had no liking for the war. He and Vendôme, disagreeing, failed to throw Cadogan's men back into the river. Nor did they prepare their defensive front on a strong natural position which existed four miles north of Oudenarde. They hesitated. When Marlborough and Eugene arrived, the two generals rode across the river with the Prussian horse.

The rest of the international army they commanded marched to the scene with extraordinary speed and enthusiasm. Men who had been detailed to guard the wagons deserted their posts in order to join the columns that were going to fight. Coaches belonging to notables were getting in the way. They were tumbled off the road without ceremony. In the end, infantry battalions were arriving at the double. This was no case of reluctant men being hounded to the slaughter. In his own way, Blackader of the Cameronians shared in the exuberance of the troops: "My thoughts were much on the 103rd Psalm, which I sang frequently in my heart." It was going to be a soldiers' battle. And the soldiers belonging to half a dozen nations were eager to get at the French who, in their opinion, had won Ghent and Bruges by fraud. As each unit hurried over the bridges, Marlborough and Eugene assigned it to its post in the line of battle.

At three o'clock the battle started. Cadogan sent in sixteen battalions and eight squadrons against the little village of Eyne, a mile from Oudenarde, which was held by four Swiss battalions, three miles in front of the French vanguard. Without much ado, the Swiss threw down their arms, all but one battalion who were summarily dealt with by Hanoverian dragoons advancing on the left under the leadership of General Rantzau. Then, in front of him, Rantzau was aware of three battalions who had been on their way to help their comrades and who now hesitated in dismay, broke and fled. The eight victorious Hanoverian squadrons now saw twelve squadrons of French cavalry trotting across their front. The chance was too good to miss. Without a moment's hesitation, Rantzau led his troops in a charge which broke the French. Prince George of Hanover, the future George II of England, had his horse killed under him in the fighting. Then, bringing in prisoners, standards, kettledrums as visible witnesses of his success, Rantzau trotted back to the main forces of the Allied army, which was coming up fast over the bridge. Eugene rode up to have a look at the forward position; he was in the highest of spirits, infected, if he needed to be infected, by the bravura of the opening battle.

Lieutenant Colonel
John Blackader
(*Radio Times Hulton Picture Library*)

Marshal de Villars
(*Mary Evans Picture Library*)

The Battle of Malplaquet (*British Library*)

John Campbell,
2nd Duke of Argyll
(*National Portrait Gallery*)

William, 1st Earl Cadogan
(*National Portrait Gallery*)

Queen Anne
(*Mary Evans Picture Library*)

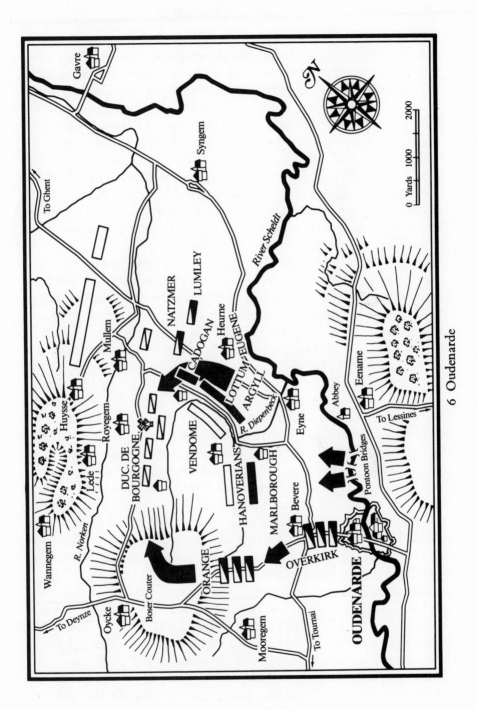

To Ghent

Gavre

Syngem

River Scheldt

N

0 Yards 1000 2000

LUMLEY

NATZMER

Heurne

CADOGAN

LOTTUM-EUGENE

Mullem

ARGYLL

R. Diepenbeeck

Huysse

Royegem

R. Norken

Lede

VENDOME

Eename

Eyne

Abbey

To Lessines

Wannegem

DUC. DE
BOURGOGNE

HANOVERIANS

MARLBOROUGH

Bevere

Pontoon Bridges

To Deynze

Oycke

Boser Couter

ORANGE

OVERKIRK

OUDENARDE

Mooregem

To Tournai

6 Oudenarde

213

The clash of the two main armies had still to come. It broke out, not as a single collision, but as a series of eruptions spreading over an ever wider front. The generals were in the heart of the battle, Argyll fighting at the head of the Buffs, Eugene overlooking the battle on the right wing where the British infantry was fighting. Marlborough, at one moment, was leading freshly arrived Dutch and Germans against a threatening French envelopment, at the next, he was pulling a Dutch brigade out of the fighting on the left wing to bring help to the right. On the other side, Vendôme, marshal of France though he was, was in the bloody mêlée wielding a pike against the Prussian infantry. There could be no question of carefully designed tactical moves in this battle. It was a matter of whose mental and physical reactions were quicker, and who was luckier in his responses to the changing emergency of the struggle.

About five that afternoon, a ferocious infantry battle was raging round the village of Gröenwald, which lay twelve hundred yards north of Eyne where the first exchanges had occurred. Vendôme sent a message to the Duc de Bourgogne to bring his left wing into the fight at that point. But the Duc was told that the ground there was boggy, so he sent a courier to tell Vendôme he would not be co-operating. The courier was killed on the way. By this time, Argyll was bringing twenty British battalions into action on Cadogan's left. But first Gröenwald was lost to the French and then Argyll was outflanked by a French attack. Lottum brought in twenty battalions to save Argyll's flank and, when this force was sent by Marlborough to take the weight off Eugene, who was fighting desperately on the right, Hanoverians and Hessians came in to fill their place. By this time, Field-Marshal Overkirk was riding over the stone bridges at Oudenarde with 20,000 Dutchmen, horse and foot. Not coming as quickly as he could have wished, for the pontoon bridges had collapsed and the stone bridges were narrow. But would his arrival be accomplished quickly enough to make possible the large enveloping movement that, in the turmoil of the battle, Marlborough was hoping for? The light was beginning to fade.

Meanwhile, on the right wing, the Prussian gendarmes had been launched in a wild charge. After overcoming the French cavalry, they had run into infantry firing from behind hedges. Badly shaken by this hail of musketry, the Prussians were charged by the Maison du Roi and put to rout, having lost three-quarters of their strength. But by this time, the Dutch, supported by Danish cavalry, were closing in on the left. The last phase of the battle was beginning. Bourgogne's brother, the Duc de Berri, and the British prince who was known as the Chevalier de St George, watched from a windmill. They saw the Dutch streaming down the hillside towards them. More alarming still, they saw the Maison du Roi about turn to fend off the new danger. They waited to see no more. Within minutes, they had mounted in reasonable alarm and were hurrying to the other wing, where they ran into their own infantry retreating before Cadogan's. By this time, darkness was falling. It was time for Princes of the Blood to take no more risks.

Soon Overkirk's men were firing into Cadogan's. The long loop thrown round the French had become a noose. It was time to stop the fighting. Marlborough ordered a cease fire. Eugene incited the Huguenot soldiers in the Allied ranks to call out in French so as to lure bewildered stragglers into captivity: "A moi, Roussillon!" Bourgogne decided that it was time to leave the field and retreat to Ghent. Vendôme, who had fought like a man and lost control of the battle, agreed with death in his heart. The Maison du Roi cut a way out through the encircling Dutch.

And so, in confusion, ended the famous battle of Oudenarde at a time when a third of the French army had not been given the chance to exchange blows with their enemies and when the rearguard of the Allies was still marching across the bridges over the Scheldt. Marlborough, the sick man of two days before, spent the night in the saddle in the pouring rain. Next day, he sent Lord Stair to London with a letter which gave Godolphin the good news: he had risked a battle in unfavourable circumstances only because he thought that the Queen's interest demanded a victory; he had won the victory. The outcome had been that the enemy's infantry had suffered a blow which would put them out of the fight for the rest of the year. While the Allies had lost 3,000 killed and wounded ("I thank God the English suffered less than any of the other troops"), the French lost 6,000 and another 9,000 men in prisoners. And, as it happened, the Allied losses were speedily made up from prisoners belonging to mercenary regiments who took the opportunity to change their allegiance. It was, as a French diplomat said, a "fatal result of the jealousy between courtiers of a young prince and the general who commanded the army under his orders".[1] Hearing the bad news from Flanders, Louis complained irritably at the dinner table about all the dishes that were offered to him.*

By dinner that night, Marlborough, in conversation with the French General Biron, who had been captured during the fighting, asked for news

---

* Report of "Marlborough's Spy", Blenheim MSS, DI 17b.

of the Prince of Wales, the Jacobite Pretender who had been with the Duc de Bourgogne. When he was told that the "Chevalier de St George", who had been threatening to invade Scotland a few months before, had behaved well in the battle, Marlborough was delighted. He was "keenly interested in this young man" whose father had been his first patron and who might yet sit on the British throne. Who could say? The Queen's health was precarious. The parties were confused.

When the Queen heard the news of Oudenarde at Windsor, she said, "Oh Lord, when will all this dreadful bloodshed cease?" It was a human, womanly reaction to the battle. And it expressed instinctively and surely the mood of the nation. About the same time, Robert Harley was writing to a friend, "Everything is run out of breath. The mines are worked out." After six years, Britain was growing tired of the war. One of Harley's correspondents witnessed the Royal procession to the thanksgiving service at St Paul's and saw "very few people in the windows and balconies". More remarkable was the scene on the steps of the Cathedral between the Queen and Sarah. The Duchess had noticed with indignation that Anne was not wearing the jewels which she, as Mistress of the Robes, had laid out for her. Indeed, the Queen was not wearing any jewels at all. At the top of the steps, the Queen said something angrily. Sarah, interrupting, told her to be silent. The astonished bystanders could only guess what had gone before. Mrs Masham, who had persuaded the Queen not to wear the jewels, had acted effectively to widen the breach between the two women. But, in truth, Sarah needed help from nobody in damaging her own cause. The day after Oudenarde, Marlborough had scribbled a note to his wife in which he thanked God for "making me the instrument of so much happiness to the Queen *if she will please to make use of it*". Sarah passed the note on to the Queen . . . The Bishop of St Asaph, who preached the sermon that day, said that Marlborough "was crowned with fresh laurels every year because they wither faster in our unkindly climate than elsewhere". The climate was to grow more unkindly still. Meanwhile, Sarah was involved in another kind of battle. After a prolonged squabble with the Commissioner of Taxes at Windsor, she was at last persuaded that it would be wise to pay a rate demand of £170 on her land there.[2]

On 28 October, two months after the service at St Paul's, the Queen's husband, the fat, stupid man whom she loved, died at Windsor. Sarah rushed to the widow's side, fussing over her and keeping Mrs Masham away. George of Denmark had not been a person of much consequence, but he had in general been a moderating influence on the Queen's political views. Grief strengthened Anne's drift towards religion.

The question was: now that the Grand Army of King Louis had been knocked out, what was to be done? On, on to Paris! thought Marlborough. Lord Orkney was sure. But Eugene shook his head. If they marched on to Paris, they would leave two French armies, Vendôme's and Berwick's, in their rear and though Vendôme's was badly shaken, Berwick's was intact. If these two united – and there was admittedly seventy miles between them – they would command an army of 100,000 strong. Besides, a French garrison of 15,000 under Marshal Boufflers held Lille, thought to be the strongest fortress in Europe. To advance on Paris an army would require to by-pass Lille, which plainly would involve risks. In detail, Marlborough's proposal was that a British force, then encamped in the Isle of Wight, should be brought over escorted by the fleet and seize Abbeville, which would then become a new base of operations in France. All the necessary stores and guns for the armies would be shipped along the coast from Holland – and Marlborough and Eugene with a combined army of 100,000 men would march on Paris, by-passing the frontier fortresses, supplying themselves from the new base and, as seemed certain, relieving Holland of the threat from Vendôme and Berwick. These generals would be summoned by the King to the defence of the capital. And the Allies would have a head start on them.

It was an attractive project, far-reaching and imaginative, like the idea he had cherished at one time of crossing the Alps, like the "Great Design" against Toulon, like the march to the Danube itself. It was a typical product of Marlborough's strategic genius – and of his longing to escape from the cramped war-zone in the Low Countries. Attractive, but – it alarmed Eugene. He was a land animal. His sole experience of combined operations, the unfortunate Toulon expedition, had given him an acute distrust of the sea. He would have nothing to do with the project. The Dutch agreed with him. But what was the alternative? There was a prolonged Council of War in the Governor of Oudenarde's house. There, Eugene prevailed, as he was bound to do. If he, the most audacious general in Europe, thought that the Paris project was too risky, it was not for others to insist on it. Instead, Lille should be besieged. It was the first and strongest fortress on French soil. It was a rich and important city whose merchants financed most of the Dunkirk privateers who were seizing so many Allied merchant ships – 1,600 before the war was ended.

Eugene would command the operations against it, while Marlborough commanded the army which was to beat off the French attempts to relieve the city. And so it was.

Sixteen thousand draught horses were assembled from owners who knew that if they failed to hand over the animals their houses would be burnt down. The horses were used to bring a hundred siege guns, sixty mortars and thousands of wagons over the seventy miles of road between Brussels and Lille. It was an operation of war on a scale commensurate with the march to the Danube. It was even more hazardous. For the vast convoy stretched over fifteen miles of road and could move no faster than the slowest draught horse tugging at the traces. Twenty miles north of the route it would follow was Vendôme at Ghent, with an army of 80,000 still licking its wounds after the Oudenarde disaster: twenty miles to the south-west, at Douai, was Berwick with 20,000. The convoy set out on 6 August and six days later was in Menin, a fortress in Allied hands. The convoy was guarded by Eugene on the one hand and the Prince of Hesse-Cassel on the other. Marlborough was ready to deal with Vendôme if he showed any sign of intervening. But Vendôme stayed behind the canals that linked Ghent to Bruges, convinced that while he had an army in being Marlborough and Eugene would think twice about an advance on Paris. On 13 August, Lille was completely surrounded by the Allied armies and the most important siege of the eighteenth century had begun. Marlborough wrote to Godolphin: "This day Lille is invested; I pray God to bless the undertaking. What I most fear is the want of powder and ball."

By 5 September, Vendôme and Berwick, carrying out peremptory orders from the King, appeared to the south of the city. They had 100,000 men against Marlborough's 80,000. But the French commanders could not make up their minds what to do and, in the end, Bourgogne, Berwick and Vendôme all sent letters to Versailles asking advice. Attack! Louis replied. While these consultations went on, the assault on the great fortress began. On the north side of the city, fourteen thousand men leapt from their trenches and moved forward. The hostile musket fire was heavy. Four mines exploded under their feet. The engineers who were to prepare the way for the second phase were killed to a man and the labourers who were to work under the engineers fled in the darkness. By the time the attack had ground to a halt, the Allied army had lost as many men as at Oudenarde. A few miles away, on the other side of the city, Marlborough awaited Vendôme's attack. He had a fever and his nerves were in a bad state, with him the normal premonitions of a major battle. It did not seem far off.

Louis sent his War Minister, Chamillart, from Versailles to urge his generals to fight. Chamillart saw how matters were and gave his vote for retreat. Only Vendôme was left in favour of attack. The French army sent to raise the siege withdrew. Then, on 21 September, Eugene was hit on the head by a spent musket ball in hand-to-hand fighting; he suffered a severe concussion. Next morning, Marlborough took over the tiresome business of bringing Lille to capitulate. By this time, both the city and its besiegers were desperately short of ammunition. In a matter of days, Boufflers must surrender. Then the Chevalier de Luxembourg set out from Douai with 2,000 dragoons each carrying a sixty-pound bag of gunpowder. They bluffed and bribed their way past the Allied sentries until an officer, more suspicious than the rest, went forward to examine them. Baron Sandreski kept him talking while the squadrons trotted past until at last the sentries realized what was happening and opened fire. After that there was a mad gallop for the city. Powder bags exploded, but sixty thousand pounds of gunpowder reached Boufflers.

On that day, Marlborough, almost dead with fatigue and anxiety, was awaiting the arrival of a convoy of munitions from Ostend. If it failed to get through, the siege must be abandoned. Marlborough had visited the dumps and, to his horror, had found they contained ammunition for no more than four days' fighting. Well aware of the gravity of the crisis, Vendôme sent 22,000 men to intercept the precious convoy. Marlborough countered by reinforcing the convoy guard with twenty battalions under General Webb. Later – too late as it proved – he sent Cadogan with cavalry. By that time Webb had fought and defeated the French at Wynendael in a gap between two woods. The convoy got through with 250,000 pounds of powder. Had Webb failed to protect it, the siege would have been called off next day. The affair had one unfortunate outcome. Webb's name was omitted from the first official account published in the *Gazette*: the credit was given to Cadogan. Marlborough did what he could to remedy the injustice, which was none of his making. But Webb was a Tory, indeed a Jacobite, and the Tory propagandists seized on what they insisted was an instance of party spite. Wynendael, however, did not end the supply battle. Vendôme flooded the country round Ostend; the besieging army was cut off from the coast by a ten-mile stretch of water. The soldiers were now short of bread as well as gunpowder. By mid-October, Marlborough's foraging parties, with orders to "play the devil", were scouring the French countryside in search of food. Boats brought supplies from Ostend; wagons with extra-high wheels brought munitions along roads that were feet under water. The French armed shallow-draught galleys to interrupt this traffic. The Allies replied in the same way. And all the time the floods were spreading to the batteries bombarding Lille and were creeping closer to the city. In a strange kind of war, the besiegers were themselves besieged. And the army of the first maritime power was cut off from the sea.

On 22 October, Boufflers offered to surrender the city on terms: his sick and wounded should be taken to Douai; he was to be allowed three days to withdraw to the citadel, where, in fact, he held out until 9 December. By the end of the year, Marlborough's troops had crossed the Scheldt and Ghent and Bruges were once more in Allied hands. "The campaign is now ended to my own heart's desire." The Duke, shivering in his lodgings, was confident that an honourable peace was now assured: he wrote to Godolphin "and as the hand of the Almighty is visible to this whole matter, I hope her Majesty will think it due to Him to return public thanks." It was unlikely that her Majesty would.

While the siege of Lille was dragging on, Marlborough began an interesting correspondence with his nephew, Arabella's son, the Duke of Berwick. Had not the time come to talk about peace? France was in a desperate state: she had lost three great battles; she was about to lose a fortress which had as much prestige as military value. Winter was coming on, at first ominous and then terrible. Marlborough, who opened the exchanges, assured Berwick that he was in favour of peace, remembering the "proof of goodwill" promised two years before by the Marquis d'Alègre. This "proof" was, in fact, the bribe of two million livres (£150,000) which the Marquis had offered in the name of King Louis. Marlborough had turned the proposal down at the time, thinking that the terms offered to Britain were not good enough. But now matters might be different. France might be ready to concede a peace more favourable to Britain. Certainly Britain's position was one of extraordinary strength.

The Whig government which had come into power seemed determined to prosecute the war and to be content that Godolphin and Marlborough should remain at their offices. The Queen might be discontented, but her grumbles were not heard beyond the little circle of Mrs Masham. The country might be bored with the war but Parliament had cheerfully voted to increase the army by ten thousand men and had sent a deputation to Flanders to congratulate the victorious general. Taxes might be high but the government's credit was good: in a few hours a huge Bank of England loan at 6 per cent was taken up. "The like I believe was never known in any country," as Sunderland said to Marlborough, his father-in-law. To an Austrian observer,* accustomed to the penury and confusion of Vienna, the situation in London was unbelievable: such wealth pouring into the coffers of the state, apparently inexhaustible, and all based on paper money and the punctual payment of the interest! It was indeed a mystery, so little were the workings of the credit system understood in those early days of the financial revolution. Not everybody thought that its benefits were unmixed:

"Blest paper credit! Last and best supply!
That lends corruption lighter wings to fly."[3]

But if, on the surface, all seemed smiling, Marlborough knew that there were weaknesses. He was all the more inclined to be sceptical because he, a Tory of the Tories, son of a man who had been wounded and ruined fighting for King Charles, was now dependent on a Whig majority in the House of Commons which a new election might at any moment destroy. When they fell, how much would be swept away with them? And there was always, most unpredictable element of all, the widowed Queen. Poor Anne, she had much to bear. The Tories tormented her by proposing to bring over the Electress of Hanover, whom she had never met and whom she hated from the bottom of her heart. The Whigs went further. With a lack of ordinary decency which is hard to credit, they passed an address in both Houses of Parliament urging the Queen to find a new husband. This, to a sick woman of forty-five, who had already had seventeen miscarriages and one son who had died! The grimy soil of party politics does not favour the growth of good manners. There was also the problem of finding recruits for the army, although the prospect of a hard winter might make the recruiting officers' task easier than it had been. "In this hard winter in all probability they [the recruiting officers] may get more men in a day than in a week hereafter."[4] And so, in fact, it did.

Before the winter was over as many as 1,087 volunteers joined the colours as well as 5,821 "pressed men", i.e. unemployed who could be legally compelled to carry a musket for Queen Anne. But, in all, more than 14,000 men were needed.[5] Parliament had already rejected general

* Philip von Hoffman, Imperial ambassador in London.

conscription, "lest it prejudice chances at the elections". The government was driven back on the old devices. Rogues and vagabonds were pulled in by the justices. The prisons, a small but useful source of soldiers, were scoured. On the other hand, desertion was rife. Indeed one writer[6] maintained that, at any time, there were more deserters than soldiers in Britain, this in spite of the severe punishment for the offence – death by the firing squad or, more mildly, a thousand lashes.

It was, however, the precarious political situation rather than any social or military factor that made Marlborough play with the notion of peace. Before the siege of Lille was over, Louis had increased his offer to four million livres – which was to be paid to Marlborough if the Englishman obtained for his grandson, Philip de Bourbon, Naples and Sicily as the price of quitting the Spanish throne. Four million livres! Three hundred thousand pounds! It was not a proposition to be lightly turned down. At the same time he was soon aware, through his intelligence service, that the French were whispering peace to the Dutch. And the Austrian prince who was nominally King of Spain was renewing the offer to Marlborough of the vice-royalty of the Netherlands. Nothing could be more embarrassing to him because there was no post in the world he coveted more. And nothing would have more effectively ruined his standing with the Dutch, who looked on the Netherlands as theirs. It would not be enough for him to reject the offer, which he had sulkily rejected once before. He proposed that Prince Eugene should become the Viceroy. Eugene was popular with Dutch and Belgians. He would like to be a Viceroy. It was an excellent idea, killed in Vienna.

At the end of 1708, then, while the great antagonists assembled their armies for a new campaign in Flanders, on a vaster scale than anything that had gone before – a hundred and fifty thousand men a side – the diplomats were busy. The minimum desiderata were plain enough. The Dutch wanted their Barrier – a zone of fortresses in the Netherlands manned by Dutch garrisons. The Emperor wanted Spain for the Hapsburg family. The British wanted some trade advantages, a recognition of the Protestant succession by the powers and the expulsion of the Stuart Pretender from France. And Louis wanted to save what he could from the wreckage of his hopes. Very soon his gloom had deepened into something like despair.

XX

The Great Cold

"Cette gloire qui endurçit votre coeur, vous est plus chère que la justice.
Vous vivez comme ayant un bandeau fatal sur les yeux."
Fénélon to Louis XIV, 1694

Men are dying of hunger to the sound of Te Deums.
Voltaire

"The cold," wrote Liselotte, Duchess of Orléans to her aunt, Sophie, Electress of Hanover, "is so grim that words fail me. I am sitting in front of a roaring fire; there is a screen in front of the door, my neck is wrapped in sables and my feet are in a bearskin sack but, all the same, I am trembling with cold."[1] The wine was frozen in the bottles; so was the ink. After three sentries on guard at Versailles had died of cold, the King ordered that the guard should be changed every quarter of an hour.* All the Paris shops were shut for five days. It was 10 January 1709. The catastrophic winter of 1709 had gripped Europe four days earlier. Probably the man who was least surprised by the thing was Pastor Matias Foss, priest of a mountain parish in Western Norway. For years he had been watching how the glacier called Nygårdsbreen had been advancing relentlessly into the valley. The climate of Norway was getting colder, the winters were becoming more severe. Snowfall was heavier. Ice was spreading.[2] And what was true of one Norwegian parish would in due course be true of Europe generally.

So the rich shivered; the poor perished. Liselotte reported from Versailles that every morning, people were found dead of cold. Partridges were picked up frozen in the fields. Plays and lawsuits stopped. Robert Walpole told Marlborough that he had been driven out of Houghton "by the severest weather and snow I can remember". He arrived shivering at his town house.[3] The Kentish mail was lost in the snow. Jonathan Swift ate gingerbread in a booth by a fire on the Thames. The river was frozen

* *Blenheim MSS, DI – 17.*

over. So were the Rhône and the Tagus and the canals in Venice. Masses of ice were seen in the English Channel. Most of the trees in the Petites Landes died, the principal European sources of turpentine and resin for the English and Dutch fleets. "All the Médoc, Graves, Sauternes are lost. The King's revenues will suffer extremely. I understand all the vines of France beyond the Loire are frozen." Thus, the spy, reporting from Bordeaux in January.* Worse was to come.

After a month, with no sign of the cold abating, it was known that the Ice Age of 1709 was going to have an even grimmer successor. The vines had been destroyed. The seed corn had been killed in the ground. Famine was on the way. The frost began to ease off in March but already it had done its work. "Il faut une paix générale" – it was the only hope, wrote the spy on 18 April. At that time, he was in Normandy. By May, Liselotte was reporting, "they say that little children are devouring each other . . . perhaps they will send all the extra mouths away, including me."4 Peasants, having eaten the last raw turnip, poured into the towns, where they found nothing to eat. The Venetian ambassador in Paris feared that soon he would not be safe in his own house.

Dogs ate corpses in the streets. The famished ate one another. And so it lasted all through that terrible summer and into autumn. "As soon as you leave the house," wrote Liselotte in October, "you are followed by the poor, black with hunger." Famine had an ally in its war on the French. While King Louis sent his gold plate to the Mint and Liselotte stoically ate off silver dishes instead of gold, so that the armies might be equipped and fed, the English navy scoured the seas in search of any grain ship that might be heading for a French port. Meanwhile, in the wastes of Russia, that extraordinary winter was freezing the heart out of the Swedish army waiting to try conclusions with Peter the Great.

In France, hunger proved to be a two-edged weapon. It goaded the peasants to the edge of rebellion and drove the able-bodied among them into the army where, at least, they would have something to eat. "They follow the bread-wagons," said the King. Marlborough, for similar reasons, thought that the gaps in his regiments would be easier to fill than usual. He was planning to put 120,000 men into the field for the new campaign. Scraping the barrel, Louis was bent on surpassing that figure. And, very soon, it was apparent that the spirit of the new French army would match its numbers. By a fatal breath, the diplomacy of the Allies blew new life into France's passion for the war.

* *Blenheim MSS*, DI – 4a.

At this moment of pause, it seemed that, if the war broke out again, it would have a new and different aspect. It was changing as the mood of the British people was changing, a fact of which they were not yet aware. The truth was that they had not yet found themselves. Indeed, with the ink on the Scots Treaty still scarcely dry, they could hardly be called British at all.

They were a people of poets and mathematicians, traders and improvers, pirates who had turned respectable, fighters who had no enthusiasm for war until they found inspiration under Marlborough. They could be as unscrupulous as the Venetians, whom they despised. But, then, they despised most foreigners, whose ideas, however, they were quick to borrow. Their religion was a habit rather than a passion. Politically, they were disappointing. Their sole brilliant dynasty had been Welsh; their stupidest, Scottish. At one time, golden opportunities had been within their grasp and they had frittered them away. Their single experiment with republicanism had left them with a deep antipathy to doctrinaire politics. Yet their political thinkers had wafted the seeds of revolution on the winds of the world. Their talent, although this was something they still did not realize, was to have the best of both worlds: to be a monarchy with an amenable king; to be democrats with an aristocracy they could look up to but need not respect; to be Protestant and Catholic. It was a part of this duality of their nature that they conceded leadership in Europe to France while continuing to think of themselves as superior to the French. In the same perverse way, they recognized in the Dutch the nearest thing to themselves in race, temperament and talent (painting taking the place of poetry), while disliking the Dutch more than most other nations. On the other hand, they had no hesitation in taking business ideas from Dutch Jews, Huguenot Frenchmen and even, of all unlikely sources, from a Scotsman named Paterson. Much good it did him; like his compatriot and fellow-ideologue, John Law, he died in poverty. But his Bank went marching on.

Ahead of this nation of hard-boiled businessmen lay the most unlikely of destinies: they were about to become a world-spanning empire. Needless to say, this empire, when it came into being, would be as different as can be imagined from earlier institutions bearing the name. An empire without an emperor, without an imperial ethos, without much imperial pride. It was another example of the British gift for being two things at once. However, the fact remains that, in this first decade of the eighteenth century, the British, like it or not, were about to be drawn into playing a wider role in the world and that one of the men who was to enlarge their field of vision was John Churchill, a gentleman by birth, a duke by his own efforts and – somewhat to the dismay of his fellow-countrymen – a soldier of genius. A man not entirely to be trusted. But that was something that did not surprise many and which shocked even fewer.

The British, as they must begin to be called, did not expect too much of their public men: ambition, a love of power, a touch of ruthlessness, industry – but honesty, fidelity to principle? Yes. But not to excess. If the state was to be efficiently governed, if its fleets and armies were to be led with skill, the executant must, of course, be adequately rewarded in one form or another, in fame which lasts, power that fades, or fortune which endures but a lifetime. Just how, and how much, reward should be given was a matter for the individual to decide. It was natural that Marlborough should want a dukedom. What Englishman did not? Reasonable that, having won the battle, he should build the palace, whatever might be thought of its architecture, and thus give employment to fifteen hundred honest craftsmen, Whigs to a man. The British understood the soldier with the cold blue eyes and the composed expression in which there was already the hint of a jowl. Not that he was popular, or would have wanted to be. Even among his officers, who had the best of reasons to admire his ability, his aloofness excluded warmth. If he fell – *when* he fell – there would be tears, but they would be shed not so much for the man as for the prospect of half-pay.

It is probable but not certain that Marlborough was unaware of the part he was playing in the development of his people. He was, however, very much a man of his time, and the time was one of revolution – the revolution which, in two generations, transformed Britain into a great commercial power, the leading capitalist state. Marlborough not only won the battles of Blenheim and Ramillies but he invested his money so prudently that he died a millionaire. (It need hardly be said that Sarah was doing even better.) He was, in other words, immersed in his time; as much at home in the City as at his headquarters, and better informed than most financiers about the shifts of power on the Continent which would influence a wise man in laying out his money.

Marlborough and money. The two are indissolubly and, so far as the man's reputation is concerned, deplorably associated. He is accused of being mean and close-fisted, of being inordinately acquisitive. It was one of the factors that stood between him and popularity. It is hard for a frugal millionaire to be loved. Finally, he is charged with being downright dishonest. What is the truth? First, that he was born poor and died very rich, and that his widow, thought to be even more unblushingly extortionate than he, died the richest woman in England. And probably the unhappiest? To think so would no doubt gratify our moral feelings, our disposition to find a balance in human affairs. Great triumphs must be followed by great retributions, otherwise the artistic picture we have formed of man's destiny is distorted. In fact, however, there is no reason to think that, in old age, Sarah was any more miserable than any woman who has reached the age of eighty-four and has her due share of the physical burdens of the years. By then, the young teenager had become an old crone.

Marlborough and money. By the time of the Revolution he had a capital of £70,000, according to his wife. This was apparently acquired by the sale of places in the army. He invested what he could spare of the money, which was probably quite a lot. And he took good advice on his finances, above all from his banker friend, Sir Harry Furnese (a "self-made" man, son of a bankrupt grocer), who had excellent reason to serve him well. Furnese, a presence in the City, a power at the Kit-Cat Club, was one of the brokers through whom army contracts were placed. During the war, Marlborough's salary exceeded £50,000 a year; he lived abroad most of the time at the public expense. By 1704, he was rich enough to use his personal credit with the German bankers to obtain a loan of 100,000 crowns for the Emperor. A few weeks later, his name was second on the list of subscribers to a London loan for Prince Eugene. When his political enemies were struggling desperately to bring him down, they found that one of the most damaging weapons against his reputation was the arrangement by which he obtained $2\frac{1}{2}$ per cent of the money for the foreign contingents to be used for his secret service, and therefore not to be accounted for. At any time, he had a great deal of money in the bank in London, Amsterdam or elsewhere. Thus, when he was trying to persuade the King of Prussia to increase the number of his troops, money from the secret fund was used – enough to obtain the services of 6,200 soldiers.

To make a great deal of money easily, it was not necessary to steal. One needed to be an official in a position where decisions were taken or delayed or became known. Decisions which would influence the movement of money. Also, one needed access to capital. In Marlborough's private office – as it would now be called – Cadogan, his Chief-of-Staff, was in close touch with Brydges, the Paymaster-General. One was likely to know about forthcoming military moves; the other's task was to supply the regimental paymasters with foreign coin to pay the troops. Two avenues of gain were open. For example, by means of a straight bet about the town next to be besieged. In 1707, Brydges bet £100 that Charleroi would be besieged, and stood to win £3,000. On that occasion he lost. The attack on Toulon was the subject of another speculation. Swift said[5] that the plan to take the town was betrayed by the "creatures of a certain great man" (Godolphin?) so that it seemed there was not only one group of gamblers in the field. There was, however, a steadier source of income open to the astute.

On the Continent, there were varying rates of exchange. The pound sterling was, usually, worth 4 per cent more in Liège or Maastricht than in Amsterdam. In consequence, it was possible to change English money into foreign coin at one rate and pay the troops at a lower rate, pocketing the difference. On one occasion, Cadogan persuaded Brigadier Palmes to take money to pay his regiment at the same rate as in the previous year. Then Cadogan borrowed 6,000 louis d'or from Jewish moneylenders at 9.10 guilders and charged the troops 9.15 guilders. In this way, he said, "we'll turn fifteen or sixteen thousands at two per cent clear of all charges." Later he reported a profit of 6,000 guilders (about £600) on an outlay of £20,000. The rate of profit was kept low so as to avoid alarming the accounting authorities in Whitehall. And, as an additional precaution, the borrowed funds passed through Mrs Cadogan's account. In the year of Oudenarde, Cadogan and Brydges did well: they had cleared 67,000 guilders so that, after the necessary deductions to "co-operative" officials, they were able to invest £6,000 in Bank stock. It seemed, too, that the future would be even rosier, for after Oudenarde Cadogan obtained from the Captain-General an order which gave wide discretionary powers to Cartwright, the deputy paymaster. When peace negotiations began, new opportunities for speculation came. Cardonnel, Marlborough's secretary, was alert to pass on to Brydges the latest inside information about the diplomatic moves. There were, of course, ups and downs, but in the end Brydges, who had started with nothing, made a great fortune, £700,000 or thereabouts,* enough to support him as the Duke of Chandos.[6] Marlborough's opportunities were greater.

"I have loved glory too much," Louis confessed on his deathbed. Now,

---

* About seven million at today's rates.

in the spring of 1709, glory had betrayed her adorer. Frost. Famine. Three great battles lost. Lille, "finest and fairest citadel in the Kingdom", surrendered. Bruges and Ghent, gone. Pillaging hussars roaming the villages of Artois. From the Mediterranean, no comfort; the English fleet established in Minorca. Crushed by an avalanche of disasters, the King sued for peace. Peace at any price? Almost.

The Marquis de Torcy, his Foreign Minister, half-frozen under his furs, drove through Brussels carrying a passport which bore no name. He was on his way to The Hague to negotiate with the victors. His mission was not quite as hopeless as at first it seemed to be. Between Marlborough and the Dutch there was something less than perfect trust. The Dutch thought that the Englishman still hankered after that glittering prize, the vice-royalty of the Netherlands. Marlborough thought the Dutch should, in any settlement, be denied the possession of Ostend, which the Netherlands would need as an outlet to the sea. Louis, who had at one stage offered the Dutch the whole of the Netherlands, now offered Marlborough two million livres to spare the fortifications of Dunkirk or, alternatively, to leave Strasbourg in French hands, and another two million should he obtain Naples and Sicily for King Philip in compensation for the loss of the Spanish throne if, as seemed inevitable, Philip were to lose it. Marlborough neither accepted nor refused the bribes. The truth was that his influence was not what it had been and that it was doubtful if he could have earned the money even if he had wanted to do so.

The governing factor in the negotiations was, however, the mounting social disaster which, during those spring months, was overtaking France. "If the people caught fire," wrote the spy on 1 March, "you would see within twenty-four hours fifty thousand armed ruffians looting and killing." Two months later, he saw a poster in Paris that made him shudder: "We seek a Ravaillac and the Jesuits have promised us one." Ravaillac was the assassin of Henri IV, the King's grandfather.[*] Torcy carried to Holland from Versailles the memory of his king in tears, crushed, pitiful, willing to give up everything for peace. As the plight of France became more manifest, the Dutch and the Germans raised their price. The wolves were closing in. "France is quite unable to prolong the war," wrote Eugene. "We can obtain everything we ask for." When Marlborough returned from England to The Hague on 18 May, it seemed that indeed it was so. Accordingly, he demanded Newfoundland for England; he heard from Torcy that Louis had reconciled himself to

* *Blenheim MSS, DI – 17b.*

the surrender of Naples and Sicily. Already the King had made known that he was willing to see his grandson, Philip, give up Spain. On 20 May, the Germans put forward their demands. They wanted Strasbourg and Alsace. The Dutch insisted on having Lille as part of their Barrier. All of this Louis was ready to surrender. And there was no question whatever of Naples and Sicily being given to his grandson, Philip, in return for the loss of Spain. The Emperor would not have it. It was over Spain, however, that the greatest trouble arose. Was Louis to be forced to use French troops to drive Philip out of Madrid? Or was Britain to be left to do the job alone? It was not at all a theoretical question. The Spaniards had shown in the plainest possible way that Philip was the king they wanted. He had become a national symbol.

Finally, the Dutch were given the task of drawing up preliminaries to a peace treaty in the form of a memorandum of forty-four articles. The Fourth Article declared that Louis and the princes and states concerned in the treaty should in concert compel Philip to execute it. And the Thirty-Seventh said that the war would go on until the whole Spanish monarchy, i.e. Spain and the Spanish Empire, was "delivered up and yielded to King Charles III", the Hapsburg archduke who was the candidate of Britain and the Empire. In other words, Louis would either be able to prevail on his grandson to step down from the Spanish throne or be bound to go to war to drive him off it. The first was improbable; the second, preposterous. As the Duchess of Orléans said, "The Allied proposals are really too barbaric. I can't think how anyone can have imagined that our King would agree."[7] Marlborough and Eugene, taking the same pessimistic view, began to plan the invasion of Spain as a joint operation by Britain and the Empire which would probably take six months. They both realized how ridiculous it was to expect Louis to make war on his grandson. "If I were in the place of the King of France I should venture the loss of my country much sooner than be obliged to join my troops for the forcing of my grandson." So Marlborough wrote to the Grand Pensionary of Holland on 10 July. Next day he told the Dutchman that Eugene believed it to be impossible for Louis to give up the Spanish monarchy. This was after Torcy had left for Versailles with the memorandum which, in Marlborough's own words, contained the terms on which the Allies insisted.

For what followed, Marlborough has therefore a degree of responsibility which he cannot escape. Admitted that his influence was not what it had been, and that he shrank from entering into controversies with the

Allies to whom he made promises which might seem to be incompatible with one another. (That was one of the reasons he had already insisted that a tame Whig nobleman, Lord Townshend, should carry on the political negotiations.) But he, Marlborough, was the Captain-General who had directed the war so far and was planning its next stage, if there must be one. His authority in Europe was unique. And his position in London was such that unless it were assailed by the Whigs and the Tories together – a highly improbable conjecture – it appeared to be safe. He could have had the two articles amended or omitted. Nobody would have resisted him. Did he, in a moment of carelessness, decide that the risk of a prolonged war, which he plainly envisaged, was one which should be taken, and that there would in the meantime be an opportunity to re-phrase, to tone down, the terms. This seems the most likely and certainly the most creditable explanation. And it is not to be doubted that during those weeks of discussion, Marlborough, because of anxiety and ill-health, was less apt to assert himself than usual. He was disposed to let things drift. That he did not foresee how acute would be the crisis which followed may be assumed. He was sure that, in the end, Louis would agree to everything that mattered. He wrote to Sarah telling her to have ready the sideboard plate and to make sure that Godolphin sent his canopy chair of state for the ceremonial signing of the treaty. Then, with a return to his customary frugality: "I beg you will take care to have it made so that it may serve for part of a bed when I have done with it here." Torcy set off for Paris, calling on Villars and disclosing the terms to him. Understandably, Villars exploded with rage. Torcy arrived at Versailles on 1 July. He was due back at The Hague in three days with the French reply.

In his great chateau the King assembled the princes of his family and the wisest of his counsellors. Together they learnt the terms with horror and brooded over them for two and a half hours. The party in favour of acceptance was evidently strong but the Dauphin, heir to the throne and father of Philip, King of Spain, spoke passionately for rejection. His vehemence carried him far beyond the deference usually shown to the King. Then he strode out of the room, slamming the door behind him. The whole palace was agitated. A few minutes later, Torcy ran after him with the news that, after all, the Council had decided that Philip of Spain was not to be abandoned. An envoy was sent to The Hague without delay carrying the news to the Grand Pensionary. The ultimatum was rejected. No counter-proposals were offered. The war was on! The news was received by the Allies with a consternation nearly as great as that which had greeted the ultimatum at Versailles. In London, stocks fell fourteen points on the day the tidings reached the City.

Marlborough tried and failed to intercept the French envoy on his way back through Brussels. Eugene thought that they should have "explained" the Thirty-Seventh Article and made it easier of acceptance. It was too late. Marlborough insisted to Townshend that they were both bound by their instructions from London, although he said that this would not save him at least from the accusation of having frustrated the peace. In fact, it did not save either of them. But should Marlborough have been saved? Had he not been weak and compliant beyond anything that he should have been in allowing extreme terms to be presented to the French King, terms which in his own opinion no gentleman would accept? With his insight into the springs of human action and his unique, secret knowledge of the state of opinion in the French court, he must have known how great was the danger of a rejection. Known it and measured it. But there was one factor in his thinking at that moment which prevented him from looking at the question with detachment. He was at the head of the biggest army he had ever gathered. He had but to give the word, the drums would beat and the army would move forward to one gigantic, final – surely final – collision with the French. After that, the troops would pour southwards over Picardy to Paris. One last battle and then peace, dictated to the King in the Salle de Glaces. This was the fatal chimera which, reborn every year, had haunted him through battles and sieges. But now, surely, to be realized. One last battle, like the ultimate crest of hill which hides the ocean from the weary traveller! In the fight with him would be his incomparable comrade Eugene, Orkney, who had cornered the French at Blenheim, Argyll, the shifty and jealous Highland chief who hated him but fought ferociously, the warlike young Prince of Orange – too warlike as it proved – his henchman, Cadogan. And, unseen but no less important, he would be riding into battle at the head of £9,000,000 of the British taxpayers' money, half of it screwed out of the Tory squires whose antipathy to the war was growing all the time. Marlborough would have been more than human if he had not been influenced somewhere in the recesses of his mind – influenced perhaps to the extent of not urging restraint as vehemently as he should have done – by thoughts of the ultimate triumph in Paris which he had cherished through the years. In the meantime, the peace was lost.

The peace was lost and the war was dragging on, and on a bigger scale than ever. In another sense, too, it had become a greater war. When

Louis took the decision to reject the Allies' terms, he appealed over the heads of his ministers, courtiers and marshals through the governors of the provinces – to whom? To the provincial gentry who through poverty or disfavour had languished for years out of the Sun King's radiance, to the Huguenots he had persecuted with such diligent and brainless cruelty, to the artisans and shopkeepers whose lives he controlled, above all, to the famished, ragged, over-taxed peasants whom his system had ground into the soil they cultivated – in short, to the people of France. He did not appeal in vain. A grandfather being asked to betray his own grandson! In a people among whom family feeling and family loyalty are intense and particular, every French father and son understood the bitterness of the King's anguish. Understood and responded. In consequence, Marlborough and Eugene had fought, the one with respect the other with hatred, against the armies of a great monarch. Now they would find themselves fighting a great nation. At this moment in history, we are seventy years before the Cannonade of Valmy* but already imagination can detect, in the ardour of the levies of Villars, the fury of the armies of the Republic. Let it be admitted, too, that France was near to revolution that year. The angry, hungry mobs might easily have turned from burning an occasional chateau to tearing down the whole social fabric. Madame de Maintenon, better-informed than most women, saw the danger and kept her fingers crossed. The danger passed. The anger switched from revolution to war.

The old voluptuary of Versailles appealed to his people: "Since the immense concessions I was ready to grant proved useless for the establishment of peace . . ." Marshal Villars was in the meantime putting heart back into a thrice-beaten army and giving purpose and confidence to a desperate people. He was using every means that occurred to good sense and his own buoyant temperament: moving among the men, speaking to them with sympathy, as one soldier to another, listening to their complaints, promising improvements, and ensuring that whoever else in France might go short – and the bread at Versailles that year was grey – they, the nation's fighting men, would have enough to eat. He was a spark of fire running towards the powder of the French spirit. And that powder might be damp but it was drying fast.

* The battle (20 September 1792) in which Dumouriez and Kellermann repelled the army of émigrés and Germans under the Duke of Brunswick.

XXI

The Lord of Hosts at Our Head

"The most deliberate, solemn and well-ordered battle that ever I saw!"
John Blackader

"France is like a hydra which is never more dangerous than when it has been wounded."
Marlborough's Spy, 9 January 1708★

The turning-point has been placed by historians some time in May when news reached Paris that the Spanish plate fleet, laden with the silver of Peru, had come safely into port.[1] Louis had money to buy grain for his people and, first of all, for his army. Bit by bit, with amazing speed when everything is considered, the change was wrought. The officers stopped trading their uniform coats for food. The soldiers straightened their backs and paid more heed to their sergeants. By the time summer had passed into autumn, France had a fighting machine once again. And what to do with it? Louis had no doubt. Fight a battle! Villars had no doubt; engage the enemy on the plain of Lens. The men in the ranks had no doubt: "We ask you for bread. We will do without coats and shirts." And so, while belts were tightened, while horses drooped and died at the picket ropes for lack of forage, Villars' army marched on its way towards the field of Malplaquet.

It suited Marlborough very well: he had the most powerful army that he had ever commanded. More Dutch Guards, five thousand more Prussians, fifteen thousand British, including the veteran regiments that had followed his drums to the Danube five years before: all told, more than a hundred thousand men and, riding at the head of them, the generals he knew.

There was more to Villars, however, than panache and ardour; there was a cool tactical brain and a shrewd awareness of how much he could reasonably ask of a resuscitated army. He prepared forty miles of field

★ *Blenheim MSS, D.I – 16.*

fortifications between Aire and Douai, while Marlborough applied himself to the task of besieging Tournai. Sooner or later, Villars would be tempted out of his entrenchments. Then would be a chance of the battle which Marlborough longed for. Meanwhile, towards the end of August, news reached him which made a momentous and, as it turned out, lasting change in the power structure of Europe. Charles XII had been decisively defeated at Poltava by Tsar Peter with the loss of 114 standards and the silver kettledrum of the Guards. As Marlborough put it, "Constant success for ten years; two hours' mismanagement!" The Swede had taken one risk too many. His magnificent army, shattered in a day, was no longer a potential threat to Vienna, no longer a factor in the calculation of statesmen. Five days later Tournai capitulated. Marlborough moved on to lay siege to Mons, while he kept a sharp eye on Villars, watching for that incautious move which would enable him to bring the French marshal to battle.

In Paris, famished people fought over the carcass of a horse on the Pont Neuf. The Duchess of Orléans was convinced that her enemy, Madame de Maintenon, was buying up food and selling it to the army at a vast profit: "Si on ne mourrait pas de faim, il en faudrait mourir de rire." Thousands of unemployed begged in the streets. The better-off, in alarm, hid their money. Versailles was vibrant with rumours: vast inundations were being prepared on the Flemish frontier, Villars was about to throw up his command, peace was being negotiated in secret. The King, to give an impression of insouciance, went about humming a tune and ostensibly devoted himself to making a new waterfall. Marshal Boufflers, hero of the siege of Lille, was given command of the alerted Paris garrison with orders to crush the rising that was hourly expected. For two days, the city gates were guarded; the musketeers slept in their boots while in the churches the clergy prayed – against some interruptions – that the King's armies should be victorious. Then – as suddenly as it had risen – the panic was over. The troops "stood down". Boufflers saved the Dauphin from attack outside the Opéra by throwing money to the crowd who cried, "Vive le roi et du pain." Then he rode back to report to the King at Marly. All of which – the true, and the not so true, and the merely imaginative – was duly carried to Marlborough by his arch-spy in the King's household. But intelligence is a two-way traffic. On the same day that Marlborough heard about the agitation in Paris, he learnt that the valet of Marshal Tallard, a prisoner of war in England since his defeat at Blenheim, had arrived in Versailles on private business. He had brought the news that in England everyone was clamouring for peace with the same eagerness as France. Peace or a march on Paris!

In the London coffee houses there was indignation that the army was wasting time in dismal sieges in Flanders when the road to Paris was open. The trouble was that the road to Paris was not open. The ground was sodden; an army sleeping in the open would be speedily ravaged by sickness. The French countryside could not supply fodder for the horses. And Villars with his army had still to be dealt with. So while the critics grumbled, the army remained entangled in the web of Vauban's fortress-belt. That summer, at the fall of Tournai, Marlborough's eye fell upon one item in the spoils, the marble bust of Louis XIV on the citadel. He coveted it for his palace. The thirty-ton bust was brought by yacht to the Tower wharf and thence by barge to Abingdon. In the process, the barge was "quite ruined" but the bust to this day stands above the south portico of Blenheim Palace.[2] Marlborough, while waiting to besiege Mons, suspected and soon knew for certain that the King had ordered Villars, who hardly needed the order, to fight a battle. In the first week of September, Marshal Boufflers had left Paris for Flanders, taking his breastplate, sword and pistols with him: when he rode into the camp, Villars offered him the command. Boufflers replied that he had come as a volunteer. The news of his arrival came to Marlborough's ears within hours. He had no doubt of its meaning. Between the armies of Eugene and Marlborough, manoeuvring outside Mons, and the French lay ten miles of country – a belt of woodland, the Wood of Taisnières and the Wood of Lanières, with a mile of open country between them near the village of Malplaquet.

Watched by Allied generals, Villars took possession of the woods. The hope of Marlborough and Eugene seems to have been that he would come out into the open, whereupon they would fall upon him and destroy him. If that was in their minds, they were mistaken. Villars occupied the Malplaquet gap (known at that time as the Aulnois Gap from a village half a mile to the north of it) and put his men to work making field-works stretching from one wood to the other and on the outskirts of the woods themselves. In the woods trees were felled by the hundred and left on the ground with their branches stripped and pointed in the direction of an Allied attack. In line after line, these formidable obstacles lay in wait for the attack. Behind the earthworks and the woods, a dense mass of French cavalry was assembling. Villars was proposing to fight a defensive action in highly favourable conditions.

That morning Marlborough had been writing a letter to Sarah, asking her what progress was being made on the house at Blenheim. Would she taste the fruit on each tree? The buildings, as he knew, had suffered in the severe frost of the previous winter but the damage had now been made good. The great court had been levelled. During August, 157 workmen had brought in Burford stone. At the very moment that Marlborough was preparing to give battle at Malplaquet, the hall and saloon of his palace had been leaded. All told, the Treasury had spent £134,000 on the work, but Blenheim's appetite for money seemed to be inexhaustible. Another matter gave the Duke greater anxiety. Sarah had been upbraiding him because he had not protested more vigorously to the Queen about her unkind behaviour. But, had he done so, what would have happened? he asked. Mrs Masham would have been shown the letter and would have used it somehow to serve her own purposes. At that point in his writing, he was interrupted. There was a clatter of horses outside, a glimpse of wild-looking hussars. Eugene had arrived. Joyfully, Marlborough called for his horse. The time had come to see what Villars was doing. Very soon it was plain. Villars was going to occupy the woods and the ground between them. Perhaps he would press further on towards Mons?

The scattered units of the Allied army must be concentrated. A battle was about to be fought. All through the remainder of that day and the next, the two armies cautiously assembled. In some places, they were so close to one another that they "had frequent and friendly commerce and conferences with one another" until, "each man being called to his post, our commerce was drowned in blood."[3] Gunfire increased in fury and, all the while, the French were strengthening their defences. At an Allied council of war it was decided unanimously to attack. After that, Marlborough continued his letter to Sarah: "Though the fate of Europe may depend on the good or bad success, yet your uneasiness gives me much greater trouble."

At nine o'clock on 11 September, after a preliminary bombardment had been going on for two hours, forty British guns fired a salvo and the battle started. Eighty-five battalions of infantry – the whole force of the right half of the Allied army – swarmed into the Taisnières Wood or assailed the earthworks that barred its fringes. They were Hanoverians, Prussians and Imperialists, with one British brigade under Argyll. Waiting for them in the forest was a French force under Albergotti. It had only a quarter of the Allied strength. But it was supported by the fire of fourteen cannon which were brought up in a hurry to rake, from the flank, the

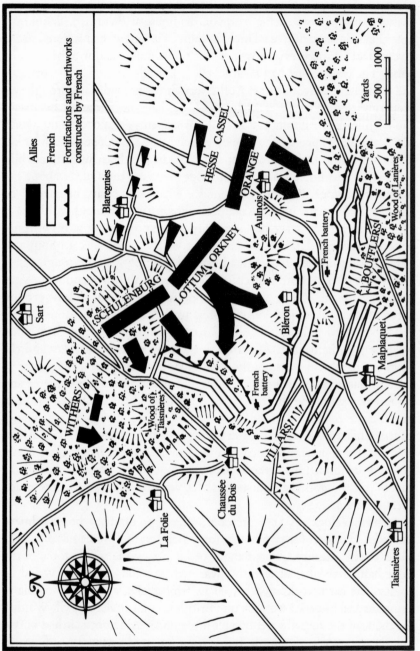

7 Malplaquet

lines of Prussian foot before they entered the wood. As a result the attack faltered until Eugene, who supervised this part of the Allied action, urged a second and a third line into the fight. Among the trees, the French, behind their improvised but effective breastworks, were ferociously resisting. Losses were appalling.

On the other flank, a similar situation had developed. Twenty well-sited field guns enfiladed the Dutch Guards as they surged forward under the young Prince of Orange to storm the earthworks covering the Lanières Wood. This Dutch onslaught, thirty battalions strong, opened half an hour after the German advance on the other flank and was swept by a hail of grapeshot even more devastating. They reached their objective but, by that time, were too few to hold it against the counter-attacks of the crack French regiments. Having lost five thousand men, including five generals, they began to fall back. So, too, did their elite, the professionals of the Scots Brigade under Gustavus Hamilton; they had suffered just as severely as their Dutch comrades. After half an hour of desperate fighting, it was clear that the Allied high command had under-estimated the usefulness of the French defences. The dominant factor in the battle had been the cunning disposition by Villars of his artillery. And the thirteen British battalions, under Orkney, who were held back in the centre of the Allied line to be used when the moment came to deliver the decisive blow, seemed to be too slight a force for that purpose. But the moment of decision was still far off. The Prince of Orange, after having two horses killed under him, snatched up the standard of a wounded general and led his Guards into a second attack.

Meanwhile, the attack on the Taisnières Wood had been renewed with no better fortune. Indeed, so shaken at one point were the troops storming the French outworks that Orkney detached two battalions, Guards and Royal Scots, from the force held back in reserve. These fresh troops were sent through boggy ground to the deadly wood. The French were about to counter-attack on their left flank when Villars became aware that a mass of Dutch cavalry was hovering in the background ready to strike. Thereupon the counter-attack was hastily called off. Orkney's two battalions, moving among the trees, fell in with Argyll's brigade (the Buffs, the King's, Temple's). Here the fighting was of extraordinary savagery. Far away was the polite image of conventional eighteenth-century war. Argyll's men had suffered heavier losses than any other British formation. In return, they reverted to a degree of barbarity which British soldiers do not often display. Meanwhile, further north in the wood, General Withers, who had brought nineteen battalions (four of them British) from Tournai, came into play beyond the extreme left of Villars' army. It seemed that the whole French position was going to be outflanked.

It had originally been Marlborough's intention that the Withers corps should join the Dutch on the left of the line. But the men who had marched from Tournai had arrived too late on the scene. They were sent into action on the extreme right of the Allied line, among the northern trees of the Taisnières Wood. About half-past ten Sicco van Goslinga, the Frisian civilian who was the only Dutch Field Deputy present at the battle, galloped up to the Captain-General, and blurted out news of disaster. The Dutch Guards, led into attack a second time by the young Prince of Orange, had been a second time swept by the murderous fire of the concealed French guns. They had reeled back and were assembling for a third onset. It would be suicide, cried Goslinga, who demanded that his fellow-countrymen should be reinforced. Marlborough, joined by Eugene, rode over to inspect the situation. They found it sufficiently grave to forbid a further attack. But no men could be spared from other sectors of the front. The Dutch must rely on the protection of a substantial force of cavalry stationed behind their starting line and commanded by the Prince of Hesse-Cassel. Having given these orders, Marlborough returned to his observation post behind the centre of the line in the Malplaquet Gap, where he meant to deliver the final thrust. Eugene hurried to the Taisnières Wood where the German fighting line was lengthened now by the arrival of Withers with his nineteen battalions. One of them was the Royal Irish. After bitter work with musket and bayonet, the Allies were beginning to reach the clear ground beyond the trees. Eugene sent a force of cavalry to encircle the wood and emerge on the further side as a threat to the French left. Villars acted promptly to meet the danger. He stripped the defences in his centre and sent them to strengthen the resistance in the wood. Among them were the Regiment Royale d'Irlande, the "Wild Geese". In the Wood of Taisnières, therefore, there took place a dramatic and fierce encounter between the two Irish regiments who represented the two halves of their nation. Captain Parker of the Royal Irish tells what followed.

His regiment was on the extreme right of the army when the Royal Irish came to a small opening in the wood on the far side of which an enemy battalion was drawn up. They "advanced gently" towards them and, at a distance of a hundred yards, opened fire. After two rounds of the platoon fire in which British infantry were trained, the enemy regiments began to fade into the trees in some disorder. A third volley and they had vanished. Among the wounded, Parker came on one Lieutenant O'Sullivan who identified his regiment. It was a fair trial of strength, says Parker, adding: "The advantage on our side will be easily accounted for, first from the weight of our ball; for the French arms carry bullets of 24 to the pound; whereas our British firelocks carry ball of 16 only to the pound. Again, the manner of our firing was different from theirs; the French at that time fired all by ranks which can never do equal execution with our platoon firing."[4]

At this stage – it was shortly before noon – Marlborough consulted with Eugene on the further edge of the wood. They saw a strong force of French infantry drawn up ready, as it seemed, to attack the Allied infantry who had fought their way through the wood and were, correspondingly, weakened. But – and this was the most important fact which a survey of the battle disclosed – the Imperialist artillery could now be brought to bear from a flank on the French entrenchments which ran across the open gap between the two woods. "Lottum," said Eugene of the Prussian general who had led the attack on the southern outskirts of the wood, "has struck a decisive blow." Said Lottum to the Duke, "The French have abandoned these trenches. Have them occupied as fast as possible." Marlborough was not a man who needed any instruction in opportunism. In a few minutes he had ridden back to his command post and given the orders which launched Orkney and his thirteen battalions (eleven British, two Prussian) in the attack on the French trenches.

"It was," said Blackader, who went forward with the Cameronians, "the most deliberate, solemn and well-ordered battle that ever I saw, a noble and fine disposition, and as nobly executed . . . The Lord of Hosts went forth at our head as Captain of our host, and the army followed with a daring cheerful boldness . . . I never had a more pleasant day in my life." On the way to the objective his colonel, Cranstoun, was killed, "A thousand shall fall at thy side and ten thousand at thy right hand, but it shall not once come near to thee." Blackader took over command of the battalion. About one o'clock, Orkney's leading troops reached the defences that Villars had built across the Gap. They found them empty. "Not that I pretend to attribute any glory to myself (for it was the nature of our situation), yet I verily believe that these 13 battalions gained us the day." So Orkney wrote to his brother, the Duke of Hamilton.[5] It was the moment for the cavalry to be brought into play.

At this time, the French sustained a severe blow. Villars, intent on restoring cohesion to the left of his army, had collected reinforcements wherever he could find them. His cavalry had routed the squadrons of Withers emerging from the Wood of Taisnières. Then news reached him that his defences in the centre were being over-run by Orkney's advance. He diverted from left to centre infantry with which he had meant to restore the flank threatened by the Germans. At that moment he and his staff became the target of an Allied battery. One general was killed, another badly wounded. The marshal's leg was smashed below the knee. He was out of the fight. Boufflers, that splendid veteran, took over command of the army, while a staff officer, named Puységusr, coolly and competently organized the fighting withdrawal of the French left wing.

Boufflers put himself at the head of the Maison du Roi. He had not brought his cuirass from Paris for nothing. Between him and the earth-works, now lined by British infantry, were twenty Dutch squadrons which British cavalry were about to join. Boufflers charged with the Maison as the British cavalry poured through the gaps in the earthworks. "Jemmy Campbell at the head of the Greys behaved like an angel." It is probably true, although it is suspect as the tribute of another Scotsman, Orkney, who was watching it all from behind the earthworks. Six times Boufflers led his horsemen in the charge. Six times the Allied cavalry in disordered groups drifted back into the shelter afforded them by the infantry lining the defences which Villars had dug the day before. Six times the controlled platoon-firing of the British infantry blasted the triumphant French. French infantry were brought back into the fight; they drove back the Dutch. The British foot were faltering, pursued by Orkney with "fair and foul language". At last Boufflers decided to call his men off. The cavalry battle was resumed in open ground where there was no interference from musket-fire. It was the greatest mounted action of the century, a clamorous, confused struggle of twenty thousand riders a side; perhaps more. Marlborough was in it, with the British and the Prussians. Eugene came up with the Imperial cuirassiers. The desperate play of sabres went on for about an hour, after which Boufflers drew off his exhausted, outnumbered but unbeaten squadrons so that they could cover the general withdrawal of the army. In the closing stage of the battle, the Prince of Orange led his heroic Guards in a third attack which carried the three defence lines in Lanières Wood, that had already cost so many Dutchmen's lives. Three regiments of Danish cavalry, falling on the retreating French, inflicted heavy casualties.

It was three o'clock. The victors had not the strength to pursue. Their horses were dropping with exhaustion. The men, sweating, panting and bloody sat hunched over their saddlebows. And were they victors? By the military conventions of that time, they might be. The French had been forced to pull back from a prepared position. But they had done so in good order and even in good spirits. They had inflicted twice as heavy casualties as they had sustained. Paris was saved for another year. Thanks to the warlike fury of the Prince of Orange, the scourge had fallen heavily on the Dutch – 8,600 casualties, or 43 per cent of the total Allied losses. So many sons of the "regent" families had fallen that the Dutch patriciate did not recover for a generation. By contrast, the British had suffered lightly – 500 dead and 1,200 wounded.[6] Those dreadful woods were strewn with dead and the groaning, writhing bodies of the wounded. "In many places they lye as thick as ever you saw a flock of sheep," said Orkney, "and where our poor nephew Tullibardine* was, it was prodigious. I really think I never saw the like." Orkney had his sailor brother, Archie, with him: "He only wonders how anybody comes off where bullets fly so thick . . . None alive ever saw such a battle, God give us a good peace." Marlborough, riding through the trees, was appalled by what he saw. Here was work utterly beyond his surgeons. He sent a messenger at once to Boufflers urging him to send transport for all the French who could be moved. When they heard the news, all Europe was aghast. This was something different from the carefully limited slaughter to which they were accustomed. Malplaquet, in eighteenth-century thinking, came to have the same dreadful significance as Passchendaele did for the twentieth. Malplaquet gave the peace party something to talk about.

From the tactical, the strategic and the political point of view, the battle was a misfortune for the Allies and, above all, for the Captain-General. He had fought on terms dictated by his opponent, Villars, who had picked the site of the action and prepared it with diabolical ingenuity. Yet there had been no reason why the Allies should have given battle there or indeed given battle at all. They had done so because Marlborough, Eugene and their subordinates under-rated the commander and the army against them. They paid a heavy price for doing so. Marlborough picked up his pen on the day after the battle to finish his letter to Sarah: "God Almighty be praised, it is now in our powers to have what peace we please." He could not have been more mistaken. Orkney wrote, "I hope to God it may be the last battle I may see."

* Marquis of Tullibardine; killed, fighting with the Scots Brigade.

Argyll, who had fought with valour and whose regiment, the Buffs, had suffered heavily in the forest fighting, wasted no time in setting off to London. There, on the floor of the House of Lords he uttered sharp disapproval of Marlborough's insistence on pressing the attack. "His High and Mighty Grace" of Argyll,★ frequenting the coffee houses with his customary retinue of swordsmen, carried on all through the town a steady campaign against his commander-in-chief, the "noble Prince of Blenheim". Liselotte, writing from Versailles, said, "There were a great many dead on both sides. You see nothing but sadness and tears." Blackader, after a spiritually uplifting tour of the battlefield in the grisly light of the morning after, thought about the command of the Cameronians now left vacant by Cranstoun's death: "I commit all to God. I know promotion comes not from the east or the west. I leave myself in Thy hands, O Lord." Next day he put in his claim. There was no harm in giving the Lord's elbow a jog. He got the job.

★ "Ambitious, covetous, cunning Scot; has no principle but his own interest" – Swift.

View of Blenheim House, the Seat of the Duke of Marlborough.

Blenheim Palace
(Mary Evans Picture Library)

Sir John Vanbrugh
(*National Portrait Gallery*)

Jonathan Swift
(*National Portrait Gallery*)

Henry St John,
1st Viscount Bolingbroke
(*National Portrait Gallery*)

Robert Harley,
1st Earl of Oxford
(*National Portrait Gallery*)

XXII

A General Infatuation

"Good God, how has this poor nation been governed in my time! During
the reign of King Charles the Second we were governed by a parcel of
French whores; in King James the Second's time by a parcel of Popish
priests; in King William's time by a parcel of Dutch footmen, and now
we are governed by a dirty chambermaid, a Welsh attorney and a profligate
wretch who has neither honour nor honesty."

Duke of Buckingham, 1714

The campaign of 1710 was a failure. Yet never at any time in Marlborough's life was it more important that he should be manifestly and
indisputably victorious. For in London in the early months of the year,
the knives were being sharpened by the politicians and, before the year
was out, they were being plied. But the war, which might have furnished
the answer to the political conspirators of the coffee houses, sank into a
state resembling paralysis. At the end of the fighting season of 1709,
Marlborough and the Allied forces had taken Mons; a year later they were
thirty miles further west, besieging Bouchain: like a noisy but futile
bumble bee, the vast army, for which the British Parliament had voted
nine million pounds before Christmas, was still caught in the web of
French fortresses. The soldiers had still to set out on the road to Paris, a
march for which it seemed nobody was ready to give the command! At
any time, this paralysis would have been serious; in that year, it was
disastrous. In contrast to the military stagnation in the Low Countries,
London was in a ferment of political activity, at an ever-growing pace
and with a steady purpose. The Godolphin ministry was threatened, was
undermined and was – but for an unlikely intervention of fate – about to
be destroyed. The brain behind the hostile operations was Robert
Harley's. But the will, without which the task of destruction could not
have been carried through, was that of Her Majesty Queen Anne.

Democracy is a female, impulsive, intuitive and implacable. That may
be one reason why queens are often more representative than kings.

Certainly in 1710 the Queen acted with the assurance and tenacity of a monarch who knew that she had her people behind her. So Harley was brought up by the back stairs into the Queen's presence; the Duke of Somerset, a great Whig nobleman, was paying furtive visits to the Tory Harley ("Don't forget to order your porter to open the door to a hackney chair with curtains drawn"); Lord Shrewsbury, who had visited Blenheim regularly to see how the work was progressing, suddenly stopped going there. And the Duke of Argyll, another Whig magnate, was spreading through the British camp in Flanders the report, backed by convincing evidence, that the ministry was about to fall. His "unquiet and ambitious spirit, never easy while there is anyone above him, made him upon some trifling resentment conceive an inveterate hatred against his general."[1] So said Swift, who disliked both men.

In his quarters, Marlborough knew most of what was going on and guessed the rest. In the autumn of 1709, just after Malplaquet, he had made a serious political blunder, asking that his appointment as Captain-General should be for life. The Queen refused but the request played into the hands of Tory propagandists. By June of 1710, he was in a state of deep depression: "My wishes and my duty are the same," he told Godolphin, "but I can't say that I have the same sanguine prophetic spirit I did use to have." In the villages around him was starvation and misery: "at least one half of the people are dead since the beginning of winter and the rest look as if they had come out of their graves." Peace, peace! With all his heart he longed for it yet Argyll, who had been one of the heroes of Malplaquet, tearing open his coat to show the Buffs whom he led that he wore no hidden breastplate – Argyll was telling everybody he met that Marlborough could have peace when he pleased. If it were only as simple as that! But Louis, who had the best diplomatic service in the world, who peered and bribed his way into every British conspiracy, put up his price every time he felt Britain's will to fight weaken. He thought that Marlborough would not be employed in the next campaign and, through his excellent intelligence service, Marlborough learnt of this belief.

In the meantime, there was nothing for it but to besiege one fortress after another at the cost of a few thousand casualties each time, and to manoeuvre across the desolate country* in the hope that one day Villars would be tricked into offering battle on something like equal terms. "I am this day three score," he told Godolphin on 25 June, "but in so good

---

* "All about is like a desert; this gives me the spleen. It must end in the plague." Marlborough to Godolphin, 21 August 1710. *Blenheim MSS*, B.II – 9a.

health that I hope to end this campaign without the inconvenience of old age." The trouble was, however, that something had gone out of him. He was no longer willing to take the risks involved in a bolder strategy. He would take no part in the negotiations which went on for a peace treaty. He would carry out his duties as a general and wait for things to develop. He did not think he would have long to wait.

Meanwhile two events had a profound and, in one case, a dramatic influence on affairs. In consequence of the disastrous harvest of 1709, the price of wheat rose by 90 per cent in a year. This inflation was something which everybody in the land could understand and which the poor felt cruelly. So far the war had been fought with a stable wheat price and with a prosperous economy. Now people felt the pinch, not as severely as in France but badly enough to make them look on the war with less enthusiasm. The other event was a sermon preached in St Paul's Cathedral by a High Church clergyman named Dr Sacheverell. He was not a clever man, but he was a demagogue who knew how to attract attention to himself. He did so that Guy Fawkes Day, preaching on the text "In perils among false brethren". The false brethren were clearly identified as the Dissenters and their friends the Whigs.

One man in particular was singled out for attack, "Volpone" the fox, which was in current abuse the nickname given to the Lord Treasurer, Godolphin. The Tories apparently knew in advance what the doctor was up to for, without delay, thirty thousand copies of the sermon were run off and distributed. It was at this point that Godolphin made a fatal blunder. Furious at the attack on "the crafty insidiousness" of Volpone, he resolved that Sacheverell should be impeached. Wiser friends like Cowper, the Lord Chancellor, tried in vain to dissuade him. Lord Sunderland and the wilder Whigs urged him on. By the time Godolphin had cooled down and wanted to retreat, it was too late. A state trial in all its panoply was being prepared in Westminster Hall. Sir Christopher Wren designed the seats for the peers and their friends, the box for the Queen.

All through the winter months the formalities of impeachment dragged on. It was March 1710 before the trial could be held. Fashionable women plagued their husbands and lovers for places. The theatre did bad business during those days. No play can compete with the drama of a trial. The Queen arrived in her chair each day of the hearing; which, in itself, was a plain indication of where her sympathies lay. Sacheverell was, in her opinion, little better than a mountebank whose style of oratory she thought inexpressibly vulgar. But he was a High Churchman persecuted

247

by her enemies, the Whigs. More important, his trial showed in a sensational way how the tide of opinion had turned against the government.
So Anne, who might have stayed at home in her palace, sallied out to be
greeted by the loyal outcries of the mob who were sure, as they told her,
bobbing past them in her chair, that she was for "the good doctor" and
"to the devil with Dissenters!" When the central figure in the drama,
"a climber thirsting for martyrdom without peril"[2] himself drove up in
his coach, surrounded by a cudgel-bearing bodyguard, the enthusiasm of
the crowd reached a climax of hysteria. It was as if a miracle-working
image were being carried in procession. Affably blessing the people,
Dr Sacheverell passed on his way to Westminster Hall where a martyr's
crown awaited him or, more likely, a bishop's crozier. "It is of the utmost
consequence in my humble opinion to put a stop to these rebellious
tumults, to prevent the mob from assembling on any pretence whatsoever
during the trial of Dr Sacheverell but especially to huzza him from his
lodgings in the Temple to Westminster."[3] The warning came too late.
The government either did not dare to interfere or could not. While the
trial droned on inside the Hall, the mob was loose outside, setting fire
to Dissenting chapels, threatening the houses of the Whig grandees, even
preparing to storm the Bank of England itself, holiest shrine of "the
money power". But at that point the Queen called out the Guards. The
Bank might be Whig but its vaults were full of gold. In the end,
Sacheverell was found guilty by 69 votes to 52 but his sentence was
light – a ban on preaching for three years. Among those who voted for
mildness were the Duke of Somerset, who had been talking lately to
Harley, and the Duke of Argyll. Sacheverell departed to a fat living. By
his trial and its result, Godolphin's government had committed suicide.
The Queen and Harley had the clearest possible intimation that England
had swung to the Tories.

When the Sacheverell crisis began, Harley was in the country. Without
delay, he came to town where, one evening, a note was brought to him,
dirty, crumpled, unsigned but in a hand he recognized, the Queen's. The
bearer said that it had been handed to him by an undergardener at
Kensington Palace or Hampton Court, he was not sure which.[4] The note
told him how, with the help of Mrs Masham, he could reach the Queen's
private apartments without being detected by that watchful dragon,
Sarah. The work of dismantling the edifice of government went forward
over the next few months. It began quite unobtrusively and progressed in
easy steps. The Duke of Somerset was successfully wooed by the Queen.

His duchess was before long Anne's closest friend. The Duke of Shrewsbury, a Whig of the highest standing who had, however, drifted away from the main faction of the party, found himself in correspondence and soon in agreement with Harley. The nation, he believed, longed for peace. Anne made him Lord Chamberlain one day when Godolphin had gone racing at Newmarket. Then it was the turn of Earl Rivers to be worked on. As a soldier he had wanted the chief command in Spain and knew that Marlborough had imposed his veto to prevent it. In January 1710, the lieutenancy of the Tower fell vacant and Rivers, encouraged by Harley, put in for it. Marlborough, acting as Captain-General, proposed to give it to the Duke of Northumberland and when Rivers asked for the post he was met with a polite rebuff. He then sought permission to take his case to the Queen. The permission was granted. When Marlborough saw the Queen for the purpose of putting forward Northumberland's name, she replied that he came too late. She had promoted Rivers. Needless to say, the news that the Captain-General had been out-manoeuvred over the command of Britain's most important arsenal was not lost on those who watched the stars in the political firmament.

Superficially, the complexion of the ministry had not altered; in fact, there had been a revolution. Marlborough's power had been exhibited as hollow; the party which wanted an early peace, and would soon want peace at almost any price, was in the ascendant. And now came a decisive trial of strength. The Queen demanded the removal of Lord Sunderland. "He is being attacked because he is my son-in-law," said Marlborough. "I am the real target of the attack!" That was the truth. Sunderland had been forced into the government by Sarah, in spite of the Queen's intense dislike which, to begin with, Marlborough had shared. Anne resisted Sunderland as a minister for the same reason that Marlborough had resisted him as a son-in-law. He was an extreme Whig, a republican, arrogant and ill-mannered. Sarah had been his champion, and the Queen, who had been humiliated when she was forced to accept the young man, had nursed a bitter grudge ever since. Now, in 1710, was the time for revenge.

The Queen had a modest preliminary triumph when, in the course of wearing down Marlborough's resistance, she ensured that Mrs Masham's brother, Jack Hill, was promoted to Brigadier. The incident was interpreted in the army as a new sign of the Captain-General's decline. In June, Sunderland was dismissed and was offered a pension, which he refused. The question now was, what would Marlborough do? Wait for dismissal, a step which the Queen said she had no intention of taking? Or go at once and throw the whole of Europe into turmoil? His colleagues in the government, and the spokesmen of England's allies abroad, begged him not to give way to vexation and, as the Emperor put it, expose the whole fruits of the war to the utmost peril: "Whatever aid, favour or authority I can ever confer shall be given to you and yours." But the Emperor soon knew, through his envoy, Philip von Hoffman, that neither Marlborough nor Godolphin could be saved: it was only a question of fixing a date for their downfall. Looking round his audience-chamber, once thronged, now deserted, in Brussels, Marlborough was equally without illusion. His old friend, the Jacobite exile, Lord Ailesbury, saw him: "My Lord, you seem melancholy. I thought you understood an English court better than to be surprised at changes. You have a fine family and a great and noble seat; go down thither, live quietly and retired and you may laugh at your enemies."[5]

It was sensible advice; if Marlborough could have taken it, he would have produced a convulsion in Europe and, in all likelihood, a political crisis in England. For, at that time, neither the Queen nor Harley's cabal was prepared to meet a situation in which, on the eve of a new campaign, the British army in Europe would be deprived of its chief, and the keystone would be knocked out of the Grand Alliance. But – and this was the deciding factor with him – France would have won the war. He would not be forgiven by his friends, above all by Heinsius and Eugene: he would not be forgiven by himself. Nor, for all his forebodings, could he imagine how far the Queen's animosity would go. Louis, who did not foresee it either, and scarcely dared to hope for it, was another who watched the British crisis with passionate interest. He did not watch it in idleness. At each new incident in the drama, his terms for peace grew harder. The immediate effect of the English anti-war movement was to postpone peace.

The Queen and Harley went on with their programme of demolition. Their choice as envoy to Hanover was preferred to Godolphin's; he was given the task of persuading the Elector that he might be offered Marlborough's place as Captain-General. However, the nominee ambassador died before he set sail for the Continent. Some time was gained in which the final blows could still be averted. England's allies, alarmed by the turn events had taken, were mobilized to intervene with the Queen. Against his better judgment ("I am of opinion, the less one meddles the better") Marlborough took part in this counter-plot. So did Godolphin. At their instigation, the Dutch envoy, Vryberg, warned the Queen that a general election which brought the peace party into office would be likely to strengthen the hands of the pro-French faction in Holland who would make a separate peace, leaving England to fend for herself. Hanover and Prussia wrote in a similar sense. They wrote in vain. In early July 1710 the Queen's letter of dismissal to Godolphin was ready in draft. While the inevitable was still delayed, a letter came from the Emperor, written in his own hand but inspired by Eugene. It did Harley's work for him.

The Queen was warned that it would be folly to dissolve Parliament and risk losing all that had been won in the war. Nothing was better calculated to stir up Queen Anne's annoyance. In the City, always sensitive to political symptoms, all this was noticed and acted on. Sir Henry Furnese reported to Marlborough that he was short by £13,000 on a loan he was floating for Prince Eugene. Could not Marlborough, Cadogan and Cardonnel increase their subscriptions? It was shameful that at such a time Britain should not support her ally. A fortnight later, the banker sent the general a present of fine palm wine to console him at a "melancholy time when all runs counter to what every honest man might reasonably expect," i.e. when there is a failure of public credit.[6]

A week after the Imperial ambassador presented the Emperor's letter, Godolphin asked the Queen bluntly, "Is it your Majesty's will that I should go on?" "Yes," she answered, lying. That night, 7 August 1710, she wrote him a letter of dismissal, giving him a pension of £4,000 a year which, incidentally, was never forthcoming. She finished, "I desire that, instead of bringing your staff to me, you will break it, which I believe will be easier to us both." So, with no excess of honesty or consideration, the deed was done. It was "the great alteration" as Walpole called it in a letter to Marlborough. Bank stock fell five points that day. Harley was now openly, as he had been in secret, the Queen's chief adviser. The Queen now turned her – or, rather, Harley's – batteries of evasion and deception on Marlborough. It would never do if he left his post before it was convenient to disgrace him. Marlborough was too old a hand, however, to be deceived.

A few days before Godolphin's dismissal, the Captain-General had written a revealing letter to his friend telling him that this would be his last campaign, "Burn this letter so that the world may continue in their error of thinking me a happy man for I think it is better to be envied than pitied."[7] He knew very well what was being planned, so well that there was no need for the usual tale-bearers in the camp to bring him Argyll's latest piece of London gossip. But Harley was not yet in a position to launch his main assault. He could, however, attack a secondary point, the money that was being spent on Blenheim – close on £200,000 by the autumn of 1710. When the building was only half completed, the Treasury stopped the money, thus driving contractors and workmen to the verge of bankruptcy, or the threat of prison. Vanbrugh proposed that Marlborough should pay. Sarah, who had already quarrelled with the contractors whom she accused of cheating the workpeople, gave orders to stop work on the building; which in any case she had never liked. Godolphin advised, "Let them keep their heap of stones." Marlborough rebuked Sarah for giving any orders about the building: Blenheim was being built with the Queen's money. She alone should decide if and when it should be finished. As for him, he was quite indifferent: what pleasure could there be for him to live in a country where, as it seemed, he had so few friends?

Preparations for a general election went forward energetically: Harley was not a man to leave anything to chance in a matter so important. Lords Lieutenant of dubious loyalty or worse were replaced by men who, for one reason or another, could be depended on to see that the desired results were obtained at the polls. On the other side, the Whigs, although in considerable disarray, did what they could. Marlborough insisted to Godolphin that for Woodstock, where his influence was paramount, his trusted military colleagues, Cadogan and Macartney, should be returned to speak for him in the Commons. His agent borrowed £300 to give to the poor of the constituency, especially those who had not been paid for the work done at Blenheim. The Tory master-stroke in the general campaign was to send Dr Sacheverell through the country to whip up the zeal of good Church people against "Volpone" and his accomplices.

In London, a pamphlet war of unexampled violence broke out corresponding to the strength of party feeling throughout the country. Journal was pitted against journal: *The Examiner* against *The Medley*, etc. The six hundred London coffee houses were drawn up in battle array: The Smyrna, Ozinda's, the Chocolate House and the Cocoa Tree were in the forefront of the Tory order of battle against the Whig St James's and Button's. Whig army officers haunted the Old Man's in the Tilt Yard kept by Jenny Man, a faithful Whig harridan. Even the playhouses were divided. Part of the auditorium of the Haymarket Theatre was reserved for members of that exclusive Whig côterie, the Kit-Cat, of which Marlborough was made a supernumerary member when he returned from Flanders. The Tories were partisans of the Italian Opera and opposed to the Whigs' favourite singer, Pilota, who came from Hanover. Organized by Robert Walpole, the ablest of a new generation of Whigs, they massed outside the theatre to prevent the Tories getting in.

The prize for the victors in the political war promised to be proportionate to the fury of the conflict. Henry St John, the new Secretary of State, swore that he would "fill the employments of the Kingdom down to the meanest with Tories". It was a promise which, in due course, he kept. It could be assumed, too, that in the general distribution of rewards, St John would not forget himself. Very soon he laid hands on the Secret Service funds of his office to pay his mortgage debts. "I pray God he will consider," wrote a friend, "that a Secretary of State must not take all those liberties one of War might perhaps think proper to his station." It was unlikely that St John took this timid view of his new opportunities.

Defoe, shrewdest of observers, thought that there had never been such heat of partisanship since the days of the Civil War. By this time, he was back on Harley's pay-roll, watching the election in Scotland, and lavishing assurances on the Presbyterians that the Union, the Protestant succession and the Kirk were all as safe under Harley as they had been under Godolphin. At the same time, he warned the new first minister that Scottish politics were very different from English. A Scottish Tory was another name for a Jacobite. And the Jacobites were strong in the north of the country, while they openly drank the Pretender's health in the Edinburgh taverns. As for the Scots nobility, they were "an odd kind of people, to say no more of them". But this was probably something that Harley had realized for himself. He was busy, just then, allocating some hundreds of pounds of the Queen's bounty among the proud aristocrats of North Britain who needed the money badly. Only one of them, his Grace of Hamilton, was a rich man by English standards; his property was worth £9,000 a year. Of the others, only Eglinton's income exceeded £4,000, and at the lower end of the scale were some sad cases: "The Earl of Home is persuaded to go up for London. He borrowed £100 sterling for the journey."

The result of the election in October 1710 was what might have been expected: in England and Wales, 320 Tories were returned against 150 Whigs and 40 of uncertain colour; in Scotland, the 45 seats were more evenly divided; some of the new Scottish members were openly Jacobite and took their orders from Saint-Germain. But the general picture was one of Tory triumph. "The infatuation is so general in the kingdom that we are beaten everywhere," wrote Walpole. "My lord Godolphin is much out of order with the stone and gravel."[8] All told, it was a landslide Tory victory. When Louis heard the news he could scarcely believe his good luck. Only a few months earlier he had faced total defeat – and the prospect of a revolution which would sweep his system into the dustbin. Now, the Duke of Berwick was arguing that the time had come for him to invade England at the head of 20,000 men. In the hour of triumph, the Tories behaved with predictable ingratitude to Sacheverell. One of the first lessons a politician must learn is how to get rid of tools after they have served their purpose. Especially tools one dislikes. In any case, another and far more interesting political clergyman had now appeared on the scene.

XXIII

We Must Have Peace, Good or Bad

"Whatever side has the sole management of the pen will soon find hands enough to write down their enemies as low as they please."
Jonathan Swift

In the whole of nature there is no force more formidable than a parson on the make. Early in September 1710, Jonathan Swift arrived in London from his Irish parish of Laracor, six miles out of Dublin, on a financial mission on behalf of the Church of Ireland, which he thought should benefit from a remission of the "first fruits" of livings as the Church of England did. The amount at stake was trifling. He put up in the Smyrna Coffee House in Pall Mall, opposite Marlborough House, from where he conducted his propaganda. With Godolphin he had no success. Harley was more sympathetic. In a little, he was on Christian name terms with the visitor, plied him with excellent wine and, after a four hours' talk, set him down at the St James's Coffee House by hackney coach. More than that, he promised Swift that his memorandum on Church finance would be put before the Queen. "All this is very odd and comical," wrote Swift to Stella, a sprightly young woman he knew in Dublin.

The truth was that he was bowled over by the great man's attentions; he was, moreover, captivated by St John's caressing ways when he met him. He was at once shocked and envious of the young man's disorderly life, appalled and admiring of one who could move so easily between the brothel and the court. Very soon he was writing for *The Examiner*, the government sheet which Harley financed and St John directed as a counter-blast to Whig propaganda. He proved to be by far the most trenchant of Tory polemical writers, as unscrupulous as the meanest hack in Grub Street, but writing with the fire of genius. In capturing Swift, Harley had brought off the greatest single *coup* of his recruiting campaign.

All the conditions in Britain in 1710 favoured a far-reaching political change. War weariness: the war had gone on through too many years and its original impulse had been lost. General social discontent, due to the inflation of prices. The burden of war taxation falling upon one class, and that the most important politically, the landed gentry. And this was taking place at a time when there was a shift in the balance of economic power. The old privileged class felt that it was losing ground to a new type of man, the man of money. There was a convenient target on which their resentments could be focused. All this might have remained within a narrow group had not a demagogue, "an ignorant impudent incendiary",[1] been able to convert it into a popular movement, emotional and religious. There were dangerous, violent demonstrations, especially in London. As Goebbels said two centuries and more later, "Whoever can conquer the streets will one day conquer the state."[2] The situation had all – or all but one – of the criteria of a coming political transformation. All that was missing was a convincing manifesto written by an inspired polemical writer. This lack Swift was about to supply. One essential quality of successful propaganda he grasped instinctively: "Hatred and contempt must be directed at particular individuals."[3]

Swift concentrated his attack on Marlborough. Swift, although a High Churchman, had been a Whig at the time of the Revolution when he fled from Ireland to escape the Irish followers of James II. He declared that King William was "the great deliverer from Popery and slavery". At that time he admired the Dutch for their tolerance and honesty. But as he came to think that the Dissenters and not the Papists were the greatest danger to the Church of Ireland, his opinions underwent a change. He moved towards a belief that the Dutch, friends and allies of the Dissenters, belonged to "a crazily instituted popular" republic, and had "from boor to burgomaster" perfected a system of "lower politics" which would have shamed any other nation. St John, who may have helped in the development of these ideas, could not match the force with which the Irish clergyman clothed them. Whatever Swift's politics may have been before he came under the spell of Harley and his flattery, he was, within a few weeks, the most convincing enemy of the Whigs. He still thought that his dazzling new friends were a little too severe on Marlborough – "although he is as covetous as hell and as ambitious as the Prince of it . . . Yet I question whether any wise state ever laid aside a general who had been successful nine years together."[4] Doubts like these did not long survive in the atmosphere of social success and political power into which Swift was plunged.

He was invited by Harley to those Saturday dinner parties at which excellent wine was drunk and the policy was as high as the company: Argyll, Peterborough, Ormonde, Rivers, the Lord Keeper and similar magnificoes; Lady Orkney, "squinting like a dragon", plied him with her redoubtable wit; Mrs Masham flattered him with the gossip of the court; if he was not actually presented to the Queen, who did not approve of him, "I am as well received at Court as perhaps any man of my level."[5] It was exciting, intoxicating stuff for a country vicar who a few weeks before had thought of little beyond the affairs of his Irish parish, and relied for conversation on two sprightly woman friends in Dublin. He still kept up that friendship, which was now sustained by the stream of exuberant letters he sent from Westminster and the answering stream for which each day his eye searched the glass frame at the bar of the St James's Coffee House. Swift was in a vertiginous upward climb which took him to a level of influence and authority such as no English man of letters has enjoyed since. With Harley and St John at his elbow to feed him with a well-selected diet of facts, he was pouring out a stream of articles for *The Examiner*, which soon made it the most widely read and most feared of political journals. They were aimed at the Whigs, "Rot 'em for ungrateful dogs."

Above all, with a shrewd tactical sense, he trained his guns on Marlborough, who had returned from Flanders looking "much changed and fallen away" and soon would look more so. While thinking – or professing to think – that the Tory leaders hit the general too hard, Swift dealt him by far the hardest blows. To the pamphlet war he brought the heaviest artillery train; his pieces were laid with the greatest accuracy. When it was alleged that the new government was not as grateful as it should be to the victorious commander, Swift replied with a list of the rewards Marlborough had received – "I shall say nothing of the title of Duke or the Star of the Garter but shall come to more substantial instances." And there they were, each with a capital value attached to it, the Woodstock estate, Blenheim Palace, the annuity from the Post Office, the German principality, the gifts from foreign princes; in addition were the Duchess' employments at court which "reckoning only the avowed salaries, are very low rated at £100,000". In all, Swift estimated that the total exceeded half a million of money, "a trifle in comparison with what is untold".[6] The list might contain errors in detail, it might assemble wildly different kinds of emolument in one impressive catalogue, but it was near enough to the truth. It was only one of many attacks launched by Swift on the Captain-General and his wife, the more scurrilous of which he passed to lower-grade hacks, like Mrs Manley, the fat, plain, hard-working journalist who had once written *Atalantis*. In the propaganda war few blows were regarded as too low; thus, on one side the Duchess of Marlborough was alleged to be Godolphin's mistress (by Swift) and on the other, Mrs Masham was accused of being over-fond of her own sex.[7] In that robust and lawless age, the most satisfactory way of dealing with such defamation was to have its perpetrators set upon in some dark alley and well-cudgelled. This was a punishment which a thin-skinned victim like Marlborough sometimes longed to inflict on his tormentors and which Swift sometimes feared; it may have been the reason why he changed his lodgings quite frequently during those months.

Marlborough, at home during the winter months of 1710–11 bore with outward patience the ill-mannered baiting of St John and the coldness of the Queen. He was aware, in a dozen different ways, that the ministry was busily undermining his authority in the army, his popularity with those whom Swift called "the rabble" and his prestige with the Allies. "Lord, what shall become of us?" wailed Pensionary Buys in Amsterdam to John Drummond, Harley's correspondent. "Lord Rivers would give me no satisfaction that the Duke shall return . . . For God's sake, let him but return for one campaign!"[8] If the Ministry did not strike him down, it was only because the time was not yet ripe: there must be one more campaign in Flanders and who should lead it – on this point, Harley, St John and the Queen all agreed, choking back their chagrin – but the Captain-General! In war, he was indispensable. But, God be thanked, war was not eternal. When the coming campaign was ended, the final disgrace would be enacted.

It is hard to imagine why Marlborough endured so much. Money, Swift thought, his vastly lucrative employments. It may be so. Or the exciting prospect of one more campaign at the head of his splendid, multi-national army against that redoubtable paladin, Villars? It seems more likely. "Cataline at the head of a mercenary army," as *The Examiner* said, losing no opportunity to remind Englishmen of the danger of another Cromwell. There is also the thought that Marlborough, knowing that the Queen's health was poor, wished to have an army at his command when the crisis of the succession came. Then the army would be decisive, as it had been half a century earlier. With exactly the same thought in mind, St John was ejecting officers of Whig sympathies from key positions in Britain and was using the Duke of Ormonde to screen the new candidates for army appointments so that only Tories or Jacobites could get through. Three generals had been dismissed on the grounds that they had drunk to the confusion of the ministers. They belonged to Marlborough's faction among the officers. One of them, a dissolute warrior named MacCartney, had rejoined the army and fought as a volunteer at Malplaquet.

While they waited to destroy the Captain-General, Harley and St John set about the easier but no less congenial task of humiliating him through his wife. Sarah was loathed by the Queen. She was hated by Mrs Masham. Her unique gift for making enemies was now at full stretch. She was conspicuously rude to St John, calling him an ungrateful rogue. And St John returned her dislike with interest. She must be forced to give up the gold key which was her badge of office as Keeper of the Privy Purse, Mistress of the Robes, Groom of the Stole. Marlborough pleaded on his knees for his wife before the gouty – or, more likely, arthritic – blotchy-faced woman who was his sovereign. But Anne would not change her mind. In three days she must have the key. Marlborough asked for ten. Anne settled for *two*. After this absurd scene, Sarah threw the key on the floor and Marlborough took it back at once to the palace. The Duchess of Somerset became the Groom of the Stole and Mrs Masham Keeper of the Privy Purse, a post which gave her access to a great deal of public money. She was irritated, however, when it became obvious that not she but the Duchess of Somerset had taken Sarah's place in the Queen's affections.

In Parliament, the political battle went on with more than usual violence. In the Commons, the Tory young bloods of the October Club bayed for the blood of Dissenters and when they were denied it, blamed this misfortune on Harley, himself a crypto-Dissenter, and the policy of Moderation. St John, already bent on ousting Harley from the head of the government, spared no art in assuring his back benchers that, when the time came, he would be their natural leader. The Lords devoted themselves to debating the disastrous campaign in Spain; Peterborough and Argyll headed the attack, which was centred on Marlborough whose real offence in Tory eyes was not that he had lost a battle in Spain, which he had not visited, but that he had won four in Flanders and Germany. The Godolphin Ministry was censured for the Spanish failure and, since James Stanhope, a prisoner of war in Spain, could not be punished, Galway, doubly unpopular with Tories as a Whig and a Huguenot, was denounced for losing a battle in Spain four years earlier. The venom spreading outside the House, Argyll fought a duel in Hyde Park with a colonel who had called him a turncoat. After that the Highland duke went off to Spain. He had always wanted to be a commander-in-chief. Now he was appointed one. But it was not at all what he had hoped for. "This day," said a letter from Barcelona which found its way to Marlborough's files, "the Duke of Argyll arrived at Barcelona with two men-of-war but brought no money with him for the army." The army was in rags, the war chest empty. A month later (10 June 1711), a tartan[9] arrived from Genoa but brought no money. His Grace had been tricked.

St John was by this time intent on an ambitious military operation of his own devising. He would capture Quebec. To do so, he would take five battalions from Flanders, thus clipping Marlborough's wings for the next campaign. He entrusted the command of the expeditionary force to Brigadier Hill who might be an incompetent soldier, as was universally believed, but was Mrs Masham's brother. And in the political conspiracy St John was preparing, it would be very important to have the friendship of the Queen's confidant. Finally, the Quebec project, and the large purchases of stores which it involved, offered St John the immediate prospect of financial gain. He was not one to disdain an easy, if dishonest, guinea although, the standards of the age being what they were, he was only bolder and more unblushing than others. And he certainly needed the money.

Peterborough fared no better than his ally in the Parliamentary battle, Argyll. He was denied a military command and had to be content with a resolution describing him as a national hero, after which he was sent on a diplomatic mission to Vienna. Then a tour of the Italian courts was planned for him, Queen Anne being of the opinion that he would do less harm there than at home. Others were not so sure. St John received – and perhaps read – his dispatches with mockery. By this time, the Secretary of State's mind was full of his Quebec scheme to which he tried by every art of persuasion to convert Harley, who, however, remained sceptical. He had the well-founded belief that St John was intent on feathering his own nest and that this was the explanation why the Secretary resisted with such heat any enquiry into the contracts for the enterprise. In spite of the division in the Cabinet, St John pressed on secretly with his plans, knowing that Mrs Masham supported him and confident that when the day came for the final struggle for power between himself and Harley, Mrs Masham would be on his side. With growing consternation, Swift watched the rift widen between his two patrons. He was, however, mainly annoyed by the influence at court of "your damned Duchess of

Somerset",[10] a moderate Tory, and therefore detestable to high-flyers like Swift and Mrs Masham. In verses which were passed from hand to hand at the palace, Swift declared that the Duchess had murdered her first husband, Thomas Thynne. It was an old and untrue tale. But Queen Anne was not amused by it. From the moment she read the lampoon she resolved that Swift would not gain preferment in the Church of England so long as she had any say in the matter.

> By an old murderess pursued,
> A crazy prelate* and a royal prude,

The parson's earthly ambitions were destined to be thwarted. But the bitterness of this had still not been brought home to him that winter of 1710/11. He was in the thick of a tremendous political conflict and his greatest triumph was still to come.

In March an event occurred, unexpected and melodramatic, which altered things considerably. A French adventurer, who called himself Guiscard, had haunted the less reputable resorts in London; there he had known St John; in fact, the two men had disputed the fatherhood of a bastard child. To supply his needs, Guiscard had been in British government pay, until Harley, who disliked him, cut down his retainer; in revenge, Guiscard began to sell British military secrets to France. Unfortunately for him an incriminating letter, which he was sending to France by way of the British Ambassador in Lisbon, was intercepted. Arrested, Guiscard was being questioned by a Privy Council Committee when he pulled out a small knife and stabbed Harley. "The villain has stabbed Mr Harley!" cried St John, drawing his sword. In the wild turmoil that followed, he and others attacked the Frenchman who died in Newgate three weeks later. St John's friends spread a story that, in fact, it was their hero whom Guiscard had really meant to kill. And with Harley out of the way for the time being, St John speeded up his preparations for the Quebec affair. The Queen made Harley Lord Treasurer and Earl of Oxford.

Before this drama, Marlborough had left for Holland in the spring of 1711 and at Scheveningen, on the North Sea coast on a bracing March day, he gave a masterly survey of the English political scene to Robethon, the Hanoverian envoy. He said that he stayed at his post against the wishes of the Whigs, because he thought it in the public interest to do so although he was well aware that the new government would be quick to blame

* The Archbishop of York.

him if the war took a turn for the worse. He was ready to risk that humiliation. There was another reason for his clinging to office; his interest in the succession. As Commander-in-Chief, he would have a part to play. He urged the Hanoverian minister not to under-rate the strength of the Jacobite party who were already in a majority in the October Club. The ministers were old and feeble, except St John who was industrious and able. Hanover would be well-advised to pay heed to him. Harley, although not a Jacobite, would probably fall in with the Jacobite scheme if that was the only way for him to keep office. As for the Queen, he was sure that she favoured the Protestant succession but she was a woman and could be deceived; to an incredible extent her mind was controlled by Harley and Mrs Masham. However, the time would come, sooner perhaps than anybody thought, when the Elector of Hanover ought to come out openly as one determined to have the succession. But not yet! On that point he was firm. Until there was a new turn in events, the Elector should seek to live on amicable terms with Queen Anne and her advisers. So, as they sat side by side in the Captain-General's coach on the windy Dutch seashore, the picture of British politics was sketched in by the expert strategist to the fascinated German official. Robethon lost no time in sending to the Elector, his master, an account of the conversation; then, Marlborough drove off to the army.

A few weeks later, three events had changed everything; St John's secret expedition to Quebec sailed, with "four-bottle" Jack Hill in command of the troops. Harley founded the South Sea Company of which he was to be governor; it was an enterprise by which the floating national debt was exchanged for shares in the monopoly of the slave trade to the Spanish Empire, the *Asiento*, as it was called. This unpleasant form of commerce was enormously profitable. For thirty years, the company would supply 4,800 Negroes a year to the Spanish colonies, buying from the Royal Africa Company at £10 a head and selling at £25. It seemed of less importance that Britain had by treaty promised the Dutch not to crowd them out of the *Asiento*. In spite of this, the creation of the company was regarded as a brilliant *coup* by Harley. The Tories rejoiced that they had, under their control, a financial institution comparable to that great Whig stronghold, the Bank of England. No wonder that Mrs Masham was furious when Harley refused to give her a share in the loot.

The third transforming event was the most important of all: the Emperor Joseph died and his natural successor was the Archduke Charles who, at that time, was fighting with no great success for the Spanish throne. The death in Vienna made it much easier to satisfy the main parties in the long war. The Austrian "King of Spain" would become Emperor – he could hardly be both. The French King of Spain could remain unchallenged on his throne, provided only that Britain was guaranteed entry into the Spanish colonial markets and that Holland was given control of enough fortresses in Belgium to satisfy her need for security. Compared with these, the other issues were of minor importance. Clearly, the whole basis on which the war had been fought was changed. As Abraham Lincoln said of another war: "Neither party expected for the war the magnitude or the duration which it has already attained. Neither anticipated that the cause of the conflict might cease with, or even before, the conflict itself should cease."★

While the German Electors assembled in Frankfurt to elect the new Emperor – a formality, but a necessary one – the war remained in a state of torpor. Eugene, as Field-Marshal of the Empire, stood on the defensive on the Rhine. Marlborough, in command of the weakened British and Dutch, faced Villars in Flanders. The English general seemed to be in the worst of humours, as well he might be for one reason and another, with the government losing no opportunity to insult him and his wife doing everything she could do – down to stripping the rooms she had occupied in St James's Palace – to deepen the Queen's rage against "the Marlboroughs". He felt his health decay so fast that for the country's sake he longed for peace. His "last journey was likely to be hastened by the many vexations" he suffered. So he told Godolphin. The military task before him filled him with gloom. Eugene was gone, five battalions of British infantry had been stolen from him by St John. Already Villars was stronger in numbers than he; the French army was posted in a well-prepared defence position running for ninety miles east to west, knitting the rivers of Flanders into a coherent system of fortifications and linking Arras, Bouchain and Valenciennes. Villars called it the "Ne Plus Ultra Line" † in testimony of his confidence that it could resist any likely attack. Early in July the Dutch general, Count Hompesch, was surprised and badly mauled by Villars. Marlborough learnt the news with fury.

The generals, British and Dutch alike, watching their commander's mood with anxious eyes, observing his tetchiness and gloom, the almost violent changes in his temper, decided that the Duke was a sick man.

★ Lincoln. Second Inaugural. 1865.
† He is supposed to have taken the name from a scarlet coat of Marlborough's, so-called from its exceptional elegance.

They learned with alarm that his aim was to make a frontal attack on the Line. This, it seemed, was the purpose of his concentration of the army at Aubigny on the western section of the Line. Villars was well-informed of all this by his agents. Marlborough, in fact, seemed to go out of his way to advertise his intention to anyone within earshot. Villars, in high spirits, awaited the attack; it would be another shambles like Malplaquet, the slaughter would be frightful but this time a French victory would not be in doubt. Captain Parker of the Royal Irish thought very much the same when he went out on reconnaissance with the Duke on 4 August and rode for three miles along the enemy lines which he could see, "very strong and high and crowded with men and cannon". Worse still, Marlborough talked with the utmost freedom about the units which would be disposed and where the assault would be delivered. Considering that "Villars had spies at his very elbow", it was hardly discreet. Indeed, some of his officers thought that the ill-treatment he had met with at home had turned his brain.

But one thing Parker found puzzling. Without warning, General Cadogan left the crowd of officers and, accompanied by his groom, rode off in the direction of the Allied camp. Nobody paid any attention to this incident. The idea that the British general was a little bit touched in the head, no doubt, reached French headquarters as, no doubt, it was meant to do. At dusk, Marlborough sent a force of cavalry towards the west. But after dark came a surprising reversal. The whole army was dispatched in the opposite direction, marching at a cracking pace parallel to the French defence line. After all, it seemed there was not going to be a frontal assault on Villars' army where it was concentrated three miles to the south. There was going to be something else. What it might be could only be guessed at. At five o'clock the vanguard came to the river Scarpe which they found bridged by pontoons just as, years before, they, as the old hands among them remembered, had found the Rhine bridged at Coblenz. At dawn, a courier galloped up to the Duke with a message from Cadogan. The Quarter-Master General had not been idle since he had vanished the day before. He had pulled in troops from villages about Douai. Now, with Hompesch in command, this hastily gathered force marched southwards and, by three o'clock in the morning, they had pierced the Ne Plus Ultra Line at Arleux, seven miles south of Douai. They had done so without losing a man. This was the news from Cadogan which was passed down Marlborough's columns accompanied by an admonition to quicken the pace. "Every regiment of foot," says Parker, "brought up as many men as they could without waiting for any that dropped behind. It was a perfect race." For, by this time, Villars had realized what was happening and was hurrying after Marlborough who was, however, a few hours, say half an army, ahead of him. Villars spurred on frantically at the head of the Household cavalry. Too late! At eleven that morning, he found that Marlborough was ready to meet him with a substantial force of horse and foot drawn up well south of the Line. There he was too strong, too well posted to be attacked by Villars' weary horsemen. Breathless and hilarious, the Allied soldiers looked at the French. Once more, the English general had won the war of manoeuvre. Corporal John had done it again.

He had done so by an elaborate display of histrionics, by a feint march, by bringing into play at the critical point a corps hastily assembled from oddments, and finally by a forced counter-march which only soldiers of the finest quality could have executed. Marlborough had done it once before when he broke through the Lines of Brabant. In spite of his political disasters and the threat of final disgrace which hung over him, in spite of age and ill-health, he was still a master of the craft of war. He had outwitted the best of the French generals. But there was no possibility of challenging Villars to battle. The Frenchman had seven thousand more men than he had and had drawn them up in a position of great natural strength. In these circumstances, Marlborough decided to content himself with besieging Bouchain, a fortress beyond which there was open country all the way to Paris.

The siege is something of a military curiosity, for the French army was as close to Marlborough as he was to the fortress and the entrenchments he dug to hold off a relieving party were thirty miles long. It was a situation of some delicacy. In the end, after a siege which lasted a month, Bouchain fell. Marlborough exacted the unconditional surrender of its commander. This he imposed in order to humiliate Villars who had been crowing over him ever since the defeat of Hompesch at Douai. Needless to say, his political enemies in England, who had been lamenting the "butchers' bill" of Malplaquet, now denounced him for cowardice in failing to fight Villars. The Whigs did what they could to whip up public enthusiasm for a new victory. "At the same time that the outed family" – the Marlboroughs – "are applauded above measure and bloated on the success at Bouchain," wrote Francis Hoffman to Lord Oxford, "I find they double their malice against your lordship . . . Whiggish libels sell best."[11]

But what had happened, meanwhile, to St John's dream, the Quebec enterprise? On 22 August, three weeks before the surrender of Bouchain, eight transports ran aground in the St Lawrence and seven hundred soldiers lost their lives. The Admiral in command of the fleet decided that the expedition should be abandoned. Brigadier Hill was denied the chance to win fame. And Lord Oxford heard the news with undisguised merriment, to the annoyance of Mrs Masham. More than £20,000 had been voted to be spent on stores for the expedition; £7,000 had been spent. St John and his cronies had pocketed the balance, which might be held to compensate them for the loss of wider hopes.

With the fall of Bouchain, Marlborough made ready to go home, aware by this time that peace negotiations were going on from which he was excluded. He and Lord Oxford were on terms of the utmost amiability, he protesting that none of the Queen's subjects desired peace more heartily than he, Oxford passing on the latest news of the Queen's health: "a fit of the gout attended with more pain than usual; but her stomach has been all the while very good."[12] Neither writer deceived the other. It was certain that Anne's health was causing her loyal servants some anxiety about this time. In June, Shrewsbury had reported that she was "indisposed with gravel" but he thought she had recovered.[13] How long was she likely to live? It was one of the most acute questions in politics. Marlborough was annoyed by the injustice he suffered in the pamphlet war which was raging in London. There, Count Hompesch alone was given credit for piercing the Line and the whole operation was derided as "the crossing of the kennel". Bouchain was described as "a dovecot" on which Marlborough had squandered 16,000 men, four times the actual casualties. Into this war, Sarah threw herself with all her accustomed zest, allowing her agents to print gross libels on the Queen and her ministers.

At this time, Marlborough often complained of the reminders of the onset of old age; perhaps it was as well that he had fought his last battle. In The Hague he was embarrassed by meeting the British negotiators when, officially at least, he knew nothing of what they were doing. He arrived at Greenwich on 17 November, the anniversary of Queen Elizabeth's accession, when, as Swift reported,[14] "a great number of his creatures thought to revive the old ceremony among the rabble of burning the Pope in effigy." Quick to seize on any chance to stir up alarm among law-abiding citizens, the ministers sent a detachment of Guards to seize the effigies of the Pope, Devil and Pretender which were stored in an empty house in Angel Court, Drury Lane. In addition, they called out the trained bands while their propagandists published a list of those who had subscribed money for the intended processions. These included prominent members of the Kit-Cat Club. Marlborough avoided all this excitement by going to pay his respects to the Queen at Hampton Court. He was not, as Swift admitted, "much turned to be popular".

So ended the Duke of Marlborough's last campaign which many good judges thought his most brilliant. It was, however, a prelude to eclipse. The government's anxiety over the political situation was to this extent justified. In spite of the Tory pamphleteers, Marlborough's return had revived his military glory; and the ministers were about to make a settlement with France which would be widely regarded as a betrayal of his achievements as a soldier. Before many weeks had passed, the ministers and their friends were in such a state of alarm that they thought of fleeing the country; Swift asked Oxford to send him abroad as a Queen's Secretary until the storm had spent itself. But in the nick of time the wind turned.

XXIV

Materials for a Little Mischief

"Today we hear of new Lords and officers created, to-morrow of some
great men deposed and then again of fresh honours conferred."
                                  Robert Burton, The Anatomy of Melancholy

Not lies but half-truths are the main ammunition of political warfare.
Lies have their place of course; so has truth. But the shrewder combatant
uses subtler weapons. This fact was very much in the mind of Swift when
he sat down in his lodging in New Panton Street to write a pamphlet
which was shortly to be read and discussed by half the politically conscious
public in England. It was entitled *The Conduct of the Allies*. Its purpose was
to whip up popular support for the Tory government at a moment when
that seemed to be much needed. Harley, now Lord Oxford, and St John,
although deadly rivals contending for political leadership, were united in
their determination to make a peace with France, apart from the Allies
and, if need be, at the expense of the Allies. Through the Jacobite, Lord
Jersey, whose Catholic wife had a French chaplain, Abbé Gaultier, they
were already far advanced in negotiations with the French Foreign
Minister, the Marquis de Torcy. To promote the business Lord Jersey was
very soon receiving £3,000 a year from the French. He had already agreed
to concessions which, were they made public in England, would have
roused the Whig, Protestant alarm which, since James II, were never far
below the surface. For instance, Jersey was willing to concede that, on the
Queen's death she would be followed on the throne by her half-brother,
the Pretender. This was kept secret.

But what was known of the "Peace Preliminaries" was sufficiently
disturbing; England was prepared to see a Bourbon prince on the Spanish
throne. "No peace without Spain!" The Tory slogan, long since abandoned by all but the more old-fashioned of the party, was taken up by
the Whigs. Five years earlier, St John had seen Spain as the military
cul-de-sac which it was. "For God's sake, let us be out of Spain!" he had

cried. Now the policy he had abandoned was taken up by the Whigs. At the same time from every Allied court in Europe came outcries of protest: England, having presided over a victorious war against the French King, was about to give Louis "a peace glorious to himself, ruinous to the victorious Allies and destructive to the liberties of all Europe." So wrote Baron von Bothmar, the Hanoverian minister, using words of protest which might have come from any of England's allies. In this crisis, Tory noblemen of the highest respectability deserted the government. And could the Queen herself be counted on? Swift, whose ears picked up all the Tory whispers from Oxford or St John or Mrs Masham, was afraid that Her Majesty was false, for which he blamed the throng of unreliable persons round her. The Duke and Duchess of Somerset were there, known opponents of the peace. If he had his way, Swift would have turned all of them out of their employments. And now, to make matters worse, here was Marlborough himself back in England, somewhat battered by hostile propaganda and with the threat hanging over him of an examination of his accounts, but beyond question the most famous Englishman of the day with a string of dazzling victories to his credit. A power therefore as well as a name.

Moreover, Marlborough was not only a presence in the land; he was an active force, priming Allied ministers with arguments and, it was believed, organizing the opposition in the House of Lords where the critical debate on policy was about to be held. It was a time, if ever there was one, for a spokesman for the government to exert the full force of his genius. Swift wrote as one in whom – as in all great controversialists – need supplied an extra spurt of imagination and ingenuity.

"After ten years' war, with perpetual success," he began, "to tell us it is yet impossible to have a good peace is very surprising." The tone was light, urbane, reasonable, ironic. As an opening to what was to be a savage attack, it could hardly have been improved. "It is natural to enquire how long we shall be able to go on at this rate." Very soon, the mood of the pamphlet altered. At the time of the Revolution, England had spent six millions annually to enlarge the frontier of the Dutch; then she had hastily engaged in this other war which had cost her sixty millions and put her in a worse condition not only than any of her allies, but even her conquered enemies. And now? Swift having prepared the ground by these appeals to just resentment and self-pity, the time had come to launch the thunderbolts: "No nation was ever so long or so scandalously abused by the folly, the temerity, the corruption and the ambition of its domestic enemies or treated with so much insolence, injustice and ingratitude by its foreign friends. Ten glorious campaigns are passed and now, at last, like the sick man, we are just expiring with all sorts of good symptoms." By this time, Swift's audience, whether Tories who were being confirmed in joyous apprehensions or Whigs appalled by what they read, must have been aware that they were in the presence of a masterpiece. A masterpiece of a special kind, admittedly. *The Conduct of the Allies* has a place not only in literature but also in the rogues' gallery of political sophistry. It should be a set piece in every sixth form as an Awful Warning against the wiles and ways of the demagogue.

But to go on with Swift's argument: while England was squandering her money on the Continent, France was grabbing the South American trade, and what had been England's reward for this abnegation? Hardly a petty prince whom she half-maintained with subsidies but was ready to threaten that he would recall his troops. It was necessary to examine how this disaster had come about. The hunter moved in for the kill. "Reputation is the smallest sacrifice those can make us who have been the instruments of our ruin so that, in exposing the action of such persons, I cannot be said, properly speaking, to do them any injury . . . The true spring and motive of [the war] was the aggrandizing of a particular family . . ." Marlborough had tolerated Dutch encroachments owing to "this immeasurable love of wealth which his best friends allow to be his predominant passion". But greed was not his only vice, there was also ambition which had already advanced far and wished to go further: "By these steps the old masters of the palace in France became masters of the Kingdom and by these steps a general during pleasure might grow into a general for life and a general for life into a King." The ghost of Oliver Cromwell walked through the phrases, alarming all good people.

By this time, Swift was in full flight; one after the other the phrases, telling and memorable, were pouring out. "It will no doubt be a mighty comfort to our grandchildren when they see a few rags hang up in Westminster Hall which cost a hundred million . . . We have lived upon [financial] expedients. We have dieted a healthy body into a consumption by plying it with physic instead of food . . . We have been fighting for the ruin of the public interest and the advancement of a private . . . The nation begins now to think these blessings are not worth fighting for any longer." And so on.

Rarely had the pedestrian business of politics been deluged with such a cataract of eloquence. Yet scarcely a word was wasted, scarcely a phrase but added force or precision to the argument. And what an argument it was! It is true that few of the steps in the course of reasoning but had been taken before. The ingredients which had been mixed in the cup were for the most part familiar enough: xenophobia; readiness to believe that one has been over-reached; distrust of an ally – any ally; jealousy of another man's success and envy of his wealth, which can be most conveniently ascribed to dishonesty or avarice or both. All this had been heard before; it had furnished the pabulum for a hundred Tory pamphlets, a score of scurrilous lampoons against the Marlboroughs. But here it was compressed into a single missile which exploded in the reader's mind with the power of a bomb. But there was, too, an effect which was novel.

"An entirely new picture emerged. Monied men who paraded their wealth while the rest of the nation was weighed down by taxes; allies who broke their compacts with impunity; the Whigs who had actually rejected peace terms with France when they were offered, a duchess who lorded it over the Queen and ranted when a few of her privileges were stripped from her; a general who had amassed a tremendous fortune and had, indeed, applied to become general for life; all these were facts, verifiable by the public with their own eyes and from accepted hearsay. Adding them together, it was not so outlandish to suggest there was a conspiracy on all sides to go on with those measures which must perpetuate the war." So writes the most learned and inspired student of those tremendous winter days of 1711.*

The effect on the political public was instant and powerful, as it had to be. *The Conduct* was published on 27 November; Parliament was due to meet on 7 December. Within a month, 11,000 copies had been sold. By that time, then, the number of its readers was at least 30,000 and in all likelihood was more. In other words, the coffee houses, the pulpits, the universities, Whitehall and Grub Street were aware and agog. When Parliament met, some doubters would have been converted to the cause of Oxford and St John and a greater number of believers would be strengthened in the faith. Just as important, there would not be enough time for an equally cogent counter-argument to be marshalled which might have shown, for example, that the Dutch had spent and suffered more than the British at Malplaquet and before Malplaquet.

For the moment, Swift had it all his own way with the public. His impact on their thinking was immense. They had suspected – some of them – that they had been wronged. But wronged on this scale! The

* Michael Foot, *The Pen and the Sword*, p. 302. MacGibbon and Kee, London, 1951.

discovery was shattering. On the day after publication, the author noted, "The pamphlet begins to make a noise."[1] The day after, he reported, "My printer came this morning to tell me he must immediately print a new edition." Men who met him and did not know he was the author urged him to read it, "for it is something extraordinary". He saw it on the First Minister's table. St John, who had supplied many of the facts, the true and the false, told him that the Dutch envoy was planning a riposte. An obscure pamphleteer could hardly ask for a higher compliment. A poor vicar from an Irish parish might be forgiven if he experienced a wave of spiritual pride.

The political drama was due to reach its climax in the House of Lords. In the Commons, the Ministry had a reliable majority, especially as the Jacobite members, obedient to their paymasters in France, were bound to support the policy of peace. In the Lords, matters were different. The Duke of Somerset, a former Whig won over by Oxford, had quarrelled with St John and left court. Disturbingly enough, his Duchess was the Queen's constant companion. Lord Nottingham, most gloomy and devoted of High Churchmen, promised to vote against the peace provided the Whigs would pass his Occasional Conformity Bill – aimed at preventing Dissenters from gaining the privileges reserved for good Anglicans through the device of taking the Sacraments now and then. This bargain had been duly struck. The Scots peers had been ready to vote for the Ministry, a service for which their lordships had been well paid. But, alas, flooding in the north had held them up. They could not reach Westminster in time.

On the appointed day, the Queen duly delivered her speech: "notwithstanding the arts of those who delighted in war [i.e. Marlborough] a peace treaty was going to be negotiated." Having performed that ceremonial task, Anne had put off her robes and taken her place in a box to listen to the speeches. Nottingham proposed an amendment to the Address of Thanks: that there should be no peace so long as a Bourbon prince sat on the Spanish throne. The government moved the previous question – and lost by one vote. In the debate on policy that followed, Lord Anglesey said that they might have had peace after Ramillies if it had not been for the opposition of some persons "whose interest it was to prolong the war" (i.e. Marlborough).

At this, the Duke who had been sitting impassively in his place, a mute reminder of military glories, got up and, with a respectful bow, "I refer myself to the Queen whether I have not constantly informed her and her Council of all the proposals for peace that have been made, and have not desired instruction for my conduct on the subject." Advanced age (he was sixty-one) and many fatigues had made him earnestly wish for retirement so that he could think of eternity. He would be ready to serve Queen and country ("if I can but crawl along") to obtain an honourable and lasting peace, but he could not take part in negotiating a peace which would leave Spain to the Bourbons. In short, he would vote for Lord Nottingham's amendment. When the vote came to be taken, Oxford and the Ministry were defeated by twelve. The Queen rose from her seat. Lord Shrewsbury, the Lord Chamberlain, asked if she would wish him to lead her from the House or would she prefer the Lord Great Chamberlain. "Neither," said Her Majesty, and beckoned to the Duke of Somerset, who had voted against the government that day and was known to believe that the time had come when the Queen should change her first minister. All Westminster buzzed with excitement at the significance which was read into the Queen's gesture. Did it mean that the Queen was about to dismiss Oxford? Most people thought so. But for whom would she send? Marlborough? And have Sarah storming into her palace? Surely that was out of the question. But what, then, was to happen? Wharton, the most sardonic jester on the Whig benches, put both hands round his neck every time a minister rose to speak. The hangman's noose was ready.

Although Swift's pamphlet, by this time in its fifth edition, was still doing its work in the country, it could not ease the apprehensions in its author's breast. "You will be beheaded," he told Oxford, "but I shall only be hanged." He thought seriously of taking refuge in Ireland from these dangerous scenes with their delusive triumphs. Only Oxford and St John remained inexplicably cheerful. "Pooh! it will be all right," said the First Minister. His confidence was not without foundation: the House of Commons remained faithful to the peace, rejecting by 232 votes to 106 the amendment which the Lords had carried. More than that, the campaign against Marlborough's reputation took a long stride forward when the report of the Commission of Public Accounts was brought before Parliament on 15 December.

Marlborough, having come out openly and, as it seemed, decisively against the Ministry, must be destroyed. Parliament would be told that he had behaved dishonestly with public money. The amount was stated. The documentary evidence was forthcoming. At the same time the Queen was being told that her Captain-General was a potential Cromwell and that she must either defend her ministers or suffer the fate of her grandfather who had failed to defend his great minister, Lord Strafford, and had in consequence followed him to the scaffold. That these were the arguments which Oxford put to the Queen can be inferred from a letter in which St John put them to the Lord Strafford of the day, who was Ambassador at The Hague. The case against Marlborough's honesty was on a different level. But before it could be answered and debated in Parliament two events had transformed the scene completely. In a bold assertion of the prerogative, Oxford persuaded the Queen to make twelve new peers. Thus it was certain that his command of the Upper House would not depend on the state of the roads to the north or the cupidity of the Scottish nobility. At the last minute, one of the proposed new lords declined the honour on the creditable, if unusual, ground that acceptance might savour of jobbery. However, a new candidate was ready at hand: Mrs Masham's husband, who was a nonentity but was willing to serve. The Queen had no wish to make her ex-Bedchamber woman a peeress but, in the crisis, she overcame her repugnance. When the twelve new barons arrived in the Chamber Lord Wharton asked, in his jovial way, if they intended to vote individually or by their foreman.

On the same day, 1 January 1712, the final step was taken. The Queen dismissed Marlborough from all his offices. The Duke of Ormonde, a Jacobite, became Captain-General and Colonel of the First Guards, a post which Marlborough had held since the triumphant days after Blenheim. Lord Rivers was Master General of the Ordnance. Swift who, as much as any man, had made possible the general's downfall, looked with some alarm at the fruit of his labours: "These are strong remedies," he wrote, "pray God the patient is able to bear them."

Sir John Vanbrugh was alarmed when the Treasury cut off the supply of money for Blenheim, " 'Twould be very hard we should be yet undone by the mere Tory mob, ignorant, furious country priests and stupid justices." The unpaid workmen threatened sabotage; Sarah shrugged her shoulders. Her views about the palace were well known. "The second greenhouse or a detached gallery, I thank God I prevented being built; nothing could be more mad than this proposal."[2] Eventually Harley decided that it would be less trouble to let the building go on. His backbenchers were displeased.

Louis XIV learned the news of Marlborough's downfall with delighted incredulity: no longer were the armies arrayed against him led by a soldier whom his generals could not beat. No longer was the policy of

Britain directed by one who, as Marlborough wrote to Queen Anne on that first morning of January, believed that "the friendship of France must needs be destructive to your Majesty". In that sombre conclusion, he was wrong. For one thing, he under-rated, in a moment of understandable annoyance, the magnitude of his own achievement in reducing the military power and political authority of France. For another, he failed to realize that the fanatical nationalism of the Spaniards, which had defeated Allied ambitions, would also work against French. A Bourbon prince on the Spanish throne would go to some pains to assert his detachment from his French relatives in Versailles. But all this was not visible to the general when, loaded with honours and rewards, he read the chilly letter which Oxford had dictated and Anne had signed. Then he threw it in the fire.

Marlborough recovered his composure very quickly. After all, some things could not be taken from him. This new Europe which was emerging was of his making as much as any man's. The glory of Blenheim – the battle – would live in history while the grandeur of Blenheim – the palace – although not yet complete, would be his monument as long as it stood in the English countryside. And it was likely to stand for long; Vanbrugh's massive design had seen to that. Besides, the game was not over yet. The War of the Spanish Succession was coming to an end in a treaty which was likely to be discreditable to England but, thanks to his victories, would not be to her complete disadvantage. The War of the British Succession, waged with the weapons of politics, intrigues, knavery, if not of those of actual battle, still lay ahead.

The dignified old gentleman with the fine clothes and the military bearing who sat at the card table in Holywell House at St Albans had other matters on his mind but basset or piquet; other sounds reached his ears besides the sharp clatter of Sarah's tongue; other reading engaged his eyes besides the spite and scurrillity of the pamphleteers. There were letters from Hanover and Vienna; echoes from the coffee houses of St James's Street; hoarse whispers from old comrades home on leave and angry about the way matters were going in Flanders; enticements of Jacobite agents that must, at all costs, be kept out of Sarah's sight. In those days, the Duke was reported to be much cast down, weary of it all, a sick man – diabetes, as Swift heard with satisfaction: in short, he was a spent force. How much truth was there in this picture of despondency, and how much of it was play-acting which had in the past so often concealed an intense activity? The Duke of Berwick, his nephew who knew him well, warned his half-brother, the Pretender, do not trust Marlborough.

Time to Leave

"Cursed apostates who taught their prince to break her word. These are
they that got the bravest general in the world degraded."

John Dunton

"I don't believe in war: there is too much luck in it for my liking."

Louis Napoleon after Solferino

When they wish to behave with incivility nobody can do the job more
thoroughly than the gentlemen of England. Thus, when Prince Eugene
arrived in London in February 1712, he was very soon made to feel that
he was unwelcome. The Queen was embarrassed (although she did give
him a diamond-hilted sword). Ministers were preoccupied, evasive, if not
downright discourteous. The City wished to arrange a banquet for him
but was forbidden to do so. In compensation, Lord Portland gave him an
entertainment so magnificent that the dinner table was served by gentlemen who had volunteered for the duty in order to see the splendour. All
the great Whig nobles were present that night. When the band struck up,
his fellow-guest, the Duke, who had once been admired in the Duchess of
Cleveland's ballroom, did not take the floor. His dancing days were over.
On another occasion, Eugene and his old friend, Marlborough, went to
the opera together; when he appeared in the box the audience gave him
three cheers, and another three on leaving. Such popular acclamation
only made the government more determined than ever to keep aloof
from the famous visitor. Eugene must be frozen out. After all, they were
at that moment engaged in secret talks with the French which involved
some betrayal of their allies.

While observing the extraordinary manners of the people he had come
among, the Prince spent a great deal of time buying rare books. He was
the greatest non-reading bibliophile in Europe, but fortunately he had
brought along with him Hohendorff, a learned connoisseur. They
haunted the booksellers' shops together. After two months, he took his
leave, having learnt much and accomplished nothing. Meanwhile, his

companion-in-arms, Marlborough, who had been dismissed, was in process of being disgraced.

This was something longed for by the enthusiasts of the October Club ("Tory when sober, Jacobite when drunk"), whose support St John and Oxford saw as necessary to carry through their projected peace. Marlborough must be destroyed. He had shown his power in the Lords debate. He must not be given the chance to do it again. And the materials were at hand. Enough to persuade the House of Commons, who did not need much in the way of persuasion, and probably enough to convince the House of Lords, too, now that Oxford had adjusted the balance in that noble assembly. On two charges, Marlborough was accused of corruption. About the same time, Robert Walpole, ablest of the younger Whigs, was charged with corruption and spent five months in the Tower. His imprisonment was quite comfortable; he used it to write *A Short History of Parliament*; his apartment was much frequented by Whig notables. But he did not take it lightly. "I heartily despise what I shall one day revenge," he told his sister, Dolly.[1] He knew that St John was the man chiefly responsible for his trouble and, in due course, he took his revenge. But Walpole was not the main target of the Tories. By striking at him they were playing "a leading card to maul the Duke of Marlborough" (Swift).

It was said that Marlborough had obtained a commission of £6,000 a year from Sir Solomon de Medina on the contract for the providing of bread for the army, and that he had received $2\frac{1}{2}$ per cent on the amount voted by Parliament for the foreign troops in British pay. All told, the sum produced by these two sources was estimated at something between £170,000 and a quarter of a million. Was this, then, the origin of the Duke's envied and enormous wealth? His political enemies did not doubt it. The simpler Tory squires were ready to believe anything against one who was in their minds clearly associated with the "moneyed interest" – and was not Sir Solomon de Medina, a Jew, born in Italy, one of those who had financed the Revolution of 1688 and one of the biggest sellers of gold to the Bank of England? More than that, was he not a member of the "Bank Parlour", the inner circle of that mysterious institution? If one were searching for an individual to embody the novel, sinister power of credit, Sir Solomon would do very well.

St John pressed the attack on Marlborough in Parliament. Swift said, "The bribery is manifest." The case for the defence as put by Marlborough was simple. The commission on the bread contract and the

2½ per cent on the pay of the foreign troops were both customary perquisites of the commander-in-chief in the Low Countries and were
intended for his secret service. For this latter purpose, Parliament had
been prepared to vote a specific sum of £10,000 a year while, in King
William's time, £70,000 had been needed to cover the actual cost of
Intelligence. For that reason the sum of £10,000 openly voted had been
supplemented in this unobtrusive and convenient way. The idea was
King William's. Queen Anne had given it her authority under her Royal
warrant. In due course – which was important – the Allied states publicly
declared that the 2½ per cent had been deducted with their consent
and approval. They might well do so. No army had ever been better
served by its Intelligence than Marlborough's. And the bread? Marlborough maintained – and nobody contested – that the British army had
as cheap and abundant a supply of good bread as the Dutch, who were
notoriously the most frugally fed troops in Europe. As bread contractors,
Sir Solomon and his brother, Moses, were equal to the best. Marlborough
had tried others and knew what he was talking about. So the case against
him had vanished in smoke? On the contrary!

The House of Commons found against him by 267 votes to 165. From
one quarter during those tense days, Oxford could count on votes from
Mrs Masham and her family, the Hills. As Sarah tells the story, "This
honest Jack Hill, the once ragged boy whom I clothed, happening to be
sick in bed, was nevertheless persuaded by his sister to get up, wrap
himself in warmer clothes than those I had given him and go to the House
to vote against the Duke."[2] Adam Cardonnel, Marlborough's secretary,
was charged with taking 500 ducats from Sir Solomon on the sealing of
each bread contract, and was expelled from the House. And Benjamin
Sweet, who had deducted 1 per cent of the forces' pay – again a customary
perquisite of his office as Paymaster – was prosecuted.

Marlborough's explanation of the 2½ per cent was not published
until the affair was all over and, by most people, forgotten. As for the
statements by the Allied governments, these were not made until the
peace conference at Utrecht a year after the Commons vote. "We are
fully convinced and satisfied that the Prince, Duke of Marlborough, has
annually applied these sums to the secret service and his wise application
of these amounts has forcibly contributed to the gaining of so many
battles." So wrote the Elector of Hanover, the future George I. But his
testimony could not alter the verdict of the House of Commons a year
earlier. One final touch of cynicism. When the Duke of Ormonde was

appointed Captain-General, the ministers who had obtained Marl-borough's condemnation by the Commons gave Ormonde the right to draw the same amount from the bread contract and the same percentage from the pay of the foreign troops and to apply the money to the same purpose.

One question remains. It is now known that Marlborough's military "family", Cadogan and Cardonnel, speculated on the foreign exchange market with money which was passing through their hands on its way to the troops. It is possible that Marlborough did the same. He would be able to do so with sums of money vastly bigger than either of his two subordinates and with all the greater impunity since his favourite banker and close friend, Sir Henry Furnese, was also a leading contractor for commercial bills of exchange in the Low Countries. But there is no evidence that Marlborough did anything of the sort and his great wealth, which was not to be forgiven him by the landed gentry, could well be accounted for by frugality, skilful investment and an enormous salary. There is no doubt, however, that during those months Marlborough was in a highly emotional and nervous state. His correspondence with Sweet shows this plainly enough.* The most probable explanation of this anxiety is, however, not a troubled conscience, but fear lest his "delicate" sources of information might be imperilled by clumsy investigations.

But St John, who had promised the French to get rid of Marlborough, was not likely to be content with his dismissal, and at St John's heels was the whole pack of the October Club, determined to pursue Marlborough "to the blood", that is, to impeachment and the scaffold – at least the wilder among them were. They were bent on rescinding the Act of Settlement and bringing the Queen's brother, James Stuart, to the throne on her death. It would be better, of course, if he would agree to change his religion – or keep it concealed, as his Uncle Charles had done. But, if he proved to be inconveniently stubborn on this doctrinal issue, as he did, there were men in the Club who were prepared to regard the question as of secondary importance and to acknowledge that steadfastness in religion

---

* *Blenheim MSS*, HJ. 34.

Marlborough to Sweet: "Never write to me but by a sure hand." 2 February 1711.

Marlborough to Sweet from Aix-la-Chapelle, 13 January 1712: "Cadogan will let you know where you and he can meet in secret."

Sweet to Marlborough, 2 May 1712: "I would sooner lose my life than disclose any transaction Your Grace has entrusted to me."

Marlborough to Sweet, 12 October 1712: "These Ministers must know that I have laid the money" (the $2\frac{1}{2}$ per cent) "out for the public good. God forgive them."

was, after all, creditable to the man. Those with longer memories, men who could cast their minds back to events in England before the Revolution, might not share this amiable view. Men like Marlborough; better still, women like Sarah! So long as the victor of Blenheim was alive and at large the odds were against a success of the Jacobite conspiracy. Against, but the margin was slight! If the army and the fortresses were in the hands of the Jacobite Ormonde (whose incompetence had not yet been measured in 1712), if a French army under Villars or Berwick were brought over the Channel with the connivance of a Jacobite admiral, if the British army were further disheartened by the removal of its best officers, then who was to say what would be the outcome of the War of the British Succession? And if, in addition, Marlborough were out of the way at the hour of crisis . . . Some important factors might be left out of this reckoning, but Jacobites have never been famous for taking a chilly view of their prospects.

In May 1712, the government's plans to strengthen the French and weaken Britain's allies took a decisive step forward: Ormonde received orders to take no part in battle alongside his allies. The orders were known to the French high command but kept secret from the Dutch, Eugene and the others. In short, the British army and its new Captain-General were involved in an act of treachery almost without parallel in British history. This was indeed perfidious Albion! It followed, naturally enough, given St John's resourceful and unscrupulous character, from the negotiations he was carrying on surreptitiously with the French Foreign Minister. When the matter became publicly known, there was a debate in the Lords during which Lord Poulett compared the courage of the Duke of Ormonde favourably with the conduct of "a certain general" who had deliberately led his troops to the slaughter so that he could fill his pockets by disposing of the commissions of officers killed in action. Poulett, who thought that the accusation was covered by the privilege of Parliament, was much taken aback when Marlborough challenged him to a duel. He carried the news of this unexpected event to Lady Poulett who implored the government to intervene. Eventually, the Queen ordered Marlborough to go no further with the business.

As the year wore on and a general election loomed, St John's campaign of calumny against Marlborough went on with growing savagery. He was accused of cowardice and of causing needless suffering to the wounded at Malplaquet by failing to provide medical supplies for which he had been given money. It is strange that charges so preposterous should have been spread, and by many believed, against a brilliantly successful general, but it is not so strange that in the autumn of 1712, Marlborough decided to leave the country. By that time, he knew that the government were preparing a case against him over money spent on his still unfinished palace at Blenheim and that he might be required to repay the money he had spent on the secret service during the war.

This was all the more likely because, since he had been driven from his command, Britain's military record had been deplorable. Her record in other respects was even more unsavoury. St John, informed by a spy in Eugene's entourage, passed on to the French the warning that the prince was about to launch a surprise attack on Nieuport or Furnes. Nor did the shame for this particularly despicable treachery belong to St John alone. Oxford, too, was a party to it, as if unwilling that his younger and more energetic rival should have a monopoly of infamy. In Flanders the unhappy British army, retreating to the coast, was humiliated as town after town shut its gates contemptuously and refused it admission. It was a miserable end to ten splendid campaigns. No wonder that the veterans of Blenheim and Ramillies ground their teeth in rage and broke their muskets over their knees. St John, for his services to the nation in that summer, was made a peer. He was now Viscount Bolingbroke. The earldom which he had hoped for was denied him, a disappointment for which he blamed Queen Anne's grudging spirit and the spite of Lord Oxford. Swallowing his annoyance, he set off for Paris where he enjoyed the most flattering attentions from the King and the court, found himself a new and beautiful mistress and – for business is business – made £3,000 by the sale of passports. The making of peace went more smoothly after the Dutch and Eugene, deserted by their British allies, had been soundly defeated by Villars.

One day that autumn, Marlborough asked Oxford for his passport, and against Bolingbroke's opposition, Oxford persuaded the Queen to give it. Bolingbroke thought, reasonably enough, that Marlborough was less dangerous at home than abroad. And the extremer Tories were furious that he, for whom they had prepared the Tower if not the block,[3] was about to escape them. There were indeed good reasons of personal safety why he should want to go. The speculation charge against him was still grinding on. The press campaign did not abate. Then, in mid-September, a personal loss disheartened him: his lifelong friend, Godolphin, who had borne half the burden of administering the war, died at St Albans.

A month later, a melodramatic incident made London an even more unpleasant place: the Duke of Hamilton, the first Scottish peer, on the eve of leaving for France where he was to be Ambassador, was challenged to a duel by Lord Mohun. When they met in Hyde Park, each duellist, without troubling to fence, killed the other. Although Marlborough had nothing to do with the affair, Mohun had been named as his second in the proposed duel with Lord Poulett and Mohun's second, General Macartney, was notoriously a member of Marlborough's faction in the army. Indeed, two years earlier, he had been broken for drinking confusion to Marlborough's enemies, as he claimed, to Harley, as the government alleged. Now he fled hurriedly to the Continent, sceptical that he would be given a fair trial. It need not be said that Tory propaganda seized on this tragic affair to assert that Marlborough, associated with two of the duellists, was the man ultimately responsible for the ruffianism of the unemployed officers who infested the drinking dens of Covent Garden and St James's.

Nine days after the duel, Marlborough left for Dover. He had arranged that £50,000 should be sent to The Hague for his use in case of need. He had settled his affairs. It was time to go. He arrived at Ostend on 12 December, greeted by salvoes of cannon-fire and welcomed by the Governor. Cadogan accompanied him on the road to Antwerp, "an indispensable duty to me who was for so many years honoured with his confidence and friendship." For this act, Cadogan was, in due course, dismissed from his post by the government. He had given the clearest possible indication of where his loyalty lay and it was not a time in which a man could serve two masters.

XXVI

How Fortune Does Banter Us!

"'Tis well an Old Age is out
And time to begin a new."
Dryden

One day in the spring of 1713, Marlborough, then staying at Aix-la-Chapelle, heard that the war was over. It had lasted for twelve years; its casualties – the dead and wounded – had numbered 180,000[1]; it had brought devastation to various regions of Europe, above all to the Palatinate and Flanders; it had worn out the patience of people who had suffered least, notably the British. It had cost untold millions in money.[2] And what had it accomplished? Who was the victor? If it were properly named as the War of the Spanish Succession, if the main object of the Grand Alliance were to prevent a French prince from sitting on the Spanish throne, then France had emerged as the victor. For Louis' grandson, Philip, Duke of Anjou, was the King of Spain, Philip V, recognized as such, willingly or reluctantly, by the states that had gone to war to prevent his succession. To that extent French policy, or, at least, the family pride of the Bourbons, had triumphed. But, in spite of its name, the conflict had been much wider and more complex than a dynastic quarrel centred on one European throne, and nobody had better reason for realizing this than the old gentleman who was trying to restore his failing health in the hot baths at Aix.

Through painful diplomacy and with the British taxpayers' money, he had created a polyglot army, owing an allegiance to ten or eleven princes, that matched the military power of France; by exercise of his personality, he had held it together through a long and tedious war; in a series of dazzling battles he had led it to victory. He had met and measured the Swedish King and had sensed that something novel and alarming was coming into existence beyond the Pripet Marshes. Through his comrade, Eugene, he had come to understand better than any English statesman the Empire, its intricacy, its ambitions, its weakness. He had seen Prussians in action, a foretaste of battles to come. In Hanover he had become a favourite of that jolly old woman, the Electress, whom Queen Anne detested so much and who wanted so much to be Britain's queen. At the same time he was in correspondence with the Stuart Pretender who had, after all, a fifty-fifty chance of following his half-sister, Anne, on the throne. Marlborough had asked his forgiveness for the past – and at the same time had offered a loan of £50,000 to the Hanoverian claimant!

Marlborough, more than most men, was capable of looking at the broad European picture as Bolingbroke's rough and brazen diplomacy had left it, and seeing it in perspective. Certainly, he was not a man to waste moral indignation on what had been done. Britain's part in the Peace of Utrecht had been contemptible. The Catalan insurgents, who had fought with such ferocious valour on Britain's side, were abandoned; worse still, a British fleet helped to ensure their defeat. The Dutch had spent more and suffered more in the war than any of the Allies; they had moreover been bullied by British statesmen; in consequence, they had stayed in the fight when they wanted to make peace and had been deserted by the British army when they tried to fight on! Now, in defeat, they were forced to accept a defensive barrier of fortresses which collapsed at the first French onslaught, thirty years later. Staggering under a war debt which she could barely carry, Holland was the real loser in the war.

The Duke of Savoy was rewarded for his cunning and courage by being given a stronger frontier in Piedmont and by the possession of Sicily. Prussia was given Guelderland which the Whigs had promised to Holland. Belgium – apart from the fortresses earmarked for the Dutch – was bestowed on Austria, which was also enlarged by the possession of Sardinia and Naples. France was given back Lille, but was under obligation to demilitarize the port of Dunkirk, nest of her privateers. This promise, however, she was in no hurry to carry out. In the delaying action the French government was abetted by Lady Masham and her brother, Brigadier Hill, who vied with one another in promoting French interests. Two Scots battalions in the Dunkirk garrison were preponderantly Jacobite, a fact which might be of importance if there was a French invasion of England in aid of the Pretender. Britain did well out of the war. Not only did she now have Gibraltar and Port Mahon in Minorca and, therefore, the command of the Western Mediterranean, but she kept her hold on the Hudson's Bay territory. Above all, she had the *Asiento* – the slave monopoly – which once she had promised to share with the Dutch. 1713 was not a year in which the British honoured their pledges.

Oxford and Bolingbroke, who had risen to power by exploiting the prejudice of the squirearchy against the "money interest", now felt that they needed to placate the merchants. The *Asiento*, as profitable as the greediest financier could wish for, was the device by which they hoped to win over the City of London. They did not hope in vain.

At the end of all the fighting, then, peace had apparently brought about only some limited re-arrangements in the political map. But, as it turned out, these modifications had set the stage for the infinitely more far-reaching transformation which was to come. Britain was now indisputably a great power, challenging France for supremacy and both richer and stronger than Holland which, only half a century before, had been her naval and commercial rival and now was so far reduced that when, a year later, the Dutch wished to escort George I to his new realm in England, they had the utmost difficulty in scraping together enough warships for the task. In contrast, British exports doubled in the fifty years after the peace. But in her reduced state, Holland could not look for compassion or even civility from her gloating ally. Instead, she was subjected to a stream of calumny from London journals, calumny which Bolingbroke encouraged but did not believe and which Swift and his fellow-hacks should not have believed.

At this time the Irish parson was still reporting to Stella the doings of Sarah on the eve of her departure to join her Duke: she "makes presents of rings to her friends worth £200 apiece; I am sure she ought to give me one." Later, he heard that the Duchess had stripped the diamonds from a portrait which the Queen had given her in happier days, and "given the picture to old Mrs Higgins, bidding her make the best of it she could. Is she not a detestable slut!"[3] Swift was in a fever of anxiety just then about his own future; having given up all hope for a bishopric, the best he could expect was a deanery. Would it be Windsor or St Patrick's? At length, the blow fell. The pamphleteer felt, as the Duke had felt before him, the sharp tooth of Royal disfavour and political ingratitude. Even Lady Masham's grief could not save him. He was to be Dean of St Patrick's. Like Marlborough, Swift went into exile, to a country he detested, but carrying with him a priceless possession, his genius. Another man of letters, Joseph Addison, was more fortunate; his drama, *Cato*, opened at the Haymarket on 14 April and ran for twenty nights. The author had intended it as a Whig propaganda play which at one time he thought of dedicating to the Duchess of Marlborough. He was somewhat taken aback when Bolingbroke handed fifty guineas to Booth, the actor, who took the leading part, "for defending the cause of liberty so well against a perpetual dictator". The run of the play ended when the actress, Mrs Oldfield, "cannot hold out any longer having had for several nights a midwife behind the scenes which is surely very unbecoming the character of Cato's daughter."[4] It had made a great deal of money for Addison.

By this time, Sarah had joined the Duke and together they had travelled to Frankfurt, greeted where they went by cheering people and saluting soldiers, alarmed on one occasion by a rumour that kidnappers were in the neighbourhood – inspired by the Jacobites? Suborned by Bolingbroke? Who could say? But on the whole life was peaceful, tranquil, which held danger for one of Sarah's ardent temperament but not, apparently, for Marlborough. He had, she complained, grown lazy. And those letters to the Pretender, begging him to use his influence with Louis XIV in order to dissuade the British government from confiscating his property, as it seemed they might do. Sarah would certainly not approve of them.

The money in the bank, the share certificates, the lands, above all, the golden walls and ordered plantations of Blenheim spread over two thousand acres, the Grinling Gibbons carvings, the pictures and tapestries he had brought from Brussels – like many rich old men, especially those who have once been poor, these possessions were very dear to him, especially now that he thought he might be stripped of them. To keep his hold on them, he abased himself to the son of the King he had helped to drive from the throne. Mercifully – so far as is known – the shaming letters were never seen by Sarah. She, who had as tenacious a clutch on her possessions as the meanest housewife in the world, who hated Blenheim as much for its extravagance as for the lack of propriety which her taste detected in it – she who loved money, hoarded money, and guarded money like a dragon, would certainly not have dropped the stiffest curtsey to the Pretender in order to save all her fortune. With another part of the Duke's correspondence she would, however, have been in full sympathy: his letters to Hanover, the plans he was making with his old friends in the army for military intervention in England when the time came. The time did not seem far off, for the Queen's health was very frail. During those months its state could be gathered from the changing value of government stocks on the London market. "The Funds rose when the Queen's illness was followed by a report of her death, fell on a sudden rumour of her recovery."[5]

The crisis of the Queen's health came and it passed, but not before Bolingbroke had spent a few days of fevered anxiety, realizing that the project to bring in the Pretender was still far from ready. Worse still, when James was begged by ministers to change his religion or, at least, to conceal it, he replied as the son of James II and not as the nephew of Charles II. Rather than play the knave he would forfeit the throne which was his by birth. But there was no possibility of Parliament accepting a Papist king. What then? That he should become king by means of a military *coup*? But the best officers were Whigs, hardened soldiers with a string of battles to their credit. It was necessary to remove them. As quickly as he could, Bolingbroke was ousting them from the key commands. But the purge was not half complete and the new men would not be as good as the old.* Villars and the French army must be shipped over. That was agreed, and suitable regiments in French pay, Irish for example, were already being moved nearer to the French Channel ports. But nothing irrevocable could be done until the Queen's death. Nothing on either side. For, all this while, Marlborough had not been idle. He had convinced the Hanoverian ministers that it would be a fatal error for him to arrive in England at the head of the Flanders army before the crisis had broken out. Until then, he would be content to act through Cadogan, arranging to store arms in secret, picking reliable officers and assigning them their tasks when the emergency arose. Of all this there was no outward sign as the retired general strolled in the streets of Frankfurt, observed with awe by the citizens, exchanging bows with visiting dignitaries.

One minor annoyance which arose out of the Utrecht settlement related to his own principality. Mündelheim had gone back to the Elector of Bavaria at the peace and with it had gone its £2,000 a year of revenue. Marlborough could well afford the loss of income. He was still entitled to take his seat in the Imperial Diet, still a Prince of the Empire. But these empty honours were not likely to please him and they certainly would not please Sarah. He pursued the Emperor with demands for compensation for the loss of his princely emoluments, but the Hofburg had centuries of experience in fobbing off complaints of this kind. Marlborough had no success. Sarah, who had never put a high price on the title, was probably not surprised by the loss of the income. What else could one expect from a foreign tyrant who was, after all, a Papist! For her, the Continental tour was at first agreeable enough – all the deference, the courtesy, the kindness!

---

* One who went of his own accord was Colonel Blackader, who sold his regiment, the Cameronians, for £2,600 and became an evangelist.

At the same time, using her sharp eyes and her keen critical sense, she observed the wretchedness in which the people lived and contrasted it with the fat, idle priests who swarmed everywhere. She had no doubt that the latter were the cause of the former. In nunneries and churches she heard of such marvels and saw so many "ridiculous things" that "strange thoughts" rose in her mind, which she checked as soon as she could. No wonder people were tempted to atheism! Her own Whiggery and anti-clericalism grew stronger every day. In the same way the sight of a regiment of Prince Eugene's marching past the Duke made her weep and wish she had been a man that "I might have ventured my life a thousand times in the glorious Cause of Liberty, the loss of which will be seen and lamented too late for any Remedy." Her thoughts were led back to England and, with a sentence borrowed from *Cato*, she cursed the men that used their greatness to their country's ruin. In time, the longing to be home grew stronger, to see how Laguerre was progressing with the battle pictures in Marlborough House, to be no longer exiled in "these dirty countries" as she ungratefully called them and, best of all, to "see justice done upon some of one's enemies". England! This most loyal and cranky of English women longed for it. " 'Tis much better to be dead than to live out of England."[6] Even in poverty and obscurity – if the worst came – under a Stuart tyrant, it was still the best place in the world. On the Continent, they used stoves to warm the rooms. Intolerable!

Britain was at this time plagued with confused politics which, if they had any meaning at all, were preparations for civil war. The clash, it seemed, could not be far off; its likely date depended on whether you measured the Queen's life in weeks or months. The strain showed in various ways. Oxford, most numb and stolid of ministers, took more and more to the bottle, was sometimes barely coherent in Cabinet, with liquor on his breath in the sovereign's presence, a thing detestable to Anne, and seized on by Abigail to weaken her cousin who had earned her hatred by refusing her a share of the *Asiento*. Bolingbroke reacted differently to the tension. His response was that of an excitable gambler; he kept on doubling the stakes. Increasingly, he was reckless in his misuse of public money; all the time, his hand was deeper in the till. He, the freethinker, won the Queen's goodwill, and Tory cheers, by an act forbidding Dissenting schools. The achievement was all the sweeter to him because it was gall and wormwood to Oxford, a dissenter by origin and loyalty. Oxford was about to be brought down. Bolingbroke was going to rule Britain. Soon. And when the day came he would not need to care about all these careful records which Oxford was compiling about the curious financial transactions in Bolingbroke's ministry. At the same time, Bolingbroke's military plans went forward. Argyll was stripped of his posts. Lord Stair, another Scottish Whig who was a close associate of Marlborough, was forced to give up the command of the Scots Greys. It was arranged that nine Protestant battalions in Ireland were to be replaced by fifteen Jacobite battalions. Bolingbroke had hoped for a Stuart successor to Anne who would agree to forget his religion. Now he seemed to be more reckless and ready to contemplate a Catholic on the throne. Any other theory makes nonsense of his policy.

On the other side of the political divide, a matching activity went on. Although Marlborough refused to commit himself to what was mainly a Whig conspiracy, that probably deceived nobody. Ex-officers drew up lists of likely men. Cadogan was the central figure in London and Argyll in Edinburgh. When the moment came, the Tower and Edinburgh Castle were to be taken. Since his humiliating experience in Spain, Red John of the Battles was as fierce an enemy of the Tory government as he had once been of Marlborough. On a given signal, armed men would gather in the wasteland north of Montagu House, a favourite rendezvous of duellists. It was understood that at the right time, that is to say, when word came of a French landing, or anarchy broke out in the country, Marlborough would put himself at the head of troops loyal to the law of the land and the Protestant succession. Meanwhile, Sarah fretted in Germany, shook her head over her husband's lethargy and dreamt of the glorious deeds she would perform for freedom were she only a man.

In December 1713, at a time when the Queen's health had become suddenly worse, an anguished appeal reached Marlborough from London. A Whig conclave meeting in Wharton's house had sent an alarm signal to that resolute old woman in Hanover, the Electress Sophie, who would be lawful Queen of England if Anne died. And Sophie had ordered Marlborough to take command of the British troops on the Continent. Dunkirk was to be seized so that it could not be used as an embarkation port for a French invasion fleet and might, instead, become the base for an intervention friendly to the House of Hanover. At this point, Marlborough did two things. He sent Cadogan to stir up the Dutch, who were bound by treaty to give military aid to a Protestant succession. And he moved himself and his household to Antwerp, from which he could intervene more promptly.

When he heard that the Dutch had begun to equip a squadron,

Marlborough accepted the Hanoverian commission as commander-in-chief. Although, in the spring of 1714, Queen Anne's health made a spectacular recovery, it was plain that the improvement was not likely to last. It was a time when Royal mortality had a disturbing effect on political calculations. King Louis' son died in 1711; his grandson died in 1712; his great-grandson, a weakly infant, was now heir to the throne of France. It was an extraordinary Royal holocaust which, in a matter of months, had raised the alarming question: If this child were to die, would not Philip V of Spain be tempted to claim that he was the rightful heir to the throne of Louis XIV? The thought was profoundly alarming to Bolingbroke who knew that, were the old spectre of a Franco-Spanish union to be raised, his foreign policy would be brought to ruin. For that policy was based on an entente with France which would be made impossible if, contrary to the Peace of Utrecht, a king of France ruled the Spanish Empire.

Now it seemed that another Royal death, that of Queen Anne, would at any moment bring new anxieties to a troubled world. With that in mind, Marlborough moved to Ostend in the middle of July and let it be known that he meant to cross over to England. The news alarmed the Tories and bewildered the Hanoverian officials, who thought it would have been more prudent for him to wait until the political dogfight between Oxford and Bolingbroke was over. They were inclined to put the blame on Sarah, never noted for excess of caution. Although it is quite likely that simple boredom was a motive in the case of both the exiles, it is possible that Marlborough was better informed than Hanover about the state of the Queen's health. On 30 July the Marlboroughs were still in Ostend waiting for a fair wind, for Sarah shrank from spending a night on one of the packets in rough weather. She sat down and wrote a letter to a friend telling her about the welcome they had received at Ghent from officers of two British regiments. She only hoped that the officers would not be punished for their demonstration. As it turned out, the officers were quite safe. In London, events were moving at a breakneck speed.

On that very day a Privy Council of crucial importance was held. Forty-eight hours earlier, Bolingbroke had, at last, driven Oxford from power. He was head of the government. Then he had invited the leading Whigs of the younger set to dinner in his house in Golden Square. Not all of them came. Walpole, whom he had sent to the Tower for corruption, "was out of town": he had no intention of forgiving Bolingbroke and every intention of being revenged on him. The atmosphere round the dinner table that evening was electric with a coming storm. Bolingbroke protested his devotion to the House of Hanover. That no longer meant the Electress Sophie. The old woman, Queen Anne's pet aversion, had died. She had missed by six weeks achieving the dream of her life, the British crown. Bolingbroke's purpose was to offer his dinner guests places in the government he was about to form. His guests did not believe him.

They had their own ideas of what was likely to happen in the near future. Plans had been made. Cadogan was going to seize the Tower and Stanhope was going to arrest prominent Jacobites. Stanhope, speaking for them all, gave Bolingbroke their terms: put the fleet under an admiral loyal to the Protestant succession; bring back Marlborough as Captain-General and give him command of the forces. After that, Bolingbroke could keep his ministerial posts for his friends until the Queen died. "Harry, you have only two ways of escaping the gallows. The first is to join the Whigs, the other is to give yourself up entirely to the French King and seek his help for the Pretender." As Bolingbroke's guests, flushed with wine, poured out into Golden Square that summer evening they left their host with plenty to think about and, as it turned out, not much time to do it.

Within hours, it was clear that the Queen was dying. Too soon for Bolingbroke's convenience. In the Privy Council summoned to Kensington Palace, the Hanoverians were few, the Jacobites perplexed. Bolingbroke himself was for once at a loss. At that moment, two members of the Council, who had not been invited, entered the room – the Duke of Somerset and the Duke of Argyll. The Duke of Shrewsbury was not surprised to see them. The three dukes at once took command of the proceedings. Almost before Bolingbroke knew what he was doing, he had proposed that Shrewsbury should be Lord Treasurer and was leading a deputation to the dying Queen with this advice. And the Queen passed Shrewsbury the white staff of office so that he now became head of the government; the whole business had taken an hour. In an hour the future course of British politics had been decided.

After that, the Council applied itself to the business of moving troops, strengthening garrisons, calling out the London trained bands, seizing the horses and arms of Roman Catholics and taking the other precautions required in an hour of gravest crisis. The Queen died at half-past seven on 1 August. As ordinary a woman as any in England, ordinary alike in her virtues and her prejudices, her reign had been more remarkable than that of any previous monarch but Elizabeth I, who was not an ordinary woman. Anne's life was unhappy, her health wretched, and now all those she loved were either dead or become unbearable; she was not clever; but by obstinacy, instinct and some hidden source of strength, she had presided over an age which came to be called glorious. "Glorious!" With what mockery the word would have sounded in the poor woman's ears!

"Oxford was removed on Tuesday. The Queen died on Sunday," wrote Bolingbroke to Swift. "What a world this is and how does fortune banter us!" Swift agreed. "Fortune turned rotten at the very moment it grew ripe." The Elector of Hanover was proclaimed King.

Next day, the Duke and Duchess of Marlborough landed at Dover. At last the wind had changed in their favour. Exile was over. The timing of the return could not have been better.

XXVII

Triumphant Return

"What a humbling reflection for our vanity! That a Condé, a Eugene or a Marlborough should have to witness the decline of their mental before their physical powers. . . . Poor humanity, boast of your glory if you dare!"

Frederick the Great

Crowned and sceptred, King George I sat on the throne in Westminster Abbey and received the homage of the peers. "Who is that?" he asked Marlborough who was standing beside him. An unfamiliar peer had just made his bow. "That is Viscount Bolingbroke," said Marlborough. Bolingbroke had already tried in vain to be presented to his new monarch. Now he overheard the exchange and, turning, bowed three times to the ground. The incident was observed by Countess Cowper, who had worked her way to one of the upper tiers of seats from which she commanded a good view of the pageantry. She was not one to miss any of its comedy. Already she had observed the behaviour of the Jacobite peeresses, "all there, looking as cheerful as they could. Lady Nottingham overdid her High Church part by kneeling facing the King and repeating the Litany."[1]

Lady Portmore, one of the Jacobite ladies, still had the sharp tongue which had made her famous in the days when she was Catherine Sedley, the ugly mistress of James II whom Marlborough's parents had once wanted him to marry. When the Archbishop made his circuit of the throne asking if the people consented to their new monarch, her ladyship was heard to ask, "Does the old fool think that anybody here will say No when there are so many drawn swords in the church?"[2] On the whole, the ceremony went off quite well. Lady Cowper even shed a few tears at some of the more affecting passages. It was a day when the nation was united; Whigs and Tories were in agreement and all the bells rang. True, there were sporadic outbursts of disloyalty here and there, in Bristol, for example. But, on the whole, the elderly gentleman who had come from Hanover had reason to be gratified by his reception among his new subjects.

For the gorgeous duke in robes and coronet who stood near him in the Abbey on that October day, career was over, although life went on. The outward insignia of fame and power – Captain-General, Colonel of the First Guards, etc. – these dignities had been restored, to the disapproval of Sarah who wanted her husband to live a tranquil life and who probably knew that he was not fit for much more than that. Few people were deceived about the real state of things, least of all the old, distinguished soldier himself. The fire had died. The power was fading fast. The business of managing the state was passing into younger hands. Townshend, Stanhope and Walpole in politics, and also his once detested son-in-law, Sunderland, whose Whiggery had mellowed with the years. In the army, Argyll and Cadogan. When danger loomed in Scotland in the following year, with the Pretender landing, the Earl of Mar joining him, and a rising that was as much Nationalist as Jacobite, it was natural that Argyll should have the task of suppressing the revolt. But this, as it turned out, was harder than might have been expected because many of his own clansmen – the Campbells – sympathized that year with a Stuart claimant who was opposed to the Parliamentary Union with England. Besides, the army in Scotland was of miserable quality. In consequence, Argyll fought a less than brilliant campaign for which, needless to say, he put the blame on Marlborough who, as he said, had not sent him enough men and money. Marlborough replaced him with Cadogan who marched north with six thousand Dutch troops. Then, as it chanced, the crisis in Scotland fizzled out.

In Versailles, a long-expected event occurred: Louis XIV died. The sun that had blazed so menacingly down upon Europe for so many decades was extinguished. A sickly child was King of France. Orléans, a prince of untested quality, was regent. In these circumstances, the danger could not be ignored that the Bourbon King of Spain might re-assert the claim to France which he had revoked. Where so much was in doubt, "James VIII" of Scotland decided that the moment had come to abandon a military adventure which, in any case, was not prospering. On his departure, the rising collapsed.

By this time Bolingbroke had fled the country. Since the opening of the new reign, his behaviour had been jumpy to a degree. He had greeted the accession with a huge bonfire in front of his London house, a loyal

demonstration which amused Lord Oxford and convinced nobody of
Bolingbroke's loyalty to the new King. He had been ready to betray his
Jacobite associates to Marlborough provided the squalid fact was kept
secret.[3] But evidence against him was being gathered, alarming to a
nervous man. Lord Strafford's papers were seized and Strafford had been
one of the instruments of Bolingbroke's foreign policy, now being
denounced as treasonable. Then James Brydges warned him that the
Whigs were planning to pursue him to the scaffold.[4] In his agitation he
called on Marlborough for advice, which was an extraordinary move in
the circumstances, although oddly similar in its combination of the
desperate and the impudent to the dinner party he gave to the Whig
leaders during the last days of Queen Anne's life. What Marlborough
said in that interview is not certainly known. All that is sure is that
Bolingbroke borrowed £20,000 from Brydges and left for France that
night disguised as a valet. Later, he denied that any ominous words of
Marlborough's had prompted his flight. It may be so. But there is a more
important question, Was Bolingbroke's life in any real danger?

He was about to be impeached, charged with betraying his country and
her allies at a time of war. Oxford, accused of less serious crimes but
pursued by no less vengeful enemies, spent two years in the Tower and
was at length acquitted by the House of Lords because of an error in
procedure. Marlborough voted against the acquittal. "Lady Marlborough," said Swift, "is almost distracted that she could not obtain
revenge."[5] If Marlborough was vindictive, the reason is not hard to
guess: Oxford had organized the intrigue which brought down Marlborough's friend, Godolphin, now dead. It is possible that Bolingbroke
would not have got off as lightly as Oxford, but would the triumphant
Whigs have taken his life? All that one can say is that in 1715 capital
punishment had not been abolished from British politics. In any case,
Bolingbroke was ruined. He spent six months as the Pretender's Secretary
of State, a severe sentence which enabled his eyes to be opened to the
gloomy realities of the Jacobite cause. He was never again allowed to
return to the Lords.

Swift, his hour of political influence over, watched from his Dublin
deanery the triumph of all he detested most, toleration, money-power
and Dissent. He mouldered into misanthropy and, at last, into madness,
but not before he had written *Gulliver's Travels*. His accomplice in the
pamphlet war, fat Mrs Manley, was now at the mercy of her creditors:
"I have nothing but a starving scene before me; Lord Mal – and all his

accomplices justly enraged; nothing saved out of the general wreck."
However, she survived until 1724, living above the printing house on
Lambeth Hill which belonged to her publisher and lover, Alderman
Barber. Another lady had already disappeared from London. Before
Queen Anne was buried, Lady Masham had left for the country
taking her winnings with her. She lived, obscure but in comfort, until
1734.

When Marlborough and Sarah went to look at Blenheim, they were
shocked to find that the gardens of which Marlborough had dreamt so
often during his stay abroad, had been neglected. What was worse,
Vanbrugh, whom Sarah had ordered to demolish the old building of
Woodstock Manor on the estate, had contumaciously failed to do so.
Instead, he had gone there to live. Sarah, therefore, forbade him entry to
the grounds, so that the architect of Blenheim could only inspect his
building by peering over the boundary wall. Sarah's resentment of the
palace smouldered on; she contrasted it with her own more modest and
vastly less expensive town house on the site in Pall Mall which her
husband had thought not good enough. And it is true that when, at last,
she took responsibility for the building of Blenheim out of the hands of
the government, she was able to cut the cost by half.

As a businesswoman, Sarah was exceptionally gifted. This virtue had
its less amiable side, as Marlborough's old comrade, Cadogan, discovered.
When the Duke went into exile, he had left £40,000 with Cadogan,
who moved the money out of Dutch funds paying $2\frac{1}{2}$ per cent interest
into Austrian loans which paid 8 per cent. When the Austrian securities
fell heavily in market value, Sarah demanded repayment of the original
capital. She also alleged that Cadogan had pocketed the difference in
interest between the two stocks, and from what is known of Cadogan's
financial habits this is probably true. "He had a passion for money that is
beyond anything," said Sarah[6] who kept all knowledge of the dispute
from the Duke, by this time a sick man. Her own passion for money was
combined with an instinct for it which was at times almost uncanny.
When all England went mad over the South Sea Bubble in 1722, her
sense of realities remained unimpaired. She argued, stormed and threatened until all the family's shares in the South Sea Company were sold.
Thus, when ruin stalked through half the mansions of the land, Sarah was
£100,000 to the good![7]

In 1716, Marlborough was living quietly at Holywell House where,
after suffering from frequent headaches, he had a stroke and for a time

was unable to speak. Sarah nursed him devotedly in conformity with the best advice of the time: "I have been told that vipers boiled in broth is an admirable thing. The Duchess of Shrewsbury says that the best in the world come from Montpellier in boxes with holes filled with bran."[8] Later, she decided that calvesfoot jelly was better. But the vipers were already on their way from France. In spite of the doctors, the Duke gradually got better and went to Bath, a resort which Sarah thought the most disagreeable place on earth. A second stroke which came in November was, for a time, expected to be fatal. Once again, however, he recovered sufficiently to go riding and to take an interest in public affairs. But he was easily tired and his speech was permanently impaired, a weakness of which he was painfully aware. It seems possible, too, that the damage to his brain had brought about changes in his personality; this might help to account for the persistence with which he, who had not been a vengeful man, pursued Lord Oxford.

"The beautiful villas of noblemen raised upon the spoils of plundered nations or aggrandized by the wealth of the public."
Alexander Pope to Martha Blount, 1722

At last, in 1719, Marlborough went to live in the palace which bore the name of his most famous victory. Not long before, he had heard with joy that his comrade, Eugene, had won his finest victory: he had captured Belgrade from the Turks. Blenheim had been long a-building; even now, only one wing of it was habitable; Sarah's irritation with the architects and builders covered but did not hide her profound distaste for the whole extravagant edifice. But here it was, as from the first he had dreamed it, as Vanbrugh with extraordinary intuition or persuasive power had realized it and as the state, by turns prodigal and grudging, had raised it to commemorate a battle which would have passed into history before the last slate was laid on the roof. Here it was, as imposing as Eugene's Belvedere in Vienna and grander than George's palace at St James's, John Churchill's home, his monument and when the time should come, his tomb. "Home?" Not everybody thought so. Said Vanbrugh, "One may find a great deal of pleasure in building a palace for another when one should find very little in living in it oneself." But even the pleasure of building was, he found, a highly qualified thing. One day Sarah found this quatrain:

Thanks, sir, cried I, 'tis very fine
But where d'ye sleep or where d'ye dine?
I find by all you have been telling
That 'tis a house but not a dwelling.

With this train of thought, Sarah was inclined to agree. But there it stood – and stands, "Roman and medieval at once", as Laurence Whistler saw it, "the Rome and Middle Ages of the soldiers, of hard campaigning and triumphant returns."[9]

One day in June 1722, after years of quiescence deepening into silence, Marlborough died at Windsor Lodge, the house that Queen Anne had given Sarah long ago for her use during life. Their daughters, the Duchess of Montagu and Lady Godolphin, arrived before the end and stayed so long with their father that Sarah could bear it no longer. She went into the room and knelt beside the couch on which Marlborough was lying. Thereupon the daughters rose and curtsied, without speaking to their mother. Sarah called for prayers which the dying man said he had heard and had joined in. Later he was carried from the couch to his bed where he sank into a coma. He died as the sun was rising on 16 June. He was seventy-two.

On any scale of reckoning his life had been an extraordinary one. He had been a skinny little boy running in the meadows beside the Axe, a pupil at the school behind the old cathedral which the Fire was so soon to sweep away; then had come a sudden turn, a door had opened and a dazzling world lay beyond. He had known how to wait and when to strike: he had mingled dissimulation with audacity while preserving all the time an impenetrable mask of urbanity; by employing the gifts of diplomacy which he had acquired at three courts with the soldier's skill that, as it seems, he was born with, he, the son of a ruined gentleman, had become the peer of princes, the employer of vast international armies, and a figure whose splendour outshone that of the Sun King himself. More than that, while remaining all his life a conformist, a mild Tory in politics, a moderate Church of England man, he had done more than most men to throw open the doors to a new age of commercial adventure and colonial expansion, in short to bring about a revolution vastly more far-reaching than the modest political upheaval he had helped to engineer in 1688. In that greater revolution, Britain would be the leader.

True, the achievement had been more or less accidental. It is doubtful if he even knew what he had done. He had set out to destroy the military power of France and, in this purpose, he felt that he had been frustrated. As Moltke after Königgratz had wanted to destroy Austria and, to his annoyance, had been forbidden by Bismarck, so Marlborough had been denied that final campaign which was to have taken him to Paris. But if France was not destroyed, her domination of Europe did not survive the constellation of victories of which the first was Blenheim. Britain was to dominate the next phase in the evolution of the world, thanks in a measure to Marlborough's victories. More than that, Oxford and Bolingbroke, who had half-betrayed his work, had also half-completed it. Their peace-making, hurried and clumsy as it was, had made the Mediterranean a British sea and had ensured that Newfoundland and Hudson's Bay – and therefore, in the not so distant future, Canada – should lie in Britain's sphere.

All this was done by one who, starting as a boy with little but good looks to commend him, had cuckolded one king, betrayed another and had become the distrusted confederate of a third. Finally, he had become a minister as powerful as any in Europe since Mazarin and a political soldier as feared in Britain as Cromwell had been. In the process, he had become enormously rich, as his will was soon to exhibit, and money always played an unduly important part in his system of values. "The great talk is now about what Lord Marlborough has left. Those who speak most moderately say above a million besides land and what separate estate the Duchess has.[10] Not one farthing is left to any charity or to any old servant." Nobody was surprised by that revelation. In a year or two the joint Marlborough–Godolphin–Sunderland holding in bank shares was the largest, valued at £166,858, although the largest single holding (£104,625) was that of Francis Pereira.[11] Few millionaires make their fortunes while making history, but Marlborough was one of those mortals in whom the ignoble greed of gold exists alongside the more respectable quest of glory.

In the mind of Sarah, his wife, no such ambivalence existed. For her, glory was empty. Rank was frivolous. Power was real but ephemeral. Money was a solid, lasting, comforting presence to be treated with respect. She insisted on bearing all the costs of the Duke's funeral. This was an expense which she would not share even with "neighbour George" in his palace next door.

The First Churchill

> "What is the business of great men that pass the stage of the world in seeming triumph? Alas, no more than to be turned into ballad and song and sung by old women to quiet children, or at the corner of a street to gather crowds in aid of the pickpocket and the whore."
>
> *Probably Daniel Defoe*

Twenty-four great families went into mourning. While a fine hearse was being made by the King's coachman and 4,000 commemorative medals were being struck at the Mint, the body lay in state at Marlborough House under a pall on which was an empty suit of armour clasping a baton and wearing a Garter and George. On the right was a ducal coronet, on the left the cap of a prince of the Empire. But all was not deference and solemnity. Business, too, had its place. Windows on the processional route were let, wine, chocolate and cold dishes to be served. Mist's *Journal*[12] had the bad taste to recall Arabella's downfall all those years ago and promised further revelations, but "certain gentlemen with greyhounds on their breasts"* raided the printing house. There was no sequel to the story in the *Journal*. For the funeral, the road between the Bell Tavern in King Street and Westminster Abbey was covered with black cloth for the noblemen to walk on.

And the procession? Guards, with colours furled and drums muffled, cannon, nine generals, Lord Cadogan in his new uniform as commander-in-chief (and, thought the censorious, looking more jovial than he should on so solemn an occasion), seventy-three Chelsea pensioners, all the heralds of England – no! all but one. Clarenceux – Vanbrugh – was not there. That must have been Sarah's doing. At last, the funeral chariot, drawn by eight horses, covered with velvet, and eight dukes in their coaches following the chief mourner, Marlborough's son-in-law, the Duke of Montagu. The sentence rang through the church, "Thus it has pleased Almighty God to take out of this transitory world into His mercy the most high, mighty and noble prince, John, Duke of Marlborough . . ." The Dean of Westminster, a Tory, claimed that the pall was his by right and quarrelled over it with the undertaker. The squabble received wide publicity in the Tory journals, probably anxious to publicize the fact that the Duchess had only hired the pall.

Sarah thought that the whole thing was, in any case, grossly overdone and far too expensive. £5,265! Ridiculous! Forty-eight yards of black cloth to cover the mourning coach: "Enough to cover my garden."[13] Worst of all, the bill included fees for seven trumpeters who were not

* King's messengers.

there. And the white plumes for the horses had been invoiced twice over. Even on so sad and splendid an occasion, the dowager's eye for an inflated bill was as keen as when, a newly appointed Groom of the Stole, she had prevented Queen Anne being cheated by her purveyors. She resolved that, when her own time came, the funeral would be no more than decent "without plumes or escutcheons". But as it turned out, that was an event which lay long years ahead. Before that day came, the Duchess of Buckingham wanted to borrow the Duke's funeral chariot for her son's obsequies. Sarah said, "It carried my Lord Marlborough and shall never be profaned by any other corpse." But just for once she did not have the last word. Her Grace of Buckingham retorted, "The undertakers tell me that I may have a finer chariot for twenty pounds."[14]

The amount left in Marlborough's will amounted to a great deal more than £2 millions, according to Vanbrugh who said that the Duke had left £10,000 a year "to his widow – may a Scotch ensign get her" to spoil Blenheim in her own way. By that time, she had quarrelled irremediably with Vanbrugh as she quarrelled with almost everyone, beginning with her daughters. She had said that Blenheim was "a chaos enough to turn her brain". "It was time to put a stop to such madness." And Vanbrugh, who could write with as much force as she, had sent his final letter: "I will never trouble you more." The break occurred in November 1716. Since then, the work at Blenheim had progressed, one wing was habitable and the old soldier whose dream it had realized had lived in it before he died.

For the widow life went on. She was handsome and spirited, attractive enough at sixty-two to be sought in marriage by Lord Coningsby and the Duke of Somerset, both of whom she rejected; more remarkably, she did it with such tact that each remained her friend. The joy of life ebbed slowly, although the quickness of Sarah's temper did not grow noticeably less. She was still forever right, forever put upon by stupid and malicious adversaries, above all those in her own family. She still believed that attack was the best defence. There is a document in her vigorous and unmistakable handwriting, extant, for all who wish to see it.[15] It begins, "There is nothing so contrary to my Nature nor that I do so unwillingly as to say anything that is a reflection upon my children, but the barbarous treatment I have lately received from two of them . . ." There follows 102 pages, thirty lines a page, twelve words a line, roughly 35,000 words of vituperation against her daughters, the Duchess of Montagu and Lady Godolphin. She had already dealt with her son-in-law, the Duke of Montagu, in a letter written to the Bishop of Exeter while Marlborough was still alive: "He has never spoken me fifty words in the whole time he has been my son-in-law." So much for his Grace.

Sarah's quarrels extended beyond the family and even crossed party lines. Sir Robert Walpole, as great a Whig as she, had the bad taste to take Vanbrugh's side in the squabble over the Blenheim money: "Being forced into Chancery by that B.B.B. old B. the Duchess of Marlborough . . . I have prevailed Sir Robert Walpole to help me . . . by which I have got my money in spite of the huzzy's teeth." Walpole had gone further: he had taxed the £5,000 annuity to Marlborough and refused to extend Sarah's lease of Windsor Lodge. While he was responsible for the Post Office, Sarah was sure that he arranged that letters to her and the second Duchess of Marlborough should be misdirected. Most infamous of all, when Queen Caroline wanted to drive in her carriage through Sarah's estate at Wimbledon, Walpole abetted the Queen in this monstrous usurpation. With Alexander Pope, on the other hand, she played a cat and mouse game because she was anxious to obtain from him the manuscript – as if the poet would have only a single copy! – of a poem in which he was believed to have referred to her under the name of Atossa:

> Atossa, cursed with every granted prayer;
> Childless with all her children, wants an heir.
> To heirs unknown descends the unguarded store
> Or wanders, heaven-directed, to the poor.*

But as time passed, even the most bitter of memories grew imperceptibly softer, the most exciting of feuds lost their appeal. When Voltaire visited her at Blenheim, which he did not much care for ("if only the rooms were as wide as the walls are thick, it would be a convenient enough château"), and asked to see her memoirs about which so many rumours abounded, she replied, "Wait a little. I am at present altering my account of Queen Anne's character. I have begun to love her again since the present set have become our governors."[16] And at Blenheim she raised a statue inscribed: "To the memory of Queen Ann under whose auspices John, Duke of Marlborough, conquered and to whose munificence he and his posterity with gratitude owe the possession of Blenheim."† Sarah could hardly have said less and, being Sarah, could not be expected to say

---

* But some scholars think that "Atossa" was another great lady of the period.

† The spelling of the Queen's name on the pedestal probably has no significance. But her expression, obstinate, almost brutal, may owe something to Sarah's feelings about the woman who had been her friend.

more, and typically she completed Blenheim according to her husband's desires.

She lived through the reign of George I and, in all her diamonds, sat on a drum in Palace Yard waiting to attend the coronation of George II. She lived on through her seventies and into her eighties, a remarkable feat for that period, although it had been achieved by another duchess, Sarah's senior by a few years and different from her in every respect but the love of money which they shared. She had once been a dark-eyed Breton girl in the suite of Madame: Louise de Keroualle, Duchess of Portsmouth. Louise died in Paris in 1734, aged eighty-five, poor and penitent; Sarah died very rich, weary at last of life but hardly penitent. After all, she was not aware of having done any wrong, however ill-used and defamed by others. Weary of life, longing for death but not afraid of it: "I cannot be disappointed when I have no hope and I fear nothing in the world but the French . . . I am going soon out of the world and I am packing." The old lady was leaving behind her everything in good order.

Having lived twenty-two years after John Churchill, she died in Marlborough House aged eighty-four. Her funeral was simple, as she had wished it to be. Her will was a businesslike document on a suitably cheap paper and was the best testimony possible to the prudence and vigilance with which she had managed her affairs through the years. There they were, the visible fruits of that long and tenacious life! Twenty-two estates or groups of properties, including Blenheim, Marlborough House, her manor of Wimbledon, her property as a Jennings heiress, money, securities and jewels in glittering heaps.[17] The whole valued at – what? People talked of four millions. Her surviving daughter, the Duchess of Montagu, was forgiven to the extent of being left a gold snuffbox containing two pictures of Marlborough as a young man. Nor were the poor of Woodstock forgotten by the richest woman in England. They got £300. One bequest has been thought to show a political motive and, possibly, political acumen: £10,000 and some land to William Pitt. Sarah, who had been the love, consort, plague and inspiration of a great soldier during glorious days, may have sensed that the glory was returning. She would certainly hope so. After all, there was something more important in life than money.

APPENDIX A

The following estimates of the official incomes of the Duke and Duchess of Marlborough appear as a *Review of a late Treatise* . . . printed for J. Roberts, London, and is bound in one volume with *The Conduct of the Dowager Duchess of Marlborough*, London, George Hawkins, MDCCXLII.

A short computation of the annual income of a certain great man. Written in the year 1704.

Plenipotentiary to the States	£7,000
General for the English forces on Mr Howe's establishment	£5,000
General for the forces in Flanders on Mr Brydges' establishment	£5,000
Master of the Ordnance	£3,000
Travelling Charges	£1,825
Colonel of the Foot Guards	£2,000
Pension	£5,000
From the States General as General of their Forces	£10,000
From the Foreign troops in English pay, 6d a day	£15,000
For keeping a table	£1,000
	£54,825

His Lady's income

Keeper of the Great and Home Parks	£1,500
Mistress of the Robes	1,500
Keeper of the Privy Purse	1,500
Groom of the Stole	3,000
A Pension out of the Privy Purse	2,000
	£9,500

APPENDIX B

Who was "Marlborough's Spy"?

He is called Marlborough's spy by Winston Churchill in his biography, in the catalogue of the *Blenheim Papers*; the description still holds. But should he not more accurately be called "Lord Sunderland's spy"? His letters were sent to Whitehall to Lord Sunderland, then Secretary of State and, as such, the natural recipient of secret diplomatic intelligence. They ranged over a much wider field than is normally covered by military intelligence. They are particularly informative on naval matters. That Marlborough saw them, or relevant extracts from them, need not be doubted. But the impression remains that the letters were addressed to Lord Sunderland (as in places they specifically say) and that they are probably in the Blenheim archive simply because Sunderland was Marlborough's son-in-law and that his son became the third Duke of Marlborough. However that may be, the correspondence remains one of exceptional interest.

At one moment, this unknown writer is giving a list of the battalions being sent to Provence when the attack on Toulon was expected, at the next he is naming the lieutenant-generals earmarked for the Flanders army. The warships at the various French naval bases are set out along with the number of guns each of them carries, and on 30 September 1707 the spy reports that Louis XIV has 350,000 men in the army, and 60,000 horses – "How can the state support such expenses?" – particularly as the King is spending so prodigally in other ways. Two millions on buildings at Meudon, two millions on planting chestnut trees at Marly, transported from the forest of St Germain, roots, earth and all, none of them less than twenty years old. Being old, notes the spy, Louis is not interested in young trees. Lord Sunderland would have observed this same weakness in his father-in-law, the Duke. "Useless expenses," says the spy, "as a result of which officers are not paid – but we are luckier than we are wise; I am astonished that this whole situation is not ruined."

And so the narrative runs on from letter to letter (in the first ten months of 1707 there are more than 130 of them), darting from grave discourses on financial problems to lighter topics – the Countess de Quailus has sent Madame de Maintenon a doll indecently dressed; and even criminal – the King's First Equerry has been seized from his coach by twenty horsemen on the road to Versailles. The English officers captured at Almanza say they would rather spend all their life in prison than go back to Spain. And so on.

Who was this intelligent, voluble, knowledgeable informant? Who was this traitor at Versailles?

All one can say is that he moved in the highest circles, dining one day with a duke, supping next day with an eminent financier. He went on a periodical tour of French ports. Apparently he was a high officer of the Crown, probably in Finance – once he says, "I know this business because it passed under my hands. It is a matter of a private loan of 100,000 écus to the King."*

It would have been quite easy at that time to identify him; the man has no hesitation in telling where he dined and who else was in the company. But he continues with the greatest insouciance to send his gossipy letters to London, written in two hands, one presumably his secretary's; the other his own. He does not write with the grace of Madame de Sevigné or the furious power of Saint-Simon, but he is an alert reporter of his times and theirs. And, as spies do, he took exceptional risks.

Who was he?

---

* *Blenheim MSS*, D1. 15 a, b and c.

Notes on Sources

The Golden Swamp

1 Thomas Hobbes, *Leviathan*, Ch. 4.
2 Princess Palatine, 4 January 1715. *Letters from Liselotte, Princess Palatine.*
3 Emanuel le Roy Ladurie, *Histoire du Climat depuis l'an mil*, pp. 15 and 16.
4 *New Cambridge Modern History*, Vol. VI, p. 764.
5 *Rutland Papers*, Vol. II. HMC. Charles Bertie to Viscountess Campden, 22 November 1681.
6 Quotation from E. M. de Jouellans, "Informe sobre la ley agraria" (1787), on p. 28 of A. Goodwin, *The European Nobility in the Eighteenth Century*.
7 Samuel Pufendorff, *Introduction to the History of the Several Kingdoms . . . of Europe*, trans. London, 1697.
8 Quoted by E. Guitard in "Colbert and Seignelay Contre la Religion Reformée".
9 Fénélon, letter to the King, dated 1694 by Renouard, who published it in 1825.
10 Sue Masterman, "The Netherlands", article in *The Times*, 10 November 1976.
11 S. Pufendorff, *op. cit.*
12 "A New Description of Holland", London 1705, p. 51.
13 Violet Barbour, *Capitalism in Amsterdam*.
14 Constantijn Huygens (1596–1687), quoted p. 162 in Pieter Geyl, *The Netherlands in the Seventeenth Century*, Pt. I.
15 Violet Barbour, *op. cit.*, p. 22.
16 John Carswell, *The Descent on England*, quoted p. 11.
17 Violet Barbour, *op. cit.*, p. 40.
18 D. S. Coombs, *The Conduct of the Dutch*, p. 43.
19 John Carswell, *op. cit.*, p. 21.
20 Daniel Defoe, *A Plan for the English Commerce*.
21 Anon, "News from Newcastle", 1651.
22 S. Pufendorff, *op. cit.*
23 John Carswell, *op. cit.*, p. 15.
24 Daniel Defoe, *op. cit.*
25 "The Conference on Gregg's Ghost", London, 1721.
26 Johnson's *Dictionary*.
27 Daniel Defoe, *op. cit.*

I

Le Bel Anglais

1 Wolseley, *Life of Marlborough*, I, p. 22.
2 Quoted in F. C. Turner, *James II*, 1948.
3 12 January 1669, *The Diary of Samuel Pepys*, Vol. Nine, p. 413.
4 *State Papers*, 631320, f. 226.
5 Pepys, *Diary*, 13 July 1663.
6 John Oldmixon, *Critical History of England*.
7 G. Steinman Steinman, *A Memoir of Barbara, Duchess of Cleveland*, privately printed, 1871.
8 *Secret Memoirs and Manners of Several Persons of Quality of both sexes from the New Atalantis, an island in the Mediterranean*, London, MDCCXLI.
9 G. Steinman Steinman, *op. cit.*, p. 235.
10 F. W. Hamilton, *History of the Grenadier Guards*, I, p. 166.

II

The Worst Woman in the World

1 *The Account of the Conduct of the Dowager Duchess of Marlborough*. It was a substantial income which would have been regarded as sufficient for a man to support an earldom.
2 *Rutland Papers*, Historical MSS Commission XIII Report to App. 5, ii, pp. 32, 33.
3 *Correspondence politique, Angleterre*, 120. f. 231, 206, 248, etc.
4 *Correspondence politique, Angleterre*, f. 206, f. 248.
5 Letter from Humphrey Prideaux, Paris, 3 February 1677.
6 Jonathan Swift.
7 *Rutland Papers*, Vol. ii, 22 November 1677.
8 Gilbert Burnet, *History of My Own Time*, ii, p. 132.
9 Andrew Browning, *Thomas, Earl of Danby*.
10 Henry Savile to Lord Rochester, *Bath Papers*, HMC, vol. ii, p. 16.
11 Savile, *Bath Papers*, HMC, Vol. ii, p. 164.
12 *Dartmouth Papers*, HMC, xi. Appendix Y.
13 *Moneys Received and Paid for Secret Services of Charles II and James II*, ed. J. Y. Ackerman.
14 *Ormonde Papers*, New Series, Vol. 7, HMC. Letter to Ormonde from Sir C. Syche, 17 February 1684/5.

III

No Penny, No Paternoster

The most convincing modern account of the Sedgemoor campaign is given in
V. I. R. Emerson's *Monmouth's Rebellion*.

1 Sir George Clark, *The Later Stuarts*, p. 120.
2 Arthur Bryant, *Samuel Pepys, the Saviour of the Nation*, p. 124.
3 "An Account of the Rebellion, etc." Appendix IV in *A Vindication of Mr Fox's Historical Work*, by Samuel Heywood.
4 Sir George Clark, *op. cit.*
5 E. E. Rich, *Hudson's Bay Company, 1670–1870*, Vol. 1.

IV

Such Bustle About Religion

The events preceding the Revolution of 1688 have been exhaustively presented in Macaulay, Churchill and later writers such as David Ogg, *England in the Reign of James II and William III*, Oxford, 1966. Witty and well-informed is John Carswell, *The Old Cause* and the same author's *The Descent on England*.

1 John Evelyn, *Diary*, 29 December 1684.
2 Louis XIV, *Memoirs*.
3 Anon, *The Lives of the Two Illustrious Generals*.
4 *Spencer Papers*, HMC.
5 John Carswell, *The Old Cause*, p. 67.
6 John Carswell, *Descent on England*, p. 73.
7 Ibid, p. 37.
8 Samuel Pepys, *Memoirs Relating to the State of the Royal Navy of England*.
9 James Johnstone, 28 April 1688.
10 Sir John Reresby, *Memoirs*.
11 John Whittle, Chaplain to the Army, *An Exact Diary of the Late Expedition*.
12 Sir John Reresby, *op. cit.*, 4 November.
13 Thomas, Earl of Ailesbury, *Memoirs*, Vol. I, p. 218.
14 *Newsletter*, Mackintosh Collection, Vol. I.
15 G. Steinman Steinman. Later, the Countess came back to England where she died in 1722.

V

The Cockpit Quarrels with Kensington

1 *The Lockhart Papers*, 1817.
2 Ailesbury, *Memoirs*. "My Lord Churchill disposes all" – remark of French Huguenot officer.

3 Sir John W. Fortescue, *A History of the British Army*, Vol. 1, p. 338.
4 *Portland Papers*, iii, 16 February 1691, HMC.
5 Hester W. Chapman, *Mary II, Queen of England*.
6 *New Cambridge Modern History*, Vol. VI, "The Rise of Britain and Russia".
  p. 400.
7 HMC 7th Report. MSS of Earl of Denbigh's 3rd Report, 26 January 1693.
8 *Portland Papers*, iii, 16 February 1691, HMC.

VI

Prisoner of State

1 "German to the last drop of her blood. With the figure of a Swiss guard,"
  Saint-Simon.
2 *Letters from Liselotte*, p. 262.
3 David Ogg, *England in the Reigns of James II and William III*, p. 379.
4 Fernand Braudel, *Capitalism and Material Life*, p. 35.
5 Sir John Clapham, *The Bank of England*.
6 Henri and Barbara van der Zee, *William and Mary*, p. 356.
7 *Cal. State Papers*, Dom., 8 May 1694.
8 *Letters from Liselotte*, p. 81.

VII

A War to Plan

1 John Nada, *Carlos the Bewitched*.
2 *Letters from Liselotte*.
3 John Nada, *op. cit.*
4 *Letters from Liselotte*.
5 Ibid, letter of 4 September 1701.
6 John Evelyn.

VIII

God Has Sent Our Heart's Desire

1 Lord Ailesbury, *Memoirs*.
2 John Evelyn, *Diary*, 30 December 1702.
3 Lord Ailesbury, *op. cit.*
4 Sicco van Goslinga, *Memoirs*, 1857, p. 2.
5 Coxe, I, p. 204.

6 Luttrell, *Diary*, Vol. vi, p. 25.
7 Daniel Defoe, *A Plan for the English Commerce*.
8 Captain Robert Parker, *Memoirs*.
9 John Evelyn, *Diary*, Vol. II.
10 Ibid.

IX

Malbrouk s'en va-t-en Guerre

1 Ferdnand Braudel, *Capitalism and Material Life*, p. 256.
2 Swift's correspondence, ed. Elrington Ball, 3 February 1703/4.
3 Laurence Sterne, *Tristram Shandy*, iii, XXV.
4 David B. Green, *Sarah, Duchess of Marlborough*, p. 94.

X

The Glorious Interview

The march to the Danube may be followed in the memoirs of several who took part in it, such as John Blackader, Sergeant Millner, etc.

1 Officers were allowed a bigger ration than privates. For these important logistical details see *The Art of Warfare in the Age of Marlborough*, David Chandler, p. 15, which draws on Professor G. Perjes' study *Army Provisioning, Logistics and Strategy in the Second Half of the Seventeenth Century*.
2 For the Medina brothers, the *DNB*, *The Sephardim of England*, Albert M. Hyamson, pp. 54, 68, 96, 103; *Encyclopedia Judaica*; and an article by Oscar Rabinowicz, published by the Jewish Historical Society of England.
3 Jean M. de la Colonie, *The Chronicles of an Old Campaigner*.
4 *Letters from Liselotte*. The most satisfactory life of Prince Eugene in English is by Nicholas Henderson.

XI and XII

"The Enemy Have Marched"
A Long, Hot Summer's Day

The battle of the Schellenberg, the preliminaries to Blenheim and that decisive action itself have been described a dozen times over, in the accounts of Frank Taylor, Wolseley, General Fuller, etc. and, above all, in the magisterial narrative of Winston Churchill. There are also the notes made at the time by Lord Orkney, John Blackader, Sergeant Millner, Captain Pope, etc., and from the

other side by La Colonie and Count Mérode-Westerloo. Saint-Simon has left a
record of the impression which the result of the battle made at Versailles.

1 G. de Mérode-Westerloo, *Mémoires*, p. 66. He lost thirteen horses that day
  as he said later on.
2 David Chandler, *The Art of Warfare in the Age of Marlborough*, p. 208.
3 Saint-Simon, *Mémoires*, Vol. 13.
4 *The Life and Diary of Lieut-Colonel John Blackader*, ed. Andrew Crichton.
5 Mérode-Westerloo, *op. cit.*
6 John Evelyn, *Diary*, Vol. 5.
7 Saint-Simon, *op. cit.*, Vol. 13.
8 Sergeant Millner, *A Compendious Journal* . . .
9 *Athole Papers*, p. 62, HMC.

XIII

Principalities and Powers

1 Parke was murdered six years later in an insurrection in the Leeward
  Islands. George Washington married his grandson's widow.
2 John Evelyn, *Diary*, Vol. 5.
3 Lady Pye to Abigail Harley, *Portland Papers*, vol. 4, HMC.
4 *The Life and Diary of Lieut-Colonel John Blackader*, ed. Andrew Crichton.
5 Far more horses died of contagion than in action. The Greys, for instance,
  had seven horses killed during the campaign while 231 died of disease. The
  same proportion prevailed all through the army. *Blenheim MSS*, A. I – 32.
6 *Cowper Papers*, HMC. H. St John to Thomas Coke, 10 October 1704.
7 Luttrell, *Diary*, Vol. V, p. 470.
8 Saint-Simon, *Mémoires*, vol. 13.
9 Ibid., Vol. 8, p. 54.
10 R. E. Scouller, *Armies of Queen Anne*.
11 Letter from Weissenburg, 8 November 1702.
12 John Millner, sergeant in the Royal Regiment of Ireland, *A Compendious
   Journal of all the marches, etc.*
13 Marlborough to Godolphin.
14 Peter Smithers, *Life of Joseph Addison*, p. 92.
15 "Nouvelles des Cours de l'Europe pour Septembre, 1704", *Blenheim
   MSS*, F. I – 19.
16 John Evelyn, *Diaries*.

XIV

"As Emphatic as an Oath"

The story of the building of Blenheim, as dramatic as the palace itself, has been told with the utmost scholarly thoroughness by D. B. Green in *Blenheim Palace*, 1951, a magnificent volume, and by Lawrence Whistler in his life of *Sir John Vanbrugh, Architect and Dramatist*. To both of these writers I am deeply indebted, for information and for the excitement which they have communicated.

1 *Blenheim MSS*, F. I – 49.

XV

"See What a Happy Man He Is!"

1 Lord Orkney. Letter to his brother, 20 July 1705.
2 *Blenheim MSS*, F. I – 35.
3 Ibid., F. I – 19.
4 Ibid., A. I – 27.

XVI

Consternation at Versailles

1 The list contains interesting names: Prince George of Denmark, £20,000; Marlborough, £10,000; Godolphin, £5,000; Sir Henry Furnese, £4,000; Adam Cardonnel, Marlborough's secretary, £2,000; Cadogan, Sir Godfrey Kneller and Moses Medina, £1,000 each. *Blenheim MSS*, F.I c – 15.
2 Captain Robert Parker, *Memoirs*, p. 108.
3 *The Life and Diary of Lieut-Colonel John Blackader*, ed. Andrew Crichton.
4 Jean M. de la Colonie, *The Chronicles of an Old Campaigner*, p. 305.
5 Saint-Simon, *Mémoires*, 26 May 1706.
6 *Blenheim MSS*, A. I – 45.
7 *Blenheim MSS*, A. II – 2 (a).
8 *Blenheim MSS*, A. II – 35 (a).

XVII

The Bonny Blue Caps

1 Beau Fielding: the *DNB*, "A Memoir of Barbara, Duchess of Cleveland", G. Steinman Steinman; *The Great Lady*, Margaret Gilmour; *My Lady Castlemaine*, Philip W. Sergeant.

2 G. M. Trevelyan, *Ramillies*, p. 314.
3 *Portland MSS* at Welbeck, Vol. ii. HMC.
4 *Portland Papers*, Vol. viii; *Harley Letters*, vi, "A News letter from Edinburgh". HMC.

XVIII

"The Wigths and the Thorys"

1 M. de Torcy, *Mémoires . . . pour servir à l'Histoire des Negotiations*.
2 *Blenheim MSS*, A. II – 20. In due course, Raby's wish was granted. He became Earl of Strafford.
3 Sweden, Poland, Prussia and the Elector of Saxony.
4 *Blenheim MSS*. Unsigned and without address, the letter seems to be directed to the French headquarters. It runs: "30th July 1707. A letter worthy of belief coming from the Army of the Duke of Marlborough gives assurance that this lord has corrupted with money a person in the office of M. de Chamillart [French Minister of War] and that, by way of this secret correspondence and another which he has elsewhere he knows all that goes on in the court of the Elector of Bavaria."
5 Coxe, letter, 4 August 1707.
6 Coxe, letter to Sarah, 21 July 1707.
7 Letter to Sir W. Cocks, July 1704. Letter Book of John Hervey, Lord Bristol.
8 Coxe, iii, p. 380. Letter to Sarah, 13 October 1707.

XIX

The Mines are Worked Out

1 Marquis de Torcy, *Mémoires pour servir* . . .
2 *Portland Papers*, Vol. IV, HMC.
3 Alexander Pope, "Epistle to Bathurst".
4 Marlborough, *Letters and Dispatches*, Vol. IV, p. 397.
5 R. E. Scouller, *The Armies of Queen Anne*, p. 375.
6 A. Hutcheson, "An Essay on the most effective way to recruit the Army", 1709.

XX

The Great Cold

1 Liselotte to her aunt, the Electress Sophie. *Letters*, p. 135.
2 Letter from William Palmer, *The Times*, 24 August 1977.

3 J. H. Plumb, *Sir Robert Walpole*, p. 144.
4 Liselotte, from Versailles, 23 May 1709.
5 Swift, *The Conduct of the Allies*.
6 Godfrey Davis, "The Seamy Side of Marlborough's War", *Huntingdon Library Quarterly*, November 1951.
7 Liselotte. Letter from Marly of 15 June 1709.

XXI

The Lord of Hosts at Our Head

1 H. G. Pitt, "The Pacification of Utrecht", from *The Cambridge Modern History*, Vol. VI, chapter XIII.
2 D. B. Green, *Blenheim Palace*.
3 Sergeant John Millner, *A Compendious Journal . . .*, p. 279.
4 Parker, *Memoirs*, pp. 138–140.
5 "Letters of the first Lord Orkney", *English Historical Review*, 1904.
6 Sergeant Millner tots up the Allied casualties: 19,692 killed or wounded, of which 5,316 were German (Imperialists), 1,783 British, 1,694 Prussian, 2,219 Hanoverian, and 8,680 Dutch.

XXII

A General Infatuation

1 Jonathan Swift, *Memoirs relating to the Change that happened in the Queen's Ministry in the year 1710*.
2 Carl von Noorden, *Europaische Geschicht*, vol. iii, p. 638.
3 Mr Shute to Lord Sunderland, *Blenheim MSS*, A. II – 2, 3, and 4.
4 Swift, *op. cit.*
5 Earl of Ailesbury, *Memoirs*.
6 *Blenheim MSS*, B. II – 1 (b). Furnese to Marlborough, 14 July 1710 and 28 July 1710.
7 Ibid., B. II – 9 (a).
8 Ibid., B. II – 1 (b). Walpole to Marlborough.

XXIII

We Must Have Peace, Good or Bad

1 Sarah, Duchess of Marlborough, *Account of the Conduct of the Dowager Duchess of Marlborough*.

2 Goebbels, quoted in Hugh Trevor-Roper's introduction to *The Goebbels Diaries*.

3 Hugh Trevor-Roper, describing Goebbels' methods, ibid.

4 Swift, *Journal to Stella*, 4 January 1710–11.

5 Swift, *Correspondence*, i, p. 291.

6 *The Examiner*, 23 November 1710.

7 "The Rival Duchess . . . a dialogue between Madame Maintenon and Madam M.", London, 1708.

8 Letter, 1/11 November 1710.

9 *Blenheim MSS*, B. II – 7 (b). A tartan is a small, single-masted vessel with a lateen sail.

10 Swift, *Journey to Stella*, 8 December 1711.

11 *Portland Papers*, Vol. 5, p. 94. HMC.

12 *Blenheim MSS*, B. II – 7 (b).

13 Ibid., B. II – 25.

14 Swift, *The History of the Four Last Years of Queen Anne's Reign*.

XXIV

Materials For a Little Mischief

The title of the chapter is drawn from a phrase of Swift's to Stella.

The extensive quotations from *The Conduct of the Allies* are from the edition published in London in 1712.

1 Swift, *Journal to Stella*, 28 November 1711 (the day after publication). Vol. II, edited by Harold Williams.

2 *Blenheim MSS*, E. 32.

XXV

Time to Leave

1 J. H. Plumb, *Sir Robert Walpole*, I, *The Making of a Statesman*, p. 181.

2 Sarah, Duchess of Marlborough, *Account of the Conduct of the Dowager Duchess of Marlborough*.

3 Louis XIV had, however, insisted that Marlborough was not to be executed.

XXVI

How Fortune Does Banter Us!

1 David Chandler, *The Art of Warfare in the Age of Marlborough*.

2 Total government expenditure in Europe from 1689 to 1714 totalled £500–

600 millions, of which three-quarters was due to war. P. G. M. Dickinson, "War Finance", *New Cambridge Modern History*, vol. VI.

3 Swift, *Journal to Stella*, Vol. II, 11 April 1713.
4 Peter Smithers, *Life of Joseph Addison*, p. 265.
5 Lecky, *History of England in the Eighteenth Century*.
6 David B. Green, *Sarah, Duchess of Marlborough*.

XXVII

Triumphant Return

1 *Diary of Mary, Countess Cowper*, ed. Hon. Spencer Cowper, 1865, and HMC 10th report. *Bagot MSS* – pt. iv, p. 393.
2 Countess Cowper, *Diary*.
3 H. T. Dickinson, *Bolingbroke*, p. 143.
4 Ibid., p. 139.
5 David B. Green, *Sarah, Duchess of Marlborough*, p. 211.
6 W. S. Churchill, *Marlborough*, IV, p. 641.
7 David Green, *op. cit.*, p. 218.
8 Ibid., p. 201.
9 Lawrence Whistler, *Sir John Vanbrugh, Architect and Dramatist*.
10 *Portland Papers*, Vol. VII, p. 330. But others thought the capital sum was bigger. For instance, Vanbrugh.
11 Sir John Clapham, *The Bank of England*, p. 279.
12 J. Sutherland, "Marlborough's Funeral", from *Background for Queen Anne*.
13 David Green, *op. cit.*, p. 228.
14 J. Sutherland, *op. cit.*, p. 204.
15 *Blenheim MSS*, F. I – 35.
16 David B. Green, *op. cit.*
17 W. Lewis, *The Will of the Duchess of Marlborough*.

Select Bibliography

In preparing a selected list of the books, pamphlets, letters, etc., which I have consulted, I have also tried to arrange them according to the subject or the period for which I have found them particularly useful. Naturally, a good deal of overlapping occurs; high politics and family life are interwoven; the diary of a Norwegian pastor becomes important in discussing the climate of Western Europe during vital years; and so on. Even so, I believe that the list, set out in this way, will be of use.

Social and Economic Conditions in the Second Half of the Seventeenth Century

BARBOUR, Violet: *Capitalism in Amsterdam*, Baltimore, 1963.

BRAUDEL, Fernand: *Capitalism and Material Life*, Weidenfeld and Nicolson, London, 1967.

GEYL, Pieter: *The Netherlands in the Seventeenth Century*, Benn, London, 1961.

GOODWIN, A.: *The European Nobility in the Eighteenth Century*, A. & C. Black, London, 1953.

LADURIE, Emanuel le Roy: *Histoire du Climat depuis l'an mil*, Flammarion, Paris, 1967.

New Cambridge Modern History, Vol. V, *The Ascendancy of France, 1648–88*. Vol. VI, *The Rise of Britain and Russia, 1688–1725* contains Jean Meuvret, "The Conditions of France, 1688–1715", and David Ogg, "The Emergence of Great Britain as a World Power", Cambridge University Press, 1970.

PUFENDORFF, Samuel: *Introduction to the History of the Several Kingdoms . . . of Europe*, made English from the original High Dutch, London, 1697.

WOLF, John B.: *The Emergence of the Great Powers*, Harper Bros, New York, 1951.

The following two volumes are parts of *A General History of Europe* edited by Denys Hay. They are scholarly and readable and, between them, provide a valuable survey of the world in which Marlborough lived and helped to shape.

ANDERSON, M. S.: *Europe in the Eighteenth Century, 1713–1783*, Longman, London, 1961.

PENNINGTON, D. H.: *Seventeenth Century Europe*, Longman, London, 1970.

Select Bibliography

The Man and His Family

The standard works dealing with Marlborough's life include:

Account of the Conduct of the Dowager Duchess of Marlborough, George Hawkins, London, 1742.

ALISON, Archibald: *The Military Life of the Duke of Marlborough*.

ATKINSON, C. T.: *Marlborough and the Rise of the British Army*, Putnam, London and New York, 1921.

BARNETT, Corelli: *Marlborough*, Eyre Methuen, London, 1974. A brief, vivid account, lavishly illustrated.

BURTON, I. F.: *The Captain General*, Constable, London, 1968.

SARAH CHURCHILL, DUCHESS OF MARLBOROUGH: *Letters*, 1875.

CHURCHILL, Winston S.: *Marlborough: His Life and Times*, 4 Vols, Harrap, London, 1933–1938.

COXE, Archdeacon W. C.: *Memoirs of John, Duke of Marlborough*, 6 Vols, Longmans, London, 1820.

GREEN, David B.: *Sarah, Duchess of Marlborough*, Collins, London, 1967.

SUTHERLAND, James: "Funeral of the Duke of Marlborough", in *Background for Queen Anne*, Methuen, London, 1939.

TAYLOR, Frank: *The Wars of Marlborough*, 2 Vols, Blackwell, Oxford, 1921.

THOMSON, Gladys Scott: *Letters of a Grandmother*, Cape, London, 1943.

The Will of the Duchess of Marlborough, W. Lewis, London, 1745.

WOLSELEY, G. F.: *Life of Marlborough*, London, 1894.

Biographies of Other Figures

BARBOUR, Violet: *Henry Bennet, Earl of Arlington*, 1914.

BROWNING, Andrew: *Thomas, Earl of Danby*, Jackson Son & Co., Glasgow, 1951.

BRYANT, Arthur: *Samuel Pepys, The Saviour of the Nation*, Collins, London, 1949.

DICKSON, Patricia: *Red John of the Battles* (John, 2nd Duke of Argyll), Sidgwick & Jackson, London, 1973.

HENDERSON, Nicholas: *Prince Eugene of Savoy*, Weidenfeld and Nicolson, London, 1964.

KENYON, J. P.: *Robert Spencer, Earl of Sunderland*, Longmans, London, 1958.

MANLEY, Mary de la Rivière: see *DNB* and Sir Charles Petrie, *op. cit.*

MARSHALL, Rosalind K.: *The Days of Duchess Anne, 1656–1716* (the Duchess of Hamilton), Collins, London, 1973.

MITFORD, Nancy: *The Sun King*, Hamish Hamilton, London, 1966.

NADA, John: *Carlos the Bewitched* (life of Charles II of Spain, whose death precipitated the War of the Spanish Succession), Cape, London, 1962.

PETRIE, Sir Charles: *The Marshal Duke of Berwick*, Eyre and Spottiswoode, London, 1953.

PLUMB, J. H.: *Sir Robert Walpole*, Vol. I *The Making of a Statesman*, Allen Lane, The Penguin Press, London, first published in 1922.

ROGERS, Pat: "Note on Sir Henry Furnese", in *Notes and Queries*, February 1971.

SERGEANT, Philip W.: *My Lady Castlemaine*, Hutchinson, London, 1912.

SMITHERS, Peter: *The Life of Joseph Addison*, Clarendon Press, Oxford, 1968.

STEINMAN, G. Steinman: *A Memoir of Barbara, Duchess of Cleveland*, privately printed, 1871.

TAYLOR, Henrietta: "John, Duke of Argyll", in *Scottish Historical Review*, Vols. 26–27, Nelson, Edinburgh, 1947–48.

ZEE, Henri and Barbara van der: *William and Mary*, Macmillan, London, 1973.

British Social and Political Events

ACKERMAN, J. Y. (Ed.): *Moneys Received and Paid For Secret Services of Charles II and James II*, Camden Society, London, 1851.

BOND, Richmond P.: *The Tatler: The Making of a Literary Journal*, Oxford University Press, 1971.

CARSWELL, John: *The South Sea Bubble*, Cresset Press, London, 1961.
    The Descent on England, Barrie and Rockliff, London, 1969.
    The Old Cause, Three Biographical Studies in Whiggism, Cresset Press, London, 1954.

CLARK, Sir George: *The Later Stuarts*, Clarendon Press, Oxford, 1955.

DEFOE, Daniel: *The History of the Union*, Stockdale, London, 1786.

EMERSON, V. I. R.: *Monmouth's Rebellion*, Yale University Press, New Haven, Oxford University Press, London, 1951.

HEYWOOD, Samuel: *A Vindication of Mr Fox's Historical Work*, J. Johnson, London, 1811.

HOLMES, Geoffrey: *British Politics in the Age of Anne*, Macmillan, London, 1967.

LUTTRELL, Narcissus: *Brief Historical Relation*, Oxford University Press, 1857.

MORRIS, Christopher (Ed.): *The Journeys of Celia Fiennes*, Cresset Press, London, 1949.

OGG, David: *England in the Reigns of James II and William III*, Clarendon Press, Oxford, 1963.

RICH, E. E.: *Hudson's Bay Company, 1670–1870*, Vol. 1, Hudson's Bay Record Society, XXI, London, 1958.

SMOUT, T. C.: *Scottish Trade on the Eve of Union*, Oliver and Boyd, Edinburgh and London, 1963.

TREVELYAN, G. M.: *England under Queen Anne*, 3 Vols, Longmans, London, 1932.

Armies and War

Two recent books I have found especially enlightening:

Select Bibliography

CHANDLER, David: *The Art of Warfare in the Age of Marlborough*, Batsford, London, 1976, from which I was led to:

CHILDS, John: *The Army of Charles II*, Routledge and Kegan Paul, London, 1976.

FERGUSON, James: *Papers Relating to the History of the Scots Brigade in the Service of the United Netherlands*, Scottish History Society, Edinburgh, 1899–1901.

FORTESCUE, Sir John W.: *A History of the British Army*, Vol. 1, Macmillan, London, 1889.

HALL, A. R.: *Ballistics in the 17th Century*, Cambridge University Press, 1952.

HAYES, James: "Scottish Officers in the British Army", in *Scottish Historical Review*, April 1958.

New Cambridge Modern History, Vol. VI, *The Rise of Britain and Russia, 1688–1725* contains David G. Chandler, "The Art of War on Land", and J. W. Stoye, "Soldiers and Civilians".

NEF, J. U.: *War and Human Progress*, Routledge and Kegan Paul, London, 1951.

PERJE, Professor G.: *Army Provisioning, Logistics and Strategy in the Second Half of the Seventeenth Century*, Budapest, 1970. (The book is, so far as I know, still untranslated.)

SCOULLER, R. E.: *The Armies of Queen Anne*, Clarendon Press, Oxford, 1966.

War and Finance

ATKINSON, C. T.: *A Royal Dragoon*, Society for Army Historical Research, 1938.

CLAPHAM, Sir John: *The Bank of England*, 2 Vols, Cambridge University Press, 1944.

COWES, W. L. C.: *The Royal Navy*, Vol. II, Samson Low, London, 1898.

DAVIES, Godfrey: "The Seamy Side of Marlborough's War", in *The Huntingdon Library Quarterly*, San Marino, California, November 1956.

EHRMAN, John: *The Navy in the Wars of William III*, Cambridge University Press, 1953.

FULLER, Major-General J. F. C.: *The Decisive Battles of the Western World*, Vol. II, Eyre and Spottiswoode, London, 1955.

HYAMSON, Albert M.: *The Sephardim of England*, Methuen, London, 1951. For the Medina brothers – see also *Encyclopedia Judaica*.

LAWSON, Cecil C. P.: *A History of the Uniforms of the British Army*, Kaye and Ward, London, 1964.

The Lives of the Two Illustrious Generals, Anon., 1713.

New Cambridge Modern History, Vol. VI, *The Rise of Britain and Russia, 1688–1725*, contains P. G. M. Dickinson, "War Finance, 1689–1714", and his "Armies and Navies".

The First Churchill

PITT, H. G.: "The Pacification of Utrecht", in *Cambridge Modern History*, Vol. VI.

ROTH, Cecil: *History of the Jews in England*, Clarendon Press, Oxford, 1949.

SCOTT, John: *The Remembrance*, Scottish Historical Society XXXVII.

VEENENDAAL, A. J.: "War of the Spanish Succession in Europe", in *Cambridge Modern History*, Vol. VI.

The Dutch and the War

COOMBS, D. S.: *The Conduct of the British*, Martinus Nijhoff, The Hague, 1958.

GEIKIE, Roderick and MONTGOMERY, Isabel A.: *The Dutch Barrier*, Cambridge University Press, 1930.

HUIZANGA, Johan: *Dutch Civilization in the Seventeenth Century*, 1968.

Soldiers' Stories

BLACKADER, John: *The Life and Diary of Lieut-Colonel John Blackader*, ed. Andrew Crichton, Baynes, Edinburgh, 1824.

COLONIE, Jean M. de la: *The Chronicles of an Old Campaigner*, trans. W. C. Horsley, London, 1904.

CRANSTOUN, Lt.-Col. James: see *Portland Papers*, Vol. IV. (Accounts of the battles of Ramillies and Oudenarde.)

DRAKE, Captain Peter: *Memoirs*, S. Powell, Dublin, 1755.

GOSLINGA, Sicco van: *Mémoires*, G. T. N. Suringar, Leeuvarten, 1857.

MÉRODE-WESTERLOO, G. de: *Mémoires*, Societé des Bibliophiles de Mons, Mons, 1840.

MILLNER, John (Sergeant in the Honourable Royal Regiment of Foot of Ireland): *A Compendious Journal of All the Marches, Famous Battles, Sieges, etc.*, London, 1733.

ORKNEY, Lord: "Letters during Marlborough's Campaigns", in *English. Historical Review*, London, April 1904.

PARKER, Captain Robert: *Memoirs*, London, 1746.

Contemporary Documents, Memoirs, etc.

Most important of all are *The Blenheim Papers*, now lodged in the British Museum, an incomparable archive with which I have spent many enjoyable and fruitful hours.

Baschet's Transcripts, 19 Nov.–29 Nov. 1676 and 27 Nov.–7 Dec. 1676.

Cal. State Papers: Treasury, 1679–80, pp. 216, 233, 240.

　　　　　　　　　Domestic, 1678, 1690, 1694–5.

Select Bibliography

HISTORICAL MANUSCRIPTS COMMISSION:
Bath Papers, Vols I and II.
Cowper Papers, Vol. III.
Dartmouth Papers, Vol. XI, p. 34.
Earl of Denbigh's MSS, 7th Report and Appendix.
Ormonde Papers, New Series, Vols IV and VII.
Portland Papers, Vols II, IV and VII.
Rutland Papers, Vol. II, pp. 32 and 34.
Letters from Liselotte, Elizabeth Charlotte, Princess Palatine and Duchess of Orléans, trans. Maria Kroll, Gollancz, London, 1970.
Newsletters of 1688, Mackintosh Collection, Add. MSS 34,487, British Museum.
The Rival Duchess . . . a dialogue between Madame Maintenon and Madame M., London, 1708.
Savile Correspondence, Camden Society LXXI, London, 1858.
State Papers, 84/206 f. 151, Add. MSS 2893 7 f. 289–291.

BARILLON, Paul: "Letters", in *A History of the Early Part of the Reign of James II* by Charles James Fox, Miller, London, 1888.
DALRYMPLE: *Memoirs of Great Britain and Ireland*, Vol. I.
DEFOE, Daniel: *A Tour through the Whole Island of Great Britain*, G. Strachan, London, 1724.
    A Plan for the English Commerce, Charles Rivington, London, 1728.
    Letters, Ed. G. H. Healey, Oxford, 1955.
DUNTON, John: *King Abigail, or the Secret Reign of the She-Favourite*, printed for the author, London, 1715.
EARL OF AILESBURY: *Memoirs*, Roxburgh Club, Westminster, 1890.
EVELYN, John: *Diaries*, Vol. V, London, 1955.
JOHN ERSKINE OF CARNOCK: *Journal*, Ed. Walter Macleod, Scottish Historical Society, Vol. 14, Edinburgh, 1893.
MANLEY, Mary de la Rivière: *Atalantis*, James Woodward, London, 1711.
MARQUIS DE TORCY: *Mémoires de M. de —— pour servir à l'Histoire des Negotiations*, A La Haye, 1757.
MARY, COUNTESS COWPER: *Diary*, Ed. Hon. Spencer Cowper, Murray, London, 1865.
PEPYS, Samuel: *Memoirs Relating to the State of the Royal Navy of England*, Ben Griffin, London, 1690.
SAINT-SIMON: *Mémoires*, Vol. 7, Ed. the Marquis de Saint-Simon, Delloye, Paris, 1840.
WHITTLE, John (Chaplain in the army): *An Exact Diary of the Late Expedition*, Richard Baldwin, London, 1689.

The First Churchill

Swift and the Political Crisis of 1710–1712

Excellent biographies of the leading figures in these events are available for the student:

DAVIES, Godfrey: "The Fall of Harley in 1708", in *English Historical Review*, April 1951.

DICKINSON, H. T.: *Bolingbroke*, Constable, London, 1970.

KRAMMICK, Isaac: *Bolingbroke and his circle: The politics of nostalgia in the age of Walpole*, Harvard University Press, Mass., Oxford University Press, London, 1968.

McINNES, Angus: *Robert Harley, Puritan Politician*, Gollancz, London, 1970.

Swift contributes vivid, partisan pictures by one who was recording history as it was being made and was himself helping to make it in his *Journal to Stella*, edited by Harold Williams, Vols 1 and 2, Blackwell, Oxford, 1974. This is a brilliant, unfair, indispensable guide to be read with pleasure and caution. There is also the decisive pamphlet *The Conduct of the Allies*, which may also be read in *Political Tracts, 1711–1713*, and, by the same author:

Contributions to the Examiner from 1710 onwards, Blackwell, Oxford, 1957.

The History of the Four Last Years of Queen Anne's Reign, Blackwell, Oxford, 1951.

Political Tracts, 1711–1719, Blackwell, Oxford, 1951, 1953.

These may be found conveniently assembled, in Volumes 3, 6, 7 and 8 of *Swift's Prose Works*, edited by George H. Davis, London, 1940–53.

Another man of letters had not Swift's exceptional back-stage insight:

DEFOE, Daniel: *Letters*, Ed. G. H. Healey, Oxford, 1955.

There is also an amusing Tory satire:

ARBUTHNOT, John J.: "The History of John Bull", see *Life and Works*, Ed. G. A. Aitken, Clarendon Press, Oxford, 1892, 1954.

And finally,

CLARK, J. Kent: *Swift and the Dutch*.

EWALD, W. B.: *The Newsmen of Queen Anne*, Blackwell, Oxford, 1956.

ROGERS, Pat: *Grub Street: Studies in a sub-culture*, Methuen, London, 1972.

Blenheim Palace

GREEN, D. B.: *Blenheim Palace*, Country Life Books, London, 1951.

WHISTLER, Laurence: *Sir John Vanbrugh, Architect and Dramatist*, Cobden-Sanderson, London, 1938.

Index

The name of the Duke of Marlborough is abbreviated to "M." within index entries.

Index

Index

Dryden, J., 20
Dublin, 15, 54, 56, 71
Dublin Free Grammar School, 16
Duguay-Trouin, R., 80
Dumouriez, C. F., 233n
Dunkirk, 207–8, 229, 284, 289
Dutch Guards, 182, 185, 234, 239f
Dykevelt, E. van, 53
Dyle, River, 179

East India Companies:
  Dutch, 8f, 30, 58, 60
  English, 11–12
Edict of Nantes, 34, 48, 195
Edinburgh, 35–6, 43, 193, 289
  Castle, 191, 208, 289
Eglinton, Earl of, 253
Ehrenbreitstein, 123
Eleanora, Empress, 128
Elixem, 170
England, seventeenth-century, 10–13
Enzheim, 24–5
Essex, A. Capel, Earl of, 39
Eugene, Prince of Savoy:
  early life, 126–7, 130
  fights Turks at Mohacs, 57, 127
  battle of Zenta, 112, 128
  at Luzzara, 112
  Bavarian campaign, 125, 131, 138–9f
  Blenheim, 141ff, 144, 149f, 156
  army wages loan, 176f
  relief of Turin, 178, 188–9
  plan to attack Toulon, 196–7f
  Oudenarde, 210–11f, 214f
  opposes Paris project, 217
  siege of Lille, 217–18f
  proposed as Netherlands' Viceroy, 222
  London loan, 227, 251
  Spanish invasion plans, 230
  Malplaquet, 236f, 239ff, 242
  on the Rhine, 263
  visit to London, 276
  defeated by Villars, 281
  captures Belgrade, 297
Evelyn, J., 27, 50, 95, 105f, 154, 162
Examiner, The, 255, 257f
exchange-rate of the £, xi, 228
Exeter, Bishop of, 301
Eyemouth, J. Churchill, Baron of, *see*
  Marlborough, J. Churchill, 1st Duke
  of
Eyne, 212, 214

famine, 2
Farewell, Lieutenant, 104–5
Fearn, D., 192

Fénelon, F. de S. de la Mothe-, Bishop of
  Cambrai, 6
Ferguson, Brigadier-General, 142, 146
Ferguson, Robert, 40
Fenwick, Sir J., 84
Feversham, L. de D. de Duras, Earl of,
  42–3ff, 46, 48, 52, 63
Fielding, Beau, 191
finance, rise of, 12f
Finland Dragoons, 64
Fire of London, 39
First Guards, 44
Fischer von Erlach, J. B., 128
Fitzharding, Lady, 76
Fitzharding, Lord, 42
FitzJames, J., Duke of Berwick, *see* Berwick,
  J. FitzJames, Duke of
Flanders, 24, 31f, 75, 112, 185, 194, 197ff,
  221, 246, 263–7, 281
Fletcher of Saltoun, A., 41f
Footguards, *see* Guards
Foss, Pastor M., 223
France, seventeenth-century, 5–6
Franche-Comté, 156
Frankfurt, 124, 176, 263, 286
Frederick I (King of Prussia), 157, 160, 162,
  175f, 178ff
Frederick IV (King of Denmark), 179
Freeman, Mrs, *see* Anne (Queen of Britain
  and Ireland)
Frome, 40
Fugger, Count, 187
Furnese, Sir H., 227, 251, 279

Galway, H. de Massue, Earl of, 190, 196, 259
Gaultier, Abbé, 268
Geete, 180f
Gell, S., 104f
geometry, 1
George, Prince of Denmark, 37, 55, 62, 88,
  96, 99, 216–17
George I (King of Britain and Ireland;
  Elector of Hanover), 137, 212, 262, 278,
  285, 293f, 299, 303
George II (King of Britain and Ireland), 303
Ghent, 186, 210, 212, 215, 218, 220, 290
Gibbons, G., 286
Gibraltar, 190, 284
Ginkel, G. de, 99, 101f
Glasgow, 43, 192
Gloucester (city), 43f
Gloucester (frigate), 36
Gloucester, W., Duke of, 87
Godfrey, C., 61, 80, 93
Godfrey, Sir E. B., 34
Godfrey, R., 44f

328

Index

Index